GREATEST AMERICAN CARS

PEPPERBOX
PRESS

Contents

Packard Model C Runabout

1901

J ames Ward Packard didn't like his Winton Automobile, and told Mr. Winton so. The reply was somewhat testy, but ran along the lines of 'if you don't like my car build one yourself'. So Packard did, and his belief that he could make a better car than Winton is borne out by history. He wisely recruited two of Winton's engineers, George Weiss and William A. Hatcher, to help build the first Packard. The car was completed in November 1899, at the Ohio Automobile Company's workshop in Warren, Ohio. The vehicle was designated as the Model A. Five cars were built that year.

The Model A and Model B followed in 1900. Both used a (for the time) conventional single-cylinder engine, producing seven horsepower fitted with two-speed planetary gears. The rear wheels were chain driven. However, two early innovations that singled out these cars were the 'H' configuration gear change slot and an automatic advance on the spark mechanism. Both of these ideas, which we now take for granted, were groundbreaking in 1900.

Packard's reputation grew quickly. William D. Rockefeller jettisoned his collection of Wintons in order to buy two new Packards at the New York Automobile show of November 1900. Henry B, Joy, a Detroit businessman, was so impressed when he bought his second Packard Model F in 1902, that he purchased quantities of stock in the company. His involvement was one of the factors that prompted the removal of the Packard factory to Detroit in October 1903. An early slogan adopted by the company was 'Ask the man who owns one' which clearly exemplified the fact that Packard had got it right where others had failed.

Our featured car, the 1901 Model C Runabout, was exhibited at the New York Automobile Show of 1900. By this time, improvements had increased the available power to 12 horsepower. This model was the first Packard to replace the spade handle lever with a steering wheel - another feature the modern motorist takes for granted. Back in 1901 somebody had to invent this leap forward. A bulb horn was added but the foot operated chime was also retained. A pair of handsome brass Dietz oil lamps replaced the original single solar lamp. Seating at the front of the car was bench style. At the back, there was an optional forward-facing rear seat.

Packard entered three cars in the 1901 New York to Buffalo auto race and received First Class certificates for their performance. These models reached the dizzy heights of 25 mph with standard gearing and up to 30mph with the higher gear option. Not bad for 1901!

■ *Left: The model has smart black paintwork with the wire wheels picked out in red. Wire wheels were an advanced feature at a time when most cars still had wooden spokes. Our car also has the optional Surrey top.*

Engine:	Single cylinder
Displacement:	183.8-cid
Horsepower:	12 at 850 rpm
Transmission:	Two-speed planetary
Base Price:	$1500
Number Produced:	81

1902 Oldsmobile Curved Dash

Ransom Eli Olds was already an old hand at the automobile business by 1902. He had tested his first car, a steamer, in 1887. His first gasoline car soon followed. His early production was mainly centered on engine manufacture. This early start earned Oldsmobile the title of the oldest surviving automobile company in America, until its recent demise.

Capitalized in 1899 by wealthy lumber merchant, Samuel L. Smith, the company was consolidated as the Olds Motor Works. Olds himself worked on the development of several different cars, including electric models, but it wasn't until the factory burned down on March 9th 1901 (fortuitously, some believed) that Olds focused his attention on the surviving car, a gasoline runabout. This was the basis for the future development of the company. It was the Curved Dash Oldsmobile.

The car was powered by a single-cylinder engine, fitted with spur geared, two-speed transmission. It quickly became America's first volume-produced car.

In those days there were no trailers and if you wanted to show your latest car at the New York Automobile Show you would probably have to drive it there. Roy Chapin did exactly this with the Curved Dash in the Fall of 1901. This was a feat, which added greatly to the credibility of the car, and its sales. 425 cars were sold in 1901. Whilst rival manufacturers like Alexander Winton were happy to rely on a lower volume of cars at higher prices, Olds went for a price that people could afford, $650, and watched his sales rocket.

Our featured car clearly shows its attractive wooden construction –the familiar curved toboggan-like front end giving the car its name. A high gloss finish in black, with cherry trim, was achieved by hand applied layers of paint rubbed down and recoated many times until the correct depth of sheen was reached. The car was available as a two seat runabout with the option of a dos a dos (literally back to back, which meant a rear facing seat for additional passengers). The car was steered by a tiller and was right hand drive. The starting crank is a fixed item protruding from the right hand side of the engine and can be used from the driving seat. The white Tubeless tires are 28x 2½ inch on wire wheels. The car has a Surrey Top. The only thing missing is the horse in front!

Engine: Single horizontal Cylinder.

Horsepower: 41/2 at 600 rpm

Transmission: Two-speed planetary gears chain drive and semi floating rear axle

Induction: Floatless carburetor- gravity fed.

Weight: 650lbs

Wheelbase: 66 inches

Base Price: $650

■ *Right: Still very much craftsman built with a wooden body the 1902 Olds lingered in the Nineteenth Century.*

1903 Model A Ford

The most famous of all car manufacturers was forty years of age when his first real mass production car was born. His previous career was, to say the least, precarious. Cars built in sheds, engines tested in kitchen sinks, was this guy ever likely to make it?

Early backers were disenchanted by Ford's seeming fixation on racing projects. The famous 999, now in the Ford Museum in Dearborn, was the first car to circle the Grosse Pointe track in less than a minute in 1901. But its construction resulted in his backers defecting to Henry Leland, the founder of Cadillac. This may have been one of the factors that resulted in Ford finally buckling down to full-scale production in 1903. The Ford Motor Company had been born. Model A's began rolling off the line by July that year, and a total of 1700 cars were built in the subsequent 15 months.

The basic layout of the Model A was that of a horse-drawn buggy. The engine was under the seat and a detachable tonneau bolted to the rear platform (which added $100 to the price) was available for accommodating two extra passengers.

It had two cylinders horizontally opposed, which was an improvement over its rival, the Curved Dash Olds, as it provided 8 horsepower as opposed to the Olds' 4-1/2 horsepower. This gave a top speed of 30 mph, only achievable in the Olds with optional gearing.

The engine was cranked by a handle inserted in the side of the body below the seat. Within a year the car would evolve into the model AC, complete with an upgraded engine. The model C came next. Unlike some of his competitors Henry Ford was not standing still!

Engine: Two-cylinder opposed.

Displacement: 100.4-cid

Horsepower: 8

Transmission: Two-speed planetary

Induction: Schebler carburetor

Body style: Open top runabout with bolt-on tonneau

Number of seats: 2/4

Weight: 1250lbs

Wheelbase: 72 inches

Base Price: $850, plus $100 for the tonneau

Number Produced: 1700

■ *Right: Finished in bright red with tasteful brass fittings, including a business-like curly bulb horn, the 1903 Model A looked the part.*

Cadillac Model H Coupe 1906

Named for Le Sieur Antoine de la Mothe Cadillac, the French explorer who discovered Detroit in the early 18th century, the Cadillac Automobile Company was founded by Henry Leland in 1902. This was the beginning of a auspicious heritage that has survived to this day.

Company sales manager William E. Metzger took 2286 initial orders at the New York Automobile Show that year, which seemed to indicate that the company had a big future.

The car proved to be a success right from the start because, by offering precision engineering at an affordable price: $750. By 1906, the original single-cylinder engined cars had been joined by a new four-cylinder unit with its 30 horsepower giving a significant increase in power.

Models available in 1906 include the Model K, a single-cylinder powered car, which sported steering column mounted spark control for the first time, and a cam-powered oiler, positioned on the hub of the flywheel. Even in these very early days, car design was under constant review.

Straight-sided Dunlop rubber tires were standard equipment on Cadillacs by 1906. The Model M was very similar to the Model K, but was built on a two-inch longer wheelbase.

The Model L was the company's first seven-seater limousine body. This was achieved by the addition of two rear-facing seats. This car had the four-cylinder engine, which was machined out to five inches per bore, and was fitted with a float-feed jet type carburetor with a centrifugal governor attached to the throttle butterfly. The L's dashboard was pressed steel in place of the more usual wood.

Finally we come to our featured model, the H Coupe. This was the first production two-door coupe offered by Cadillac. It was based on the Model L mechanical package, and like the Buick Model G, its styling was still heavily rooted in the era of the horse-drawn carriage.

■ *Left: Aerodynamic design wasn't really a consideration when the H Coupe was built. Nevertheless, the result is an extremely pretty little car.*

Engine: Vertical inline four-cylinder with L-head.

Displacement: 392.7-cid

Horsepower: 40

Induction: Float-feed jet type with governor.

Body Style: Two-door Coupe

Number of Seats: 2

Weight: 2500 lbs

Wheelbase: 102 inches

Base Price: $3000

Number produced: 509

Ford Model T

At last, here was the car that Henry Ford meant to build all along! Its dual hallmarks were simplicity and reliability. Launched in the fall of 1908, the first Tin Lizzie two-person runabout (as the car became affectionately known) went on sale for just $825. This was an entirely new car compared to the previous Fords. It had a four-cylinder side valve power unit, with a cast iron block and removable cylinder head. Many of the ancillary engine and transmission parts were stamped, or drawn, rather than cast. This kept down both the weight and cost. Essentially, Ford had approached the building of his car as an engineer, not as a financier or marketing person. The revolutionary techniques displayed in the model were the result of two decades of engineering trial and error. The car's suspension was by way of two transverse leaf springs. Although this was basic, it gave long service and little trouble, contributing to the car's longevity and popularity. Childe Harold Wills, one of Fords leading metallurgists, had developed Vanadium steel. This was a lighter and more durable steel, which was used for the Model T chassis and engine components. This gave the car an enormous weight advantage over its competitors. Ford strongly believed in innovation, and many of his chosen comrades (like Edison) helped to keep him on the cutting edge of new technology.

The Model T wheels were 30x3 inch on the front and 30x3-1/2 on the rear (giving extra grip to the driving wheels). This was an innovation, which is still in use in high-performance cars almost a century later.

The hood was plain and fabricated from sheet aluminum. A wide range of factory-fitted options was available including headlamps, tops, windshields, speedometers, Prest-o-lite gas tanks, footrests and autochimes. This made the car eminently flexible to the requirements of the individual customer. This was a lesson that other manufacturers had yet to learn.

■ *Left: Many Model T's found their way into rural locations as this picture depicts. The car's rugged simplicity, coupled with good mechanics, kept it running down on the farm for many years.*

Engine: L-head four-cylinder

Displacement: 176.7-cid

Horsepower: 22 at 1600 rpm

Transmission: Planetary two-speed

Induction: Kingston five-ball carburetor

Body style: Open Top Tourer

Number of seats: 5

Weight: 1200lbs

Wheelbase: 100 inches

Base Price: $825

Number Produced: 10,660

1909 Maxwell Model A

The Maxwell Company got started when backer Benjamin Briscoe diverted his cash away from Buick. He believed that the Buick Company would never amount to much. He now invested his money in company with Jonathan D. Maxwell an engineer who had worked at Olds. With further support from Banker J. P. Morgan, they launched the Maxwell-Briscoe Motor Company in 1904.

The company started manufacturing at a factory in Tarrytown, New York and this was where Maxwell's first model, designated the 'H', started production in 1904 when ten units were produced. Their design featured a twin-cylinder water-cooled engine, with a honeycomb radiator mounted up front, and with thermosyphon cooling. This was a system that Henry Ford also adopted on his Model T. The car also had two-speed gears, and in common with many other cars at this time, was equipped with right hand steering.

The company's early years were enhanced by a series of sales stunts organized by Sales Manager Cadwallader Washburn Kelsey. In the year we are featuring, Kelsey persuaded a party of young society women to drive across the country, from Hell's Gate in New York to the Golden Gate in San Francisco, in a Maxwell (of course). At the time, this raised unprecedented interest, as it was considered almost impossible for women to even attempt such a thing.

Largely as a result of this kind of publicity 20,000 Maxwells were sold in the following year. By 1909, a four-cylinder 30 horsepower engine had joined the range, but the two- cylinder engine (with a slightly up-rated power output) still accounted for most of the sales.

Maxwells were available in a number of different body options: a touring car and limousine, a tourabout, runabout and most notable the 'Doctor Maxwell' a car which was specially designed for physicians. This was a new slant on targeting your car to suit the customer. Our example is a rare delivery car, a utility vehicle converted from Maxwell's basic Model A runabout with an out-sourced aftermarket body. It uses the reliable two-cylinder ten horsepower unit, which seemed low on power even at the time. However, a team of Maxwell's had cleaned up in the Light Car race preceding the Grand Prize in 1908. The on-paper performance might not have looked so good, but it worked well in practice. Maxwell were now third in the car sales league behind Ford and Buick, but in subsequent years the company suffered mixed fortunes, and later became Walter P. Chrysler's platform from which to launch his eponymous company in 1925.

Engine: Water-cooled Opposed Two-cylinder

Horsepower: 10

Induction: Float-feed carburetor

Wheelbase: 82 inches

Base Price: $500

Number produced: 9,460

■ *Right: Red paintwork and artillery-spoke wheels really show off the jaunty lines of this Delivery Car, based on the 1909 Model A Runabout.*

1912 Buick Model 36 Roadster

Buick's success in intermediate-level automobile racing was an undoubted factor in their growing popularity. Pressure on cash had led to the company's bankers to force Billy Durant to step down as President of General Motors, which he had built up on the foundation of Buick. Durant made sure that the job of Buick President went to Charles W. Nash who occupied the Chair until Walter P. Chrysler took over in November 1912. The early days of the Automobile industry saw a kind of musical chairs for the top positions of famous name companies.

Durant now linked up with Louis Chevrolet, and took off to pursue his other interests. But he left a legacy of belief in racing behind him. This acted as an important shop window for the company products, and contributed to Buick's strong reputation in the marketplace. By 1912, Buick was placed fourth in the top eight manufacturers. Needless to say, Ford was number one! A choice of four-cylinder engines was on offer for the year: a 165-cid of 22.5 horsepower, a 201-cid unit with 25.5 horsepower and the big daddy of 318-cid that developed 48 horsepower. All these power units featured spark plugs, canted into the head at forty-five degrees instead of the old horizontal position.

Other improvements included improved oil ways in the engine block that increased push rod lubrication, and beefed up lubrication points for suspension, steering and clutch controls, which allowed for a smoother ride and longer life. It could also be argued that these small improvements were the result of lessons learnt in competition. Our featured car is one of three roadsters on offer. It is finished in its original paint colors of blue and gray with blue/black hood, fenders and fuel tank. The wooden artillery wheels are picked out in white. By this time, the doors on all Buick Models were fully functional opening doors, unlike the false doors offered on the Ford Model T, or the cutaway coach style bodies of the early 1900s. The doors gave the car a more finished and modern look.

This car has the 201-cid engine, fitted with a three-speed gearbox, a powerful option for the times.

Engine: Four-cylinder Inline

Displacement: 201-cid

Horsepower: 25.5

Transmission: Three-speed sliding gear

Induction: Marvel E carburetor

Body Style: Two-door Open Top Roadster

Wheelbase: 101.75 inches

Base Price: $900

Number Produced: 1,600

■ *Right: 1600 of these handsome Buick Roadsters were sold in 1912 and the car looks at home outside this period building.*

Chevrolet Classic Six

When Billy Durant was forced to step down as head of General Motors in 1910, he teamed up with Louis Chevrolet to form a powerful new force in the automotive world. It was his intention to regain control of GM at some future point. Chevrolet was already well known for his motor racing exploits. Durant considered that Chevrolet's European background and motor racing prowess made him the ideal person to produce a groundbreaking new model with European-styling.

By 1910, intense competition between the leading nations in Europe had produced a forward surge in design that was led by France and Germany. Durant hoped to tap into these technological advances to give his cars an edge in the American domestic market. He assembled a collection of factories to help him found the new company, including the Little Car factory in Flint, Michigan and the Republic Motor Company in New York City. A car had already appeared under the Little banner in 1912, but where was the Chevrolet? When the car finally appeared later in the year, it was a monster. The 120-inch wheelbase made the car one of the largest Chevrolets ever produced. This massive 299 cubic inch power plant was not overtaken by another Chevrolet engine until 1958! It was configured as a six-cylinder T-head twin overhead camshaft. Despite the engine's size and advanced technical design, its power output was a modest 40 horsepower, which rendered the car a sluggish performer.

The car's size and specification meant that it had to be marketed at well over $2000, which limited sales. This over-specified model was the unfortunate result of giving an engineer free rein to produce the kind of car of his dreams rather than designing the car with the customer in mind.

Despite this, the car featured many excellent modifications such as dual ignition, self-starter, a gas gauge, speedometer with illuminated dial, electric lights, forged front axle, cone clutch with three-speed gears, semi-elliptic front springs and three-quarter rear platform springs. The engine was mounted at three points. All of this added up to a very well engineered car, which was just too expensive.

■ *Left: The distinctive Silver Radiator cowl and nickel-plated electric headlights give the first Chevrolet a very modern appearance.*

Engine:	T-head twin cam six-cylinder
Displacement:	299-cid
Horsepower:	40
Induction:	Stromberg carburetor
Body Style:	Four-door Roadster
Number of seats:	5
Wheelbase:	120 inches
Base price:	$2250
Number produced:	2,999

Hudson Model 33

1912

The men behind the Hudson Company were seasoned graduates of the 'Olds' school. Roy D Chapin made his name when he drove from Detroit to New York City for the National Automobile Show in 1901 in record time in an Olds Curved Dash and was joined at Hudson by fellow Olds veterans Howard E. Coffin, George W. Dunham and Roscoe B. Jackson. The latter was most important to the success of the enterprise, as his wife was the niece of the wealthy Joseph L. Hudson, the owner of Detroit's most successful department store. Hudson gave his name to the car company as well as a $90,000 investment.

The resultant car –the nippy little Model 20 Roadster-arrived in 1910 with a good turn of speed (50 mph) and an affordable price tag of just $900.With the Olds team's combined knowledge of the market the car had been developed to hit it dead right first time. In fact over 4000 cars were sold in the first trading year making Hudson the most successful auto company start up yet encountered. Joseph L must have been pleased indeed.

In 1912 the Model 20 was dropped, and a new upgraded car was introduced – the Model 33. A choice of seven different body styles was offered, including the sensational Mile-A-Minute Roadster, which guaranteed a heady 60 mph. A stripped down version of the normal roadster, this was the first factory Hot Rod with 32-inch special wheels, a 100mph speedo, and was supplied minus doors and windshield.

At the same time the company raised the issue of safety standards in the minds of the customers by mounting a campaign warning of the dangers of buying other makes which the folks at Hudson took it upon themselves to regard as 'unsafe motor car purchases'. You were quite safe if you stuck with them! Quite how much this was swallowed in 1912 is a matter for conjecture.

Prices of the Model 33 averaged out at $1600 except for the coupe and limousine versions, where specially made bodies increased the price.

■ *Left: This two-door Roadster looks very much at home outside a grand mansion. The distinctive triangular Hudson badge can be clearly seen. It was an inexpensive car with a lot of class. Note: Non-standard wire wheels and electric headlamps which are later additions.*

Engine:	Four-cylinder inline
Displacement:	226-cid
Horsepower:	33
Transmission:	Three-speed sliding gear
Induction:	Stromberg carburetor
Body Style:	Two-door Roadster.
Weight:	2631 lbs
Wheelbase:	114.5 inches
Base Price:	$1600
Number Produced:	5708 [based on actual shipments to dealers]

1912   Oldsmobile Autocrat

Paradoxically a company that set out under its original leadership to become a volume-producing budget car manufacturer, was the maker of some of the most gargantuan monsters in the history of American cars by 1910. Under the influence of the Smith family, who ousted R.E. Olds from the company, production turned to large models with extremely low production runs. By 1912 and now under the ownership of General Motors the trend had reached it's most extreme conclusion in terms of large, opulent cars. Names like The Special, The Autocrat, The Defender, and The Limited gave an instant clue to the intention of this series of cars. These were cars that appealed to buyers who valued exclusivity and elitism.

    The cars were outrageous in every way, an affront to the man who bought the

■ *Below: A splendid piece of machinery- the 1912 Autocrat sits confidently on its 38-inch Firestone tires.*

unostentatious Olds Curved Dash. The Autocrat, not even the worst of the bunch, sported a total length of just below 15 feet, making the Chevrolet Classic Six look like a compact. Its four-cylinder 471 cubic inch engine produced just 40 horsepower and one can only guess at its gas mileage. Its sister car, the Limited, equipped with the six-cylinder variant of the Autocrat's engine [same bore and stroke –just two more cylinders] inspired the famous action painting by William Hamden Foster - 'Setting the Pace'. The pace was 70 miles per hour even in 1911. The Limited's engine was 706 cubic inches! In years to come this trend was reversed, but this period left us with some of the most remarkable cars in our collection.

Engine: Four-cylinder inline

Displacement: 471-cid

Horsepower: 40

Induction: Rayfield Model D carburetor

Wheelbase: 126 inches

Base Price: $3500

Number Produced: 500 across the entire model range

Mercer Raceabout

'The Steinway of the Automobile World' was how the Mercer was described in 1914, and this title gives us a clue to the rather exclusive world that the car belonged to. Clearly, the model's very name tells us what the car was about. No comfort for starters. Everything was sacrificed on the altar of performance and you could certainly 'raceabout' in it. At least, you could if you had the necessary $2500. This was steep for a fairly basic car.

The Mercer Automobile Company, named for Mercer County, NJ, was established by the wealthy and entrepreneurial Roebling Family. This was the family, which gave us the Brooklyn Bridge so they were used to thinking big. Their first cars were manufactured in Trenton, New Jersey in 1909.

The Mercer started out with a four-cylinder L-Head Beaver engine, which was upgraded in 1911 to a T-head design, then all the rage, as President C.G. Roebling's son, Washington, pointed out. Washington Roebling took a keen interest in the company and provided much of its marketing thrust, knowing the kind of car that people in his 'set' would respond to. Stalwart engineer Finlay Robertson Porter sourced the better engine, and became a leading light in the company for the next three years. As well as the celebrated Raceabout, the company also offered a five-seater touring car, a Roadster and a Sport Touring model. 1914 production was 600 cars, of which around 90 were Raceabouts. The capable T-head four-cylinder engine was nominally rated at 34 horsepower. When this was coupled to a stripped-down lightweight body (with very little in the way of creature comforts) and power delivered smoothly and precisely by way of a four-speed selective transmission and oil immersed clutch, it made for an exhilarating driving experience.

But shadows fell across the future of the company. Company guru Washington A. Roebling went down with the Titanic, and from that moment in time, it seemed as though the company was drifting. Engineer Findlay Porter departed in 1914 and his replacement Eric H. Delling seemed obsessed with adding uncalled-for comforts to the car such as full-length windscreens, cumbersome faired in bodywork and a bench arrangement instead of the old bucket seats. This was all moving away from the essential spirit of the car. Our featured 1914 model captures the spirit of the company before these changes had taken effect. Spartan bucket seats, monocle windshield, strapped-down hood and gas tank and raked-back steering column all combine to give the car a street-racer look.

■ *Left: The Mercer Raceabout in 1914 captures the spirit of fun motoring before the First World War. The Red paint job with black detailing makes the car a real head turner to this day.*

Engine: Four-cylinder T-head.	
Displacement: 300-cid	
Horsepower: 34	
Wheelbase: 108 inches	
Base Price $2600	
Number Produced: 90	

Stutz Bearcat

1914

Ideal had an outstanding success at the inaugural Indy 500 race in 1911. Its first car, the 'A' series roadster, was driven to an 11th place finish by racer Gil Anderson. The Ideal Motor Car Company was now set up for full-scale production to capitalize on the reputation gained. The 'car that made good in a day', stemmed from the collective experience of Harry C. Stutz. Stutz was an automotive engineer, who started out in much the same way as Henry Ford, bolting agricultural scrap parts together in a home workshop in Dayton Ohio. He produced an engine by 1902 that somebody wanted to manufacture under license and he moved to Indianapolis that year to supervise its production. This didn't last long - like many of Stutz's jobs in this period. He moved around the industry working in tire, carburetor and engine plants gaining experience and giving him a clear industry overview, which came in very handy when he started to make his own cars.

The 'A' model was followed-up with a more comprehensive model range in 1912. This included the car that would make his name famous for all time. The Bearcat was a true hairy-chested, macho sportscar. Rumor had it that Stutz specially designed the clutch with extra strong springs to prevent females getting behind the wheel. There was a choice between four- and six-cylinder power units, both of these were outsourced T-head Wisconsin engines. Stutz didn't make its own engines until 1917. Power outputs were competitive with 60 and 70 horsepower respectively developed by the two engines.

Solid racing success was quick to follow. Of thirty events entered in 1912 the Bearcat triumphed in twenty-five. The 'White Squadron' as the Stutz racing team came to be known was the deadly rival of the Mercer Runabout boys. A whacky races scenario!

As can be seen in our featured model, the steering wheel was on the right hand side and remained there until 1922. Artillery wheels with detachable rims were standard in 1914, but wires were available in the following year.

■ *Left: The Bearcat was an uncompromising sports carriage with few creature comforts. This model is now one of the most collectible cars in America.*

Engine: Four-cylinder T-head

Displacement: 389-cid

Horsepower: 50

Transmission: Four-speed rear axle mounted

Induction: Schebler carburetor

Body Style: Two-seater Sports

Number of Seats: 2

Wheelbase: 120 inches

Base Price: $2000

Number Produced: 647

1915 Cadillac Type 51

This model was the lucky recipient of the new V-8. The use of four cylinder power units was now banished for the next 67 years establishing Cadillac firmly as a luxury car manufacturer that didn't dally with economy engines. Although not the first to come up with a V-8 option, this was certainly the first engine to go into serious production in the US. It displaced 314 cubic inches and produced a healthy seventy brake horse power. The engine remained in service until 1927.

The Type 51 also saw the change to left drive (although right drive was still available as an option). This was a gradual process, which slowly filtered through the car industry. Henry Ford's early decision to go left on the Model T must have had a big influence on those who followed on, but some die-hards like Stutz held out 'on the right' until 1922.

Type 51 also showed modern influences in its body styling. The hood was more rounded off with top panels blending smoothly into side panels, unlike the sharp-edged, box-like shapes of yesteryear. Closed bodies like the Landaulet coupe were sleeker with shallow profile glass in side windows and windshields and lower rooflines. The overall effect was that the closed car compartment now appeared as an integral part of the design - rather than a square cabin bolted onto a chassis. Type 51 offered no less than nine body styles. Two touring cars with either 5 or 7 seats, a two-door salon with a passageway between the front and rear seats, a two-door roadster, the pretty two-door Landaulet coupe, the remarkable center-door 'sedan for five passengers', two limousines and an Imperial. The latter model had a glass partition between the seats for really grand people.

All closed cars had three-piece 'rain vision' windshields, a kind of early wraparound design. Open cars with the 'one man top' had side curtains, which opened with the doors.

A lot of thought had gone into the Type 51!

Engine: 90-degree L-head V-8

Displacement: 314.5-cid

Horsepower: 70

Transmission: Three-speed sliding gear selective

Induction: Cadillac carburetor under CF Johnson patents.

Body style: Two-door Sedan

Number of seats: 5

Wheelbase: 122 inches

Base Price: $2800

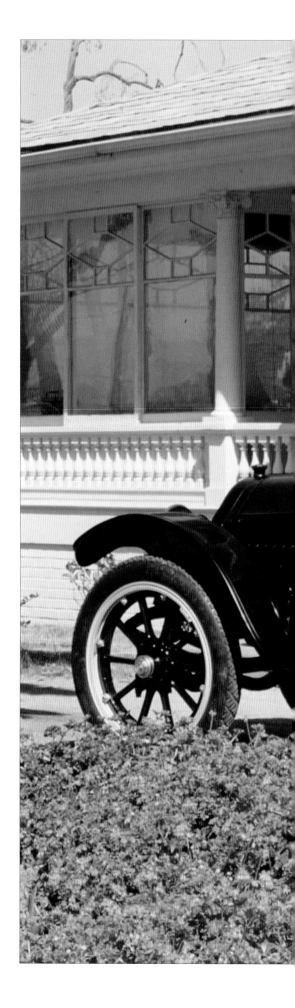

■ *Right: The all-new Type 51 center-door 'sedan for five passengers'. Its 'rain vision' windshield and the latest Cadillac V-8 engine made it a cutting-edge car in 1915.*

1915 Chevrolet H Series Roadster

William C. Durant had learned some lessons from the launch of his first Chevrolet, the Classic Six. Designed by Louis Chevrolet, the car was over-priced and over engineered.

He made more money from the launch of the Little, a budget car assembled at one of the many Chevrolet plants. Durant now planned to consolidate his efforts back in Flint Michigan –his old stamping ground. He had Arthur Mason, a former Buick engineer who now ran the Mason Motor Company (an engine facility already owned by Chevrolet), design a down to earth four-cylinder unit. The side benefit to the arrangement was that it resulted in Louis Chevrolet storming off to make Frontenacs. Under Chevrolet's leadership this company ultimately went bust. Durant was probably relieved at his departure.

The new overhead valve unit that Mason designed produced a respectable 24 horsepower out of 171 cubic inches. But most importantly, the engine was economical to produce. A much more practical proposition than Louis Chevrolet's complicated 299 cubic inch twin cam six-cylinder monster!

Coupled with the H series compact body style with a wheelbase of 106 inches (against 120 inches for the Classic Six), Durant had got back into the real world of volume car production. He was able to price the new range at under $1000. Small improvements also found their way into the H series design. Concealed door hinges, larger tires, no windshield braces, electric starter and headlights all conspired to give the car a modern appearance. Three model options were offered: a two door roadster with a flat deck, named The Royal Mail, a four-door touring car called the Baby Grand (this car was notorious for a stunt where it climbed the State Capitol steps at Des Moines, Iowa), and a Roadster known as the Amesbury Special.

Engine: OHV four-cylinder inline

Displacement: 171-cid

Horsepower: 24

Transmission: Three-speed selective sliding gears

Induction: Zenith two-jet carburetor

Body style: Two-door Roadster

Weight: 2100 lbs

Wheelbase: 106 inches

Base Price: $985

Number Produced: 13600 total for series

■ *Right: The very attractive Amesbury Special Roadster version of Chevrolet's 1915 'H' series. The car has the optional rear dickey seat with separate windshield and Houk Quick-detachable wire wheels.*

1915 Dodge Brothers Model 30-35

John and Horace Dodge established a small machine shop in Detroit in the early years of the century. They had already made a good living and a reputation for themselves by supplying the likes of R. E. Olds and Henry Ford. Their products were respected for quality and reliability. The brothers were smart enough to see the writing on the wall when large players like Ford sought to control costs by manufacturing their own components. The days of outsourced engines, and gearboxes in particular, were drawing to a close. Interestingly, the Dodge brothers were also Ford shareholders at a time when Henry Ford was planning to implement his dream of buying out non-family shareholders so that total control of FoMoCo would revert to the Fords.

When The Dodge Brothers announced that they would be introducing their own line of cars in 1914, the automobile industry was delighted. Their reputation gave them an enormous advantage.

The first Dodge offering was developed from their direct experience of competitive products. They knew exactly how their models could improve upon what was already available. Of course, they were particularly knowledgeable about the Model T, having supplied many of its components. Their Model 30-35 was sturdy in both body and design. It had an all-steel body made by Budd, and an early 12-volt electrical system, which included headlights and a self-starter as standard. An 'unburstable' L-Head engine of 212.3 cubic inches gave a reliable 35 horsepower. The three-speed gearbox was enclosed, and employed vanadium hardened gears. Oddly, its configuration was back to front. Leather seats were also standard on the car, as were a folding top, windshield, speedometer and demountable wheel rims. The Model T wasn't fitted with these options until well into the '20s.

Two model options were offered, a four-door tourer and a two-door roadster. Priced at $785, the models were an outstanding package, and the range immediately jumped into the number three sales slot for the year.

Engine: Four-cylinder L-Head

Displacement: 212.3-cid

Horsepower: 35 at 2000 rpm

Transmission: Three-speed

Body Styles: Four-door Tourer, Two-door Roadster

Weight: 2200 lbs

Wheelbase: 110 inches

Base Price: $785

Number Produced: 45,000

■ *Right: The neat looking Dodge Brothers Model 30-35 sold 45,000 units in its first year.*

1918   Cadillac Type 57

World War 1 was a busy time for Cadillac. After rigorous testing, they were awarded the status of 'standard model' for war service. This special status involved the supply of staff cars, ambulances, hearses, and police patrol vehicles for the services. Much of the reason for this was the recognized strength, power and reliability of the V-8 engine, which the company had adopted as its standard powerplant three years earlier. Busy too, because the founding Leland family finally left the company. This was also portrayed as a war-related issue. The Lelands left the company as a protest, over the fact that William Durant, (head of parent company General Motors) had refused to build much needed Liberty Aero engines for the war effort. Whether the family feelings on this matter were governed by patriotism, or the desire to profit from war work is a moot point. But the ultimate result of their dissatisfaction was that the family left to found Lincoln, which immediately tooled up to produce Liberty engines. Once the Lelands had gone,

■ *Below: Our featured model is an Open tourer, clearly showing the modern styling and spacious interior, which made it the 'standard model' for service in World War 1.*

Billy Durant relented and he also agreed to make the engines...

Type 57 was a larger, more comfortable car than earlier Cadillac models. Styling improvements meant that the hood flowed more smoothly into the windshield cowl, in a continuous straight line. Nine louvers adorned each side of the hood, raked back at a subtle six degrees. The windshield on open cars was slanted at a matching angle. This was a gradual move away from the upright boxiness of earlier cars. Other small improvements were also incorporated into the car, such as tilting headlight reflectors controlled by a lever.

The V-8 was also subject to modernization. It now had detachable heads and ultra-lightweight pistons together with a brand new transmission arrangement. Priced at under $3000 this car represented excellent value for money.

Engine: Ninety-degree L-head V-8

Displacement: 314.5-cid

Horsepower: 31.25

Body Style: Four-door Open Tourer

Number of Seats: 5

Weight: 3925 lbs

Wheelbase: 125 inches

Base Price: $2590

Number produced 45146 (including war production)

Chevrolet Series D

1918

Billy Durant, by now a regular player in our drama, had managed to buy back General Motors in 1915 with the aid of Chevrolet. But while he was maneuvering it seems that he took his eye off the ball at Chevrolet. The result was that the Model D, an admirable new project, didn't get the full marketing thrust that it deserved.

The car, which came in two models: a five-passenger Touring and a four-passenger Roadster. The Roadster was offered in Chevrolet Green with pleated French leather upholstery and had lots of exposed mahogany, varnished to a fine finish. Materials alone lift it out of the under $2000 category that it actually occupied. At just $1400 for the launch model the car was astonishingly good value.

Its body style was very much in vogue with its upscale big brother, the Cadillac Type 57. Hood and cowl now flowed smoothly into each other without an obvious step and there were slanted louvers on the hood sides. At 120 inches, the wheelbase was only 5 inches down on the Cadillac. This meant that the Chevrolet offered roomy accommodation too. The open car was well equipped, with a one-man waterproof top and side curtains. The body was described in advertising copy of the time as a 'delight to the eye' and 'a series of curves that blend harmoniously'. Whatever the value of the purple prose this was a good-looking set of wheels. Technologically too, the car was all there. Its floor pan was pressed steel and all its metal parts were now nickel-plated. The real kick came from the spanking new V-8 designed by Arthur Mason, the man who baled out the company with his sensible four-cylinder engine in 1913. It was an ambitious ninety-degree V-8 with overhead valves and detachable cross-flow cylinder heads, probably the most advanced engine of its kind around at the time. Its 288 cubic inches gave a guaranteed 55 brake horsepower.

By 1919 the model had disappeared. 'Why' is a complete mystery. Perhaps customers just couldn't get their heads round paying over $1000 for a Chevrolet, a lesson already learnt with the Classic Six. Personally, if I had been around at the time I'd have bought one. Chevrolet would not offer V-8 power again until the fifties.

■ *Left: The D4 Roadster resplendent with leather, wood, 16 candle electric headlights and distinctive 'bowtie' radiator badge. It looks every inch a Chevrolet.*

Engine:	Ninety-degree overhead valve V-8
Displacement:	288-cid
Horsepower:	55
Induction:	Zenith Double jet carburetor
Body style:	Two-seater Roadster
Weight:	3150 lbs
Wheelbase:	120 inches
Base Price:	$1550
Number Produced:	2781

1922 Duesenberg Model A Roadster

This manufacturer's roots can be traced back to March 1903 when one Fred Duesenberg, 'a bicycle builder from Iowa' filed for bankruptcy. Like all good businessmen, Fred bounced back, realizing that the demand for bicycles was about to be eclipsed by that for automobiles. To this end, he threw himself into the design of the Mason, which was named for Edward R Mason, a local attorney in Des Moines who put up the money. The 'Mason' featured a two-cylinder unit to begin, with but this was replaced by a four-cylinder unit designed by Dusenberg himself. At this time he enjoyed a good deal of success racing the cars including almost qualifying for the 1912 Indy 500.

By 1913 he had teamed up with his brother, August, to form the Duesenberg Motor Company in St Paul, Minnesota. This was the first of many different locations and incarnations of the company that bore their name. Strangely the brothers were never actually the owners. They preferred to remain as employees, while the owner/financiers did the worrying for them. This left them free to get on with the design, production and racing of the cars. This was what they really enjoyed.

By 1920 the Duesenberg Automobile and Motors Corporation was incorporated with funding of

■ *Below: Only 600 of the classic 'Model A' were built in five years. The result is that this Roadster model is now one of the cars most sought after by American collectors.*

$1.5 million, and was about to launch its first car. The prototype, which had its debut at the Hotel Commodore, created a sensation. It had four-wheel brakes, which was a first. The car was powered by a 260-cid eight-cylinder overhead valve engine, which produced a respectable eighty-eight. In another quirky move Dusenberg decided that he would upgrade the engine to single overhead camshaft for the production model. The prototype used the Duesenberg patented horizontal valve and rocker arm set-up. This change delayed the flow of cars into the dealers until late 1921.

The new 'Model A' as it was designated, came in a variety of factory bodies including a Tourer, Roadster, Sedan and Town car. All these models were all based on a 134-inch wheelbase chassis. The featured car is probably the nicest, a very attractive two-door Roadster with a host of chrome-plated details set off by the dark coachwork. White wall tires on spoked wire wheels and a white hood also add glamor. The rear deck is in an early boat style. The car heralds the classic styling of the 20s.

Engine: Single overhead camshaft straight eight-cylinder.

Displacement: 260-cid

Horsepower 88 at 3000 rpm

Transmission: Three-speed Manual

Body Style: Two-door Roadster

Number of seats: 2

Wheelbase: 134 inches

Base Price: $6500

Number Produced: 600

Studebaker Light Six

1923

According to company boss Albert Russel Erskine, six-cylinder cars 'were what made Studebaker famous'. Indeed, the Light, the Special and the Big Six were legends in their own lifetime. But the Studebaker Company had been around a lot longer than that. The company was around during the Civil War, and supplied the North with horse-drawn vehicles. It continued to prosper. There were plenty of small wars around the globe in the late nineteenth century, where the company's product was in demand. Their entry into the gasoline automobile business was rather more tentative. John M. Studebaker was something of a die-hard. He thought gas cars were smelly, and that electric was the way forward. But he was finally persuaded to go into car production by his rather more go-ahead son in law, Fred Fish. Studebaker subsequently took over the General Car Company in 1911. The Studebaker Corporation was now formed with Fred Fish as President.

The company continued to manufacture worthy, medium priced cars - profitably. Fred Fish retired in 1915, and Albert Erskine took over the management of the company. World War1 had begun in Europe and there was a great demand for military vehicles. Studebaker got their share of government supply contracts, which put the company in a healthy financial position to face the changing times in the '20s. Studebaker Corporation had some very able engineers on board, including Fred M. Zeder, Owen R. Skelton and Carl Breer. These men were responsible for designing the six-cylinder powerplant that kept the company's sales buoyant in the '20s. Subsequently, this engineering team defected to Chrysler, taking their know-how with them.

The Light Six had a new all steel body for 1923, in common with many other cars of the time. Studebaker held out against four-wheel brakes, considering them dangerous, so the car retained the two-wheel brakes at the rear. Body options were the two-door roadster, four-door tourer, two-door coupe, and four-door sedan. Our featured car is the cute coupe. Standard wheels were the artillery wood spoke type and the windshield on open cars was raked back provocatively. The engine was an L-head Inline six with an aluminum head, of 207.1 cubic inches, giving a credible forty horsepower.

Like all straight sixes, the resultant smooth power of the engine mounted in a relatively light body must have made the car a delight to drive.

■ *The next light six coupe in black awaits its owner.*

Engine:	L-Head inline six-cylinder
Displacement:	207.1-cid
Horsepower:	40 at 2000rpm
Induction:	Stromberg one-barrel carburetor
Weight:	2730 lbs
Wheelbase:	112 inches
Base Price:	$1395

Cadillac V63 Brougham

Since the introduction of V-8 power to its lineup in 1915, Cadillac hadn't looked back. Valuable contracts in World War 1 had boosted the company's position as one of the most profitable divisions of the General Motors group. With the departure of the founding Leland family, however, there was a period in the late teens and early '20s when the top management was in some disarray. Richard L. Collins, Herbert H. Rice and Lawrence P. Fisher all occupied the 'number one' position at the company during this period, and only the latter survived longer than a couple of years. Luckily, the Chief Engineer's job remained stable with Ernest Seaholm in charge from 1923 up to World War II. He kept things moving forward technologically.

By the time of our model, the V-8 had detachable heads and a balanced crankshaft. This, together with other detailed improvements would carry the engine right through to 1936. The V63 was also was the first Cadillac to be fitted with four-wheel brakes. New too was the Custom concept –a special collection of non-standard body styles. Sedan, Imperial Sedan, limousine, Imperial Suburban, Town Brougham, and a brace of coupes were all available for either two or five passengers.

Choice was the hallmark of the Custom. Today's car buyer expects a wide range of options, but back in 1923 this was remarkable stuff. To have a choice of twenty-four different color combinations, plus ten upholstery types was a new experience. New technology in paint finishes meant that many more colors were available, and this launched cars forward into a new realm of brighter hues leaving behind years of drab motoring. Nickel-plated radiator shells and headlights also improved the look of most model ranges. The Custom series also pioneered the scrolled-style radiator detail, which was soon adopted by the entire Cadillac range.

The result of all of this was to produce a car that needed to be sold at around $4000. This high price had the potential to have had a negative effect on sales. But customers loved the whole 'Custom' concept, and sales actually rose steadily. Cadillac found buyers for as many as 20,000 units per year throughout the middle years of the '20s.

■ *Left: The Cadillac V 63 Brougham shows clearly the new nickel-plated scrolled radiator shell and headlights. The hood is adorned with 27 louvers. Despite the racy color choices available on the model, the customer has opted for a discreet green.*

Engine:	L-Head V-8
Displacement:	314.5-cid
Horsepower:	85
Induction:	Float fed carburetor-Cadillac M/F to Johnson Patent
Weight:	4530 lbs
Wheelbase:	138 inches
Base Price:	$4950

1925 Hudson Super Six

Hudson powered out of the postwar sales slump in fine style. Profitability was a given at Hudson. The company was properly financed by Joseph Hudson from the word go, and was properly run by a strong and stable management team led by Roy D. Chapin. This was unlike the fragmented management pattern at many other car manufacturers who hired and fired top people after a couple of years, or else they became disaffected and left to found their own companies. Hudson was either very wise or very fortunate, as they managed to keep a great team together over a long period. The family-feel of the company may have contributed to this. Roscoe B. Jackson was President for many years, alongside Roy Chapin, who had married into the Hudson Family. This happy situation meant that shareholders were also well looked after. The regularly paid dividends resulted in increasing confidence in the company. This feel good factor enabled the company to weather periods of depression better than most. They also cut prices to boost sales whenever necessary.

Hudson now had a good foothold in the domestic market, thanks to its marketing strategy. The Hudson marque took care of mid-section sales whilst the Essex line, launched in 1919, provided budget-end sales. The combined sales of the two divisions put the company at third place in the year's sales charts, behind Ford and Chevrolet. The Essex range was not a cheapened form of Hudson but a completely unique range, with its own separate design and power options. Essex also had a reputation for sportiness. Hudson, on the other hand, relied on a more solid, well-heeled image.

The car that sustained Hudson sales in the '20s was the Super Six. It was based on the company's L-Head inline 289 cubic inch six-cylinder power unit, which gave an impressive 76 horsepower. The car offered fantastic value, priced at just over $1000. Hudson continuously developed the standard power plant, and by 1925 it sported aluminum pistons and chain timing actuation instead of helical gear drive. Car bodies were built by Biddle & Smart- many with aluminum panels, which kept the weight down considerably. In 1925 a new brougham body from this company became an overnight success because at a mere $1450, it looked every bit as good as a $3000 Cadillac!

The popular Coach model was also redesigned in this year, and was given slimmer side pillars and a curving windshield base. Tires were changed from 33 x 6.2 to 33 x 6.00. The overall appearance of the car is that of a solid and well-engineered vehicle, which was no slouch either, with its smooth six-cylinder engine.

Engine: L-Head Six-cylinder Inline

Displacement: 289-cid

Horsepower: 76

Base Price: $1165

Number Produced: 109,840

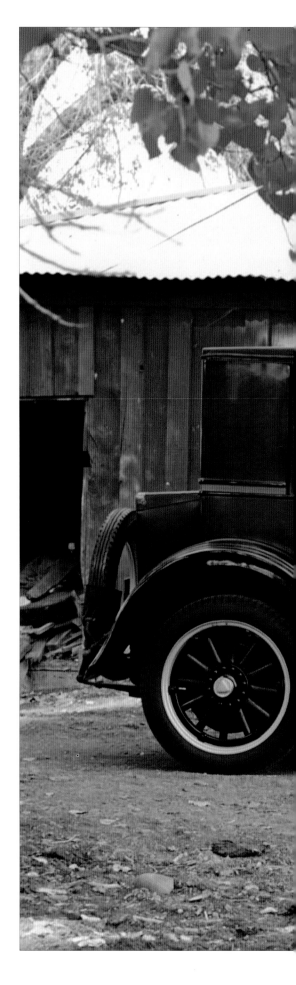

■ *Right: The commanding Hudson Super Six exudes confidence.*

1925 Hupmobile Series R Touring

In 1909 Robert Craig Hupp began his company with a small cute runabout, which was surprisingly well equipped with a four-cylinder engine of 16.9 horsepower and two-speed sliding gears. Priced at only $750 it was designated the Model 20. Thus began a marque that was to last for thirty years and always provide interesting value-for-money cars. Sadly, Hupp himself parted from the company quite early on in its history. He was gone by 1911. Like Ransom Eli Olds, who had parted early on from the company he had named, Hupp had to resort to using his initials for future car exploits but RCH doesn't really have the same resonance as REO and after a few years he disappeared from sight. The two board members he quarreled with were Charles Hastings and J. Walter Drake. Both men would be involved with the company for a good many years to come. Early sales success was credited to Hastings hard work in establishing the car's reputation. Sales rose quickly, going from 1,617 in 1909 to 6,079 in 1911.

A 1910 car straight off the production line took part in a round-the-world promotional trek covering 48,600 miles and traveling through 26 countries. The man responsible for engineering the car following Hupp's departure was Emil Nelson, who left the company in 1912 and who formed his own manufacturing company - Nelson in 1917. Following Nelson's departure, Frank E. Watts took over and remained in charge of engineering for the next 26 years - virtually to the end of the company's life. By 1916, Hupp was in some disarray. Drake had led the company into developing an over-complicated model range and some large, ambitious vehicles that were moving away from the company's founding ethic of value for money cars. A parallel to what happened at Olds following R. E.'s departure.

The only man who could stand up to Drake was his former colleague Charles Hastings. Hastings had retired to California some three years earlier. He was recalled by the board and invited to serve as President from 1917 onward. In that first year he was responsible for a new, smaller model – that put the company right back at the popular end of the market. This, 'Series R' car was given the familiar four-cylinder power unit that had been the mainstay of the company all along. The model revived the company's fortunes, reaching an apogee in 1923 with 38,279 cars sold.

The series R was available in 5 body styles: a touring model, roadster, coupe, club sedan and regular sedan. It was well finished, with two-piece bumpers, nickel-plated drum headlights and radiator shell, and had a louvered hood. But by 1925 the body style was looking dated.

Engine: Four-cylinder in-line

Horsepower: 39

Transmission: Three speed selective

Base price: $1225

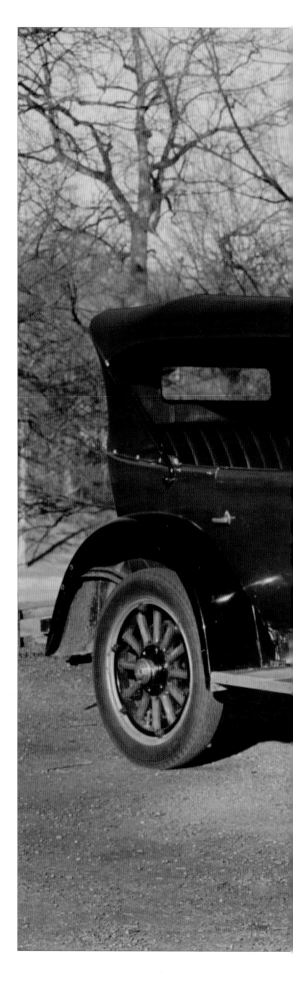

■ *Right: The last of the Four-cylinder Hupmobiles. The following year the company went straight-eight!*

Chrysler Series 70 Royal Coupe   1927

Walter Chrysler lived the original American rags to riches story. The one time farmhand, grocery boy, silverware salesman and roundhouse sweeper for Union Pacific was 'discovered' by Billy Durant in 1910 when he put him in charge of Buick as works manager. He learnt his craft well. When he left General Motors just nine years later, he was already a millionaire. Durant reportedly paid Walter Chrysler $10 million to buy out his share of Buick. By 1919 Chrysler had had enough of Durant, and his next job was at the Chase National Bank. The bank had many big customers in the automotive industry and by the early '20s many of these companies were ailing. It was Chrysler's knowledge of the industry that got him the job to help straighten these out. Firstly, he was asked to try to put Willys-Overland back on track. In the course of this job one thing – a new six-cylinder power plant – caught his eye. It was lying fallow at the Elizabeth, New Jersey plant that Willys were forced to sell. The creators of this interesting piece of engineering were a team we have encountered already at Studebaker, Fred Zeder, Owen Skelton and Carl Breer.

In the meanwhile, Chrysler had moved on to sort out the equally unstable Maxwell company, and it was this that he used as his final platform to launch Chrysler. He hired the Maxwell team and set them up at the Chalmers-Maxwell factory in Detroit to further develop the engine that he had decided would power his first car - the Chrysler B 70. He launched his first model at the Hotel Commodore in 1924.

Chrysler's marketing strategy was simple –to sell a car for $1500 that provided the same kind of motoring pleasure for which people were willing to pay $5000. This strategy worked well and the car soon evolved into 'Series 70' with nine different body styles. These included a roadster model, phaeton, the Royal Coupe, a sedan, brougham and Crown Sedan. All the models were all based on a single 112-inch wheelbase and the same basic chassis. Four-wheel hydraulic brakes were standard on the entire series.

The engine was an impressive six-cylinder, with 218.6 cubic inches and a high compression rating (for the time), with cylinder heads giving a 4.7:1 ratio. This developed a respectable 68 brake horsepower. Quite a package!

■ *Left: The aristocratic prow of the Royal Coupe decries its comparatively modest price of $1695. This closed car retains the drum-style headlights that were soon to be replaced with the bullet type.*

Engine:	L-Head Inline Six-cylinder
Displacement:	218.6-cid
Horsepower:	68 at 3000 rpm
Transmission:	Three-speed manual
Body Style:	Two-door Coupe
Weight:	2935 lbs
Base Price:	$1695
Number Produced:	72039

1927 Ford Model T Pickup

Henry Ford was in an unassailable position within his company by 1925, he owned it, he was President and he decided what went on. He certainly wasn't going to listen to anyone criticizing his revered Model T. When critics called it old fashioned he had the company's leading position in the car sales chart to reassure him. That, and a few million dollars in the bank. But his management team recognized the threat posed by Ford's competitors, particularly Chevrolet's Superior range. The defection of the Head of Ford Production, William S. Knudsen, over to Chevrolet was also worrying. But instead of making any radical changes, Henry Ford introduced cosmetic adjustments in an attempt to silence his critics.

The tires for the 'T' were upgraded to the balloon type in 1925. The most radical departure for '26 was the reverse of the 'black as the only color option' diktat. Other minor changes to the Model T that had been announced in 1925 as part of the 'Improved Ford' promotion, included new fenders, running boards and a modified chassis. Extra models were also added to the range. This was probably the most significant number of changes that anyone could remember in the car's history. But such measures were actually too little, and certainly too late.

By 1927 the Model T line was shut down with no replacement planned. There were six long months of feverish speculation before the line began rolling again. However, some smart marketing had come out of the 'Improved Ford' package, in the shape of the Roadster Pickup. Because of their rugged practicality and low price, people had been using Model Ts as utility vehicles all along. The option had been to buy the chassis-only version, which gave customers the option to construct their own buckboard style back, modified to carry fence posts, livestock or whatever was required. Ford now marketed a ready-to-buy package for practical hauling. This was a great product that, in years to come, would be marketed as a vehicle in its own right, and become an essential part of American transport culture - the pick-up.

Engine: L-Head Four-cylinder

Displacement: 176.7-cid

Horsepower: 20 at 1600 rpm

Transmission: Two-speed planetary

Body Style: Roadster Pickup

Weight: 1736 lbs

Wheelbase: 100 inches

Base Price: $381

Number Produced: 75,406

■ *Right: A Roadster Pickup from 1927 – the final year of Model T production. In this year alone over 75,000 units found buyers.*

Hudson Roadster

1927

The late '20s were a good time for Hudson. Adding together Hudson and Essex sales, the company was always in the top five producers. Essex had been created specially to pioneer models for the budget end of the closed car market, and it had been recognized as such by no less a force than the New York Times. In an article of January 1926, the paper expressed a view that: 'the flood of new, small closed sixes is one of the outstanding features of the year... That the light economical six makes a definite and potent appeal cannot be doubted. Indeed the Hudson and Essex organization has one of the most remarkable achievements of 1925 to its credit in the production of 250,000 cars of both makes, almost entirely closed models'. That year, Hudson invested a massive $3 million in a new production plant. Hudson's Model 'O' of 1927 demonstrated the same commitment to strong investment in the company's future. This was a completely new model with a host of improvements on its predecessors.

Astonishingly, the holy of holies - Hudson's trusty L-Head Super Six engine was also revamped, with a tasty new F-Head, better manifolding and improved valve design. Whilst it was of identical bore and stroke to the old unit, the improvements took the power up to 92 horsepower. This was transmitted to the rear wheels via an improved single plate clutch. In fact, many experts regard the horsepower rating as a conservative estimate of the engine's output. Claims of 100 mph plus were not unusual from drivers of the car. The brakes were also beefed up. These were four-wheel mechanical. A new rear suspension, 18-inch wheel rims, full-crown fenders, reshaped hood profile, a four-inch lower bodyline and bullet-shaped headlights all contributed to the truly racy look of the new car.

But why was all this undertaken? Hudson already had a pretty good market share with a proven car. The explanation may lie in Chairman Roy D. Chapin's mission statement of the same year. He noted that 'buyers are now insistent that cars shall excel in appearance and convenience as well as in the fundamental qualities. The demand for improved performance is widespread and is being met by better design, materials and workmanship'.

■ *Left: A hot rod in the making. The sporty looking Hudson Roadster just invites you to climb in!*

Engine:	F-Head Inline six-cylinder
Displacement:	288.5-cid
Horsepower:	92 at 3200 rpm
Transmission:	Three-speed sliding gear
Body Style:	Two-door Roadster
Weight:	3480 lbs
Wheelbase:	127 3/8 inches
Base Price:	$1500
Number Produced:	66034

Studebaker Big Six President   1927

Albert Erskine, President of Studebaker was worried. He just didn't feel that South Bend, Indiana, the location of the company plant, had enough style and class for his enterprise. He had designs on the prestige car market. Erskine's solution was to book space at the Plaza Hotel in New York that summer, in order to present the company's range to the socialites of Manhattan.

But the presentation wasn't a great success. So instead, he launched a new model, the Erskine, styled with so-called European flair. This model also failed to impress. As a last resort, he decided to rely on the Studebaker product speaking for itself, at least for the time being.

The six cylinder cars had made Studebaker famous, and the company planned an impressive, all new 'six' for 1927. The President Big Six model was restyled to include a lower body line, sloping rounded roof, double-side body moldings, a two-tone paint job, steel disc type wheels, 'acorn' shaped nickel-plated headlights and nickel-plated double bumpers. The cars also had 'Atlanta-style' hood mascots and 'French' windshield visors.

Two wheelbase lengths were offered, 120 and 127 inches. A host of extras could also be ordered, which could put the car firmly in the luxury category. These included a no-draft ventilating windshield, Watson stabilizers, engine thermometer, clock, hydrostatic gas gauge, coincidental lock, oil filter, Alemite chassis lubrication, automatic wiper, double rear vision mirror, armrests, toggle grips, auto dome light, rear signal light, emergency lamp on an extension cord, four wheel mechanical brakes, balloon tires and even a Vanity case smoking set!

The famous six-cylinder engine was boosted to 354 cubic inches, giving 75 horsepower at 2400 rpm. Three body styles were now available: a four-door custom sedan, four-door limo and a four-door duplex phaeton. The entire range could accommodate seven passengers in great luxury.

■ *Left: The 1927 restyled President four-door sedan in dark red with distinctive nickel-plated features.*

Engine: L-Head inline six-cylinder	
Displacement: 354-cid	
Horsepower: 75 at 2400 rpm	
Transmission: Three-speed manual	
Induction: Ball & Ball one-barrel Model SV 33 carburetor	
Body style: Four-door Sedan	
Weight: 2495 lbs	
Wheelbase: 120/127 inches	
Base Price: $2245	
Number Produced: 7949/9405	

1928 Cunningham Series V7

Just like Studebaker, Cunningham was another auto producer that started out by manufacturing high quality horse-drawn vehicles. The company's origins went back to the mid-nineteenth century. Joseph Cunningham inherited his fathers carriage business in 1886 and consolidated the company's worth by concentrating on a range of superbly handcrafted vehicles, from dogcarts to Berlins. But like many smart businessmen at the turn of the 20th century, Joseph could see that there was a wind of change sweeping through society, and that horseflesh would soon be replaced by horsepower of a different sort. His intention to produce a horseless carriage was realized in 1907 when he completed a vehicle using a Continental engine. By 1911 the Cunningham full production model was ready. The 'Model J' had its own four-cylinder engine, which developed 40 horsepower.

Joseph Cunningham obviously thought big. Only two years later, he graduated to a large, 442-cid V-8 capable of a modest 45 horsepower. The cars themselves were also big, with no wheelbase smaller than 130 inches, and were to grow even larger in subsequent years.

By 1919 Cunningham cars were winning speed trials, and the famous racing driver Ralph De Palma, drove one at a reputed 98 mph in a speed trial at Sheepshead Bay. As well as performance ability, the cars also had a reputation for the immaculate style and finish of the coachwork, a reflection of their pre-engine heritage. The cars were long and sleek and their good looks and classy reputation attracted a rich and famous clientele. Hollywood movie stars and celebrities, such as William Randolph Hearst, Mary Pickford, Cecil B. DeMille, Fatty Arbuckle, Blanche Sweet and Harold Lloyd all drove Cunninghams in the '20s. Unsurprisingly, the price of the cars was very steep – buyers had to pay between $5,000 and $9,000 for the privilege of ownership. Such lavish cars had their time and place. When the economic downturn arrived in the 1930s, conspicuous consumption was no longer considered smart, and the company was forced to retrench into ambulance and hearse production.

1928 Cunningham models included a touring car, cabriolet, roadster, two-door coupe and Town car. A choice of wheelbase was offered, of either 132 or 142 inches.

■ *Right: The 1928 Cunningham with its exclusive styling and superb build-quality. Arguably, it was one of the best-looking cars of the '20s.*

Engine: V-8

Displacement: 442-cid

Horsepower: 106

Transmission: Three-speed manual

Body Style: Two-door Touring

Wheelbase: 132 and 142 inches

Base Price: $7000

1928 Ford Model A

So here it was at last! The first all-new Ford model for nineteen years. Years in which Ford had completely failed to develop a replacement for their one and only model. Instead of having a new lineup ready and waiting in the wings, Ford were left with a gaping lack of product, and were forced to shut down their entire production line in May 1927. This allowed Chevrolet to take over as the number one-selling manufacturer. In the ensuing six months, rumors circulated about the introduction of a Linford model - a cross between a Lincoln and a Ford. This was not entirely surprising. Ford had purchased the Lincoln Company out of receivership in 1922 from the Leland Family, and Henry Ford's son, Edsel, had run the company very successfully from that time, developing a model range that Ford now desperately needed to access.

The new car was inevitably compared to its predecessor, and its heritage was recognizable in some regards. The same four-cylinder L-Head engine was present, but this time it displaced 200 cubic inches and generated twice the horsepower. The 'A' also shared the semi elliptic front and transverse leaf spring rear suspension that Henry Ford so passionately believed in. He defended the re-cycled suspension by saying 'we use transverse springs for the same reason that we use round wheels - because we have found nothing better for the purpose'. However, beyond these similarities the two models had little in common.

In place of a magneto, the Model A had a modern electrical system, complete with battery and coil type ignition. Nickel-plated electric headlamps were standard. The car also had four-wheel mechanical brakes and double action shock absorbers. In place of the old two-speed planetary gears, a three-speed selective sliding type gearbox was now fitted. The wheelbase was also up by 31/2 inches. The new bodyshell had an attractive longer, lower look that the Model T, with sleeker windows and a high beltline. The fenders had arched cross sections and welded wire wheels replaced the old wood spoke artillery type. Two-piece nickel-plated front and rear bumpers were added, and the radiator shell now had a distinctive 'V' shaped dip over the top front of the radiator core. Nine body options were offered, something for everyone, including a two-door roadster, phaeton, Tudor and fordor sedan, sport coupe and even a taxicab. Strangely, the taxi was the most expensive car that year, priced at $600. Maybe Henry figured they made up the money with the extra tips.

All in all, it is fair to say that the Model A was in every way a more than worthy successor to the crown of America's number one selling car.

Engine: Inline L-Head Four-cylinder Inline

Displacement: 200.5-cid

Horsepower: 40

Base Price: $550

Number Produced: 633,594

■ *Right: Model A Tudor, Walton-style outside a lumber mill.*

Pontiac 6-28 Roadster

1928

Depending which way you look at it, Pontiac is either a suburb of Detroit or an Indian Chief. Either way, it's a good name for a car. The Pontiac Buggy Company was originally part of the Oakland Motor Company, started in 1907 by Edward Murphy and Alanson P. Brush. When Oakland was bought by Billy Durant in 1909 to join the General Motors empire, the company continued to produce mid-priced models. The General Manager, George Hannum, decided that the company needed a lower priced market entry model and code-named his idea 'Relot'. Alfred P. Sloan who was managing GM, after the departure of Billy Durant, recognized the sense of this. After all, Hudson had started Essex for the same reason a couple of years earlier. Having two car marques at completely different price points made good economic sense. This strategy had pole-vaulted Hudson several rungs up the sales ladder. Experimental engineers Ormond E. Hunt and Henry M. Crane were asked to develop the idea. Their proposal was to graft a six-cylinder engine onto a Chevrolet chassis. At this time, Chevrolet's engines were almost universally fours. Essex's success had been won by six-cylinder 'closed cars' and this was the target to beat. Hannum's leadership wasn't to last. He was succeeded by Alfred Glancy, who hired his own team to see the task completed. The 'four horsemen' as they were known Ben Anibal, Fenn Holden, Herman Schwarze and Roy Milner were all seasoned professionals, having spent a decade at Cadillac learning their craft. The Pontiac name was already part of the company's heritage, and it provided the excuse for an Indian head hood ornament to hang the publicity on.

The sales launch was designated 'the Pow Wow with heap big eats at lunchtime'. This took place in 1926 at the New York Automobile Show. Although Series 6-27 was hardly remarkable, it was well designed for its purpose, and in its first year it set a sales record by finding 76,696 buyers.

The car's chassis was conventional and its L-head six was decidedly unexciting (with a meager forty horsepower developed from 185-cid), but it was well targeted to compete against other low-priced sixes. At $825 only the Essex was cheaper. The sales just kep on coming - by March 1929 100,000 Pontiacs had been sold. The formula was obviously working.

By 1928 Pontiac had a fully fledged range, with seven models on offer. Its body styling now had more sweeping lines, a raised panel on the top of the hood, deep crowned fenders. Mechanically, other improvements included four-wheel mechanical brakes. Pontiac was here to stay.

■ *Left: The Two-door roadster in blue with later type Jaxon ten-spoke wood wheels and a standard front bumper.*

Engine:	L-Head Six-cylinder inline
Displacement:	186.5-cid
Horsepower:	48
Base Price:	$775
Number Produced:	80,000

Auburn Speedster 120

The origins of Auburn lie in a small carriage company started by Charles Eckhart back in 1874. Eckhart had previously worked for Studebaker in South Bend where he picked up the skills of his trade. His sons Frank and Morris took over the family firm in 1893 and started the Auburn Automobile Company. A single-cylinder, chain drive runabout soon gave way to a two-cylinder car in 1905, and in they manufactured a four-cylinder version in 1909. Sales continued throughout World War I, but by 1919 the company had began to lose direction. A consortium of Chicago businessmen led by William Wrigley Jr. (of chewing gum fame) bought the Eckharts out.

Despite restyling the range to add the Auburn Beauty Six, the company got caught in the post war sales dip. In four model years, just over 15,000 cars were sold. By 1924 the company was producing fewer than 10 cars a day. Enter hotshot salesman Erret Lobban Cord, who had made over $1,000,000 selling Moon cars for the Chicago based Quinlan Car Company. He was now looking to invest. First he took a lowly paid position as General Manager of Auburn, on the understanding that he could acquire stock if he could get the company 'off the bottom'. He authorized some cosmetic restyling, adding a touch of nickel plate here and a custom paint job there. Thus beautified, the backlog of cars on the Auburn lot finally began to sell. In 1925 he began buying straight eights from Lycoming and he had James Crawford (Auburn Chief Engineer) bolt these into the existing six-cylinder chassis. He then commissioned an outstanding 'boat tail' design by Al Leamy. A combination of the two factors, an improved engine plus and eye-catching looks, really made Aurburn sales take off.

At about this time, the demise of Mercer left a gap in the market for somebody to challenge Stutz, and the new Auburn wanted the slot. The car was well engineered for the times, with four-wheel hydraulic brakes and Bijar lubrication.

Seven models were on offer for 1929: a speedster, cabriolet, phaeton, Victoria, sedan (both five and seven seat), and sport sedan.

■ *Left: The superb 1929 Boat tail Speedster styled by Al Leamy in two-tone red/black, complete with aerodynamic 'split' windshield.*

Engine:	Eight-cylinder inline
Displacement:	298.6-cid
Horsepower:	125
Transmission:	Three-speed manual
Body Style:	Two-door Roadster
Number of seats:	4
Wheelbase:	136 inches
Base Price:	$1895

1929 Chrysler Imperial L Sedan

Walter Chrysler had been busy. To consolidate his position in the motor industry, he had improved his model range dramatically, widening the number of models available and moved toward the upper end of the market, while selling at prices that undercut those of his rival Cadillac. He had bought Dodge in 1928, not for cash, but paid for in Chrysler stock. This move would provide him with the distribution outlets he needed to crack the volume market.

He then created Desoto and Plymouth to give him access to all other market sectors. This meant that, as Chrysler approached the '30s he was in a very strong position to weather the storm of the Depression. His combined companies thrust him high in the industry sales chart taking him to third place in 1928, behind only Ford and Chevrolet.

The Chrysler Imperial was Walter P's prestige car, which had been originally launched in 1927. Styling was long and low based on a 136-inch wheelbase chassis. The car had a scalloped hood and radiator shell, a style some say was 'borrowed' from Vauxhall of England. In fact, Chrysler was not averse to incorporating all kinds of elements from other cars in his designs.

It was hoped that here was a series of cars that could take on Cadillac head-to-head. In fact, although the Imperial worked out about $600 cheaper than an equivalent Cadillac model, in many ways the Chrysler was more technologically advanced. For example, the Imperial had four-wheel hydraulic brakes, while the Cadillac was still using mechanical brakes. Also, the beefed up 309 cubic inch version of the Chrysler six engine block, complete with the high compression Red Head (5.2:1) was churning out a stunning 110 brake horsepower, whereas the Cadillac's 314-cid V-8 scraped together a mere 85 horsepower. The Cadillac probably would have had the better torque of the two cars, but hey, not everybody drove like their granny even then. Chrysler even offered the same kind of options on special custom-built bodies that Cadillac did: versions by LeBaron, Dietrich and Locke were all available (at a price) in addition to the eleven factory-listed bodies.

Last but hardly least, the car looked great, with its cadet-style windshield, its long lines accentuated by the new two-tone color scheme, bullet style headlamps, body-colored wire wheels and distinctive Viking's head winged radiator cap.

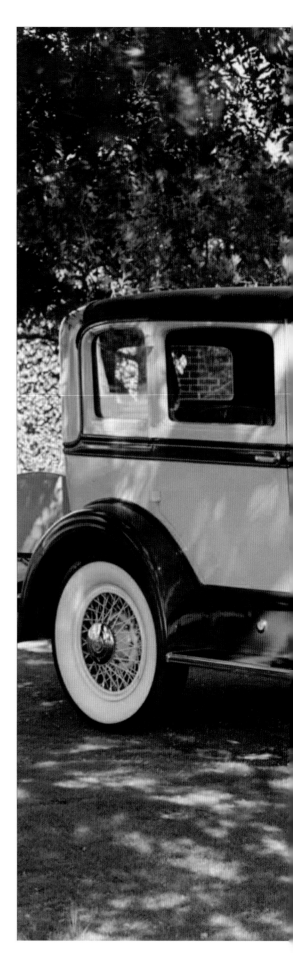

■ *Right: The 1929 Chrysler Imperial Sedan, with an immaculate two-tone cream and brown paint job shows how serious Chrysler's threat to more established prestige car manufacturers really was.*

Engine:	L-Head Inline six-cylinder
Displacement:	309.3-cid
Horsepower:	110 at 3200 rpm
Weight:	$4460
Wheelbase:	136 inches
Base Price:	$3095
Number Produced:	2506

1929 De Soto Series K

At the same time that Walter P. Chrysler was trying to buy Dodge Brothers from bankers Dillon Read and Co., he thought it would be smart to hedge his bets by creating his own division to bridge the gap between the top-end sales of Chrysler and his budget priced Plymouths. This was the inspiration behind De Soto. De Soto was named for the Spanish explorer Hernando De Soto who had explored the Mississippi Valley some centuries earlier, along with La Salle. But by the time the first De Sotos were ready in 1929, Walter Chrysler had managed to buy Dodge and it could have been thought that De Soto was surplus to requirements. But first year sales for the line set an all-time record, one that wasn't even approached for another 30 years. A massive 81,065 cars were sold in the model year, beating Chrysler's own sales and those of Pontiac.

The Series K was not the most outstanding car around, but at $845 it offered a lot for the cash. Seven models were available all with the L-Head six of 174.9 cubic inches, giving a respectable 55 horsepower. This was enough to give the Series K models a lively and enjoyable performance. Four-wheel hydraulic braking was by manufactured by Lockheed. Wood spoke wheels were offered as standard, but wire wheels were an option taken by most customers. Lovejoy shock absorbers and rubber engine mounts contributed to a smooth ride quality and passenger comfort. Externally, there were also some nice styling touches. Chrome-plated bullet headlights were mounted on an upward curving tie-bar, triple groups of hood louvers, built-in cowl lamps and a host of special paint jobs all went to suggest a car of quality. The fact that the car was on sale at under $1000 was a real incentive.

Engine: L-Head Six Cylinder in line

Displacement: 174.9 cid

Horsepower: 55

Transmission: Three-speed selective sliding gears

Induction: Stromberg IV carburetor

Body style: Four-door Phaeton

Number of seats: 5

Weight: 2445 lbs

Wheelbase: 109.75 inches

Base Price: $845

Number Produced: 81,065

■ *Right: The magnificent 1929 De Soto Series K four-door Phaeton was a great buy at $845.*

Dodge Senior Six

A fter the untimely end of both of the roistering Dodge brothers in 1920, the famous company was left to the two widows. Uncertain how to continue the company and concerned by a marked downturn in sales, the two women decided to sell out to New York bankers Dillon Read and Company. Dillon Read paid $146 million for the company, which was then the largest transaction ever known in auto trade banking.

The bank put accountants in charge of the company, who had no knowledge of the auto business. The company's fortunes continued to wane. Walter P. Chrysler was finally able to gain control of the company in 1928, having been rejected on his earlier attempt. Chrysler's vision for Dodge was to allow the company to operate without any drastic change of image. Dodge had good customer loyalty in the lower end of the mid-priced market. More importantly, the company had a great dealer network. This asset would help Chrysler increase his penetration into a wider market segment.

Dodge had always abreast of current trends. The Senior Six had had four-wheel hydraulic brakes by 1927. Further improvements for our featured year of 1929 included a restyled radiator shell, vertical hood louvers, automatic radiator shutters, a cadet-type sun visor, frosted silver-finish dash panel with full instrumentation, automatic windshield wipers, front and rear bumpers, interior courtesy lights, velvet mohair upholstery, smoking cases and mahogany finish steering wheel. The option list is very extensive.

More substantial changes were made in the lengthened chassis, which gave a four-inch increase to the length of the wheelbase. A more powerful six-cylinder engine was now fitted. Lovejoy brand shocks were also added to improve the ride and handling.

No less than nineteen different body options were now available, too many to list. In short, the car was an astonishing package for under $1000!

■ *Left: This dark red two-door Roadster Senior Six looks like a car that should cost over $2000. In fact, it was available for just $995.*

Engine: Six-cylinder L-Head inline

Displacement: 214.6-cid

Horsepower: 78 at 3000 rpm

Transmission: Three-speed selective sliding gears

Induction: Stromberg one-barrel carburetor

Body Style: Two-door Roadster

Number of Seats: 4

Weight: 2695 lbs

Wheelbase: 120 inches

Base Price: $995

1929 La Salle

Cadillac was named for the French explorer who discovered Detroit. So what was more natural than to dip back into history once again to name Cadillac's new brand for 1927. Another Frenchman this time, a Monsieur La Salle, who explored the Mississippi valley in the 1600s gave his name to a model that was to turn out to be a flop for Cadillac and GM.

Created to fill the price gap between Buick and Cadillac, the La Salle brand should have worked well. A young, up and coming designer, J. Harley Earl, was working at the Don Lee Corporation in California when he came to the attention of Cadillac's President Lawrence P. Fisher. Fisher had taken over as President in 1924. He quickly recruited Earl to design the new cars.

Cadillac knew that they had to increase sales. Adding a division with more cutting-edge design and less staid looking models seemed a good idea. To achieve this, Fisher founded a new department 'art and color' which was an attempt to disentangle the design function from engineering considerations. Earl always hated the department name, which he felt sounded superficial. When American auto manufacturers want their product to look better, they often turn to Europe for inspiration. Earl did exactly this, and was impressed with the looks of the Hispano-Suiza. But Earl's designs far exceeded anything that Europe could offer, and the La Salle styling was always one of the strongest aspects of the range.

Because La Salles were engineered to Cadillac's high standards, their customers were buying into a high-quality range. Indeed it has been suggested that if the cars had been badged as Cadillacs, theirs could have been a success story. The 303 cubic inch V-8, capable of 75 horsepower pushing along Harley Earl's elegant body very nicely. Test ace Bill Rader drove a stripped La Salle stock car at the GM proving track for 951 miles at an average speed of 95.3 mph.

The La Salle experiment initially looked good. Combined sales took Cadillac over 40,000 units for the first time ever in 1928. By 1929 sales were at over 50,000 cars.

Engine: Ninety-degree L-Head V-8

Displacement: 328 cid

Horsepower (Estimated): 80

Body Style: Two-door Roadster

Number of Seats: 2/4

Weight: 3990 lbs

Wheelbase: 125 inches

Base Price: $2345

Sales: 22,961

■ *Right: This dark red 1929 La Salle Roadster is an example of classic Harley Earl styling.*

Lincoln Model L

1929

Henry Martyn Leland, the founder of Cadillac was already 74 when he stormed out, leaving the company after a quarrel with Billy Durant. Durant insisted that he had fired the Lelands. They maintained that Durant had refused to do his patriotic duty by producing Liberty Aero Engines for the War effort. Whichever version was true, Leland subsequently set up a company to make the engines, receiving a government contract and a ten million dollar advance to do so.

But towards the end of the war, the Lelands ended up with a huge factory, 6000 workers and mounting debts. To power their way out of these financial problems, they did what they knew best - manufacture cars. Within three hours of announcing his return to auto manufacturing, Henry Leland had raised $6.5 million worth of stock.

Naming the new company 'Lincoln', for the first president Leland had voted for, might have indicated the era Henry Leland was most comfortable in. The auto market had moved on by this time, and the first Lincolns were very old-fashioned looking. Precision engineering was his watchword with the new cars and due to Leland's attention to detail, the cars were also late in getting to the market. Two demerit points already! After 17 months of trading, only 3400 cars had been sold against projections of 6000 per year. A panic-stricken board of directors called in the receivers.

Henry Ford was immediately attracted to Lincoln for three interesting reasons. Firstly, the company would give him instant access to the upper end of the market with a good basic product line that could be quickly overhauled. Secondly, he was looking for a task to occupy his son Edsel. Edsel had a strong instinct for style and taste, which was unsatisfied by his work on the Model T. Thirdly, was Ford's long-standing enmity for Henry Leland .

Cadillac had sprung from the ashes of one of Henry Ford's first companies. It was also Leland who had persuaded the shareholders to desert Ford in his favor. Buying Lincoln out of trouble cost Ford $8 million, but he probably enjoyed spending the money. A picture survives of the signing of the agreement. White-bearded Leland and his son Wilfred both look thoroughly dejected. Edsel Ford stares confidently at the camera and even Henry wears a tight-lipped smile. Appropriately, a portrait of President Lincoln looks down on the scene.

■ *Left: By 1929 Lincolns had become handsome and tasteful, thanks to Edsel Ford. He chose the greyhound hood mascot personally.*

Engine:	60-degree V8 L-Head
Displacement:	384.8 cid
Horsepower:	90 at 2800 rpm
Induction:	Stromberg 03 Updraft carburetor
Base Price:	$4800
Number Produced:	7,641

1929 Plymouth Model U

Plymouth was named for the Plymouth Rock, an enduring symbol of New World spirit, and associated with the Pilgrim qualities of integrity, simplicity and honesty. The name exemplified the ambitions of the brand. Walter P. Chrysler designed the Model U as a no-nonsense entry into the budget end of the car market. It was launched to go head-to-head with Ford and Chevrolet. The model's first year sales were respectable at 50,000, but this hardly swamped the opposition. The second year was better and the 100,000-unit mark was crossed. Times were tough in the ensuing years, with the Wall Street Crash and the economy-minded Plymouth came into its own, entirely justifying Chrysler's strategy.

The Model U was the first real Plymouth, as the earlier cars bore the Chrysler prefix. But both models are virtually interchangeable. The 'U' offered no breathtaking surprises but was well appointed for a car in this class. Power was provided by a four-cylinder unit, equipped with aluminum pistons and full-pressure lubrication. The 175.4 cubic inch displacement generated a steady 45 horsepower. Four-wheel hydraulic brakes were fitted as standard, and the car had an independent handbrake. The competition didn't offer these specifications for a few years. The model prices were also competitive, at between six- and seven-hundred dollars. The car came with fitted wood spoke wheels as standard but wires were an option, with two-piece rounded bumpers and Twolite headlamps. Seven body options were offered, including a roadster and coupe with rumble seats, two- and four-door sedans, plus a touring car.

Engine: Four-cylinder Inline, Valve in block

Displacement: 175.4 cid

Horsepower: 45 at 2800 rpm

Transmission: Three-speed sliding gears

Induction: Carter 103 S Carburetor

Body Style: Two-door Roadster

Number of Seats: 2/4

Weight: 2285 lbs

Wheelbase: 109¾ inches

Base Price: $675

Number Produced: 108,345

■ *Right: The Two-door Roadster with Rumbleseat in two-tone brown and yellow on a day at the beach.*

Duesenberg Model J

1930

W as the Model J the finest American car ever built? E. L. Cord described it as "the world's finest". This was a typically modest remark from the showman empire builder. The Duesenberg Company was formed by bothers Fred and August Duesenburg in 1913. They quickly achieved a reputation for brilliantly engineered race engines. In 1921, their Model A arrived – a good, solid car but no style-setter. The lack of business success resulted in Duesenberg Motors being sold to the charismatic Cord who immediately put the company to work. In 1928, the stupendous Model J emerged, to countrywide acclaim. The Model J came with a 420-cid straight eight designed by Fred Duesenberg, and built by Lycoming: it was an engine capable of 265 horsepower – truly exceptional for the time.

But it wasn't only their sublime power, which gave these cars their reputation. The specifications both interior and exterior were something else and aimed at only the rich. The engine had overhead camshafts driven by chains to four valves per cylinder. Engine fittings were finished in exotic, shiny nickel, stainless steel or chrome. Aluminum was used throughout to keep the weight down – even in the gas tank. Models J's were massive with a standard wheelbase of 142.5 inches but they weighed in at only just over 5,000 pounds. In high gear, they could reach 116 mph and could achieve almost 90 mph in second. For the comfort of the driver, the cars were equipped with a range of instruments to satisfy any enthusiast: a speedometer calibrated to 150 mph, ammeter, water and oil pressure gauges, split second stopwatch, tachometer, barometer and break pressure gauge. More detail was found in the car's warning systems designed by Fred – reminders to add or change oil, or top up battery water. And the cost of this luxury and attention to detail? Well, you didn't buy a finished car, but only the chassis, which cost a stupendous $9,500 in 1930. The bodywork was added later. This all added up to a finished price of around $17,000. A few cars were as expensive as $25,000, crazy money at the time. Between 1929 and 1936, only 470 chassis and 480 engines were built. This exclusivity was another selling point. The Model J was a rare and fabulously opulent car.

■ Left: A king among cars: the mind-blowingly expensive 1930 Duesenberg Model J.

Engine:	Eight cylinders
Displacement:	420-cid
Horsepower:	265 at 4250 rpm
Transmission:	Selective manual, floor mounted lever
Compression Ratio:	5.25:1
Induction:	Schebler carburetor
Weight:	5200 lbs
Wheelbase:	142.5 inches

REO Flying Cloud Model 25 Sport Sedan

Mr. Olds left his eponymous company in 1904, after a major fall-out with the controlling Smith family, who wanted to phase out the beloved Curved Dash and bring in some more up-market models. They were furious when he tried to use his name as a moniker for a rival company, and it was this argument that resulted in Old's new company being named REO, after this initials, Ransom Eli Olds. Ultimately, REO was a victim of the Depression, but not before the company produced the Flying Cloud Sixes. The 1930 versions were little changed from the previous year - the Series 25 was the Flying Cloud of 1929. It had a six-cylinder 268.3 cid engine capable of producing 80 horsepower at 3200 rpm and this was fed fuel from a 21-gallon tank. The wheelbase was 125 inches and the car's braking system was the Lockheed hydraulic brake system. In one respect the REO 25 stood out, it had outstanding styling and a dynamic, desirable profile. The body design was in the hands of the talented Amos Northup. He turned out a style that was both formal and as a result, classic in line and proportion.

The REO cars were beautifully finished. The workman-ship on the car was solid and all the furnishings and appearance detailing were of the highest quality. The Model 25 was the upscale version of the three models and drove quietly and smoothly not least due to the silent second transmission. The junior REO car for the year was the 115-inch wheelbase model 15, complete with a 65 horsepower, 214.7 cid continental engine sitting on a shorter 115-inch wheelbase. Then came the first of the senior models, the model 20 and the model 25. The catalogue for the year lists seven body types ranging in price from $1,125 for a small series 15 Coupe, to $1,845 for the top of the range model 25, a five-passenger sedan.

The most fabulous REO of all arrived in 1931: the Royale, a 125 horsepower straight eight with brilliant coachwork by Northup. In 1936, REO announced it would cease building cars, Olds had given up control two years earlier. He died in 1950.

■ *Left: The fender mounted, rather than on the cowl, parking lights were a feature of the 1930 REO Model 25s - a detail from Amos Northup's design.*

Engine:	six cylinder
Displacement:	268.3 cid
Horsepower:	85 at 3200 rpm
Body Style:	Sports Sedan
Number of seats:	5
Wheelbase:	125 inches
Base Price:	$1845

1931 Buick Model 54

Buick's Marquette, a basement priced car rose with the dawn of 1930... and rapidly disappeared from sight – gone after a fruitless year. Not the greatest start to a decade. By 1931, most autos were powered by straight-eight engines. The company was hard hit by the Depression, but owners General Motors employed Harlow H. Curtis to bring Buick back from the edge and five years later, he had built up a strong line. The decision to go for the eight came just before the Crash. The mid-range series 50's were built on a 124-inch wheelbase, and used a 331.3-cid engine, which developed 99 horsepower. The 50 series offered just a four-door sedan and a four-place sports coupe.

The line up in 1931 was expanded and saw the introduction of the first eights, which were possibly the most advanced power unit of the day. They were smooth and reliable engines designed by division chief engineer F. A. Bower. The 50 included a 77 horsepower, 220.7 cid power plant, and was now the cheapest model in the range. The top of the line offerings, Series 80 and 90 had a lengthy roster of models that including roadsters and a seven seat 90 limousine. The 50 line included a second series group announced early in the year, which rode on a 114-inch wheelbase taken from the deceased Marquette. The straight eight remained Buick's mainstay power plant for the following 22 years.

The new 1931 engine proved itself at the Indianapolis 500 that year, powering racer Phil Shafer to qualify at a speed of 105.1 mph averaging 86.4mph during the race. All the showroom cars of '31 were quick for their day: 0-60 mph took about 25 seconds and a top speed of 90mph was possible. The canny Scot David Dunbar Buick had evolved a successful series of cars that put him back into the auto business. Buick had come a long way from the his origins in bathtub enameling. Even his first car of 1903 had had the well-known Buick feature of overhead valves, then a rarity, but still uncommon even in the 1930s.

■ *Right: A pristine, green Buick Model 54 from the 1931 50 Series.*

Engine: eight cylinders

Displacement: 220.7-cid

Horsepower: 77

Body Style: Two-door Sedan

Number of seats: 4

Weight: 2935 lbs

Wheelbase: 114 inches

Base Price: $1055

Number produced: 907

Cadillac Fleetwood Phaeton   1931

Even in the thirties, Cadillac kept its blue chip image and continued to build outstanding luxury cars. The surprise for 1930 was the introduction of the sixteen-cylinder, a magnificent brute of a power plant. It was only nine months old when Cadillac introduced another multi-cylinder engine, a 368-cid V-12. Essentially, this was a V-16 with four fewer cylinders generating 135 horsepower, used to power slightly smaller cars such as the Fleetwoood phaeton. The V-12 was fitted onto the Cadillac eight's 140 inch wheelbase. The twelve's engine was free revving, and delivered smooth and even power. Most twelve's could cruise all day at 70 mph. However, in the market the cars fell short of being best sellers. They were staggeringly expensive, although beautiful to look at. At this time, cars with more than eight cylinders seemed like too much of an extravagance.

Cadillac designed and built most of its bodies in house through either Fisher or Fleetwood. These were two highly respected coachbuilders that GM had acquired. Classic Cadillac styling was a big feature of all the 1930-31 models with the distinctive and grand thick collar, vertical radiators, stunning rounded hoods and crisp but flowing lines.

There were fourteen Fleetwood custom models of this period with the most elegant and breathtaking being the Madam X models (fitted with the V-16). These cars were named after a stage play of the time. They had sleek chrome windshield and door mouldings. The design of both the V-12 and V-16 engine was credited to Owen Nacker. Cadillac's early '30's V-8 was based on a 341-cid unit, which was first introduced in 1928. It was resized to 353-cid for 1930-35 and delivered between 95-130 horsepower. It continued to be used up to 1949 in one form or another. It was the best selling line for the fortunes of Cadillac - the great V-16s and V-12s remained low volume after an initial sales spurt, as customers preferred the less showy and cheaper V-8 configuration. Ultimately, the big engines simply went out of fashion, overtaken by advances in technology.

■ *Left: A dream car with great poise, Cadillac's Fleetwood Phaeton looks elegant in creamy buff, with its characteristic low-slung top and piercing headlight array.*

Engine:	Eight cylinders
Displacement:	353-cid
Horsepower:	95 at 3000 rpm
Transmission:	Selective, synchromesh
Compression Ratio:	5.35:1
Body style:	Four-door Fleetwood Phaeton
Weight:	4395 lbs
Wheelbase:	152 inches
Base Price:	$2945

Oldsmobile F-31 1931

Oldsmobile, who was America's leading automaker by 1903-4, hadn't lost their desire to meet a challenge. During the Depression year of 1931, they introduced the pioneering synchromesh transmission. Many of Oldsmobile's technical advances in the '30's were down to Charles McCuen, who was first the chief engineer and then general manager of the company. The Olds F-31 followed the general styling fashion of the time, with a typically squared shape. The '30 and '31 lines offered popular styles in the Standard, Special and Deluxe trim and all sixes came on a 113.5-inch wheelbase. The cars were all powered by the tried and true six-cylinder power plant with 197.5-cid producing 65 horsepower at 3350 rpm. Both Standard and Deluxe models were offered in a variety of open and closed body styles, and the Deluxes came with front and rear bumpers, twin side mounts and a rear platform designed to carry a trunk.

Prices started at around $900 and rose to $1000. Oldsmobile suffered less from the economic effects of the Depression than many carmakers. This relative success was attributed to conservative and recognizable styling cues, which the customers could identify with and even more importantly, trust. The performance was adequate, and reliability was just as good as any other make. Perhaps it is no accident that this solid profile for the manufacturer remains intact, as it is now America's oldest car nameplate. The six-cylinder engine served the cars well, and it was only in 1932 that the first straight eight arrived while in the same period the six grew to 213.3-cid, developing 74 horsepower for 1932.

■ *Left: A 1931 Oldsmobile F-31 two-door Roadster, with bright-eyed headlamps. Over 3,000 were built, selling for just below $1000.*

Engine: Six-cylinder

Displacement: 197.5-cid

Horsepower: 65 at 3350 rpm

Transmission: Synchromesh

Compression Ratio: 5.06:1

Induction: mechanical Stomberg downdraft carburetor

Body Style: Two-door Roadster

Number of seats: 2

Weight: 2965 lbs

Wheelbase: 112 inches

Base Price: $995

Number produced: 3,500

1931 Stutz SV 16 Model MA-23

Harry C. Stutz left the company in 1926, he was replaced by European born and influenced Frederick E. Moskovics. The new owner had introduced the 'Safety Stutz' models in the same year. These cars displayed beautiful styling. The cars were powered by Stutz's first eight-cylinder engine, an inline configuration with a single overhead camshaft and dual ignition with two plugs on every cylinder. It was known as the Vertical Eight.

Moskovics resigned from Stutz in 1929. From this time, it was Charles 'Pop' Greuter who engineered power plant development for the company. Stutz couldn't afford to invest or build a 12- or 16-cylinder engine they needed for 1931 so they experimented with a supercharger that lifted the Vertical Eight to 143 horsepower. It did the job, but was ungainly and had fuel feed problems. So, after looking around the industry, Stutz decided to follow the Duesenberg solution by introducing a 32-valve twin-cam cylinder head. This engine abandoned the dual ignition system, and was named the SV-16 (single value). The company also produced a DV-32 (dual valve) assembly, which could produce 161 horsepower at 3900 rpm. Stutz attempted to enter the low price car market, but did not have the product so they were left trying to market cars that were high-priced and uncompromising with a sports-like finish.

This made Stutz an oddity in the marketplace and an expensive option. Standard body models sold for around the $3,500 level. There were at least thirty custom styles available on the SV-16 chassis, all from high-end coachbuilders such as LeBaron, Rollston, and Waterhouse. One customizer was Waterhouse who offered fabric bodies, which were strong but light, safe and durable. Compared to the steel shells, the fabric bodies absorbed the road noise well, lasted longer and were easier to repair.

The MA series used a 322-cid, eight-cylinder power plant, which developed 113 horsepower at 3300 rpm. The wheelbase was 135 inches and the engine was fueled from a twenty-gallon tank. Sales for the year and the series were both very low. By 1935, the company had discontinued car production.

Engine: eight-cylinder

Displacement: 322-cid

Horsepower: 113 at 3300 rpm

Wheelbase: 134-1/2 inches

Base Price: $3495

■ *Right: A stunningly elegant, customized 1933 two-door Stutz SV-16 Model MA-23.*

1932 Buick 96C Convertible

The company had big news for 1932. They introduced 'Silent Second Synchromesh' transmission and included more horsepower for all their engines. But sales were not so clever, and by 1931 they had a new president in Harlow H. Curtice. He demanded 'more speed for less money' - not a bad start for a consumer driven business. He backed up his dictum with an all-new 117-inch wheelbase series 40 for 1934. The result was an upturn in sales and a modern streamlined styling that broke with the now dated square designs of the '20s that beleaguered the early 30's models. Also featured in the line up was GM's new knee action independent front suspension, which was then a great step forward. Curtice also launched a $64 million factory modernization program.

The 1932 cars came in four series: 50, 60, 80 and 90. The 90 series was Buick's largest and had nine models and horsepower was rated at 104 mph at 2900 rpm. The 96C convertible coupe was powered by a straight eight, 344.8-cid engine. Innovations in 1932 included adjustable shock absorbers, 'wizard control' freewheeling and an automatic clutch. By then end of the year they had discontinued the use of wooden spoke wheels on the 50 series. But by 1932 wooden spokes were not the only things being dumped.

The economy was also dumping on the people and with almost everything at a standstill, Buick's sales slumped by more than 50 per cent with only 40,000 plus units built for their 2,000 odd outlets. This made them the third largest auto dealership of GM but there were very few buyers around, and sales slipped to seventh spot nationally. But there was always the glamorous and the imposing sight of a stunning 96 convertible to raise the spirits and drive the company on. It was an outstandingly comfortable and powerful car to drive, with all the qualities expected from a top of the range model.

Engine: straight eight-cylinder

Displacement: 344.8 cid

Horsepower: 104 at 2800 rpm

Transmission: Sliding gear synchromesh

Compression Ratio: 4.5:1

Induction: 2-barrel Marvel updraft carburetor

Body Style: Convertible Coupe

Weight: 4460 lbs

Wheelbase: 126 inches

Base Price: $1805

Number produced: 289

■ *Right: Graceful and imposing, this convertible 2 door Buick 96C has a 134 inch wheelbase length, a top speed in excess of 100 mph, brakes on four wheels, painted wire-wheels and 18 x 7.00 tires.*

1932 Chrysler Imperial Speedster

Walter P. Chrysler was not a man to have anything get in his way. Having jumped into the luxury car market in 1925 with the Chrysler Imperial E80 he wasn't going to let a little thing like the Depression of the early thirties stop him from going ahead with his plan to develop luxury cars.

Chrysler's stability was underpinned by solid sales of yeoman models like Plymouth and Dodge, which allowed Chrysler to continue development when other manufacturers were retrenching. Walter Chrysler established the experimental Custom Body Shop in 1931 with engineer Carl Breer at its head. This was a move in keeping with the company's dedication to research and development. Even so, some of the department's projects seemed somewhat self-indulgent. A special car was created for the boss's son, Walter P. Jr. The design for the car was credited to Herbert Weissinger, head of the Chrysler Art department. Although it has been mistaken for a Le Baron of the same vintage, it is in fact a totally redesigned one-off model, using stock Chrysler parts of the day. Its long low sweeping lines, accentuated by the long uncluttered hood stretching from radiator shell to windshield, gave the car the sleek and powerful appearance of its twelve- and sixteen- cylinder contemporaries, such the Cadillac V-16. A cut-down, swept-back windshield added to the illusion. The body panels were crafted in aluminum to keep the weight down.

Beneath the skin lurks the Chrysler Straight-Eight of 384.84-cid, fitted with a cast-alloy, high-compression head, which boosted the power from a standard 125 to 160 horsepower. Bringing this powerful cast-iron monster to life was a gas pedal actuated starter with an automatic stall restart system exclusive to Chrysler. The whole rig sat on a reinforced double-drop boxed frame for rigidity. With its collection of experimental gadgetry, combined with tried and tested mechanicals, the car is every bit as impressive on the road as it looks parked.

The result is probably one of the most beautiful cars of all time.

Engine: Eight-cylinders inline	
Displacement: 384.84-cid	
Horsepower: 160 at 3500rpm	
Transmission: Three-speed manual	
Compression Ratio: 6.2:1	
Induction: Stromberg Model DD 3	
Body style: Two-seat Sports Convertible	
Wheelbase: 135 inches	
Number Produced: 1	

■ *Right: The beautiful1932 Speedster remained in the ownership of Walter P Chrysler Jr. for thirty years.*

1932 Packard Dietrich Body

The co-operation of a luxury producer like Packard with a coachbuilder of the stature of Dietrich was always going to result in the creation of a very special car. Leading the Packard line-up for 1932 was the new twin six, which later became the twelve. The car was equipped with a new V-12 engine that had been specially developed for a front wheel chassis model that had never actually materialized. This new 445.5-cid engine purred. It was designed to produce a smooth and sustained pace rather than high-speed motoring. The Packard factory boys claimed that the car could cruise at 100 mph, but that was in test conditions.

A more normal driving experience was for the car to run beautifully at about 90 mph, if it was pushed much harder than that, it ran out of breath. The optimum speed for comfort was between 60-70 mph, when the car almost seemed to glide along. The 1932 cars were designated the ninth Packard series. Although these cars were more streamlined in their styling and had a lower profile, they were essentially similar to the previous year's models. The 1932-34 V-12s shared the same wheelbases and most of their body features with the Eighth series, now designated 'Deluxe' for 1932. The 160 horsepower engine produced a level of performance similar to that of KB, another twelve-cylinder car. Lincoln was Packard's head-to-head competitor throughout the 1930s.

Packard had not planned to build many of these cars, but the Packard twelve became a classic model, and was built in various, ever more impressive, configurations from 1932 right through to 1939. Sales of the twelves began to really take off in 1934 when almost a thousand cars were built. This was double the production total for the previous two years. By 1935 the engine was stoked up to 473 cid, and developed 175 horsepower. The car became more and more powerful and spectacular, both to drive and be seen in. Among its many distinguishing features was the cormorant mascot that perched on the hood. Dual rows of hood louvers aided engine cooling and were a styling addition. Together with these features, the bullet headlights and further streamlining characterized the Packard style of this vintage.

Engine: V-12, modified L-head

Displacement: 445.5 cid

Horsepower: 160 at 3200 rpm

Compression Ratio: 6.0:1

Induction: Stromberg-Duplex carburetor

Wheelbase: 142⅛ inches

■ *Right: A 1932 Packard Twelve with a custom Dietrich body found fewer than 500 buyers during the Depression years.*

1932 Pierce-Arrow Model 54

The Pierce-Arrow Company always had a sense of drama associated with its cars – epitomized by the single, radiant red sports phaeton trimmed in stainless steel that was shown and stood out even against the pomp and ceremony of the annual Princes' Convention in New Delhi, India, in March 1931. A typical act of flamboyance and panache that was the spirit of Pierce-Arrow came in the 700 shades of beige offered on the 1930's car. The 1932 cars were significant. First, there were two lines of twelve-cylinder cars, Pierce decided to cut back on the eights.

The flagship of the fleet was the model 52, offering five body types on 142 and 147-inch wheelbases. Both cars were powered by the new 150 horsepower 429-cid V-12, designed by the chief engineer, Karl M. Wise. It was a super smooth engine with an 80-degree cylinder bank angle and dual downdraft carburetors. A smaller 140 horsepower engine was used in the model 53. Anchoring the line was the model 54. Effectively, this was Model 53 with an improved 366-cid straight-eight power plant generating 125 horsepower. Common to all '32 models was solid, eight-point engine mounting, stronger frames and adjustable shocks for a fantastic ride.

The first common model produced with Studebaker also dates from this time. Studebaker now owned Pierce-Arrow and had successfully managed to expand the market for the company's product, despite the Depression. The car they produced jointly was a two-door sedan sold as the Club Brougham. The car incorporated the first recognizable exterior design changes for three years. Looking at the car's profile you can see that the radiator shell was now V-shaped and the side windows were more curved. As three-dimensional body moldings were now used in manufacturing, a more pronounced curve was put into the rear fenders. When all of these changes were put together, the result was the transition to the aerodynamic styling that would be at its zenith in the 1934 cars.

Engine: straight eight

Displacement: 366-cid

Horsepower: 125 at 3000 rpm

Transmission: Three-speed

Wheelbase: 137 inches

Base Price; $2,385

■ *Right: The distinctive radiator of the 1932 Pierce-Arrow Model 54.*

Studebaker Dictator Eight

1932

The Dictator line-up for 1932 was the same as in the previous year. The president of the Studebaker was now the company's former accountant A. R. Erskine, who brought with him all the imagination that accountant's tend to have when faced with a product requiring vision and style. None, in other words. Erskine led the company from one production disaster to another. The first car he launched was named Erskine. Unsurprisingly, it failed.

Then came the exquisite and much-sort-after name-choice of the 1930s, the Dictator. Erskine oversaw the design and production of the model's eight-cylinder engine. Studebaker engineers Max Wollering and Guy Henry objected to this strategy, and they were, therefore, bypassed. Erskine brought in Delmar G. 'Barney' Roos who was happy to follow orders. The result of their combined endeavors was the Studebaker straight-eight power plant, capable of delivering 100 horsepower. The cars were styled by Ray Dietrich.

In 1928, Erskine sent the new cars to the races, where they cleaned up and caught the eye of the public. The 1932 Dictator eight-cylinder engine had 230-cid that produced 81 horsepower mounted on a 117-inch wheelbase. Under the hood Delco Remy ignition was fitted, as were mechanical Bendix brakes, a Synchomesh transmission and a vacuum advance distributor. Fuel was fed to the engine by a Stromberg carburetor. Exterior styling included a slanted windshield, oval headlights and one piece fenders.

The big brother of the Dictator was the President (a more inspired choice of name) eight-cylinder model, which took on the 1930 Indianapolis 500 course in two private specials. These cars went well enough for Studebaker to enter a factory team in the 1932 Indy – a rare event for an American manufacturer. The Studebaker was driven by Cliff Bergere, and finished third.

■ *Left: A two-tone Studebaker Dictator Eight with the trademark V-shaped radiator and single bar bumpers.*

Engine: straight eight	
Displacement: 221 cid	
Horsepower: 81 at 3200 rpm	
Compression Ratio: 5.0:1	
Induction: Stromberg carburetor	
Wheelbase: 117 inches	

1933 Ford Deluxe Model 40-720 Coupe

Ford's first V-8 was introduced in 1932, the famous cast-iron flathead first delivered 65 horsepower from 221-cid. The new V-8 was a great bargain and had a top speed of 78 mph from 75 horsepower and caused a storm of interest. Millions were drawn to its March unveiling but it was launched too quickly for the engineers and without an ideal engine-testing program because of the need to get the V-8 into the market as quickly as possible. There were durability problems, such as cylinder head cracks and a rapid oil burn off. In some cars, the engine mounts worked loose and ignition problems came to light. Ford ended up having to replace thousands of these, and the engine problems were reflected in lower sales for the year. But Ford didn't allow themselves to be deflected by these teething difficulties. They were soon resolved, and the V-8 gained a reputation as a solid power unit that could that could withstand a considerable assault from being driven hard and fast. Everything was sweet by 1933. The generic Detroit style now consisted of streamlined models. Edsel Ford was now the force

■ *Below: The Ford 1933 Ford Deluxe Model 40 coupe successfully completed economy runs under various conditions, ranging from the Catskill Mountains to the Mojave Desert.*

behind the company's design, and came up with a balanced new look for the 1933 Ford line-up that was very well received. The hood extended back to the windshield and the sharp corner on the fender was rounded off. The V-8 durability kept improving and the line was now named the model 40. The speedy new V-8 was attracting many new enthusiasts, amongst them Public Enemy Number One, John Dillinger. Dillinger actually had the cheek to write to Henry Ford, praising the new engine. The '33 wheelbase was 112 inches, now increased from the short 106.5-inch version. All models were delivered with black fenders and 17-inch wire spoke wheels. With improved reliability and aluminum cylinder heads, the engine now delivered a performance comparable with the detailing of the interior, which featured a new dash arrangement with the gauges arranged directly in front of the driver. Ford was finally getting in tune with its customers.

Engine: eight-cylinder

Displacement: 221 cid

Horsepower: 75

Transmission: Sliding gear

Compression Ratio: 6.3:1

Induction: Mechanical, Detroit Lubricator Downdraft, single-barrel carburetor

Weight: 2538 lbs

Wheelbase: 112 inches

Base Price: $540

Number produced: 15,894

1933 Lincoln KB Convertible Coupe

Lincoln was founded by Henry Martyn Leland, the man who gave America the Cadillac at the end of the Great War. But by 1922 he had to sell up, to Henry Ford. Henry and his son Esdel brought out the Model K in 1931. It had a new 145-inch wheelbase chassis with an upgraded 120 horsepower V-8. The colossal chassis had side rails that were nine inches deep, and six cross members with cruciform bracing.

The K also had a floating rear axle, torque tube drive, Houdaille hydraulic shocks and Bendix mechanical brakes. It accelerated well and had a good top speed. The K chassis was designed for the new V-12 that arrived in 1932 for the KB series. This new engine was a 448-cid with 150 horsepower. The KB was a machine that stood apart from its rivals, both as an efficient town car and as a fast open road tourer. On the outside of the car, Esdel had been to work. He transformed the Lincoln, updating the standard factory built bodies and securing many custom or semi-custom styles from the very best of America's coach builders - Brunn, Dietrich, LeBaron and Willoughby. Between them, they styled, designed and produced some of the best examples of shapes from this classic era. A cautious approach to streamlining had begun in 1932, but by 1933 the KB had a distinguished radiator with a chrome grille, hood louvers, skirted fenders, vee'd front fender and new truck racks.

Sales for the KB, as for so many models of the period, were difficult because of the effects of the Depression. Lincoln consolidated power in '34 by boring out the old 414-cid KA engine to produce the same 150 horsepower as the KB. They also introduced aluminum cylinder heads, which were quite revolutionary for the time. This was made possible by the arrival of 70-Octane fuel, which was almost as refined as aviation fuel. The top speed for the Lincoln was 95 mph.

Engine: V-12

Displacement: 447.9 cid

Horsepower: 150 at 3400 rpm

Transmission: Sliding gear

Compression Ratio: 5.25:1

Induction: Stromberg DD downdraft carburetor

Number of seats: 2

Weight: (estimated) 5500 lbs

Wheelbase: 145 inches

Base Price: $4,200

■ *Right: The elegant, head-turning, twelve-cylinder 1933 Lincoln KB convertible coupe with custom bodywork.*

Plymouth PD

1933

Plymouth was a success from the outset. The company prospered throughout the 1930's with a strong marketing combination of low prices, eye-pleasing styling, and engineering that was often more advanced than that of its competitors, such as Chevrolet. By 1932, Plymouth was American's number three auto manufacturer. 1933 was one of the roughest industry years on record, but Plymouth came through unscathed. This was no accident, the cars had features customers wanted, such as all-steel construction, at a time when wooden framed bodies were still in production, four wheel hydraulic brakes and rubber engine mounts that gave 'the economy of a four and the smoothness of an eight'.

The 1933 PD was launched in the second period of the year as a two series line of standard and deluxe Sixes on wheelbases of 108 and 112 inches. A convertible coupe came in the Deluxe line and the cars began to follow the industry trend by moving towards a streamlined profile, with skirted fenders and a rounder hood assembly. On top of the hood came the new winged-lady mascot.

The PD grew out of the not-so-popular PC launched earlier in the year. Plymouth engineers took the Dodge Model DP frame, modified the wheelbase, added a redesigned front end and then manipulated the hood panels, front fenders, running boards and splash aprons. In this way, they ended up with a new car without too much retooling or expense.

The PD on its longer wheelbase corrected all the perceived faults of the PC. Some of the design details included: a painted or chrome grille with the hood stretched back over the cowling to the windshield. Bullet shaped, chrome plated headlamps helped the look and wire wheels gave the car a styling image. Many were fitted with trumpet horns to give the car's profile a lift. Not surprisingly, sales rocketed, not least because of the lower $495 price.

■ *Left: A 4-door 1933 Plymouth PD sedan, showing the first silver flying lady radiator-cap mascot.*

Engine:	six-cylinder
Displacement:	189.8-cid
Horsepower:	70 at 3600 rpm
Transmission:	Sliding gear
Compression Ratio:	5.5:1
Induction:	Carter C6A-C6A2-C6A3 or C6A4
Weight:	2545lbs – 2645lbs depending on body type
Wheelbase:	112 inches
Base Price:	$525
Number produced:	49,826

Pontiac Eight

1933

Pontiac veered towards collapse in 1932 but was saved by the effective leadership of GM President Alfred P. Sloane. He integrated Pontiac's manufacturing with that of Chevrolet early in 1933, which resulted in shared bodies, chassis and other main components. He achieved economy of scale. The resurgence of the company was overseen by Pontiac general manager William S. 'Big Bill' Knudsen, chief engineer Benjamin H. Anibal and chief designer Franklin Q. Hershey. Anibal became known as the father of the Pontiac Eight, whilst Hershey was responsible for its unique styling. The engine for this year was a 223.4-cid inline-eight, generating 77 horsepower. The car rode on a 115-inch wheelbase. Its body styling was in a transitional phase - moving from the boxy shape of the early 30's towards the streamlining that followed in the mid 30's. In fact, the new Pontiacs were amongst the most attractive looking cars of the year.

The Economy Eights looked unique due to the design skills of Hershey and chief body engineer Roy Milner. Both were strong-willed men who were looking to make a lasting mark. Hershey collaborated with famous styling director Harley Earl to achieve more streamlined and showy Pontiacs. They subsequently designed a distinctive new radiator and added skirted, front fenders with horizontal go-faster speed streaks. Milner also gave the open models a smooth deck. The car was equipped with a Fisher body with beavertail rear, plus a slanting V-shaped radiator with vertical bars. The hood had four wide louvers slanting backwards towards the cowl. Inside the car, airplane style instrumentation appeared on the dashboard. This excellent style and profile package, combined with the powerful straight-eight and knee action independent front suspension gave Pontiac a winner that was to pull the company through the effects of the Depression and secure its future.

■ *Left: The hood ornament on the company-saving Economy Eight features an Indian brave's head in silver.*

Engine:	Inline eight-cylinder
Displacement:	223.4 cid
Horsepower:	77
Transmission:	Muncie synchromesh
Compression Ratio:	5.7:1
Induction:	Carter IV carburetor
Body Style:	Four-door Sedan
Number of seats:	5
Weight:	3020 lbs
Wheelbase:	115 inches
Base Price;	$695
Number produced:	90,198

1934 Nash Ambassador

Automaker Charles Nash believed in offering a lot of car for your money. His Nash cars were full of innovations and extras. For example he produced aircraft-type instruments for his customers in 1934. But, like most auto companies, Nash was hit hard by the Depression and in the previous year had recorded his lowest ever output, with less than 15,000 units produced. The company needed a new approach, look and improved performance. However, difficult economic conditions delayed the planned 1934, which was postponed for a year. Despite their problems, Nash produced its millionth car in 1934, but also recorded losses of over $1.5 million...

The Ambassador model continued with a revised twin-ignition eight-cylinder engine delivered between a 100 and 115 horsepower. By 1934, these power plants had evolved into two engines of 260.8 and 322 cid delivering either 100 or 120 horsepower. The styling of the model remained classically upright even though the industry was turning towards rounder and

■ *Below: In a troubled year, the 1934 Nash Ambassador held its own in terms of stature and comfort even though the styling was looking its age as most cars entered the slipstream age.*

more streamlined shapes by this time. Some other innovations that
Nash introduced in his cars during the early '30s included sports cowl
ventilation, a dashboard starter button, shatterproof glass, downdraft
carburetors, and a Syncro-Safety Shift. The latter featured a dash-
mounted gear lever in 1931. Freewheeling was introduced, followed by
an ignition and steering wheel lock. The Ambassador body was
designed by Count Alexis de Sakhnoffsky and featured a high styled
body, deep-skirted fenders and chrome, bullet shaped headlamps with
a full beavertail back end. The model ran on the larger Nash engine,
which produced 125 horsepower at 3600 rpm. It had mechanical brakes
on all four wheels and Baker Axleflex independent front suspension.
The wheel size was 17- inches and the wheelbase was either 133 or a
massive 142 inches.

Engine:	eight cylinder
Displacement:	322 cid
Horsepower:	125 horsepower at 3600 rpm
Transmission:	Selective sliding gear
Induction:	5.25:1
Wheelbase:	133 inches

Auburn 851 Salon Coupe 1935

Auburn's offer was a car with value and amazing style. They was one of the few automakers that produced higher car sales immediately after the 1929 Wall Street Crash . They had beauty and power, and great prices matched to outstanding performances from the eight- and twelve-cylinder engine configurations. But this success did not last, and sales plunged in 1932.

The 1933 model eights and twelves continued with little change into 1934. Streamline styling was then added by Alan Leamy of Cord L-29 fame. But little changed – nobody wanted the twelve. After Auburn's owner, the charismatic E. L. Cord, fled to England in 1934, the marque was handed over to Duesenburg president Harold T. Ames. His arrival also bought in the designer Gordon Buehrig and engineer August Duesenburg. By now both men were legends in the industry. Buehrig was given the brief and a limited budget to improve the Auburn styling for 1935. Augie was briefed to design a new eight working with Lycoming and supercharge specialist Schwitzer-Cummins. And what came out of this partnership? A beautiful line of cars, with the superb 851 Speedster at the helm. It turned out to be Auburn's final moment of glory. The new design by Buehrig was a reworked 1934 twelve giving the old bodies a new radiator, sleek hood, eye-catching curved fenders and flamboyant exhausts. The engineer Duesenburg added two cylinders onto the '34 six to come up with a 280-cid eight at 115 horsepower, or supercharged with the blower to 150 horsepower. It could hit 100 mph straight from the showroom to the road. As ever the price was great – just $2245. Fifteen models were available starting with the bargain priced five-seater, six-cylinder Brougham for a modest $695 through to the two-seater Speedster. The year turned out to be a poor one – just over 5,000 units were built, putting the company in 18th place on the industry sales ratings, little return for the creative skills harnessed to build this line of inspiring cars. These breathtakingly beautiful cars were duds in the market. They were also Auburn's final flourish. The fleet was brilliant in concept – the cabriolets, broughams, phaetons, sedans and the magnificent supercharged Speedsters – but production was very low. Cord returned from exile to face a crumbling empire and personal financial investigation. The 1937 range was cancelled – the make was now dead in the water.

■ *Left: A power blue soft-top, two-door 1935 Auburn 851 saloon coupe with its distinctive radiator design and Duesenburg engineered eight-cylinder powerplant.*

Engine:	Eight cylinders
Body style:	Coupe
Weight:	3,105 lbs
Wheelbase:	120 inches
Base Price:	$1221

1935 Chevrolet Suburban

Chevy introduced America's very first SUV in 1935. This foray into fun and functionality was such a success that it allowed the model to remain at the cutting edge for over sixty years. In fact, Suburban is one of Chevy's best-loved nametags to this day, and is the longest-running model name in automotive history. The vehicle was extremely versatile, with both off-road and hauling capability, while having a comfortable ride for long-distance travel.

Chevy's core engine product for 1935 was based on an original design from 1929 when it had been introduced as the 'Stovebolt Six', better known as the cast-iron wonder. The names were drawn from the engine's cast iron pistons and slotted head bolts. It was not pretty but it was effective. The Stovebolt was designed and built by Ormond E. Hunt. By 1930, it produced around 50 horsepower from 194 cid. The engine then underwent year on year improvements and as a result remained as Chevy's only power plant for almost thirty years. The solid, overhead-valve engine came in two versions for 1935. The less powerful version was the 181 cid, which developed 60 horsepower, the other was a 206.8 cid which blew out 80 horsepower. It was a heavy engine but in the following year it was redesigned as a six that was both shorter and lighter than the original. At this point, the public relations people stepped in.

They wanted to change the public's perception of the 'Old Stovebolt' and attempted to rename this venerable power plant in 1934. First they tried to get 'Blue Streak' to catch on, then Blue Flame Six in 1935. The thinking was of Ford's publicity success of that year when they introduced their 90 horsepower V-8 engine to the market with great pizzazz. But the Stovebolt name resisted the change. The Master Deluxe of the year had an extra inch on the wheelbase and a much slimmer body with a vee'd windshield and streamlined fenders. The radiator was a new raked back design with the cap positioned under the hood – innovative for the time.

This was also the year of the steel Turret Top construction, so not all the glory went to FoMoCo that year. The 1935 Chevrolet models were the last models with any styling throw back to the classic era of the early 30's

Engine: Six-cylinder OHV inline	
Displacement: 206.8 cid	
Horsepower: 80	
Body styles: Suburban Carryall	
No of seats: 8	

 Right: A two-door 1935 Chevy Suburban in a brilliant red livery with the silver hood-mounted mascot gleaming in the sun.

1935 Chrysler Airflow C1

Chrysler came of age in 1934 when it made a major production and design decision. It looked into the future and saw the time was right for a big step up. Chrysler attempted to build the most radical car ever attempted by a US auto manufacturer. In 1934 came the Airflow, an engineer's car that the conservative Walter Chrysler had approved without a care as to what the public would think of it. Wind tunnel tests on the concept, built by the design triumvirate - Fred Zeder, Carl Breer and Owen Skelton - had suggested a modified teardrop shape. An eight-cylinder engine placed over the front axle, rather than behind it, freed up passenger space. The seats were a generous 50 inches across. A beam and truss body engineered along aircraft design principles provided strength with less than normal weight.

Body styling was directed by Oliver Clark who had designed the first Chrysler and although the aerodynamic considerations really styled the Airflow. It had a hood that cascaded into a grille and looked like a waterfall with flush mounted headlamps on each side. 'The beauty of nature itself' was the description given to it by Chrysler, 'breathlessly different-looking' was a comment from Harper's magazine. Then came the outstanding performance. On the Bonneville Salt Flats, an Imperial coupe motored the flying mile at 95.7 mph. Over 500 miles it clocked a constant 90 mph and set 27 new American speed records. Sadly, 1934 sales were under-whelming.

But the cars lost money. Unfortunately, the public found the model too bizarre or just plain ugly. The 1935 Airflow C1 was powered an eight-cylinder 323.5 cid engine developing 115 horsepower. On the outside, the car had a new hood that extended forward in the shape of a Vee, and single broad bumpers. The new grille had a great top to bottom slope. Standard equipment included Autolite ignition, hydraulic brakes, Floating Power, automatic choke and a stabilizer in the back of the front axle.

Engine: inline eight cylinders

Displacement: 323.5 cid

Horsepower: 115 at 3400 rpm

Transmission: Manual

Compression Ratio: 6.2:1

Induction: Stromberg IV model EX-32

Body style: Coupe

Weight: 3883 lbs

Wheelbase: 123 inches

Base Price: $1245

Number Produced: 379

■ *Right: A 1935 Chrysler Airflow C1 Two-door coupe.*

1935 DeSoto SG Airflow Coupe

By 1933, DeSoto sales were in decline but a new engine was planned to boost performance for the 1934-36 models. The original six had never been exciting. It was now upgraded to 100 horsepower at 3400 rpm and an increased displacement of 241.5- cid. It was, however, sturdy and reliable and would run for long spells with little maintenance other than oil and water. It was also good with gas consumption, turning in 22 mpg with steady use.

By the end of 1934 the Chrysler Airflow was in retreat and although DeSoto had their version, they also produced an Airstream model for 1935 to go alongside the unpopular Airflow design. The Airstream proved to be more saleable. The DeSoto Airflow disappeared after 1936, a year ahead of the Chrysler model. The Airflow series SG was a six and in an attempt to make it appear less radical, the DeSoto Airflow was given a new front end with a V-shaped radiator. It followed that the grille would also change and it became more sloping than rounded which served to increase the length of the hood and give the car a more acceptable look. This meant that there were now only three horizontal hood louvers instead of eleven. Freewheeling was no longer used but the car had the anti-sway stabiliser bar moved from the rear of the car to the front.

There were now more standard features such as the centifuse brake drums and Autolite ignition. By 1935 DeSoto was America's 13th largest car producer and for the second year in a row, the Airflow won the Grand Prix Award for aerodynamic styling at the Monte Carlo Concours d'Elegance. DeSoto also provided dealers with a kit that could upstage the 1934 Airflow to give them the same general appearance as the 1935 models. Over 400 SG coupes were sold at around $1015 each.

Engine: six cylinders

Displacement: 241.5 cid

Horsepower: 100 at 3400 rpm

Transmission: Manual synchromesh

Compression Ratio: 6.5:1

Induction: Ball & Ball IV E6F2

Body style: Coupe

Weight: 3390 lbs

Wheelbase: 116 inches

Base Price: $1015

Number Produced: 418

■ *Right: A 1935 DeSoto SG Airflow Coupe, with twin windshield wipers and a split screen. Note the 'modern' door opening.*

Duesenberg Model JN Coupe   1935

Fred Duesenberg died after a car smash in 1932. Before this tragic event he had supercharged the Model J to create the spectacular, powerful model SJ. His brother, Augie Duesenberg, wanted still more power and fitted a set of ram's horn manifolds. He was astonished to see the horsepower reach 400. In late 1934, A. B. Jenkins drove a special Roadster on the Bonneville Flats, and averaged 135 mph over 24 hours, clocking 160 mph for one lap. Yet again, it was an incredible car.

Only two Model Js could be described as sports cars. These were the Specials, designated Duesenberg Model SSJ. Both of these cars were first owned by Hollywood stars: Gary Cooper and Clark Gable. Then came another development in the life of the J, the 1935 JN. Only ten of these were ever built, all with Rollston coachwork. They had a 153.5-inch wheelbase and 17-inch-diameter wheels. The bodies were set below the frame rails for a lower profile. Superchargers were added to two of the cars but were removed later. This set up some confusion. Not all cars with Duesenberg plumbing on the outside had blowers and some superchargers were added to originals, so confirming specifications and accurately cataloging the cars is difficult. The face of the JN also changed. Some versions had a shorter running board apron, which meant that the battery carrier and toolbox were redesigned to give a lower door line. The bullet-shaped tail lamps were finished with the fender color. The headlamps, designed in the same recognizable style, were factory fitted, rather than dealer installed. On several JN's, the cowl lamps were absent. Engine-wise, the car was virtually the same as the J, with a 256 horsepower. A 320 horsepower version was also available. To control this engine power, the cars were fitted with Lockheed hydraulic brakes. The top speed was reported at 130 mph but for several models there were no records of how they could perform when pushed to the limit.

The Duesenberg was more than a status symbol – it was in a class all of its own – with owners ranging from robber barons and gangsters to an evangelist preacher. Duesenberg finally went out of production in 1937. Today, the company's cars are worth hundreds of thousands of dollars.

■ *Left: A unique 1935 Duesenberg Convertible Coupe, one of only ten examples of the JN.*

Engine:	eight-cylinder
Horsepower:	256
Body style:	Rollston
Wheelbase:	142.5 inches
Base Price (Chassis only):	$9,500
Number Produced:	10

Ford Coupe Roadster

1935

The 1935 Fords looked rounded and squat in shape, with smaller windows and a grille Vee that stood out more than in previous years. Few Ford enthusiasts would dispute Ford's claim of 'Greater Beauty, Greater Comfort, and Greater Safety' for this years models. The lively V-8 power plant was further enhanced by the addition of a new camshaft and better ventilation through the crankcase. Modifications were also made to the frame and the rear axle, both of which were strengthened.

The suspension was still extremely simple and effective, in fact it was a design retained from the old Model T, and had all the Ford benchmark qualities of durability and efficiency. It was a primitive set up of a solid axle bar on a transverse leaf spring in both the front of the car and the rear. Ford was also still using mechanical brakes, so the combination of a crude suspension and out of date brake technology left the impression that Roadster was behind the times, design-wise.

Henry Ford was renowned for his inflexibility and desire to keep things simple, but this approach was not helping his company plan for the future. He did sanction one development: the 1935 cars now had 16-inch steel wheels to replace the old traditional wire designs. Styling for the year was credited to Phil Wright at Briggs Company and there was a vast range of 16 different Model 48s to consider.

The most expensive Ford of the year was the new convertible sedan at $750. It featured roll up windows if the weather turned, and when the collapsible top was lowered, the B-posts could be removed and stored in a bag underneath the trunk. A more practical car for warmer climates was the Deluxe four-door phaeton which cost $170 less than the convertible sedan. A special feature on this car was the side curtains that could be packed away beneath the rear cushion. The cabriolet convertible had rumble seats, which had the effect of keeping the passengers isolated from the driver when the top was up.

■ *Left: A 1935 Ford Coupe Roaster with its distinctive large driving lights, curved mirrors and fully enclosed rear wheels.*

Engine:	eight-cylinder
Displacement:	221 cid
Horsepower:	85 at 3800 rpm
Transmission:	Sliding gear
Compression Ratio:	6.3:1
Induction:	Stromberg EE-1 carburetor
Body Style:	Coupe Roadster
Number of seats:	2
Wheelbase:	112 inches

1935 Packard Model 1201 Victoria Convertible

Packard started an exciting year in 1935. They had a new management team in place. Max Gilman came in as the front man and George Christopher as the production king who had to be coaxed out of retirement. Gilman wound up the press and public while Christopher went through the plant modernizing it for high volume builds. The result of this activity and dynamism was the launch of the One Twenty, a car for the medium priced field.

But alongside this new model was the Twelve Series Eight that included the 1201 model. For this series, aluminum cylinder heads were standard and the compression ratio was 6.5:1, horsepower was up to 130 and the top speed was over 90 mph. On the outside of the car there was a completely new look: beginning up front, where there was a five degree slant to the radiator, carrying on to the pontoon fenders in the rear. Chrome was added to the side louvers as a feature.

For the 1201 model with the 134-inch wheelbase, ten body styles were available, which included the LeBaron Cabriolet and the Packard Victoria convertible. The eight cylinder power plant was fitted, the car had Bendix mechanical brakes, rode on 16 x 7 inch tires and had a fuel tank that could take 25 gallons. The two-door Victoria had the spare on the outside and a pair of prominent headlamps backed up with lower spots. Performance was smooth, with an easy ride and enough power for controlled speed.

■ *Right: Packards's own designers created this seductive 1935 Packard Model 1201 Victoria Convertible.*

Engine: straight eight-cylinder

Displacement: 320 cid

Horsepower: 130 at 3200 rpm

Transmission: Selective synchromesh

Compression Ratio: 6.5:1

Induction: Stromberg-Duplex

Body Style: Victoria Convertible

Number of seats: 5

Weight: 4835 lbs

Wheelbase: 134 inches

Base Price: $3200

1936 Cord 810

Erret Lobban Cord was the force behind some of the most magnificent cars ever built. In 1929 he built the Cord L-29 which proved less than he had hoped for, but it was the foundation for the 1936 Cord 810. The original L-29 was chiefly engineered by race car builder Harry Miller. It was a special design and according to one Cord authority it had over 70 unique parts. Fabulous though it looked, sales limped along and by 1935 one used car guide priced it at $145. But in 1936 the idea for the 810 was originated, using a V-8 rather than the original V-12, and incorporating front wheel drive, good weight distribution and better contraction than the L-29. Everything rode on a 125-inch wheelbase. There were many advanced features on the new 810. The front suspension, for example, was made up of independent trailing arms joined by a single transverse leaf sprint. The transmission had four forward ratios instead of the usual three and a Bendix Electric hand pre-selector. The power plant was a V-8, 288.6 cid unit made by Lycoming - another Cord company. The engine generated 125 horsepower, but with the aid of a Schwitzer-Cummins supercharger, it was boosted to 170 horsepower. This up-rated the engine to 190 horsepower. The basic 810 could top 90 mph and do 0-60 in 20 seconds. The supercharged car weighed in at 111 mph and hit 60 mph in 13 seconds.

Four models were launched in series 810. These were the Westchester and Beverley sedans (where the only real update was in the upholstery patterns) a two-seater sportsman and a four-passenger phaeton sedan convertible. 1,174 Series 810 cars were registered in 1936, all with prices around the $2000 mark. The coffin nosed car had first made its debut on 2 November 1935. These first cars were all hand built for auto shows around the country, where small development problems were ironed out (especially with overheating and an unreliable transmission).

Engine: eight-cylinders

Displacement: 288.6 cid

Horsepower: 125 at 2500

Transmission: Selective synchromesh, Bendix electro-vacuum system

Compression Ratio: 6.5:1

Number of seats: 2

Weight: 3,715 lbs

Wheelbase: 125 inches

Base Price: 2000 lbs

Number Produced: 1,174

■ Right: The magnificent Cord 810, evolved from the Cord L-29. A 20 gallon tank gave it the freedom to roam the roads.

Willys 77

1936

Long before John North Willys's company built the Jeep, they were a visionary and inspired carmaker in the twenties and early thirties. But this was not enough to stop the company being obliged to declare bankruptcy in 1934. It took a further three years before they emerged from receivership. In the meantime, Willys-Overland as the company was called, had to make a decision about its future and they decided to produce a low-priced small car. In fact, one could assume that this was all they had the funds to contemplate.

Harnessing all their ingenuity, they managed to develop and build the Willys 77 for very little money. It was given its first public viewing in 1932 and at that time they had a 100-inch wheelbase and a four-cylinder engine capable of producing 48 horsepower from only 134.2 cubic inches of displacement. The car survived and remained the only model sold by the company up until 1936. The 1933 reorganization of the company had bought in a new chairman, the bespectacled Ward Canaday, a Canadian with a strong sense of civic duty and a strong empathy with the workforce. It was he who wanted to get things moving again but his first real chance did not arrive until 1937 when he decided that enough had been achieved by the sturdy 77 and ordered a full restyle. The result was less than ideal. The cars had a lumpy appearance and an oddly bulging front end. The new sheet metal construction increased the overall length to 175.5 inches.

But the cars were moderately priced, at just below $600, and met with some success despite their odd appearance. But the general recovery of the car industry was also a turning point for the company. Although Willys produced twice as many cars in 1936, so did the rest of the industry. Willys only managed to improve their industry standing by one place, to 14th.

■ *Left: The 1936 Willys 77 with dashing yellow, spoked wheels and large driver lights. The doors had front and rear hinges.*

Engine:	Four-cylinder
Horsepower:	48
Body Style:	Four-door Sedan
Wheelbase:	100 inches
Base Price:	$540

1937 Buick Century Sedan

Sleek new styling was one of the many changes that occurred in 1936 as Buick adopted GM's all-steel turret top construction, which did away with the traditional fabric roof insert. Engines became more and more powerful and technological advances included aluminum pistons. The lexicon of car names began to take on a character that remained until the 1950's. 'Century sedan' was one of these, being the renamed series 60. Styling was a big factor in the resurgence of the brand. It was directed by Harley J. Earl, the founder and head of GM'S Art and Color Section, the first dedicated styling department opened by a mainstream carmaker. Streamlining drove Earl's styling in these years and Buick had it in full force for the 1937 models. The lines were rounded and set off by swept back features, fully integrated trunks and vertical bar grilles. 1936 was the first year that production returned to something like pre-Depression levels. The new Century was a fast car with a cruising capability of over 100 mph and a 10-60 acceleration of about 18 seconds. The cars quickly became known as 'factory hot rods' and were

■ *Below: One of the great Buick's, the four-door Century Sedan of 1937 is a renamed '60' with an official top speed of 101 mph.*

indeed about the fastest thing you could buy for around $1000. But was Buick impressed by this success? Hardly. They pressed on to introduce turret tops that had longer fenders and horizontal grille bars that became industry trendsetters. The 1937 models were more refined than any seen before with additional headlights in the same style as the fender parking lights. The line proved to be a real winner. 1937 was also the first year that Buick used plastic on some of the interior fittings. The door handles, dash knobs and steering wheel were all built in an ivory-yellow plastic. A modern horn was also designed into the steering wheel. Stabilizer bars front and rear gave the four-door sedan a better ride and windshield defrosters were added to make winter motoring more comfortable. The car was one of the most impressive of all the 1937 models. The Century's engine developed 120 horsepower from the 320.2 cid power plant. There was an optional dash-installed radio for the interior.

Engine: straight eight cylinder

Displacement: 320.2 cid

Horsepower: 120 at 3200 rpm

Transmission: Sliding gear

Compression Ratio: N/A

Induction: Two-barrel Stromberg downdraft EE22 carburetor

Number of seats: 5

Wheelbase: 122 inches

Base Price: $1090

Number produced: 17,806

Cord 812 Cabriolet

1937

The styling of the 812 came from the synergy of the design teams. The team was made up of Cord regulars, Gordon Buehrig, assisted by Dale Cosper, Dick Robertson and Paul Laurenzen. Between them they came up with many innovations, and pushed the Cords graceful lines to the limit. Particularly striking design elements were the smoothly formed 'coffin' nose hood, the low silhouette, the unusual wraparound horizontal louvers instead of a standard radiator, the minimal trim and pontoon fenders. On the supercharged models, the racing style exposed exhaust pipes. The concealed headlamps on the car were an industry first. These flipped up when needed by cranking a handle. Equally eye-catching design features were the full wheel covers and the concealed gas cap. The style impact then moved to the insides where turned-metal was used on the dash in needle gauges and a ceiling-mounted radio speaker. What became apparent was that Beuhrig and his team had 'borrowed' many of the appearance items from existing proprietary bits including leftovers from Auburn.

The engine was the V-8, 288.6-cid developing 125 horsepower power plant. The supercharged version could develop 190 horsepower. The 812 came in six models: Westchester sedan four-door, Beverley sedan four-door, cabriolet, phaeton, Custom Beverley sedan four-door and the Custom Berline all with or without a supercharger. The custom cars came on an extended 132-inch wheelbase. But the Cord registered only 1,146 sales which just wasn't enough to keep the company out of trouble. As a result, the Cord Corporation had to work on a shoestring budget, and cut costs. This didn't work either. The company's problems moved to the production line, where haste became waste. Although build quality problems were ultimately resolved, the damage had been done, and unhelpful rumors circulated in the industry. Eventually, the E. L. Cord empire collapsed in 1937 and the Cord models followed the business into oblivion.

■ *Left: A mean machine of outstanding beauty, the 812 Cord cabriolet with exposed exhausts and supercharger.*

Engine:	eight cylinders
Displacement:	288.6 cid
Horsepower:	125 at 3,500 rpm
Compression Ratio:	6.5:1
Body style:	Cabriolet
Weight:	3,715 – 4,170 pounds
Wheelbase:	125 inches
Base Price:	$2,445
Number Produced:	1,146

1937 Ford Five-Window Coupe Model 78-770

Ford got the fashion message right in 1937. In a year of questionable styling throughout the industry, the Model 78 cleaned up. Ford produced one of the best looking cars of the decade. Even President Franklin D. Roosevelt bought a convertible sedan for use at his Georgia retreat.

The familiar 221 flathead was also given a new lease of life: becoming known as the V-8/85 after the development of the V-8/60 for the European market. A configuration that didn't work – fewer horsepower and better economy and a cheaper price wasn't what people wanted – power was king. The '37 engine had improved cooling due to the redesign and relocation of the water pump and new cast-alloy pistons.

Ford also made a radical change to the construction of the body. In response to GM's Turret Top bodies Ford made an all-steel body for closed models, dumping the old fabric roof inserts at long last. Headlamps were sunk into the new bodies. These were now buried in the fenders. A prominent grille, composed of fine horizontal bars which swept backwards as it approached the top, was also fitted. The styling reflected the strong influence of the Lincoln-Zephyr. The sedans came in two body shapes, one with a trunk back and the other with the slant back.

The new coupe also came with a rear seat. All the models came with a rear-hinged hood, they were described as opening 'alligator-style'. With a larger V-8 under the hood, the model 78 Sedan proved to be formidable when equipped for Police duty. The mechanical breaks now had cable linkage and were advertised and promoted as being 'all steel from pedal to wheel'.

■ *Right: An eye-catching red 1937 Ford Model 78 coupe, which by all contemporary accounts was the style champion for the year with its bold but smooth lines demonstrating that streamlining wasn't the only option.*

Engine: V-8 cylinder

Displacement: 221 cid

Horsepower: 85 at 3800 rpm

Transmission: Sliding gear

Compression Ratio: 6.3:1

Induction: Stromberg downdraft carburetor

Body Style: Coupe

Weight: 2506 lbs

Wheelbase: 112 inches

Base Price: $660

Number produced: 26,738

1937 Studebaker Coupe Express Pickup

The pickup truck is an essential part of the American auto experience. It was a practical workhorse designed to take the place of the original four-legged transport. By 1930, all of the Big Three manufacturers had active truck divisions producing pick-ups, factory complete all-steel, half-ton trucks. Studebaker had also dabbled in big trucks prior to 1930, but the company made its first entry into the world of the light-duty truck in 1937. The Depression had played a large role in the pickup's growing prominence, as the market for big trucks had contracted, so Studebaker felt that the time was right for them to enter this market. Their car-derived pickup was based around the 116-inch wheelbase Dictator, and had a handsome car-like shape and good lines for a working vehicle. The models were actually constructed by speciality body building firms. But from the doors forward the 1937 Coupe Express was a Dictator passenger car. The pickup was an attractive hybrid that reminded many witnesses of Hudson's Terraplane pickup model that had been introduced three years earlier. Its good lines were hardly surprising considering that the original design had come from the pen of Raymond Loewy.

This was a period when Studebaker's car production was going up and down. In 1937 some 98,000 cars were produced. This was up by a considerable 40,000 from the year before, and profits for the year were $812,000. An optional fully automatic overdrive followed in 1937, a further refinement of the semi-automatic that had been developed two years previously. The new hypoid rear axle had now become standard.

More innovations followed over the next few years and they too were incorporated into the pickup. 1938 saw windshield washers added, for example.

The Coupe Express 'half-car, half-truck' stayed in production for three years before this hauler was retired in favor of an 'all-pickup' pickup in 1940.

Engine: Inline six-cylinder

Displacement: 217.8 cid

Horsepower: 90 at 3400 rpm

Induction: Stromberg carburetor

Number of seats: 2

Wheelbase: 116 inches

■ *Right: The American motorized workhorse: the pickup truck. This bold yellow 1937 Studebaker Coupe Express Pickup was based on the Dictator chassis.*

Chevrolet Master Deluxe Sedan   1939

Chevy's Master Deluxe model was a fancy version of the Master with its longer 1939 hood and fenders. The wheels and running boards were lowered for a more streamlined, longer appearance. The body shell was retained from the '38 model, but was restyled to look more modern. The grille extended back along the fender line at the top and then tapered to about four inches at the bottom. The car had a rounded look with horizontal grille moldings and a horizontal bar effect on the splash on aprons. The Deluxe Sedan had bumper guards as standard equipment as well as twin taillights. The four-passenger coupe was an all new body style, with folding opera seats replacing the rumble seat. The 'knee action' coil spring front suspension was another feature. Despite all this cosmetic buffing, the Master Deluxe was reported to be the fastest accelerating American passenger car of the year. It went from 10-60 in high gear.

Even with this speed advantage no cabriolets were built in 1939 but the 15-millionth Chevrolet was completed. As you would expect there were a hatful of options for the deluxe; radio, heater, clock, cigar lighter, radio antenna, seat covers, external sun shade, spotlights, fog lights, wheel trim rings, and a slip in coupe pick-up box. The power came from the Chevy six-cylinder engine with a 216.5 cid displacement. This developed 85 horsepower at 3200 rpm. The especially rare models from this year included the Master Deluxe Coach and the four-door, slant-backed Sedan of which only 68 were produced. The Master Deluxe Sports Coupe cost $715 and an identical body was used for the Business Coupe, which sold for $684.

■ *Left: A Chevrolet 1939 Master Deluxe Sedan 4-door with gleaming white walled tires races along confirming its speed advantage in 1939 specifications.*

Engine: six cylinders	
Displacement: 216.5 cid	
Horsepower: 85 at 3200 rpm	
Transmission: Manual	
Compression Ratio: 6.25:1	
Induction: Carter IV model W1 carburetor	
Body style: Four-door Sedan	
Number of seats: 5	
Weight: 2875 lbs	
Wheelbase: 112 inches	
Base Price: $745	

Nash Model 4081

N ash Motors was twenty years old in 1936 and Charlie Nash, now 72 years of age, was feeling his age. The company continued to produce fine cars and to hold their spot in the top fifteen auto manufacturers. Nash invited George W. Mason, Vice President of Kelvinator Fridges, to take over as Nash President. Mason agreed, provided that Nash took over Kelvinator. The sale duly took place with jokesters predicting Fridges with four-wheel brakes and cars with ice cube trays! The joint companies were a good fit and Mason was a good President.

Nash sold 86,000 cars in 1937, making a $3.5 million profit. Nash's cars always kept up with the times, and innovations of the late thirties included both overdrive and the unique Weather Eye ventilation system. The 1940 model range for the Ambassador series had improvements such as Sealed Beam Headlamps, a redesigned grille with closer spaced bars and Nash scripts on hood and trunk. There were 18 different model options including a one-off special cabriolet designed by Alexis de Sakhnoffsky with distinctive cutaway doors.

Although 1940 was a disappointing sales year with only 52,855 registrations, Nash remained profitable.

■ *Left: An Ambassador Eight Cabriolet. The cut away doors identify it as a Sakhnoffsky-modified car.*

Engine: Straight-eight OHV

Displacement: 260.8-cid

Horsepower: 115 at 3400 rpm

Transmission: Three-speed selective sliding gears

Induction: Carter 485S carburetor

Body Style: Two-door Cabriolet

Number of Seats: 3/5

Weight: 3640 lbs

Wheelbase: 125 inches

Base price: $1,295

Number Produced
(Ambassador models): 63,617

1941 Lincoln Continental

Edsel Ford, a man of style and discerning taste is responsible for perhaps the most enduring of the Lincoln Models. The Lincoln line was running out of steam in the late 30s and Cadillac were challenging its position at the luxury end of the market. Edsel returned from a trip to Europe in 1938 and asked designer Bob Gregorie to build him a personal custom special that would look 'strictly Continental'. Using a Lincoln Zephyr, 125-inch wheelbase chassis, Gregorie created a fabulous car that caused a flurry of admiration wherever it went. So it was decided to put the design into production. The car was unveiled at the Ford Rotunda in Dearborn on October 2nd 1939.
The first 'Continental' was a cabriolet, this was followed by a coupe in May 1940. Twelve-cylinder power provided by the 292 cubic inch L-Head unit amounted to 120

■ *Below: What the well-dressed couple of 1941 drive to their country weekend.*

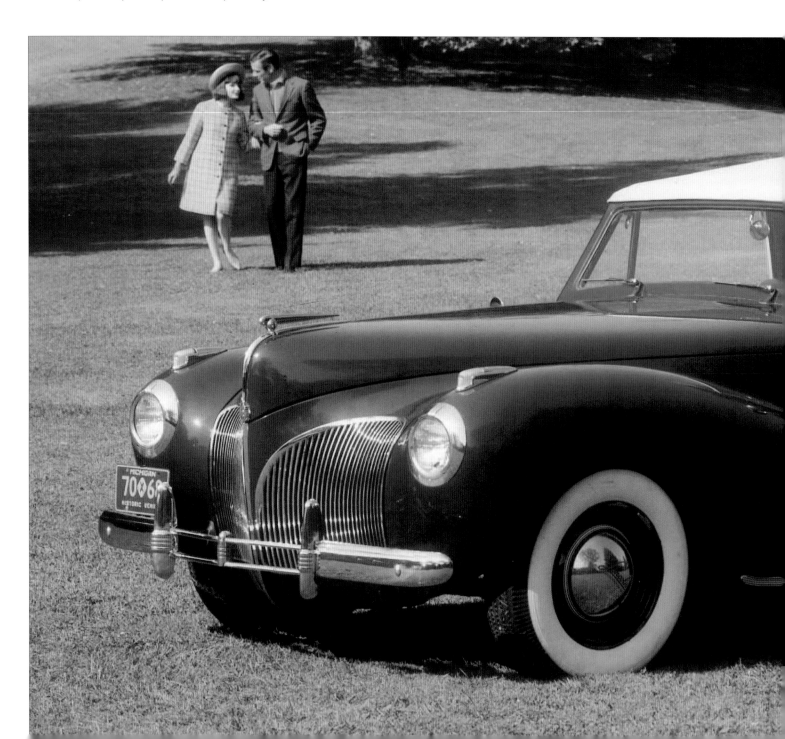

horsepower. The aluminum alloy heads were polished and had nice touches like the chrome plated acorn head nuts. The car's body was three inches lower than the Zephyr and the hood was seven inches longer, creating a sinuous, sleek look. The distinctive rear spare wheel cover was also present. The new model also had press button door operation.

The 1941 models were the first to be officially designated as Continentals and had their own tooling. 1,900 Continentals were manufactured produced up until production was suspended on the outbreak of war in 1942. Model production was resumed after the War, but very sadly, its inspiration, Edsel Ford had died in May 1943.

Engine:	75-degree V-12 L-Head.
Displacement:	292-cid
Horsepower:	120 at 3500 rpm
Body style:	Two-door Coupe/Cabriolet
Number of Seats:	5
Wheelbase:	125 inches
Weight:	3635 lbs
Base price:	$2840
Number Produced:	404

Oldsmobile Series 98

'The Car Ahead' was the cry from Oldsmobile's publicity department in 1941. 'The car that has everything modern' was another sales line, and indeed the range did have a lot going for it. New fastback styling was evident, as were redesigned grilles and simulated wood finishes. Oldsmobile also first offered a four-speed automatic gearbox option called Hydramatic. Over fifty percent of customers opted for this for an extra $100.

The company passed a couple of personal milestones in the year 1941. The two-millionth car left the production line and overall sales of 270,040 cars for the year was the best in the company's history.

The series 98 represented the top end of the Olds range. Powered by the straight-eight engine, it generated 110 brake horsepower at 3400 revs.

The relatively light two-door fastback coupe version was heading in the direction of an early musclecar. Other models on offer were the two-door convertible, four-door sedan, and the most expensive car in the Olds range, the four-door Phaeton (at $1,575).

These were amongst the last truly pre-war cars. The line was to be closed down in favor of ammunition production for the duration of World War II.

■ *Left: The two-door coupe version of the Olds 98 series, complete with fastback styling. The car looks like it's doing seventy when it's standing still!*

Engine: Eight-cylinder inline

Displacement: 257-cid

Horsepower: 110 at 3400 rpm

Transmission: Three-speed manual/ Hydramatic

Induction: Dual downdraft carburetor

Body Style: Two-door Fastback Coupe

Number of Seats: 2/4

Wheelbase: 125 inches

Weight: 3430 lbs

Base Price: $1059

Number Produced: 23,463

Packard Clipper Touring Sedan

Packard recognized that something drastic needed to be done about their styling as they introduced a completely different shape for mid-year 1941. Whilst the old 120 series harked back to the 30s, the new Clipper was making a bid for the 50s! As a result this styling would see the company through the immediate post war sales period.

The Clipper was designed by staff stylist Howard 'Dutch' Darrin and modified by Werner Gubitz. The design was lower and much wider with faired in fenders, running boards and horizontal grille styling giving the car a mean low-slung look.

Although it shared chassis dimensions with the earlier 120 series, having an identical 127-inch wheelbase, the new chassis was of a completely new design. Under the hood, but not so apparent with the new styling, was the well-proven straight-eight power unit, adjusted to provide an extra five brake horsepower, courtesy of a higher compression ratio and an upgraded carbureter. A futuristic column-mounted gearshift for the three-speed manual transmission marked a new trend for the forties.

An optional Aero Drive overdrive was offered to take advantage of the straight-eight power on a long drive. The new car was strategically priced to fit between the 120 and 160 series cars, and was priced at $1420.

■ *Left: Classic black paintwork shows off the clean lines of Dutch Darrin's design for the Clipper.*

Engine:	L-Head straight-eight
Displacement:	282-cid
Horsepower:	125 at 3600 rpm
Transmission:	Three-speed 'Sychronized'
Induction:	Carter Model WDO 512 S
Body Style:	Four-door Sedan
Number of Seats:	5
Wheelbase:	127 inches
Weight:	3725 lbs
Base Price:	$1420
Number Produced:	16,600

1941 Pontiac Torpedo

The whiz behind Chevrolet's success came to Pontiac in 1934 as General Manager. Harry Klingler was a super salesman. Pontiac had had some tough years but Klingler quickly restored their fortunes, taking them from an all time low of 42,000 cars in 1932 to a production of 175,000 by 1935. He introduced a six-cylinder engine option to reduce costs and give the company a crack at the lower-priced market.

In 1937 he beefed up the engines, the six now had 223 cubic inches and 85 horsepower. The eight had 249 cid, which was good for 100 horsepower. All of Klinglers 'gut reaction' changes to the business seemed to bear fruit. The company had its best sales year so far with 235,000 cars. But there was still something missing. Klingler asked his design team (Bob Lauer and Joe Schemansky) to dream up a new streamlined style for the 40s. This became known as the Torpedo. The customers seemed to like this model because sales continued to rise, to 249,000 in 1940 and 282,000 in 1941 when the whole range went Torpedo!

Twelve different body options were offered with the new styling. The cars were built with either six- or eight-cylinder engines. Only a subtle hood badge distinguished between them. The new styling included faired-in fenders, running boards and a wide horizontal grille that accentuated the width of the cars. Both cars were priced under $1000, which made them widely affordable.

■ *Right: This Torpedo shows off Frank Hershey's Silver Streak side detailing.*

Engine: L-Head six- or eight-cylinder.

Displacement: 239.2 /248.9-cid

Horsepower: 90/103

Transmission: Three-speed synchromesh

Induction: Carter one-barrel /two-barrel

Body style: Four-door Sedan

Number of Seats: 5

Wheelbase: 119 inches

Weight: 3235/3285 lbs

Base Price: $921/ $946

Number Produced: 117,976 / 37,823

1942 Hudson Super Six Station Wagon

In 1942, the Hudson line got a substantial styling uplift. The grille was restyled to look wider with chunkier, spaced horizontal bars, restyled fenders with chrome trim and two body-length chrome strips (one at belt level one at the bottom of the doors running onto front and rear fenders). Quite unique to Hudson were the two illuminating triangular badges on either side of the hood, towards the front. This was the final year for such frivolities - the War saw to that. In future 'Blackout Specials' (manufactured from January 1st 1942) would be limited to chrome bumpers only. Everything else would have to be coated in body-colored plastic. Running Boards were gone for good, just leaving a vestigial flare on the door bottoms. This year also saw the final model-year of Station Wagon production at Hudson.

Since people had become more mobile in the thirties, many people had been obliged to migrate to get work during the Depression, the automobile had become a vital part of the American way of life and culture. As the recession faded, people still had the desire to travel, and this was transmuted into vacation breaks using the automobile. The need grew for rugged powerful vehicles, which could transport entire families and their possessions over vast tracts of the USA. Not since the Mormon trek had there been so much mobility. The Station Wagon was part of this 'road' culture.

The wood bodies were made by the Cantrell Company and grafted onto the 121-inch Super Six wheelbase. The wagon seated eight passengers. The rear and center seats could be removed for even greater carrying capacity. Drive Master automatic transmission was available as an option.

Engine: L-Head Six-cylinder

Displacement: 212 cid

Horsepower: 102

Transmission: Three-speed manual with Drive Master auto as an option

Induction: Carter Duplex Downdraft carburetor

Body Style: Four-door Station Wagon

Wheelbase: 121 inches

Weight: 3315 lbs

Base Price: $1486

Number Produced: 40,661

■ *Right: A superb Cantrell wood-bodied Super Six with black paintwork, ready for any load.*

1946 Mercury Sedan Coupe

When production resumed on the Mercury line on November 1st 1945, it was without the guidance of its creator, Edsel Ford. Edsel had died of stomach cancer in 1943 (some say of a broken heart because of his poor relationship with his father) and Henry had taken back the reins of both Lincoln and Mercury at 80 years of age.

In 1946 Mercury became a separate division of the Ford Motor Company. But the cars took a few more years to cast off their image as 'glorified' Fords. At this time, the company was still suffering from 'war shortages' and new model production was held up. The Mercurys on offer were cosmetically restyled 1942 models, with new hood pressings and a new grille with thin vertical bars.

The model range included a Sportsman's Convertible with fancy wood paneling but priced at $2209, it was the most expensive Mercury to date. The model was not a success and was not repeated in the following year. The one model that did extremely well, with sales of over 24,000 cars, was our featured car, the very attractive notchback two-door sedan coupe. This was by far the most tasteful and understated design of the model year, and if Edsel had been looking down from on high, he would have approved of it. At $1495, it also represented great value, particularly when compared to the over-the-top Sportsman's convertible. The V-8 was still an L-head, but this was eminently tunable and many of these cars saw service as hotrods in the '60s.

The overall sales total for the entire model range was 86,603 cars. This made Mercury America's twelfth largest manufacturer.

Engine: V8, L-head

Displacement: 239.4-cid

Horsepower: 100

Transmission: Three-speed manual

Induction: Holley 94 two-barrel

Body Style: Two-door coupe

Number of seats: 4

Wheelbase: 116 inches

Weight: 3190 lbs

Base Price: $1495

Number Produced: 24,163

■ *Right: The sleek and understated black two-door Mercury Sedan Coupe*

1947 Ford Super Deluxe Tudor Sedan

Whilst nothing very momentous happened to Ford's model lineup for 1947, and the pre-war body shape was still very much in evidence, the death of its 83-year-old founder, Henry Ford, made front page news around the world. Credited by many as the inventor of the automobile and of mass production itself, he was certainly the man who gave every American the chance of owning a car. Despite his egocentric style of management and his occasional failure to keep up with the times, he was the Citizen Cane of the auto world. The company was temporarily disorientated by his loss, and for a while, no 1947 models were announced at all.

It's possible that the management was floundering, with no Henry Ford to tell them what to do. But finally, a range did appear. Sales of 429,674 for the year put the company well behind Chevrolet. Our car, the Super Deluxe, offered the top range trim level and came with a new hood emblem, chrome body strip, chrome moldings on all the window frames, two sun visors, a chrome horn ring, a dash mounted electric clock, armrests on all doors and passenger assist straps.

Other small revisions made to the styling consisted of a red tracer removed from the grille and new round rear parking lights. There was a choice of six or eight-cylinder power across the range. Most people opted for the latter for an extra $73.

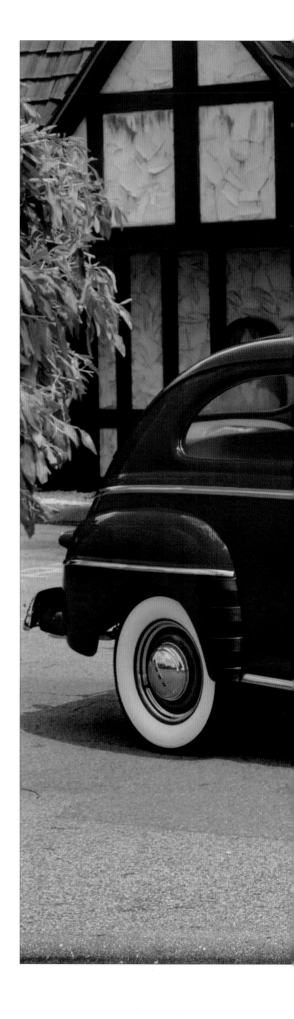

■ *Right: Despite the prewar styling, the bright red finish shows a bit of postwar cheer.*

Engine: L-Head Six-cylinder or V-8

Displacement: 226/239-cid

Horsepower: 90/100

Transmission: Three-speed manual

Induction: Holley Model 847F single barrel/Mod.94 Two-barrel

Body Style: Two-door Sedan

Number of Seats: 6

Wheelbase: 114 inches

Weight: 3183 /3216 lbs

Base Price: $1309/$1382

Number Produced (Series total): 385,109

1947 Plymouth Special Deluxe Business Coupe

With the return to the civilian economy in the late 40s, there was an increased demand for salesmen to promote new products in a rapidly expanding consumer goods market. The concept of a traveling salesman became a phenomenon. The Plymouth two-door coupe was ideal for this purpose, as it was relatively inexpensive to buy at $1200, and had a large trunk and good carrying capacity. It also had a lively 95 horsepower six-cylinder engine and looked great too.

Our model is identifiable as a Special Deluxe by the lettering at the rear of the hood, below the belt line trim, by the chrome windshield surround. Larger 10-inch hubcaps were fitted to this model and it also had a lot of useful extras like dual wipers and glovebox locks. The car was unusual in that it had proper rear quarter windows as many business coupes had blind rear quarters.

The rear fenders were re-flowed from earlier models to be more streamlined, and had smaller wheel apertures. The bumpers were wrap around and the grille had horizontal chrome bars. Options included an external sun visor and a light up hood ornament. Although the overall design was clearly pre-war in origin, sales boomed, and over 350,000 cars were produced in the model year maintaining Plymouth's third place in the auto industry.

■ *Right: The neat Plymouth business Coupe. Great lines, drab color!*

Engine: Six-cylinder L-head inline.

Displacement: 217.8 cid

Horsepower: 95 at 3600 rpm

Transmission: Three-speed manual

Induction: Carter Type BB one-barrel carburetor

Body Style: Two-door Coupe

Number of Seats: 3

Wheelbase: 117 inches

Weight: 2982 lbs

Base Price: $1209

Number Produced (Series): 350,327

Greatest American Cars

Pontiac Streamliner Station Wagon

1947

Full production resumed at Pontiac in June 1946, and 131,000 cars were produced in the first postwar calendar year. Pontiac's General Manager was Harry Klingler who had joined the company back in 1934. In those days, he had a reputation as a super-salesman and had restored the company's fortunes with a series of smart marketing moves. But it his energy may have been burned out by this time, as his model range was looking positively elderly.

Another Pontiac old timer, Ben Anibal, who had designed the company's cars back in the late '20s, now retired. He was replaced by designer George Delaney. One can only imagine how hard it would have been for Delaney to make substantial changes in a conservative company like Pontiac.

Despite their stylish names, such as Streamliner and Torpedo, the Pontiac models were deeply pedestrian and predictable. However, they were also reliable.

The 'woodie' wagon is an American classic however. Ash framing over dark maple paneling compliments the dark cherry body color. The vehicle could carry eight passengers in comfort, although the third row of seats was removable to allow give the model a greater luggage capacity. The eight-cylinder power option would gave the car both rugged reliability and long-legged pulling power on a cross-country journey. Aluminum fender panels were available for the 1942-48 model years and many owners fitted these to reduce weight.

■ *Left: A Streamliner body with custom wood styling makes the eight-cylinder Station Wagon a collector's dream.*

Engine: L-head, Eight-cylinder inline

Displacement: 248.9-cid

Horsepower: 103 at 3500 rpm

Transmission: Three-speed Manual

Induction: Carter WCD two-barrel carburetor

Body Style: Four-door Station Wagon

Number of Seats: 8

Wheelbase: 122 inches

Weight: 3845 lbs

Base Price: $2037

Number Produced: 86,324

1948   Cadillac Series 62

Nervous Cadillac dealers entertained doubts about the radical new design for the 1948 '60s' series. Although the inspiration for the styling came from a wartime theme , that of a P38 Lightning Fighter, it was beautifully translated into a great line of the postwar luxury car market. As the Cadillac ads said, the new models were 'The New Standard of the World'. The Harley Earl design team had done General Motors proud and dealer anxiety soon gave way to pleasure at sharply rising sales figures. Rising from around 30,000 cars in 1942, to 52,000 sales in 1948. Earl's new 'Futuramic Styling' had certainly done the trick.

Fins inspired by the 'twin boom' fighter's distinctive appearance made their first appearance

■ *Below: The handsome black Series 62 Convertible showing off the side stone shield trim to its beat effect.*

with this design. They were to rise to a crescendo of extravagance in the following decade. Windows and windshield were curved, as was the dashboard, complete with a rainbow shaped instrument panel. The wheelbase decreased by 3 inches to 126, and the body had handsome stone guards, which began behind the rear wheel and ran back along the rocker panel with a matching trim at the base of the rear fender. The rear tailfin on the driver's side flipped up to reveal the gas-filler. The front of the car had a redesigned grille, and torpedo shaped over-riders on the bumper. Everything about the car made it stand out from the opposition, making Cadillac the style innovator in the luxury market.

Engine: L-Head V 8

Displacement: 346-cid

Horsepower: 150 at 3400 rpm

Body Style: Two-door Convertible

Wheelbase: 126 inches

Weight: 4449 lbs

Base Price: $3442

De Soto Custom Club Coupe

1948

It was a struggle for De Soto to return to civilian manufacture after a wartime spent producing much needed Martin B26 Marauder Airplanes, nose-sections for B29 bombers and parts for Bofors Anti-aircraft guns. Converting the factory back to car production took longer than expected, and it wasn't until March 1946 that the plant was back in action.

Like most manufacturers the 'new cars' on offer after the war were really revamped 1942 models. In fact in De Soto's case, they were actually somewhat less exciting than their forebears. Gone was the neat 'Hidden Headlight' feature, conventional exposed lights were fitted instead. The cars also had rather predictable restyled grille and body trim. Moves toward some form of automatic transmission were catered for by Fluid Drive and the Vacumatic options. Fluid Drive was not a fully automated system, the driver had to 'Tip-Toe' to shift and spend an extra $121 for the privilege.

Low-pressure tires were adopted in 1948, as were stainless steel wheel 'beauty rings'.

The company's brief flirtation with plastic whitewall tires was discontinued at the same time. Body weights came down this year, just as prices went up. The postwar car boom was gathering pace and an average of $300 was slapped on the price of most models, according to the principal of supply versus demand. Nobody seemed to mind because sales were over 98,000 in the year. This gave DeSoto a twelfth place in the sales charts. Standard wheelbase (121½ inch) models were a four-door sedan, a two-door sedan, our featured car, the two-door Club Coupe and a two-door Convertible Coupe.

■ *Left: This Cherry-red Custom Coupe with Fluid Drive badge on front panel would have been good value at $1874.*

Engine:	L-head Six-cylinder
Displacement:	236.60-cid
Horsepower:	109 at 3600 rpm
Transmission:	Three-speed manual
Induction:	BB EV1 carburetor
Body Style:	Two-door Coupe
Number of Seats:	6
Wheelbase:	121 ½ inches
Weight:	3599 lbs
Base Price:	$1874
Number Produced:	98,850

1948 Plymouth Convertible Special Deluxe

Plymouth was the Chrysler Company's budget division, and things were looking good for the company in the late '40s. Model-year production of 412,000 cars lifted them to second place in the auto producers' charts for 1948. Although there were no major styling or mechanical alterations made this year, and despite the fact that the car was essentially a pre-war design, sales kept up remarkably well.

In fact, nearly all US manufacturers were still peddling models designed at the end of the 30s, so Plymouth was in good company. Prices did go up this year by an average of $200 but in the optimistic glow of the immediate post war years this didn't seem to matter either. Customers seemed actually more inclined to pay more for the upper level model choices, such as the featured Special Deluxe. Plymouth offered six different body styles in the Deluxe range: a two and four-door sedan, a two-door Club Coupe, two-door Coupe, two-door convertible and a four-door station

■ *Below: The handsome profile of the convertible Special Deluxe in Chevron Blue, one of ten colors available for 1948.*

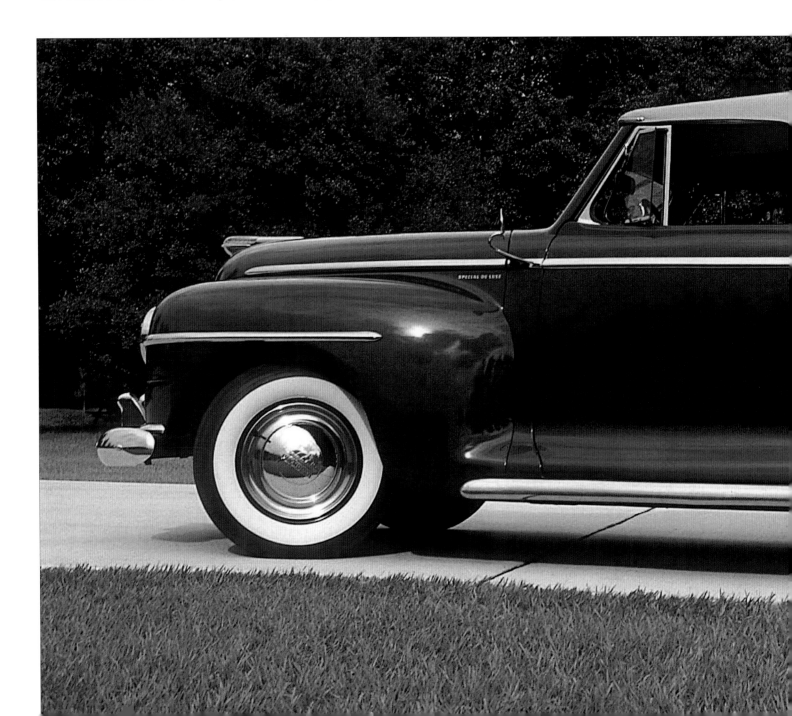

wagon. The station wagon was the most expensive model at $2,068, the least expensive was the two-door coupe at $1440. The former was a splendid creation with white ash framing contrasting to dark maple paneling. These 'woodie' bodies were largely made by hand, hence the extra cost. Next down the list was our featured car, the convertible Special Deluxe, priced at $1857. Powered by the L-head inline six, it was good for 95 horsepower. The car had all the extras associated with the series: a bright metal surround on the windshield and front quarter light windows, dual windshield wipers and sun visors, glovebox locks, and bumper fender guards. The convertible also had leather seats, a body colored painted dashboard and the pre-war style 'blind' top in white. Upholstery for the rest of the range was done in pencil-stripe broadcloth. Special Deluxe emblems on the hood identified the models in the range.

Engine: L-head Six-cylinder

Displacement: 217.8 cid

Horsepower: 95 at 3600 rpm

Transmission: Three-speed manual

Body Style: Two-door Convertible

Number of Seats: 5

Wheelbase: 117 inches

Weight: 3225 lbs

Base Price: $1857

Number Produced: 15,295

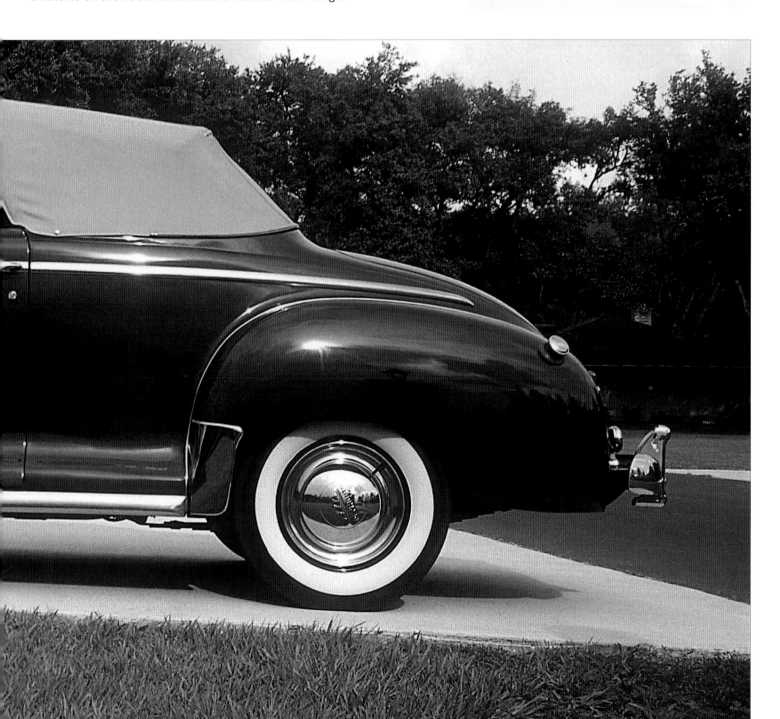

1949 Lincoln Series 9EL

The Continental was dead! The car that The Museum of Modern Art was to judge as one of eight great automotive works of art had been cast aside. Edsel Ford would not have been pleased. In its place was the Cosmopolitan, which critics said looked too much like the basic Lincoln series 9EL, which in turn was judged to looked too much like its cheaper brother, the Mercury.

As Lincoln headed toward the '50s it had at least one good card in its hand. The re-designed body shape was a huge improvement on the early '40s series 876H styling. The body was sleeker, and slab-sided with a wide horizontal grille and loads of chrome. The Cosmopolitans had a single-piece windshield, but the series model retained the two-piece.

In keeping with the times, the base model had its wheelbase cut to 121 inches, whilst the Cosmo stayed at 135 inches. Weight was still high at over 4000 pounds, so the car's performance required every ounce of strength that the 337 cubic inch L-head V8 could muster.

The Lincoln range comprised of seven different models, three Series 9EL cars and four Cosmopolitans.

Our featured car is the base model convertible, recognizable by its two-piece windshield. At $3116, this car represented better value for money than the comparative Cosmo model, priced at $3948. Eighteen different body colors were available, including seven metallic options.

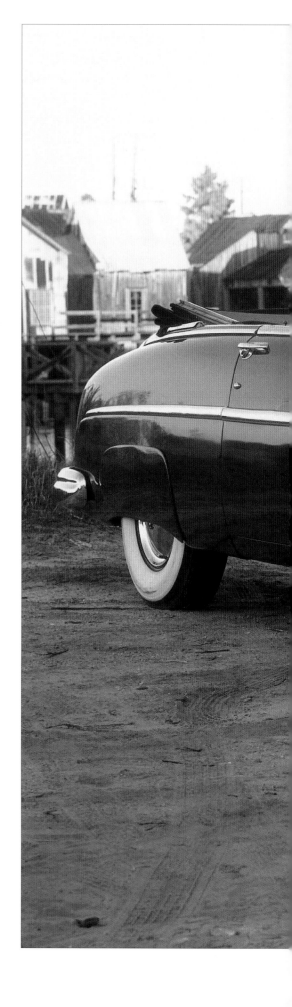

■ *Right: A Lincoln Convertible in Teal Blue.*

Engine: L-head V-8

Displacement: 336.7-cid

Horsepower: 152

Transmission: Three-speed manual

Induction: Holley Two-barrel carburetor

Body Style: Two-door Convertible

Number of Seats: 6

Wheelbase: 121 inches

Weight: 4224 lbs

Base Price: $3116

Number Produced: 38,384

1950 DeSoto Two-Door Hardtop Sportsman

The DeSoto division of the Chrysler Group had been very active in war production, assembling aircraft and cannon components for the USAF. But a return to civilian production in the post-war years was fraught with labor problems, shortages of raw materials and difficulties re-converting plant to auto production.

Their first post-war model, the 1946 Deluxe arrived in 1946, but it wasn't until 1949 that the company launched a fresh, practical look – 'The Car Designed with With You in Mind' ran the advertising slogan. This new look was to remain in production until 1954.

By 1950, the company was twelfth in the ranks of auto producers, with an output of 136,203 vehicles in the year. 39.6 million passenger cars were now on the American road, with 60% of families owning at least one.

The new top-of-the-range Custom Series was launched in 1950, and the cars reflected the same minor styling changes as the Deluxes to the original 1949 design. There were six six-seated Customs models, and two eight-seat examples that had a longer wheelbase and extra seats.

The Two-door hardtop version was the only body style with the 'Sportsman' logo. In fact, the car marked DeSoto's sole return to the hardtop market for this model year. It was an all-new pillarless coupe, with whitewall tires and full wheel covers fitted as standard.

■ *Right: DeSoto re-introduced hardtop coupes with the all-new pillar-less Sportsman.*

Engine: L-head six-cylinder, cast iron block

Displacement: 236.7 cid

Horsepower: 112 at 3600 rpm

Transmission: Tip-Toe Hydraulic shift with Gyrol Fluid Drive

Compression Ratio: 7.0:1

Induction: B-B E7L3 or B-B E7L4

Body Styles: Eight Custom styles in all, including a sedan, coupe, hardtop, convertible, two station wagons, long-wheelbase sedan and suburban

Number of Seats: 6/8

Weight: (Two-door Hardtop) 3735 lbs

Wheelbase: 125.5 inches

Base Price: $2489

Number Produced: 4,600

1950 Ford Custom Deluxe Two-door Convertible

Like so many car producers in the post-war period, Ford production relied heavily on slightly re-styled 1942 models. The cars sold very well into a car-starved market, and were only slightly tweaked until the newly designed 1949 cars. These were the first totally new cars that Ford had produced since the end of the War. They were built on a wishbone chassis, and had smoother and lower body shells than those of the early to mid-1940s. Slab-sided, the cars had now lost the unappealing bulge over the rear wheels. Horizontal chrome moldings, and a heavy chrome grille were simple and attractive adornments.

The 1950 cars were essentially unchanged, though minor trim changes were made. The ad slogan for the year was '50 improvements for '50' but these consisted of tiny adjustments in the styling rather than anything substantial. Things like a redesigned hood ornaments and push-button handles. Three model series were marketed in the year, the Deluxe, Custom Deluxe and Custom Deluxe V-8. Between them, they

Below: At just under $2,000, this convertible V-8 was a lot of fun.

accounted for sales of over 1.2 million cars. This was partly accounted for by the general upsurge in demand for automobiles, a hitherto unheard of number of 6.7 million cars were sold in the year. The fear that entry into the Korean War would result in the same consumer shortages as WWII had done fuelled demand for autos, as had the general return to civilian life.

The convertible Custom Deluxe V-8 in our photograph was one of six models in this range. It also included a four-door sedan, four-door station wagon, two-door sedan, two-door Crestliner, two-door club coupe and two-door station wagon. The Club Coupe has a short top, and the Crestliner was a special model with vinyl roof covering, extra chrome trim, a special steering wheel, special paint and full wheel covers. They all came with V-8s.

With model year updates, this body style lasted until 1955, when the entire Ford range was substantially restyled.

Engine: L-head, V-8 cast iron block

Displacement: 239 cid

Horsepower: 100 at 3600 rpm

Compression Ratio: 6.8:1

Induction: Holley two-barrel Model AA-1

Body Style: Two-door Convertible

Number of Seats: 6

Weight: 3263 lbs

Wheelbase: 114 inches

Base Price: $1948

Number Produced: 50,299

1950 Ford Custom Deluxe V-8 Sedan

Despite President Truman's order to US troops to enter the Korean 'conflict' in 1950 and the pressure to conserve raw materials exerted by the National Production authority, 1950 nevertheless saw a huge increase in car production and purchasing. Despite a slip from first to second place in the league of auto producers for the year, and trailing Chevrolet by nearly 300,000 units, Ford were still riding high from their restyle of 1949. As a company, Ford sold slightly more cars than in the previous year, but the increase in Chevy sales was enormous, nearly 50% in fact, as the company improved their output by nearly half a million cars. Traditionally however, Fords appealed to customers whose priority was performance.

Part of Ford's problem was that there were still gaps in their model line-up – they had no pillar-less hardtop, for example. Their Crestliner model (a two-door sedan in the Custom Deluxe V-8 series, with wild two-toning and deluxe interior) was a slightly half-hearted attempt to resolve this particular omission. This gap was finally filled in the following year by the Custom Deluxe Victoria, which sold a staggering 110,286 units in its first year of production.

The two-door sedan Custom Deluxe was available with both of the 1950 engine options, the L-head six-cylinder and L-head V-8. Like the other (five) models in the line-up, the body was only slightly modified from the re-designed cars of the previous year, with minor styling changes. The Custom Deluxe models had the top trim for this model year.

The two-door sedan was by far and away the best-selling model in the Custom Deluxe range, (which had total sales of 818,371 units). In fact, sales of this option were nearly 50% more than the next best-selling model, the four-door sedan ($47 more expensive). On numbers alone, the highly specified Crestliner was the least successful, with a total number of 8,703 sales. Both the Crestliner and convertible models were only available with V-8s.

Engine: L-head six-cylinder, cast iron block

Displacement: 226 cid

Horsepower: 95 at 3300 rpm

Compression Ratio: 6.8:1

Induction: Holley one-barrel Model 847F5

Body Style: Two-door Sedan

Number of Seats: 6

Weight: 3031 lbs

Base Price: $1590

Number Produced: 396,060

■ *Right: This two-door sedan version of the Custom Deluxe series was available with both six-cylinder and V-8 engines.*

Oldsmobile 'Rocket' Deluxe Holiday 88

1950

Oldsmobile has the longest heritage of any U. S. auto manufacturer, its handbuilt, wooden carriage-style vehicles having arrived on America's roads in 1897. This Lansing, Michigan based division of General Motors was successful right from the start, and its Curved Dash was the most popular car manufactured in the US in the early part of the twentieth century. In the '50s, Olds was benefiting from the 'Futuramic' restyling of 1949 and technological advances of the '40s. The latter included Hydra-Matic transmission (the first version of which was actually introduced back in 1940) and the new high-compression overhead valve Rocket V-8 under the hood (first offered in '49). This engine continued to roar around the racetracks in 1950, winning 10 out of 19 major NASCAR stock car races, handing the championship to driver Bill Rexford. Fitted to a Rocket 88, the engine broke a class speed record at Daytona, averaging 100.28 miles per hour, developing 263 lbs of torque per foot at 1800 rpm.

These assets contributed to Oldsmobile's sixth position in the league of motor manufacturing output for the year, of 408,060 cars. This was achieved under the management of General Manager S. E. Skinner.

The 88 series was Oldsmobile's mid-range line-up, with a total of seven body styles available. The 88 Holiday was introduced as a new hardtop body style to the junior series, and accounted for part of Oldsmobile's 8% share of the US hardtop market. Deluxe and standard trim versions were available. The series was now in its second year, and continued to be one of the hottest performing ranges available. One-piece windscreens were added to the range in the middle of the year, as exemplified in our photographed car. The less expensive 76 series would be discontinued in 1951, and the 88 would become the standard Olds. The top-of-the-range 98 series was Olds first slab-sided car, and was larger and more luxurious, but less performance orientated than the slightly smaller 88s. Both series had the 'Rocket' V-8 engine, but the 98 had nearly 250 lbs more to haul, and a seven-inch longer chassis to move.

■ *Left: This 'Rocket' 88 looks 'red' hot. The 88 Olds were the kings of the road in 1950 with their big engines and small bodies.*

Engine:	Overhead valve vee-block, cast iron block
Displacement:	303.7 cid
Horsepower:	135 at 3600 rpm
Compression Ratio:	7.25:1
Number of Seats:	5
Weight:	3535lbs
Wheelbase:	119-1/2 inches
Base Price:	$2035
Number Produced:	12,682

1950 Plymouth Deluxe Sedan

All-new Deluxe and Special Deluxe Plymouths had been introduced in 1949, so 1950 was a quiet model year for the company as it was for many other American motor manufacturers. K. T. Keller, who had succeeded Walter Chrysler in 1940, had introduced 'box styling' as thephilosophy behind Plymouth products. This meant that comfort and practicality were valued over beauty. His dictum was that the Plymouth autos should be practical transportation pieces in which one could sit bolt upright, wearing a hat. Although many buyers appreciated this common sense approach, and Plymouth's reputation for reliability, it did mean that the Chrysler styling fell behind that of its competitors until the mid-fifties. The cars were efficient and roomy, and modestly priced, true people's cars. These simple merits were emphasised in their 1950 advertising campaign, which offered the buyer 'spacious travel comfort'. Keller was promoted to being Chairman of the Board in this year, and Tex Colbert succeeded him as the President of Chrysler Corporation.

The '49 models were still pretty fresh in 1950, so the styling up-date for the year was limited, of the 'bolt on' type. Despite this, the cars were promoted as the 'Beautifully New Plymouth'. They were still using the L-head six-cylinder engine of the 1940s, however, and this contributed to a slow down in sales growth, combined with the general slackening of consumer demand. The Deluxes were available in both short and long wheelbase versions. The latter was seven and a half inches longer. The evolutionary changes to the Deluxes consisted of trim updates, and the rear fender was now attached with bolts so that it could be replaced if subject to collision damage. The fender design was also simpler than that of the previous year, with plainer moldings. The grille was modernised, and the rear windows were enlarged and widened. The windshields were unchanged. So were the dashboards, but these are a design classic that many people consider to be the most attractive ever used on a low-priced car.

Minor styling changes were also made to the higher priced 'Special Deluxe' line. The cars in this series were just over four inches longer than the junior models, (based on the longer wheelbase) and were more lavishly appointed, with more bright metal trim and interior comfort. The other model change in 1950 was the discontinuation of the 'woodie' wood-bodied station wagon.

The company retained its third position in the producers' league, but sales grew by a minimal half of one per cent in the year.

■ *Right: This DeLuxe Sedan is based on the shorted Plymouth wheelbase.*

Horsepower: 97 at 3600 rpm

Transmission: Manual with optional overdrive

Weight: 2946 lbs

Base Price: $1492

Number Produced: 67,584 (Two-door Sedan)

1950 Studebaker Champion

Studebaker entered the 50s in great shape, in eighth position in the auto manufacturers production league table. Having gone bust in the Great Depression – mostly through serious mismanagement at a corporate level – the company management was taken over by the successful team of Paul G. Hoffman and Harold S. Vance. Between them, these two able men guided the company through the Depression, and introduced the Champion in 1939. They were still running the company when car production resumed in 1945, and were responsible for Studebaker becoming the first major US auto manufacturer to introduce new styling in the post-war period. The fact that it was a 'seller's market' in the late '40s meant that their striking new car could really fulfil its potential, and the company made healthy profits in the final years of the decade.

There was a superficial re-style of the successful models in Studebaker's line-up to welcome the new decade. The famous, if rather bizarre, 'bullet-nose' grille at the front end and unusual vertical taillights were new, and looked very futuristic. Studebaker coined the phrase 'next look' to describe this styling and their advertising pictured the car parked next to a USAF F-86 Sabre jet fighter to emphasise its aerodynamic sleekness, the blurb describing their model as a 'beautifully flight-

■ *Below: The Champion may look quite bulky to modern eyes, but in 1950, it lines were extolled as having the 'going-somewhere distinction of a jet-plane'.*

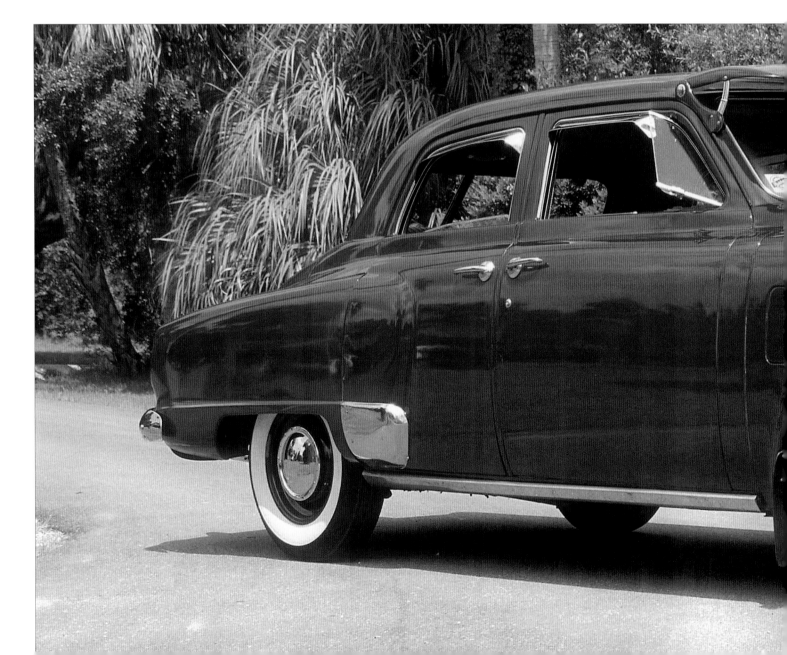

streamed car'. This was promoted as the gas-saving virtue of 'thrift'. Two model lines were now on offer, the base model Champions were available in a total of thirteen different body shapes in three trim levels (Custom Line, Deluxe Line and Regal Deluxe Line), mostly sedans and coupes with a single convertible model. The cars were economically priced, most being around fifteen hundred dollars. The Top line, the Commander Series had seven body styles in three trim levels. A single model in this series, the Land Cruiser, was built on a slightly longer chassis base.

Interestingly, the 1950s advertising also emphasised the importance of Studebaker's workforce, proudly claiming how many father and son teams worked on their assembly line. Ironically, this generous paternal attitude made it difficult for the company to react to changing times. When it became obvious that the market had switched to a 'buyer's market' in the early '50s, outdated plant and poor productivity meant that the company was operating in the red by 1953. The company was taken over by Packard in the following year.

Engine: Champion Six-cylinder L-head, cast iron block

Displacement: 169.6 cid

Horsepower: 85 at 4000 rpm

Compression Ratio: 7.0:1

Induction: Carter Model WE-715S one-barrel

Body Style: Four-door sedan

Number of Seats: 6

Weight: 2730 lbs

Wheelbase: 113 inches

Base Price: $1519

Number Produced: 16,000

Buick Special (Two-Door Coupe) 1951

The '51 Special was launched as one of four members of an 'All-Star (Fireball powered!) Line-Up for '51'. The advertising copy hailed the car as 'the newest car in the world – new in structure, new in power, new in dimensions, new in thrift – and potent in price appeal.' '51 versions of the Roadmaster and Super models were launched simultaneously.

The 1950-'52 General Motors Buicks were solidly built and heavily trimmed, so solid in fact that they are affectionately know as 'lead sleds' to this day. The heavy chroming, especially the cheesy grimace of the 'toothy' vertical-pillar grille was followed through in all the models of that year, plus a row of three chrome dimples on each front wing of the car that render the Special instantly recognisable as a Buick. The Specials were introduced with two- and four- door versions, all with Ned Nickles's 'hardtop convertible' styling, and all with side-opening hoods. A full convertible two-door model (the Special Deluxe) was also available for a further $515. Standard and Deluxe trim versions were offered (the photograph shows a Deluxe model). Interiors on Standard and Deluxe cars were cloth, but of a plusher grade in the latter.

Specials had a unique instrument panel, with speedometer and gauges housed in two large round units flanking the steering column notch. Controls were centered vertically, flanking the radio speaker grille. Standard Specials were the only 1951 Buicks to retain a split-windshield, the Deluxe models had the new one-piece version.

The cars often appeared in classic pastel two-tone combinations, pale blue and cream being especially popular, with white wall tire options. Wheels came with either solid chrome hubs or wires, which look particularly sporty.

In fact, this post war period was a great era for Buick styling, engineering and sales. Sales in 1950 reached 550,000 cars, fuelled to some degree by the fear that the impending Korean War would result in a shortage of consumer goods, as the Second World War had done.

With their straight 8-cylinder 4.3 litre engine block and dynaflow automatic transmission (first introduced on the 1948 Roadmaster, and the first torque converter automatic transmission), the cars still managed to impress original owners with their gas mileage. Yet, they were somehow a bit lacking in excitement and, even today, are not ranked among the most popular Buick models of this decade. The straight-eight era ended for the larger cars in 1952, when a four-barrel carburetted, 170-hp Roadmaster version made a fitting farewell.

■ *Left: This 1951 Special is in the classic pale blue and white wall tire combination, the chrome grille more massive than ever in the post war era.*

Engine: Straight-eight cylinder	
Displacement: 263.3-cid	
Horsepower: 120 at 3,600 rpm	
Compression: 6.1:1	
Number produced (two-door coupe): 2,700	

Lincoln Capri Convertible

1952

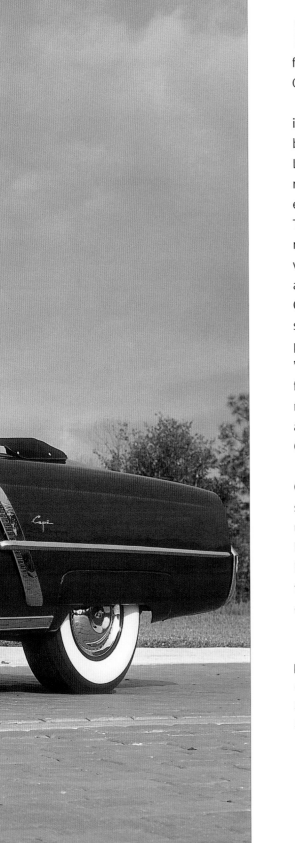

Like virtually every other US car manufacturer, Lincoln entered the post-war years by re-offering their pre-war models. However, they were still fantastically luxurious up-market cars and even in 1946, the top-of-the-range Continental model was selling for a staggering $4474.

But in 1952, Ford was the only one of the 'big three' car manufacturers to instigate a complete re-design of its entire model range, and Lincoln was a beneficiary of the 'All new for '52' look. For the first time at FoMoCo, both Lincoln and Mercury offered true pillarless hardtop models in their respective ranges. At Lincoln, this was the Capri two-door hardtop model. In fact, the entire '52 range shared the Ford corporate styling, and had a lean racy look. The bumper and grille were integrated in the car bodies instead of being recessed. All the new Lincolns were fitted with Ford's first modern overhead valve, 5.2 litre V-8s. Hydra-Matic auto transmission was fitted as standard, and Ford is reputed to have fitted the first ball-joint front suspension to these Capri models. Their reputation for performance was reflected in the racing successes of the marque. Lincolns took first, second, third and fourth positions in the 1952 Pan American 2,000 mile Road Race in Mexico (although '53 cars were used). A 'maximum duty kit' was available as an optional extra for owners who wished to race their own cars. The watchword of the Lincoln range was that they were fine cars with outstanding performance. But although Lincoln was to retain its reputation for luxury and comfort, the Chrysler 300 letter cars were about to steal it's racing crown.

The 'Capri' badge was first used in 1950 as a limited edition version of a Continental, but became a product line in its own right as the new top Lincoln series for '52. The cars were well appointed, featuring fabric and leather upholstery. The gas tank filler was hidden behind the rear licence plate. The line remained virtually unchanged for a further three models years, until the heavy re-style of 1956. Cosmopolitan was the base line model for '52, though this being Lincoln, the cars were very well equipped and sold for well over $3,000.

■ *Left: This Capri Convertible was the top model in the new Lincoln range.*

Engine: Overhead valve V-8, cast iron block	
Displacement: 317.5 cid	
Horsepower: 160 at 3900 rpm	
Transmission: Hydra-Matic automatic	
Compression Ratio: 7.5:1	
Number of Seats: 6	
Weight: 4350 lbs	
Base Price: $3665	
Number Produced: 1,191	

Buick Roadmaster Convertible   1953

Whatever excitement had been missing from Buick in the 1950-'52 models was back in 1953. The big news was under the hood – a 322-cid overhead valve V-8 for Super and Roadmaster models. For the first time ever (except for two sedans), all Buicks shared a common wheelbase. Celebrating it's 50th, anniversary (and sharing it with the Ford Motor Company), the Buick Division of General Motors was locked into aggressive price war with Ford – its most direct competitor. GM retained a 7.9% market share, with a model year total of 488,755 cars built. The seven-millionth Buick came off the production line in the June of that year.

The company owed its success in part to the upsurge in consumerism that resulted from the end of the Korean War. Detroit accurately reflected the national desire for good times by launching an endless stream of dazzling new models onto the market. The average family now aspired to owning two cars, and as the middle classes became increasingly better off, this became a reality for many.

The 1953 Roadmaster (series 70) was the top of the Buick's range of cars. Their finest model had a fore-shortened nose to emphasise the compact power of the newly introduced 'Fireball' V-8 engine under the hood. Roadmasters sported chromed rear fender gravel shields and the same sweepspear side detail that appeared on the slightly less expensive Super models. Four chromed ventiports adorned each wing. The interior options were nylon, broadcloth or leather with Roxpoint nylon carpeting as standard. Colour co-ordinated instrument panels were incorporated into the dash, which followed the glittery jukebox look favoured in the American cars of the period. A selectronic radio was optional on the Roadmaster, but an electric clock, left-hand remote control outside mirror, handy mats, air conditioning, tool kit and fold-down tissue dispenser were all fitted as standard.

Mechanically, power steering, power brakes and Dynaflow transmission were all standard on this model, as were full wheelcovers.

■ *Left: This 1953 Roadmaster two-door convertible looks stunning in yellow, with red interior. Complete with simulated wire wheelcovers, with black vee hubcab design.*

Engine: V-8 overhead valve. Cast iron block	
Displacement: 322 cid	
Horsepower: 188 at 4,000 rpm	
Transmission: Dynaflow fitted as standard	
Compression: 8.5:1	
Number of Seats: 6	
Weight (two-door convertible): 4250 lbs	
Price (two-door convertible): $3506	
Number produced (2-door convertible): 3,318	

1953 Buick Skylark Anniversary Convertible

Designed as a model to celebrate Buick's 50th Anniversary, the Skylark convertible (style 53-4767SX) was based on the top-of-the range Roadmaster chassis, but had its own fenders with open wheelhouses painted white or red. It also did without the classic Buick ventiports, and looked all the more streamlined for that.

Designers were the true kings of Detroit in the '50s, supplying the increasing market for cars with a new selection of models every year. This hugely increased the American car market, as the average driver now did in excess of 10,000 miles a year. Motels now outnumbered hotels two to one, catering for the needs of an increasingly mobile population. Special editions like the Skylark, which weighed in at a fairly punchy $5,000 stimulated the market, and pushed design and specifications further on. Even at this price, the model proved immensely popular, and the cars are still very collectible today. A total of 1,690 cars were produced.

The Skylark sported a shapely lowered topline to its body, 40-spoke Kelsey-Hayes wire wheels and a full complement of luxury accessories were included. The interior of the car was leather, and the car was trimmed with slim-cast sweepspear moldings and special bodyside emblems on the rear quarters. The seats, windows and convertible tops were all controlled hydraulically.

The Skylark was an essentially '50s car, adorned with the glitter, go and gadgets that the American car buyer of the time insisted upon. With gas at a quarter a gallon, fuel economy and safely features were fairly tertiary considerations when car buying, glamour being the most important at this end of the market.

Engine: V-8 overhead valve. Cast iron block

Displacement: 322 cid

Horsepower: 188 at 4,000 rpm

Transmission: Dynaflow

Compression: 8.5:1

Induction: Stromberg 4AUV267 carburetors, or Carter 996 or 2082S four-barrel

Body Styles: Convertible, two-door

Number of Seats: 6

Weight: 4315 lbs

Price: $5,000

Number Produced: 1,690

■ *Right: This elegant cream and cherry Skylark demonstrates the elegant flowing lines of this anniversary model.*

1953 Chevrolet Corvette Roadster

The Corvette was launched in 1953 and was a huge departure from the norm for the American car industry. It is said that GIs returned from the War were the inspiration behind the car, as they looked for American models that reflected their enthusiasm for British and Italian sports cars. It is ironic, therefore, that the Chevrolet division of General Motors– famous for its stable of family cars should become the manufacturer of such a unique and sporty car. Two men were the inspiration behind the car – chief stylist Harley Earl and chief engineer Ed Cole anxious to prove that GM could build a car to emulate the Jaguars and Ferraris they revered.

The original concept car behind the Corvette brand, the EX-122, had toured the States in the GM Motorama and generated huge interest, having also appeared in the GM promotional film 'Halls of Wonder'. The car was consequently put into production with few alterations. A tiny run of 300 cars was built in 1953. But cost saving in the manufacturing process somewhat diluted the original concept, and the engine in particular was disappointing compared to the European cars that had inspired it. Ironically, the convertible top for the first Corvette was very much an afterthought and it looked awkward and inelegant. It was also tedious to put up and down – the sidescreens had to be stored in the trunk, and the hood reduced the driver's visibility considerably.

The first cars were roundly criticised by the high-profile customers who were lucky enough to receive them, and at nearly $1,000 more than an imported MG the price tag meant that the car was well out of reach of the young drivers it was aimed at. The 'Blue Flame Six' engine was particularly derided. But Cole and Earl refused to accept that the car was a failure, and they gradually developed the model line into the American classic it remains to this day. Their first attempts are now regarded as Fifties classics, and the forerunners of a breed of true sports cars.

Engine: Inline six, overhead valve.

Displacement: 235.5 cid

Horsepower: 150 at 4200 rpm

Transmission: Powerglide automatic

Compression: 8.0:1

Body style: Convertible

Number of seats: 2

Weight: 2705 lbs

Wheelbase length: 102 inches

Price: $3498

Number Produced: (1953) 300

■ *Right: '53 'Vette in Polo white with a stunning background of Montana scenery.*

1953 Dodge Coronet Convertible

Like every other auto manufacturer, Dodge entered the post-war auto market with face-lifted pre-war models. Like the other Chrysler lines, the cars changed very little until 1949, when the 'Second Series' cars, with their rather boxy exteriors, were introduced. Venerable model names like Deluxe and Custom were replaced by the newer names of Coronet, Meadowbrook and Wayfarer. In fact, they were some of the first Chrysler models to be designed by Virgil Exner (who had formerly worked for Studebaker).

Introduced in 1949, the Coronets were the most expensive cars Dodge produced in the year, and received the top level of trim. The basic body shell for the model was identical to the Meadowbrook, but was more richly appointed inside and out. Six models were introduced, ranging from a two-door convertible to an eight-seat four-door station wagon.

President Eisenhower lifted production controls on domestic cars in February 1953, opening the gates to hugely increased production levels from all the major manufacturers. Dodge retained its position of seventh in the league table of car producers for the year.

Apart from a general Dodge price cut in March 1953, the big news for the Coronets was the introduction of a hemi head overhead valve V-8 under the 'Red Ram' hood ornament. Despite the extra sizzle introduced by the V-8, the six-cylinder engine was still much in evidence. In fact, the V-8 was fitted to only two out of the five Coronets, the four- and two-door sedans. The convertible was only ever available with the six-cylinder option.

The Coronet remained the top trim level Dodge model in 1953; the new six-cylinder models were launched in March. The cars were assembled in three Dodge plants, Detroit, San Leandro and Los Angeles.

Dodge outperformed all other American eight-cylinder models in the 1953 Mobilgas Economy Run (achieving 23.4 mpg), whilst Dodges also set 196 AAA stock car speed records at the Bonneville Salt Flats, as well as clocking up six NASCAR victories in the year.

Engine: Inline, L-head, six-cylinder

Displacement: 230 cid

Horsepower: 103 at 3600 rpm

Compression Ratio: 7.1:1

Induction: Carter one-barrel Model D6H2

Number of Seats: 6

Weight (Convertible): 3480 lbs

Base Price (Convertible): $2503

Number Produced: 4,100

■ *Right: This ragtop version of the Coronet was only ever available with a six-cylinder engine.*

1953 Ford Customline Two-Door Sedan

The Year 1953 was the 50th anniversary of Ford production. A special Ford crest appeared in the center of the steering wheel hub of cars manufactured in the year, containing the words '50th Anniversary 1903-53'. The company celebrated its birthday by manufacturing a greatly increased number of cars, and closing the gap between itself and the number one manufacturer, Chevy, to less than 100,000 cars. This despite a Chevy restyle. One major innovation for the year was the introduction of Master Glide power steering

1952 had seen the introduction of the first completely new Ford body shape since 1949. The new shape was introduced to make the company's cars more effective competitors to their Chevrolet and Plymouth rivals. The new models featured a one-piece curved windscreen, full-width rear window, protruding parking lights and new body trim. Inside, there was a completely redesigned control panel and suspended clutch and brake pedals. Under the hood, the six-cylinder Ford engine was overhauled, but the flat-head V-8 remained. Customline had been

■ *Below: Ford celebrated its 50th anniversary in 1953 by leaving the range pretty well unchanged. This two-door sedan sold 305,433 units.*

introduced as part of the general re-style as the mid-price range model in Ford's new line-up. This continued to be the case in the following year. Mainlines were the base Ford model, and the Crestline had the top trim option. In the second year of the new shape Fords, the body panels were used, but the grille was redesigned, and elongated to wrap around the front of the car, whilst parking lights became rectangular instead of round.

The Customline series hugely outsold the other Ford series, accounting for 761,662 units of the total years production of 1,244,540. Mainlines accounted for 302,714 cars, and Crestline 180,164. The four-door sedan was the most popular Customline model with sales of 374,487 units. Customlines were available with both six-cylinder and V-8 engines in three of the four body styles offered. Only the Country Sedan station wagon option was exclusively fitted with V-8s. Out of the year's output, 876,300 Fords were powered by the V-8.

Engine: six-cylinder overhead valve or L-head V-8. Both had cast iron blocks

Displacement: 215 cid/ 239 cid

Horsepower: 101 at 3500 rpm/ 110 at 3800 rpm

Compression Ratio: 7.0:1/ 7.2:1

Number of Seats: 6

Weight: 3067 lbs/ 3133 lbs

Base Price: $1724/ $1809

Number Produced (division between V-8 and 6-cylinder sales not shown in Ford sales figures): 305,433

1953 Henry J

The Henry J was a low-priced, compact economy car introduced by Kaiser-Frazer in 1951. Henry Kaiser had been very successful in his manufacturing career, and believed that there was an untapped mass market for a car that could be sold on price alone – just as the Model T Ford had been. 'Dutch' Darrin had styled other Kaiser models, and wanted the commission to design the Henry J prototype along the lines of these earlier models. But the temperamental Kaiser employed American Metal Products of Detroit instead, with a brief to evolve something completely different. Something that he hoped would change the fortunes of the company. AMP named the new model line after their patron, and the 'Henry J' was born. The car was perched on a short hundred-inch wheelbase and the car had optional four- or six-cylinder power options.

The rather sweet little car was fundamentally a two-door fastback sedan, and had miniature bench seats inside. The New York Fashion Academy named the car 'Fashion Car of the Year' and this initial model sold 81,942 units of the Standard and Deluxe models. But only the top of the range car that had an opening trunk lid, which gives an idea of exactly how basic a car this was.

The 1951 model was marketed as a Vagabond in the following year, and had some modest styling updates. A second Henry J, the Corsair, replaced it later in '52. The cars were manufactured at Willow Run, Michigan. But sales figures were following the pattern for the rest of Kaiser's automotive production – downwards - to around 22,000 units. Sales remained similarly depressed in 1953, with 17,505 units produced, despite a general 'tweaking' of the car's styling. This consisted of a new hood ornament, new chrome wheel discs and a curved rear bumper. Kaiser had managed to get a deal on with Sears to market the car in their stores, using their Allstate brand name. But the associate failed miserably, and Sears pulled out of the deal in '53 after two unsuccessful sales seasons.

In May that year, a Henry J won the Mobilgas Economy Run, but this was about the only unqualified success enjoyed by the car. The Henry J experiment collapsed in 1954, and is estimated to have cost Kaiser in excess of a hundred million dollars.

Engine: Inline six-cylinder, valves in block

Displacement: 161.04 inches

Horsepower: 80 at 3800 rpm

Compression Ratio: 7.0:1

Number of Seats: 5

Weight: 2445 lbs

Base Price: $1561

Number Produced (Corsair Six): 8,172

■ *Right: This 1953 Corsair Deluxe proved to be the final model in the Henry J line-up. Sales continued into 1954 with low sales of 1125 cars.*

Mercury Monterey Sedan   1953

Ford had formed the Lincoln-Mercury division in 1945, but it wasn't until the 1949 models were introduced that Mercury shed its image of being a line of glorified Fords. Ford had intended to introduce an updated overhead valve V-8 to replace the old flathead in 1952, but it wasn't ready in time, so the old engine was retained until '54. That was only one of the innovations in the 1954 models, but in 1953 this was all still to come. The entire line was to be restyled in 1955.

The Monterey model name was introduced in 1952, as an up-scale version of the base model Custom. This was the first time Mercury offered two distinct model lines in the same model year. Standard features included a two-tone paint job, and a leather and vinyl interior. Suspended pedals were also standard in both series. Mercury introduced three body styles in the original series, a hardtop coupe, sedan and convertible. The following year, the car was almost identical, and a station wagon was also added to the Monterey range. The car had a smoother cleaner look than the earlier Mercury series, being designed with 'unified' styling. Essentially, this meant a one-piece rear window, one-piece windshield and down-sweep hood for better forward visibility. The bumper and grille were now combined in a single unit, as were the rear lights and bumper. The Monterey interior was roomy and comfortable, and simply designed. The truck was a capacious thirty cubic feet. The model was available in fifteen solid and metallic paint colours.

'53 was also Ford's 50th anniversary year, and a Monterey convertible was used as one of the promotional vehicles for the celebrations. It was supposedly the 40 millionth car to roll off a FoMoCo production line. Ford brothers Henry II, Benson and William Clay were photographed driving the car.

Mercury sold a total of 305,863 cars in the year, and came eighth in the league of motor manufacturers.

■ *Left: This two-door sedan has a very distinctive roofline, shading the driver's eyes.*

Engine: L-head V-8, cast iron block	
Displacement: 255.4 cid	
Horsepower: 125 at 3800 rpm	
Transmission: Three-speed manual, with overdrive and Merc-O-Matic as options	
Compression Ratio: 7.2:1	
Induction: Holley 1901 FFC two-barrel	
Body Style: Two-door sedan	
Number of Seats: 6	
Weight: 3425 lbs	
Base Price: $2,193.50	
Number Produced: 50,183	

1953 Muntz Jet

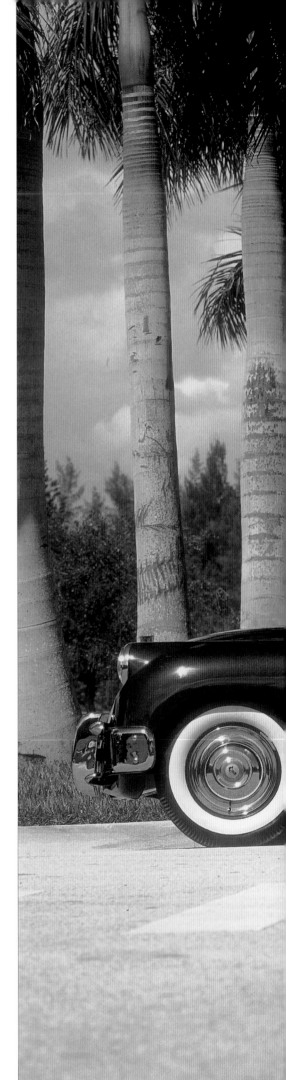

Muntz began life in 1951, when the television magnate Earl 'Madman' Muntz bought the California-based Kurtis-Kraft business. He modestly gave the car his own name, and made some relatively superficial changes. He moved production of the car to Evanston Illinois.

Frank Kurtis had begun the original business in 1949, having built many winning cars for the Indy races. He used his performance know-how to go into general production cars, aiming to offer a high-performance sports car to the public. He launched a two-door roadster that was practically custom built. Although there was a standard Kurtis bodyshell, any kind of technical kit could be fitted. When the customer didn't specify an engine, Kurtis fitted a modified Ford Flathead V-8. In this option, the cars were retailed at $4,700. He produced 36 cars in this incarnation of the business.

Muntz launched the Jet two-door hardtop coupe in 1951. The styling looked virtually identical to the Kurtis, but the wheelbase was stretched by three inches to make it a four-passenger car. He also changed the standard engine to a Lincoln V-8, which gave the 1951 Muntz a top speed of over 108mph. The car changed again in 1952 to a roadster-convertible with a removable hardtop, retaining the Lincoln engine. The final version of the car, launched in 1953 remained as the '52 model in every respect, except that the bodies were now constructed from steel rather than aluminum, and were consequently 260 pounds heavier, as well as being $178 more expensive than in the previous year. Muntz ceased car production in '53, but leftover stock was designated a '54 model. Kurtis returned to car production in the same year, basing his new model on the victorious Indy 500 car he had constructed for Bill Vukovitch. The new car was equipped with a Cadillac V-8 in a McCulloch Motors-supplied body. He put 20 of these 500M two-door roadsters together, which were capable of 135 mph, before discontinuing sales to the general public in '55.

Engine: Lincoln L-head V-8

Displacement: 336.7 cid

Horsepower: 154 at 3600 rpm (218 at 4200 rpm option available)

Transmission: GM four-speed Hydra-Matic

Compression Ratio: 7.5:1

Body Style: Two-door Convertible

Number of Seats: 4

Weight: 3560 lbs

Base Price: $5114

Number Produced: 136 (includes sales for '54)

■ *Right: This 1953 Muntz Jet had simple and elegant lines. The hardtop was removable to make it a truly versatile convertible.*

Oldsmobile Fiesta Convertible   **1953**

The year 1952 had been great for Oldsmobile. They had risen to fourth in the league of automotive producers, which was a new high for the company. During the year, they also continued to be the top-selling automatic range in America. Oldsmobile also continued to be prominent in the NASCAR stock races, winning the Southern 500 at Darlington, South Carolina on Labor Day 1950, which was one of three NASCAR victories for the year.

Things weren't quite so rosy in 1953. Despite an increase in cars produced, the company fell back to seventh in the production league. There was also a terrible fire at the General Motors Hydra-matic plant that completely destroyed the factory. This meant that many automatic Oldsmobiles produced in the year were actually fitted with sister GM company Buick's Dyna-flow transmissions.

On the positive side, the sporty fibreglass-bodied Starfire concept car (complete with aircraft-inspired oval grille) toured with the year's GM Motorama car show for six months, winning acclaim from 1.7 million visitors. In fact, the Starfire name was destined to become the inheritor of the Fiesta legacy. At NASCAR events, the '53 Olds, complete with heavy-duty factory parts, were victorious in nine races, whilst Bob Pronger set a new speed record of 113.38 mph in the Flying-Mile at Daytona in an 88 two-door sedan. Bill Blair drove another Olds to victory in the 1953 Daytona stock car race (run over 160 miles).

Oldsmobile launched a trio of flashy limited-edition convertibles in 1953, the Fiesta appearing mid-year. Classed as part of the Ninety-Eight series, it joined a range of already luxury cars, but was even plusher than the other models with 1954 styling advances such as the 'panoramic' wraparound windshield, sloping windows and virtually every other Oldsmobile option as standard (with the exclusion of slightly redundant air conditioning). If required, Oldsmobile/Frigidaire air conditioning was available at $550. The fitted options included Hydra-matic transmission, a padded dashboard, windshield washers, and a deluxe steering wheel with a horn ring. The upholstery in the photographed model is white leather. The Fiesta V-8 engine was slightly more powerful than that fitted to other ninety-eight models, developing 170 horsepower at 4000 rpm rather than 165 at 3600. But considering that the car was priced at nearly double that of the regular ninety-eight convertibles, it is hardly surprising that it only achieved 6% of the sales volume of the cheaper model.

■ *Left: This 1953 Fiesta became a milestone convertible car.*

Engine:	Overhead valve V-8 with cast iron block
Displacement:	303 cid
Horsepower:	170 at 4000rpm
Compression Ratio:	8.3:1
Base Price:	$5715
Number Produced:	458

1953 Packard Caribbean Custom Convertible

The Packard Motor Car Company had had an up-and-down time of it in the '40s, and it took some while to get the company back to full level peacetime production. President George T. Christopher steered the company through the worst of these problems, and PMCC launched its first post-war model, the Twenty First Series, in 1946 (although production was still limited by the availability of raw materials). PMCC celebrated its Golden Anniversary in 1949, and was poised for the '50s as the oldest fine-car company in America.

During its illustrious history, Packard had been responsible for many automotive innovations, including the 'H' shaped gear slot, hydraulic shocks and pressurized cooling. The first car to beat the mile a minute record was a Packard, and a Packard Thirty was the first automobile to drive coast to coast in 1908.

Unfortunately, the resolution of the war-imposed production problems could not disguise the fact that the automobile market had undergone a radical change. Packard, 'a gentleman's car built by gentlemen' did not revise their styling or models on an annual basis, relying instead on traditional values of elegance, efficiency, distinction and prestige. The company believed that their customers wanted durable cars of quality, and that they were uninterested in the vagaries of fashion. But by 1949, Packard realised that this was no longer the case, and that they had to keep abreast of new trends. Ironically, this realisation was the root of the company's ultimate demise, as the expense involved was unsustainable for an independent auto manufacturer.

The Cavalier/Packard Eight-cylinder series was introduced in 1953, and its sedan model was directly comparable to the Packard 300 of the previous model year. However, the series also included some more sporty Packards, including the new semi-custom Caribbean convertible inspired by the Pan American show car of 1952. This ragtop was introduced in January '53 as a midyear model, as the most expensive car in the series. The Caribbean was powered by an eight-cylinder engine, which pointed to another of Packard's problems, the lack of a modern overhead valve V-8. Its body was designed by the Mitchell-Bentley Corporation of Michigan, and the car listed a host of standard luxury features including a full-leather interior, chrome-plated wire wheels, a de-chromed body style, integrated fishtail rear fender, continental tire kit and custom paint finish.

Engine: Cavalier/Mayfair Eight. Inline eight-cylinder L-head engine, cast iron block

Displacement: 327 cid

Horsepower: 180 at 4000 rpm

Compression Ratio: 8.0:1

Base Price: $5210

Number Produced: 750

■ *Right: Produced in just four custom paint finishes, this lovely Caribbean is resplendent in Gulf Green Metallic with white leather interior.*

1954 Buick Century Estate Wagon

Buick launched its hot new Century series in 1954, shoehorning the powerful Roadmaster engine into the lightweight Special body for extra performance. The company was joining the national horsepower race, fifteen out of eighteen makes announced improved performance and higher engine ratings in the year. GM were also locked in a damaging price war with Ford, and were anxious to compete as aggressively as possible by offering new models to a newly-prosperous American public.

The Century name was revived for the first time since 1942 for a new range of high performance cars. The line was launched with four model options, a four-door sedan, a two-door hardtop coupe, a two-door convertible coupe and a four-door station wagon. GM show car styling was visible on all four cars. Some of the distinctive Ned Nickles's Buick styling from the early '50s was retained however - the 'toothy' vertical grilles and ventiports for example. In fact, the Specials and Centurys were virtually identical in their exterior trim, with the exception of the different model scripts. But the actual dimensions of the Special/Century chassis was larger than in the previous year, having grown lower and wider. A new Panoramic windshield was also fitted, with slanting side pillars. The Century/Special models also shared the new dual bullet taillamps. The interiors were also very similar, with identical instrument panels (gauges set into twin round housings), and upholstery cloth.

Some of these design modifications were to accommodate the new overhead valve V-8 powered engine block, which was fitted to the Specials, and shared by the Centurys. But the Centurys were far more powerful beasts than their stable mates. Even in the station wagon, the new powerhouse developed a respectable 195 horsepower at 4100 rpm (200 with Dynaflow transmission), compared to the 143 at 4200 rpm achieved by the Specials.

Engine: V-8 overhead valve, cast iron block

Displacement: 322 cid

Horsepower: 195 at 4100 rpm

Compression Ratio: 7.2:1

Number of Seats: 6

Weight (Station Wagon): 3975 lbs

Wheelbase: 122 inches (206.3 overall length)

Base Price (Station Wagon): $3470

Number Produced (Station Wagon): 1,563 (out of total of 81,982 Century models manufactured in 1954)

■ *Right: This Century Station Wagon shows its Buick styling heritage, whilst demonstrating the larger chassis for 1954.*

Chevrolet Bel Air Convertible   1954

Like almost all American manufacturers, Chevrolet had entered the postwar years with a warmed over version of a 1942 model. However, Chevrolet quickly assumed its position as the best-selling American marque, earning their reputation as value leaders in the low-price field. Chevrolet manufactured 1,143,561 units in 1954 and outsold Ford (even though Ford actually produced more cars). This was the last year for the exclusive use of six-cylinder power plants in all Chevrolet models. The only two engine options were Inline Six Syncromesh and Inline Six Powerglide.

Styling improvements for 1954 Chevrolets' although limited' gave the impression of wider, more modern cars. The full-width wraparound grilles with their five vertical 'teeth', newly designed front bumpers headlight rims and hood mascot were all introduced in this model year. The taillight housings were also brought up to date with contemporary looking tailfin styling.

The new 1954 Bel Air convertible (in fact, all the new models were introduced in December 1953) had the traditional assortment of extra equipment and features such as full genuine carpeting, newly designed full wheel discs, two-tone vinyl trimmed interiors, snap-on boot cover and an electric clock. Instead of the inconvenient dashboard-mounted rearview mirror, this was now mounted at the top of the bright metal windshield frame. Full-length chrome sweepspear moldings identified all the Bel Air models, and double moldings on the rear fenders enclosed the Chevy crest and Bel Air name badge.

■ *Left: This two-door convertible looks good in Romany Red. The model was updated with new styling and a V-8 engine in 1955.*

Engine: Inline Six, overhead valve

Displacement: 235.5 cid

Horsepower: 115 at 3700 rpm

Transmission: Syncromesh or Powerglide

Compression: 7.5:1

Induction: Rochester one-barrel 'B' type

Model 7007181 or Carter one-barrel 2102S

Body Styles: Two- and Four-door sedan, two-door Sport Coupe, Two-door Convertible, four-door Station Wagon

Number of Seats: (Convertible) 5

Weight: 3445 lbs

Wheelbase Length: 115 inches

Price: $2165

Number Produced: 19,383

Ford Ranch Wagon

1954

The 1954 Fords were introduced to the public on January 6. They utilized the 1952 bodyshell, with a few cosmetic trim changes. The grille was redesigned with a central spinner and horizontal chrome bar, with round parking lights at either side. Several new convenience options were also introduced, including power windows, power seats and power brakes. Ford was also the first low-priced marque to update their suspension with ball-joints.

But the main change to the 1954 Fords was under the hood. The old flathead V-8 was replaced linewide by the more modern Y-block engine with overhead valves. This engine was nearly 25% more efficient than the previous power source, and followed the national trend towards more powerful autos. For the first time in years, Ford was number one in the auto production charts, beating Chevy into second place by a slim margin of 22,381 units and keeping their fifteen manufacturing plants busy. The new V-8 got the credit for this reverse in fortune; economy and safety were still rather peripheral ideals in the auto industry.

The main news for the Ford Division itself was that the following year would see the introduction of the completely new Thunderbird concept in the 1955 Ford model line-up.

The Ranch Wagon was one of three new models introduced to the line-up. It was a two-door station wagon in the base trim Mainline V-8 series, but with Customline appearance features. These included the body-long chrome accent strip, and a chrome stone shield at the bottom of the back quarter panels. The 1954 hood ornament was also rather more streamlined and 'aeronautic' in appearance. The station wagon was still a staple of the American car market, and the vehicle of choice for the average suburban family in need of practical, flexible transport. There were three other options in the Mainline V-8 series, a four-door sedan, a two-door sedan and a two-door business coupe. A total of 233,680 units were sold in the series, including six-cylinder and V-8 options.

■ *Left: The 1954 Ranch Wagon looked good with the new Crestline trim.*

Engine: V-8 overhead valve, cast iron block

Displacement: 239 cid

Horsepower: 130 at 4200 rpm)

Compression Ratio: 7.2:1

Body Style: Two-door station wagon

Weight: 3459 lbs

Base Price: $2106

Number Produced: 44,315 (this includes sales of six-cylinder two-door station wagons)

1954 Packard Panama Hardtop

Packard took Studebaker over in 1954. The new company was known as Studebaker-Packard Corporation. This was a common phenomenon at the time, as small independent carmakers were finding survival so very difficult. The main problem was generating high enough profits to fund annual restyling and re-tooling. Being unable to do so made competing with larger manufacturers impossible. James Nance (President since 1952), had been forced to seek a financial partner, and had formulated a plan to merger four independents, Packard, Studeback, Nash and Hudson, so that the resulting company would be able to compete directly with the 'big three' car companies. Ironically, Studebaker turned out to be a disastrous acquisition, effectively dragging its parent company into oblivion. This was largely because the appalling financial position at the company was not fully disclosed. One of the Packard board members likened the merger to the captain of a sinking ship trying to save his craft by tying it to another sinking ship.

By 1954, Packard was down at sixteenth position in the league of auto producers, on a production of 31,291 units. The company had hoped to be able to afford a complete styling revision for this year, but were obliged to carry over the '53 models. There were name changes – Pacific replaced Mayfair as the top hardtop line for '54, with a larger straight eight engine (212 rather than 180 horsepower) to distinguish the car from the earlier version. The Caribbean returned as the glamor leader for PMCC, but with a price increase to a staggering $6100, the company was only able to sell 400 of these.

However, there were positive aspects to this shaky year. Packard had established a tradition of introducing a show car for each new model year. The supercharged Panther-Daytona (Grey Wolf II) experimental car, the first fibreglass-bodied car, was driven by Dick Rathmann at the Datona Speed Weeks, and clocked an unofficial time of 131 mph. This was the fastest time ever recorded by a car in this class. Two '54 models, the Caribbean and Patrician, were honored as Milestone Cars. A new automatic transmission, Twin Ultramatic, designed by Forest McFarland and John DeLorean was also introduced in the year.

The Panama Sports Coupe was part of the Super Clipper line, which Packard introduced in November 1954 as a strong contender for the 'hot' medium-priced market. It used the same roofline as the all-new Pacific, and strongly resembled the outside appearance of the Deluxe and Super Clippers. But inside, it was a different story, as the car was richly embellished with a luxury trim.

Engine: Super Clipper Eight-cylinder, Inline, L-head, cast iron block

Displacement: 288 cid

Horsepower: 150 at 4000 rpm

Compression Ratio: 8.0:1

■ *Right: The two-tone Panama was the top sub-series of the Super Clipper line.*

Chevrolet Bel Air

1955

In economic terms, 1955 was a boom year. It saw the opening of the first McDonald's drive-in restaurant and Disneyland California. Rock and Roll was now in its infancy, and Bill Haley and the Comets topped the charts with 'Rock Around the Clock'. The automotive industry experienced a record production year - 7,920,186 units being churned out by Detroit. Chevrolet was still outperforming Ford by over a quarter of a million cars, selling over 1.7 million with the advertising slogan 'The Hot One!' The average car now cost $2,300, with average pay running at $3851 per annum, so instalment buying is becoming more and more common for the average family.

The Chevy cars of '55 are some of the most popular restoration projects in the world – the combination of great 'fifties styling and the superb new V-8 engine. They were difficult to improve upon.

The Bel Air was the company's top series, and standard equipment was generous and interiors comfortable and stylish. The exterior styling was also sharpened up, and the chrome accents were far more subtle. But the most important change by far was the introduction of the V-8 engine to the series. Although all the models in the Bel Air range were still available in the six-cylinder engine type, the V-8 was so fundamental a change that It was classed as a separate series rather than an option. In fact, this remained the case for at least some of the model shapes until the Bel Airs were eventually phased out.

■ *Left: This 1955 Bel Air Two-door Convertible model demonstrates the lighter styling that was introduced in that year.*

Engine: V-8 overhead valve, cast iron block

Displacement: 265 cid

Horsepower: 162 at 4400 rpm

Transmission: three-speed manual with column mounted gearshift standard, overdrive available as an option. Powerglide two-speed automatic transmission available as an option at $178 extra, optional V-8 'powerpack' also available with dual exhaust

Compression: 8.0:1

Induction: Rochester two-barrel carburetor two-barrel Model 7008006

Number of Seats: 5

Wheelbase Length: 115 inches

Price: $2305

Number Produced: (V-8 and 6-cylinder Convertibles) 41,292

1955 Chevrolet Corvette Roadster

Car sales for the decade peaked in 1955 with record-breaking sales of seven-million plus. The frantic GM/Ford price war of 1953-54 had resulted in the mortal wounding of several surviving independent manufacturers, and the market was polarising in the hands of the three great companies – GM, Ford and Chrysler. Throughout these years, Detroit was in a 'horse-power race' to rival the technological Cold War between the East and West.

At Chevrolet, the big news for 1955 was the introduction of the V-8 engine in nearly all of the cars produced in that year. An enlarged golden 'V' embellishing the Chevrolet logo on the front fender was a quick way to identify cars fitted with the new engine, and a 12-volt electrical system. The earlier cars had had a six-cylinder engine and six-volt electrical system. In this transitional period, Chevrolet used three engine number suffixes to denote the three types of car available - YG for the six-cylinder engines, FG for V-8 and automatic transmission models and GR for V-8 cars with manual transmissions. Ironically, although the six-cylinder engine was offered as standard, with the V-8 as an extra (costing $135), only six non V-8s were sold. The V-8 'Vettes could go from 0-100 miles per hour in 24.7 seconds.

The car retained its original styling for '55, and the distinctive Corvette grille was now established as an identification trademark of the car's design – the thirteen chrome 'teeth' were originally designed to carry the Chevrolet family identity. The very first '53 models had had only three, which had led to concerns that the fibreglass bodywork was unprotected against parking knocks.

Various (rather basic) options were available for the car at extra cost – signal seeking AM radio at $145.15, windshield washer at $11.85, heater at $91.40 and parking brake alarm at $5.65.

However, the continuing low volume of sales – just 700 for 1955 meant that, yet again, Chevrolet came close to dropping the model from the range. So ironic, in view of its continuing success to this day, when so many better selling contemporary cars are remembered only in the archives.

Engine: (Most popular for this model year) V-8 Overhead valve. Cast iron block

Displacement: 265 cid

Horsepower: 195 at 6000 rpm

Compression: 8.0:1

Body Style: Two-door convertible roadster

Weight: 2705 lbs

Price: $2934

Number Produced: 700

■ *Right: '55 Corvettes were available in a range of colours including Gypsy Red with a beige top.*

1955 Chevrolet Nomad Station Wagon

As the newly affluent middle classes increasingly moved to the suburbs, the station wagon became a more and more popular form of transport for the typical American family – shopping, dropping the kids off at school – everything now involved driving.

Chevrolet introduced the Nomad to the Bel Air range as a midyear model addition, pioneering the introduction of the 'hardtop' wagon to the US market. Although the car was really groundbreaking, the model attracted only 6,103 buyers in 1955. The four-door Beauville station wagon was also available as part of the Chevrolet Bel Air series, and outsold the Nomad by about 4 cars to 1 in that model year.

The front-end styling was classic Bel Air, but although the designers carried through the tailfin design of the other range models at the back of the car, it seems somewhat anachronistic with the tailgate arrangement.

Interestingly, 2004 saw the launch of a brand new Chevrolet Nomad concept car. In a wave of retro nostalgia that has seen many automakers dusting off their family jewels, Chevrolet have chosen to reinterpret the very original Nomad concept (a lightweight sporty two-door wagon) for a twenty-first century generation of customers. Similar in style and function to the 1955 model, the styling of the new car is fresh, whilst paying direct homage to the original in many details – the toothy (typically Chevy) front grille, and the seven chrome ribs that adorn the tailgate, for example. But the engine is completely modern in conception – four-cylinder and turbocharged. If the new design goes into production, it will be almost fifty years to the day since Nomads first graced the suburban streets of America. That really would be a case of back to the future…

Engine: V-8 overhead valve, cast iron block (also available with six-cylinder engine)

Displacement: 235.5 cid

Horsepower: 162 at 4400 rpm

Compression: 8.0:1

Induction: Rochester two-barrel Model 7008006

Number of Seats: 6

Weight: 3270 lbs

Wheelbase Length: 115 inches (overall length 197.1 inches)

Price: $2571

Number Produced: 6,103

■ *Right: This two-tone Nomad looks very at home in front of suburban white clapboard and manicured lawns*

1955 Chrysler C-300 Coupe

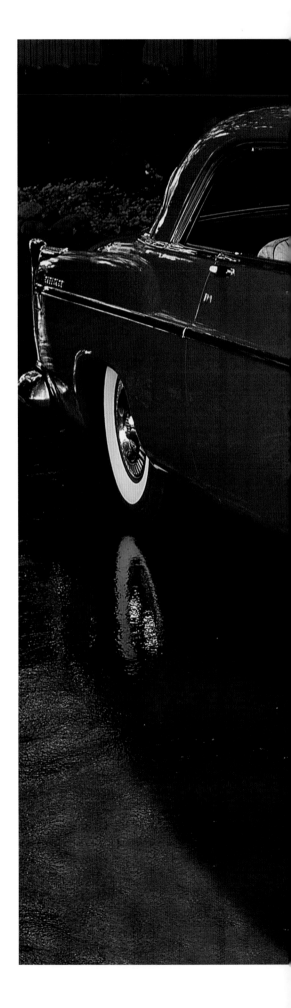

Chrysler had a difficult start in the post-war return to manufacturing consumer goods rather than military hardware and offered only warmed over pre-war models until managing to get some truly new cars off the blocks in the mid '50s. However, Chrysler had introduced three major mechanical improvements in the first half of the decade, the Firepower V-8 engine (with hemispherical combustion chambers), power steering and fully automated PowerFlite transmission. But the company failed to be counted amongst the top ten automotive producers during these years, and remained out of this select coterie until design supremo Virgil Exner launched the company's 'Hundred Million Dollar Look' in 1955. A major new model was launched in this year, the 300 Letter Car. It was to become known as Chrysler's 'beautiful brute', with a brilliant synthesis of performance and luxury styling that would be successful for more than a decade. Exner's innovations took the company to second place in the high-priced sales field for this year, and ninth overall in the sales war.

The C-300 was designed to be a 'sports touring car designed to bring Chrysler the benefit of a high-performance reputation.' Although it was a big, heavy car based on the existing New Yorker body shell, the original 1955 model was still almost as fast as Chevy's much lighter newly introduced Corvette. In fact, the C-300 was named after its stunning performance statistics – it was the very first American production model to deliver 300 horsepower as standard. The 'C' is reputedly a reference to the racing driver Briggs Cunningham who had used Chrysler's V-8 hemispherical engine in the early '50s.

The statistics are truly impressive, the C-300 could go from 0-60 mph in 9.5 seconds and cover a quarter-mile in 17.6 seconds at 82 mph. The slightly revised 1956 version of the car, the 300B, broke the world's passenger speed record in competition at Daytona Beach, Florida, with an average speed of nearly 140mph. The production model was fitted with a 150-mph speedometer to underline the latent power available under the hood.

All the 1955 C-300s were two-door hardtop coupes fitted with Powerflite transmission, power brakes, and optional power steering. Only three model colours were introduced, Chrysler Platinum White, black and the colour of our car – Tango Red. The styling of the model was comparatively modest for 1955 with discreet tailfins and only a moderate amount of chrome ornamentation - although flashy wire wheels were optional. The interior was truly luxurious, with full leather trim.

Engine: Firepower 'Hemi' V-8

Displacement: 331.1 cid

Horsepower: 300 at 5200 rpm

Compression: 8.5:1

Base Price: $4109

Number Produced: 1725

■ *Right: Successful as both a race and stock car, the C-300 has been described as America's first musclecar*

1955 DeSoto Fireflite Two-Door Convertible

The year 1955 saw the introduction of a driver's education course for the first time, and such luxuries as air-conditioning becoming more popular. Seven out of ten new cars were now supplied with automatic transmissions, and 78.6% had V-8 engines.

At DeSoto, as in the rest of Chrysler, Virgil Exner's aircraft-inspired 'New Look' was introduced, with streamlined body styling and wraparound windscreens (though the rather toothy front grille remained). The re-style was applied in its most extensive form to the top-of-the-range Fireflite series. Under the hood, the Firedome V-8 became the standard power train, with two hundred horsepower, a four-barrel carburetor and hemispherical segment combustion chambers.

Identification features included Fireflight front fender script, chrome fender top ornaments running back from headlamps; and rocker panel beauty trim. Special side beauty panels were

■ *Below: This DeSoto Fireflite has elegant aeronautic lines and sweeping body trim.*

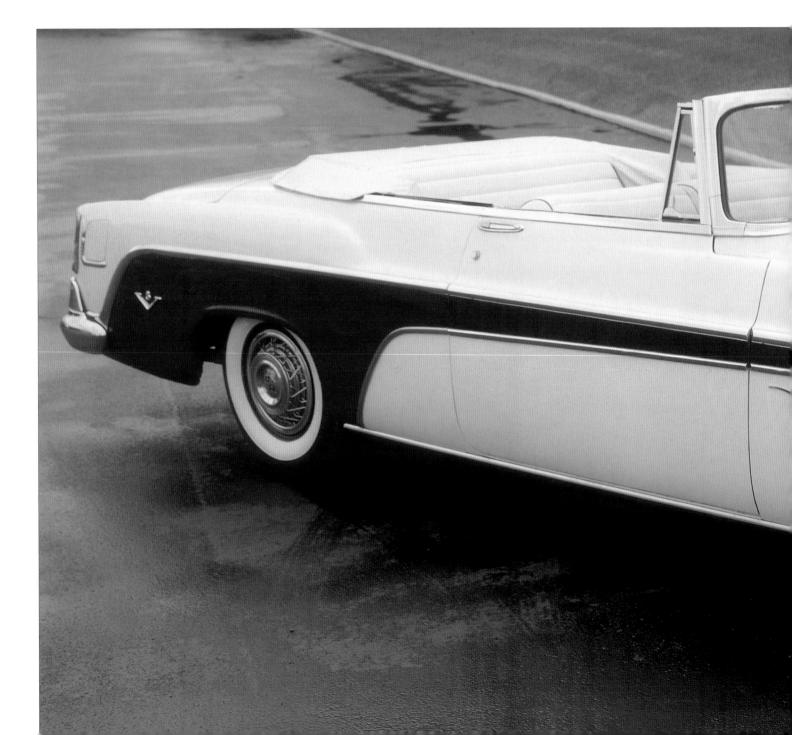

standard on Fireflite convertibles. Interior styling was of 'cockpit' inspiration, with standard upholstery of silky nylon with nylon carpeting. This was also the year when DeSoto pioneered the use of triple-tone paint jobs, introducing this trim on the Fireflite Coronado. Distinctive 'Flight Control' gearshift levers protruded from the dash in the automatic models from the range.

As a company, DeSoto remained at twelfth position in the league of auto manufacturers, but even in this bumper year, when general production leapt by 44% to 7,920,186 units, the company's output fell to 115,485 cars. Both of DeSoto's model lines were considerably more expensive than the average car price of $2300, and the marque seemed to be struggling for a distinctive identity.

Engine: V-8 overhead valve, cast iron block

Displacement: 291 cid

Horsepower: 200 at 4400rpm

Compression Ratio: 7.5:1

Number of Seats: 6

Weight: 4090 lbs

Wheelbase: 126 inches

Base Price: $3151

Number Produced: 775

Greatest American Cars

Dodge Royal Lancer Hardtop   1955

D odge slipped to eighth place in the production stakes in 1955, despite the introduction of several new models and a 160.3 percent jump in sales. In fact, even more cars could have been sold, but for the fact that Dodge shared their V-8 plant with Plymouth. The 1955 models were grouped into three series and all had longer, lower, wider bodies; new hardtops, three-tone paint and increasingly plush trim variations. Some of the economy Dodge models were discontinued. The Royal series had been originally introduced as the top trim Dodge series for 1954, and was constructed at plants in Detroit and San Leandro. A total of four Royal models were introduced: a four-door Sedan and three assorted two-door models. This was reversed in the following year, with one two-door model (the Lancer) and three four-door cars, a sedan plus two versions of the Sierra Wagon.

By 1955, the Royal was the mid-range trim model, with the Custom Royal Series now Dodge's top range. Even so, the Royals were at least 50% more expensive than the average new car.

The 1955 Royals had all the Coronet features, plus hooded, chrome headlights and the Royal name in script on the front fenders. The series was now fitted with V-8 'Red Ram' engines with overhead valves and polysphere combustion chambers.

The two-door, hardtop Royals were designated as Lancers, and had a special trim a standard. The cars were ornamented with narrow chrome strips trailed back from the hood scoop, dipped at the C-pillar, then continued high on the rear fenders to the taillight housings.

■ *Left: This two-door Lancer Royal Hardtop demonstrates the elegant two-tone colour schemes available.*

Engine: Red Ram V-8 overhead valve, poly-shpere combustion chambers, cast iron block

Displacement: 270 cid

Horsepower: 175 at 4400 rpm

Transmission: three-speed manual fitted as standard, overdrive and two-speed PowerFlite automatic available as optional extras

Compression Ratio: 7.6:1

Induction: Stromberg two-barrel

Model WW3-131

Body Styles (Lancer): Two-door Hardtop

Weight: 3425 lbs

Wheelbase: 120 inches

Base Price: $2370

Number Produced: 25,831

Ford Victoria

1955

The year 1955 was important in Ford history. Not only was their range completed restyled inside and out, but some truly beautiful new lines were also introduced. The Fairlanes (named after Henry Ford's Dearborn, Michigan mansion) were instantly popular, and sold better than any other model introduced since the end of the War. They replaced the Crestline as the top trim series. The line had particularly attractive chrome and tone-tone trim, and included the popular Sunliner convertible. Wagons were now designated as a separate Ford series. The Country Sedan remained the most popular station wagon, selling 106,284 into the market, but five other wagons were also available with six- to eight-seat options.

Of course, the Thunderbird was also introduced in this model year – a two-seater for the young market.

Despite all this positive change, Chrysler's 'Hot One' – the Virgil Exner-styled C-300 complete with small block V-8 engine – was the biggest automotive news of the year. Chevy also got 'hot', aiming the new range at the young buyer for the first time. Their 1955 'renaissance' thrust the company back into their habitual first position in the league of auto manufacturers, with Ford in second. Despite this, 1955 was Ford's second production best year, so far.

Over at Ford, the bodies were longer, lower and wider and the instrument panel and interior trim were substantially new. The powerblocks were even more powerful in this model year, with the introduction of a larger overhead V-8, and the majority of the 1955 cars were sold with this option.

The Victoria model was a Fairlane two-door pillarless hardtop. A Crown Victoria model was also available, with 'tiara' foor trim. The Crown Victoria Skyliner is a similar model with a forward roof panel constructed from transparent green plexiglass.

■ *Left: This Fairlane Victoria is fitted with the new, more powerful Ford V-8.*

Engine: Overhead valve V-8, cast iron block	
Displacement: 272 cid	
Horsepower: 162 at 4400 rpm	
Transmission: Manual with overdrive and Ford-O-Matic optional	
Compression Ratio: 7.6:1	
Body Style: Two-door Victoria Hardtop	
Weight: 3318 lbs	
Wheelbase: 115.5 inches	
Base Price: $2195	
Number Produced: 113,372 (including the 6-cylinder engine version)	

Hudson Custom Hornet Sedan 1955

By 1955, Hudson had lost its independence, and was a part of the American Motors Corporation. As production had ceased at the Hudson factory in Detroit, and been transferred to the Nash plant at Kenosha, Wisconsin, the models were really little more than AMC model lines. All but Nashes in disguise, the cars became known as 'Hashes'.

The 1955 Hornets were based on Nash bodies, but retained the Hudson model names – Wasp and Hornet, whilst the Nash Ramblers were re-badged as Hudson Ramblers.

The '55 Hornets has the same styling as the Wasps, but were built on a longer wheelbase. High quality interior trim and continental spare tire carriers fitted as standard distinguished the Custom level cars. A new V-8 engine option was now available, bought in from Packard. George Mason, the President of Nash, had intended to continue his automotive acquisitions by adding Packard and Studebaker to the AMC group, but his early death in 1954 meant that only the engine made it. In cars where the V-8 was fitted, Packard Twin Ultramatic transmission was mandatory.

Model sales for the year actually increased, partly due to various dealer and customer incentives, including free trips to Disneyland. Dealer incentives were also widely used, with promotions such as the 'Dealer Volume Investment Fund' and 'Sun Valley Sweepstakes'. Of course, Nash models were also now included in the sales figures. Although these tactics did have something of a ring of desperation about them, the company climbed 7% in the automotive sales league. In 1956 AMC introduced its own V-8 engine. But only modest styling and engineering updates to the range, in an era of huge revision, conspired to undermine sales dramatically. Wasps and Hornets were the models most severely affected. AMC decided to discontinue these models in 1957, and concentrate on Rambler production. This proved to be a very good move for the company, and AMC continued in production for nearly three more decades, until the company was finally taken over by Chrysler in 1987. Sadly, the company name has now ceased to exist.

■ *Left: The continental spare tire carrier can just be seen at the rear of this Hornet.*

Engine: Hornet 'Big' Six: Inline six. L-head, chrome alloy block	
Displacement: 308 cid	
Horsepower: 160 at 3800 rpm	
Compression Ratio: 7.5:1	
Body Style: Four-door Sedan	
Wheelbase: 121-1/4 inches	
Base Price: $2760	
Number Produced: 5,357	

Mercury Montclair Two-Door Sun Valley Hardtop

1955

Mercury and Lincoln became separately managed companies in spring 1955, as befitted their differing aspirations. The entire Mercury output was restyled in 1955, their Ford-based body shell was completely overhauled, and the Montclair range was introduced as the top line model. Generally, the cars were bolder, brighter, longer, lower and wider. But they were still recognisable from the '54 models. Montclairs were built on the same chassis as the rest of the lineup, and were similar in body style, though slightly lower than the other Mercurys.

Having first appeared in the Monterey series, the Sun Valley was now placed in the Montclair line. This was a true all steel pillarless hardtop, unlike its Ford rival the Fairlane Crown Victoria. Like the other Montclairs, (which included a four-door hardtop model), the Sun Valley cars were trimmed with an additional narrow band of chrome under the side windows, but also had a tinted plexiglass section in the front of the roof. This led to them being nicknamed the 'bubbletop'. This unique styling conceit got a mixed reception. Some customers complained that it made the cars uncomfortably hot, a serious problem with no air-conditioning available on Mercury models. Custom remained the base model for the year, whilst Monterey now became the mid-range series.

Chevrolet and Mercury shared the 'Car of the Year' title awarded by Motor Trend magazine. This was substantially due to the mechanical improvements (begun in the previous year) – the enlarging of the updated overhead valve V-8 engine to 292 cid, and the upgrading of the front suspension to ball-and-socket joint. Dual exhausts were standard on Montclairs. The cars managed a reasonable fuel efficiency of 16 miles per gallon. Sadly, the Sun Valley was discontinued in this, only its second year, with a production total of fewer than 12,000 units.

Mercury was an impressive seventh in the table of 1955 car production, with sales of 329,808 cars.

■ *Left: This Montclair Sun Valley is painted in Artic white and Gulfstream blue metallic. The plexiglass roof is blue-tinted, and matching window glass was available as an option.*

Engine:	Overhead valve V-8, cast iron block
Displacement:	292 cid
Horsepower:	198 at 4400 rpm
Compression Ratio:	8.5:1
Body Style:	Two-door hardtop
Weight:	3560 lbs
Wheelbase:	119 inches
Base Price:	$2712
Number Produced:	1,787

1955 Packard Caribbean

Things looked as though they were picking up in 1955, Packard climbed to fourteenth in the production league, output climbed to 55,247 units. Packard Styling Director, Dick Teague, conjured a remarkable facelift for the year that almost made the '51 body look like new. The new models were introduced in January 1955.

Packard continued to introduce technical innovations in this model year. The most important development was the replacement of the eight-cylinder engines with modern V-8s. This massively improved the performance of the Packard range, and generated a lot more buyer interest in the cars. Packard's innovative 'Torsion Level' suspension (designed by William D. Allison, formerly of Hudson) was also introduced in '55. This consisted of full-length motor-controlled torsion bars (instead of springs) with electric ride-height control. Allison had touted this excellent invention around the motor industry, but Packard was the first manufacturer to realise its potential. Exterior running lamps were added to the senior Packard models, including the 'Four Hundred' hardtop, named after the 'four-hundred' members of the social elite of a bygone era.

The two-door custom convertible Caribbean topped the Packard line again. The car also topped the industry power league with twin carburettors and other tuning adjustments enabling the car to achieve 275 horsepower. The Packard line models had the same shaped grille opening

■ *Below: This Caribbean's three-tone paint job is in White Jade, Fire Opal and Onyx.*

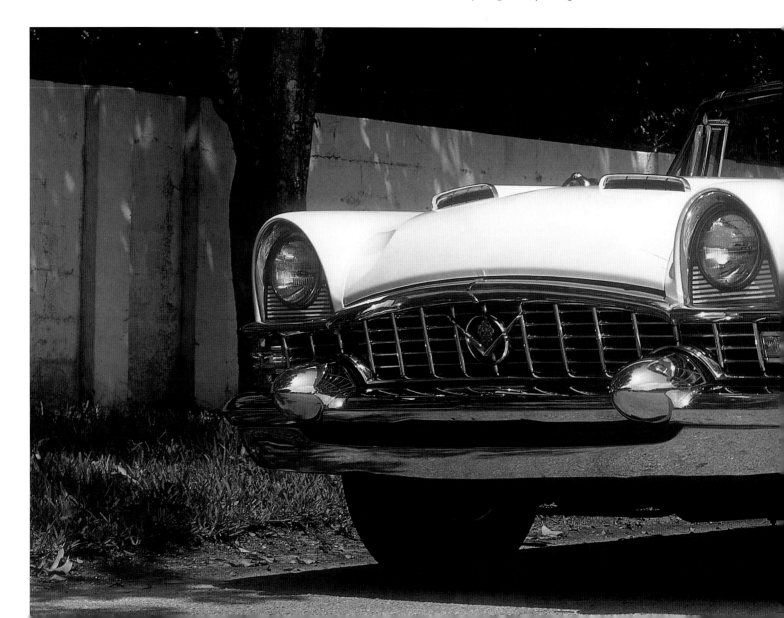

as the Clippers. New features included wraparound parking lamps and sweep-around windshields. Teague also introduced brand new cathedral-shaped taillights and a flat-rounded tailfin. The two chrome sidespears allowed for a three-tone paint finish, with one color on the roof, one between the panel moldings, and one below the lower bar. The car also had a twin scoop hood with no ornamentation, except on the front edge of the scoops. Except for air conditioning, almost every cost-plus option was offered as standard on the car, including dual outside mirrors and rear antennae and the new Twin Ultramatic Drive.

Other highlights for the year at Packard included a 25,000-mile run for a Packard Patrician at the company's Packard Proving Ground in Utica, Michigan. The car averaged 104.737 mph. More negatively, Pan American Airlines started a suit against the company for its use of the names 'Caribbean', 'Clipper', 'Pan American', 'Constellation' and 'Panama'. The suit lingered on until 1958 when, sadly, the names had lost any relevance to Packard.

The Packard Division made a profit this model year, but the Studebaker-Packard Group as a whole made an operating loss of nearly $30,000,000. The writing was on the wall.

Engine:	Packard Line V-8, overhead valve, cast iron block
Displacement:	352 cid
Horsepower:	275 at 4800 rpm
Transmission:	Twin Ultramatic
Compression Ratio:	8.5:1
Induction:	Two Rochester Type 4GC four-arrel carburettors as follows: (front) Model 476010; (rear) Model 476011
Body Style:	Two-door Convertible
Number of Seats:	6
Weight:	4755 lbs
Wheelbase:	127 inches
Base Price:	$5932
Number Produced:	500

1955 Plymouth Belvedere Sport Coupe

The 1955 Plymouths were completely redesigned, with longer lower wider bodies. Every panel of the high-priced Belvedere line, including the hardtop was revised, from the side the car is one long gentle sweeping arc stretching uninterrupted from headlight brow to tail light tip. The highlights were hidden from side-view by forward-canted hoods. At the opposite end of the car, the taillights are also hooded with a complimentary rearward cant. The whole design gives an impression of the car moving forward, and this design style is labelled 'Motion Design'. The competition at Ford and Chevrolet had also come out with great new styling and some excellent new models in the year, including the Thunderbird.

The revision came not a moment too soon. Plymouth had been dumped from their tradition third place in the car producers' league and had gone down two full places to fifth position. They had been caught in the crossfire of an extremely vicious price war between Ford and Chevrolet. Both companies had been overproducing to flood the market with their product, to top up their production figures, then dumping the overproduction on the market. By comparison to the early 1950s offerings from these two companies, the Plymouths looked clunky and old-fashioned. But the '55 re-style was expressly designed to make the cars appealing to the 'young at heart'. So determined were they to make the cars more youthful in appearance that they even gave up their hat-wearing premise by decreasing the height of the vehicle.

The wheelbase of the car was an inch longer than in the previous year, but the overall length of the car was a full ten inches greater. The tri-sectional grille was a continuation of the '53 theme, and would continue until the early 1960s. The hood ornament is a very abstract sailing ship motive indeed, and was due to disappear altogether in 1956. The windshield was now wraparound, 'The New Horizon' Plymouth called it, and the backward A-post contributed towards the 'Motion Design' effect.

The dashboard came in for some criticism with a rather bizarre layout of the instruments and dials. There was also a dash-mounted gearshift lever. Most 1955 Plymouths were still fitted with six-cylinder engines, but all the Belvederes were available with a 'Hy-fire' V-8 option, except for the convertible, which only came with a V-8.

Engine: Overhead valve Hy-fire V-8

Displacement: 241 cid

Horsepower: 117 at 3600 rpm

Compression Ratio: 7.6:1

Weight: 3261 lbs

Base Price: $2192

Number Produced: 47,375

■ *Right: Both the Sports Coupe and convertible Belvederes had contrasting 'color sweep' panels as standard.*

Studebaker President Speedster 1955

By 1955, Studebaker's fortunes appeared to be in something of a decline. The company had been taken over by Packard in 1954 and became the Studebaker-Packard Corp. of America. They had slipped to eleventh place in the league of auto manufacturers, on a reduced production level of 116,333, but this was a huge improvement on the 68,708 cars produced in the takeover year.

After an absence of thirteen years, the top-line President name was revived. The original Studebaker President had been styled by industrial designer Raymond Loewy. His design partnership with the company stretched from his original partnership with company President Paul Hoffman in 1938 to the iconic 1962 Avanti. In fact, he started the eponymous 'Raymond Loewy Design Division' at Studebaker, working with bright young engineers such as Harold Churchill (who became company President in 1956). Loewy's design principle for Studebaker was 'simplification', effectively streamlining the cars to remove visual and literal weight and 'drag' that obliged manufacturers to fit more and more powerful powerplants to maintain performance in big heavy models. Through his work with Studebaker, Loewy is credited with the introduction of many design features that seem obvious today – the down-slanted hood, the integrated bumper, and the replacement of the grille by an air scoop. He was passionate about the aerodynamic wedge-shaped superstructure, with uncluttered body styling, and seems to be one of the first car designers to consider designing safety into the structure of the car itself. Many design elements by which Studebaker's are instantly recognisable, like the 'bullet-nose' came from Raymond Loewy's pen, and the classic 1953 model line was his, from the coved body styling down to the plain conical hubcaps.

Loewy was finally dropped by Studebaker after their merger with Packard. To secure a release from their contract with him reputedly cost the company one million dollars.

The 1955 Studebakers were fundamentally restyled '53 models, but the President Speedster was probably the closest in appearance to the classic Starliner, retaining the overall grille style (although this was now more massive). The tri-level painted hardtop model was introduced in January 1955, and featured the 'butter knife' side trim. The Speedster was the top-of-the-range President model and was loaded with every conceivable extra including an engine turned instrument panel and Automatic Drive or overdrive as standard.

■ *Left: Although the grille has been beefed up and chrome beauty bars added, the basic Raymond Loewy styling of '53 is clearly visible in this '55 model President Speedster.*

Engine: President V-8 overhead valve	
Displacement: 259.2 cid	
Horsepower: (later version) 185 at 4500 rpm	
Compression Ratio: 7.5:1	
Base Price: $3253	
Number Produced: 2215	

1956 Cadillac Eldorado

In 1956 the Federal government approved a massive building programme for 41,000 miles of Interstate Highway. But car production eased slightly to around 6.3 million units. Cadillacs accounted for 154,577 vehicles, moving from tenth to ninth position in the American sales race. Eighty per cent of all cars manufactured in America in 1956 were fitted with classic V-8 engines.

The postwar years were good ones for Cadillac, as they competed with Packard for the luxury American car market. The trademark aircraft inspired tailfin look debuted on selected 1948 models and from then, Cadillac became the style innovator at this high-priced end of the market. Sales hit 10,000 in 1950, outselling other prestige makes, and were at 265,000 by 1975.

Cadillac's Eldorado was introduced in 1953 (when 532 examples were produced), but – like all Cadillacs – the 'Eldo' was re-designed and re-blended almost every year. The 1956 Eldorado retained the distinctive shark fins, but benefited from the deft restyle given to its sister models, with a new grille and the repositioning of the parking lights in the bumper below the wing guards. The convertible now carried the Biarritz name to distinguish it from the first Eldorado hardtop, a new two-door named Seville, which sold 3,900 copies to the ragtop's 2150. Both models were priced at a princely $6501. For the first time since 1949, all Cadillacs had a larger V-8, a bored-out 365-cubic-inch unit with 285 horsepower. With dual four-barrel carburetors, the figure rose to 305 bhp for Eldorados.

Various luxury options were also available including air conditioning, gold finished grille, and E-Z eye safety glass.

■ *Right: This 1956 Cadillac Eldorado was manufactured in the year when a superhighway was finally completed between Chicago and New York.*

Engine: V-8 Overhead valve, cast iron block

Displacement: 365 cid

Horsepower: 305 at 4700 rpm

Transmission: Hydra-Matic

Compression: 9.75:1

Induction: Two Carter WCFB four-barrel carburetors , Model 2371

Body style: Two-door hardtop coupe, two-door convertible Biarritz model

Number of Seats: 6

Weight: 4880 lbs

Wheelbase Length: 129 inches (overall length for Eldorados 222.2 inches)

Price: $6501

Number Produced: 2,150

1956 DeSoto Fireflite Two-Door Convertible

In a year when general manufacturing production was eased, DeSoto moved up to number 11 in the output league table, but the company's sales fell yet again to 109,442 cars. A refined Fireflite convertible was introduced to the market in 1956. To re-inforce the more widespread use of the V-8, the new perforated mesh grille with a large central 'V' dominating the front aspect of the car. The taillight clusters were redesigned, but color sweep two-tone remained a feature (although the shape of the panels was redesigned). The headlamps still had chrome plated headlamp hoods.

Mechanically, all Fireflite models were now fitted with PowerFlite automatic transmission as standard. This was now controlled by push-button gear selection.

On January 11 1956, DeSoto announced that a Fireflite convertible with heavy-duty

■ *Below: This official pace car of the Indianapolis 500 Race of May 30 1956 is resplendent in gold and white.*

underpinnings, but standard engine, would act as a pace car at the Indianapolis 500 and that a limited 'Pacesetter' convertible would be available to the public. These cars had the same special features and a heavy complement of power accessories but were not lettered like the authentic pace car shown in the photograph.

The gold and white trim of this limited edition car was commemorated in the slightly later 'Adventurer', an exclusive sub-series of the Fireflite range launched to compete with the Chrysler 300-B, Dodge D-500 and Plymouth Fury. The convertible pace car carried a premium of $110 over the regular convertible model in the Fireflite range, but no separate production total was released.

Engine: V-8 overhead valve, cast iron block	
Displacement: 330.4 cid	
Horsepower: 255 at 4400 rpm	
Compression Ratio: 8.5:1	
Weight: 4070 lbs	
Wheelbase: 126 inches	
Base Price: $3565	
Nos. Produced (All Fireflite Convertibles): 1485	

Dodge D-500 V-8 Two-Door Custom Royal/Lancer Hardtop

1956

Dodge began a major restyling project in 1956, with back fenders sprouting fins, and technologically, a push-button PowerFlite automatic transmission was introduced to both Dodge and Chrysler models. The D-500 model was launched as a flag-waving performance car for the Royal range. But the re-style did nothing to improve sales, which actually tumbled by 22.4% to just over 200,000 units, and gave the company a market share of exactly 3.7%. M.C. Patterson became the President of the Dodge division in 1956, with a brief to improve its performance.

The 1956 Custom Royal was Dodge's top-of-the-range and most prestigious line, with the most intense trim options. They had everything the Royal models did and more – hooded and painted headlight housings, and extra grooved taillight assemblies. Several special models were introduced as part of the Custom Royal two-door hardtop Lancer line-up for the year, including the Golden Lancer and the rather bizarre Dodge La Femme. The first American car specifically introduced to appeal to women buyers, the 1956 La Femme appeared in a sickly livery of two-tone lavender, and gold-flecked interior. It also had a patronising array of matching feminine accoutrements such as a cap, a pair of boots, an umbrella, a shoulder bag and floral upholstery fabric... sales were reassuringly miniscule. The almost equally tasteful Golden Lancer has a Sapphire white body, with a Gallant Saddle Gold exterior and interior trim.

At the other end of the Custom Royal market, the D-500 (complete with hemi V-8) was introduced to demonstrate the performance capabilities of the marque. These were underlined by the Dodge performance at the year's NASCAR races, where they won eleven victories. A Dodge Custom Royal four-door sedan was driven 31,224 miles in 14 days, and set 306 speed records at the Bonneville Salt Flats in Utah. Dodge was thus saved from a potentially embarrassing year.

■ *Left: The D-500 was the highest performing Dodge of 1956*

Engine:	D-500 V-8 overhead valve, hemispherical combustion chambers, cast iron block
Displacement:	315 cid
Horsepower:	260 at 4400 rpm
Compression Ratio:	9.25:1
Induction:	Carter four-barrel Type WCFB
Weight (Two-door Lancer Hardtop):	3505 lbs
Wheelbase:	120 inches
Base Price:	$2658
Number Produced:	40,100

Ford Convertible Sunliner V-8　1956

The Ford Motor Company became a publicly owned company on February 24 1956, and immediately gained about 350,000 additional stockholders. This was part of Henry Ford II's vision for the future of the company, and was the platform for a great expansion of FoMoCo in the 1960s.

1956 saw a general easing of industrial production, but a stepping-up of the horsepower race. Like several other manufacturers, Ford offered a 'power pack' option consisting of a four-barrel carburettor, dual exhaust and slightly stronger camshaft to boost the power of the new V-8 as an option. Ford's version displaced 312 cid.

FoMoCo manufactured in excess of 1.4 million units in this model year, but Chevrolet achieved an output of 1.56 million to take first position in the league of car producers for '56.

So far as model revises went, Ford re-used the '55 body shell with new grilles and trim, but the car interiors were completely new. Safety was now an important sales feature, and a padded dashboard, sun visor and less aggressively shaped steering wheel were all designed to lessen injuries in an accident. Seat belts were also offered for the first time. A twelve-volt electrical system and 18mm anti-fouling spark plus were also introduced.

The Fairlane series was the top trim for the 1956 model year, and included chrome window moldings, chrome 'A' pillar trim on the Sunliners, and simulated exhaust outlets. Chrome side sweep bars were similar to those used in the previous year, but subtly revised. All seven versions of the Fairlane series came with either six-cylinder or V-8 engine options, and sold a combined number of 645,306 units in the year. Apart from the Sunliner convertible, the 1956 Fairlane model range comprised the four-door Town sedan, a two-door Club Sedan, a four-door Town Victoria, a two-door Club Victoria, a two-door Crown Victoria and a two-door Crown Victoria Skyliner. The Town Victoria was released in direct competition to Chevy's established range of hardtops, but with limited success. Mainline were the base models for 1956, Customline the intermediate. The Thunderbirds were considered separate to the main Ford output.

■ *Left: The Skyliner didn't have the performance of the new Y-block T-Bird, but out sold its sister car almost four to one.*

Engine: Overhead valve V-8, cast iron block

Displacement: 272 cid

Horsepower: 174 at 4400 rpm (176 at 4400 rpm with Ford-O-Matic)

Compression Ratio: 8.0:1

Wheelbase: 115.5 inches

Base Price: $2459

Number Produced: 58,147 (6-cylinder and V-8s combined)

Packard Executive

'Ask The Man Who Owns One' was the Packard advertising slogan for decades, the most famous in the motor manufacturing world. Through the strength of this 'word of mouth' recommendation, Packard became the car of Rockerfellers, Vanderbilts, Astors, European royalty, the last Russian Czar, movie royalty and US Presidents. The Packard crest (featuring roses and a pelican) became a graceful symbol of success.

From its humble beginnings in Warren, Ohio, Packard moved to the forefront of the motor industry, opening the first gas-filling station (the 'Red and White' in Los Angeles), and was very active in the national 'good roads' movement. Even their showrooms were elegant and impressive.

The Packards built for 1956 may have been the company's best ever products, when measured by their advanced engineering and styling, an outstanding and beautiful car. Packard was intensely proud of its lineup for '56, but buyer interest was reduced in a generally depressed market. Packard had always had an excellent and close relationship with its dealer network, but the dealers now began to defect in droves, feeling that they might be pulled down if the company crashed. The company was now completely lacking in direction, and decided to commission a report from the management consultants Ernst & Ernst. Their shock recommendation was that Packard production should cease immediately, and the Studebaker-Packard Corporation should go into liquidation.

The Executive Line was introduced in 1956 as a replacement for the entire Clipper Custom lineup, and was designed to bridge the gap between the lower price Clipper and top line Packard ranges. The Clipper V-8 was used for power, and was available in two-tone color schemes.

The company name continued on some redressed Studebaker models until 1958, but 1956 was the final year for true Packard-built automobiles. Sadly, a car of enduring quality and style could not survive in this era of planned obsolescence.

■ *Left: This Packard Executive sports a two-tone paint job of Corsican Black and Jamaican Yellow.*

Engine:	Clipper Custom/Executive V-8, overhead valve, cast iron block
Displacement:	352 cid
Horsepower:	275 at 4600 rpm
Compression Ratio:	9.5:1
Number of Seats:	6
Weight:	4185 lbs
Wheelbase:	122 inches
Base Price:	$3560
Number Produced:	1,031

1956 Plymouth Fury Hardtop

Plymouth was number four in the production league in 1956, very slightly behind Buick in the number three position, with an output of 571,634 vehicles. J. P. Mansfield was Chief Executive Officer of the Division.

Introduced in 1956 with a 240-horsepower 303 V-8, the Fury had sharply peaked tail fins, a Cadillac-like logo and special side trim. It was a great example of Plymouths 'All new Aerodynamic' styling for the year, which was instigated as part of Virgil Exner's 1955 Chrysler-wide 'Forward Look' re-style. The front and rear windshields were wraparounds, and the side windows were pillarless.

The Fury was introduced to heat up Plymouth's performance image, for '56 was a seminal, power-orientated, year for the entire US automotive industry. Effectively, it was the Division's first muscle car. Plymouth chose to introduce the production version of the car with a 240-horsepower 303 V-8, a polyspheric head engine, rather than the 'hemi' used by the other Chrysler divisions.

Sister company Chrysler introduced its 300 'B' letter car in the same year, which was specifically designed to outperform every other US production car, including newly-introduced Corvette and Thunderbird rivals. But at the Daytona Beach February Speed Week, the Plymouth Fury FX, driven by Phil Walters beat even the 'B', with a 'resounding boom and a flash of gold', by achieving a

■ *Below: The new Fury was introduced for '56, loaded with custom features and trim.*

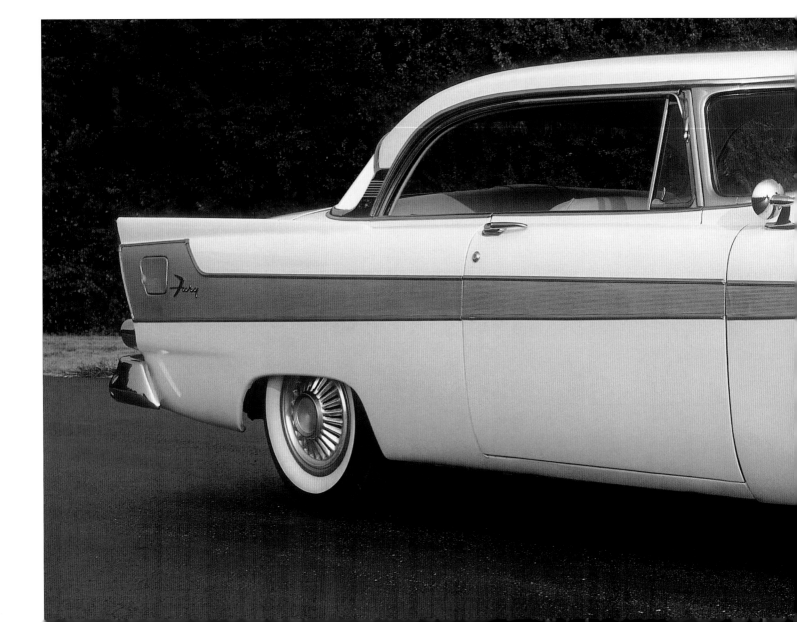

record pace of over 149 miles per hour. This made it the fastest Plymouth every built. Evidently, this was not a source of unalloyed joy to the board at Chrysler, who had hoped the 'B' would be totally invincible by all-comers, including their own. As well as being truly quick, the Fury also handled well, with its body lowered an inch from the other Belvedere models.

The production version Fury was a sub-series of the top of the range Belvedere. A single Fury model was available, the two-door Sports Coupe, all examples of which were painted eggshell white with a gold anodised aluminium trim. Plazas were the base models for the year, and Savoys were the Plymouth mid-range series.

1956 was also an important technological year at Plymouth, with the introduction of Push-button PowerFlite automatic transmission controls. An experimental turbine-powered Fury sport coupe was also constructed. The company would have to wait until '57 for the introduction of their phenomenally successful Torsion Air Ride suspension, which remained in use until 1980.

Engine: Overhead valve Fury V-8

Displacement: 303 cid

Horsepower: 240 at 4800 rpm

Transmission: Three-speed manual with optional overdrive and automatic

Compression Ratio: 9.25:1

Body Style: Two-door Sports Coupe

Number of Seats: 6

Weight: 3650 lbs

Wheelbase: 115 inches (overall length 204.8 inches)

Base Price: $2807

Number Produced: 4485

1956 Studebaker Golden Hawk

Engineer Harold Churchill was selected as Studebaker's President in 1956. He was a loyal company man, who had worked in the company since 1926, and had cooperated with Raymond Loewy in his Studebaker Design Divison. He was determined that the company should survive, even with its difficulties.

These were pretty legion in this year. Model production slumped to 69,593 units, despite a full-on restyle of every model range. Studebaker fell back to thirteenth position in the league of auto production. The California plant was mothballed, leaving only two factories in production, at South Bend, Indiana and in Canada. The company also diversified somewhat, manufacturing the Ambulet (based on the station wagons) was launched and the Custom four-door sedan (the cheapest Stude at $1717) was marketed as a police/taxi vehicle. This model was also available in a Canadian 'export' edition.

The Loewy 1953 design classic, the Starliner, was the chief inspiration behind the pillarless Hawk quartet - the Golden Hawk, Power Hawk, Sky Hawk and Flight Hawk hardtops. Loewy himself supervised their deft makeover into a line of family sportscars with an effective restyle. The cars in this vein ran from the six-cylinder Flight Hawk, priced at a reasonable $1986 to the Packard V-8 equipped Golden Hawk at $3061. The big block Packard engine displaced 352 cid, and there was a dealer option to install a dual four-barrel set up borrowed from the Packard Caribbean. The 160 mph speedometer and matching 6000 rpm rev-counter made it clear that this was one car at least that Studebaker did not consider an economy model. But true to his principles, Loewy also designed safely into the car, and with a padded dash and floor-anchored seatbelts, it excelled in this area.

The Golden Hawk was the top-of-the range Studebaker for 1956, and its styling and equipment reflected this. Exclusive fibreglass fins were fitted on top of the rear fenders, which did not appear on the other Hawk models. Like the President Classic the Golden Hawk had wide grooved horizontal moldings just above the rocker panel. The interior specifications were also high, with all vinyl interiors or vinyl with cloth inserts in a variety of colors and patterns, with co-ordinating carpets. The fiberglass dashboard was also attractive, with its engine turned facing, featured black dials with white numerals and indicators. Standard items fitted to the Golden Hawk included a cigar lighter, glove compartment, electric windshield wipers and a dual exhaust system. A long list of cost-plus options was also available, including an AM radio, power seats and windows and tinted glass.

Engine: Golden Hawk V-8 Packard engine.
Overhead valve, cast iron block

Displacement: 352 cid

Horsepower: 275 at 4600 rpm

Compression Ratio: 9.5:1

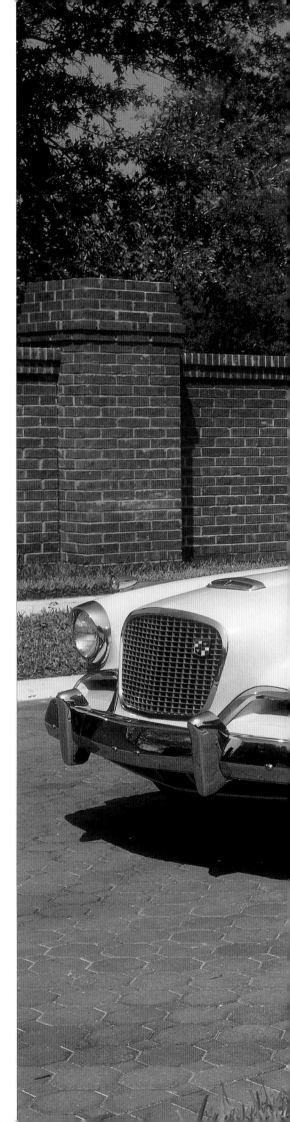

■ *Right: This 1956 Golden Hawk is the only car produced by the Studebaker-Packard Corporation that combines the key elements of each company – Studebaker styling and Packard power.*

Chevrolet Bel Air Sport Sedan   1957

Jack Kerouac published 'On The Road' in 1957, a book that was to set the mood for a whole generation, demonstrating how Road Culture was now a subliminal part of America's national psyche.

Chevrolet and Ford reversed their sales positions in 1957, Chevrolet slipped to second position manufacturing just over 1.5 million vehicles, but nearly 1.7 million Fords came off the production line that year. In fact, by the end of the year, symptoms of the economic recession of 1958 were already beginning to appear. But so far as automotive history goes, the Chevrolet Bel Air goes down as the most important car of the year, examples are treasured to this day and the model may well be the most highly regarded car of the decade: a style and performance classic.

1957 was also the year when Chevy introduced optional fuel injection - 'Ramjet' - for the first time on its V-8 engines. They claimed that the innovation made them the first American car manufacturer to deliver one horsepower for each cubic inch of displacement. But at $500 the system was tremendously expensive, especially as a basic Chevy came in at just a tad more than $2,000. Rivals Pontiac also introduced fuel injection in '57. Turboglide transmission was also introduced as an optional update to Powerglide. It was based on Buick's successful Dynaflow system, but proved less reliable. Safety seat belts and shoulder harnesses were also offered as options for the first time that year. Just as well.

Extra richness characterised the update styling and trim for the Bel Airs, which were now three years old. The marque seemed to be looking towards Cadillac for its influences, with more style and go fitted as standard for the new models. The massive front bumper became an integral part of the lower profile body. Chrome sidespears formed branched on the rear wings, and were filled with silver anodised aluminium beauty panels. Three gold chevrons accented the forward sides of the front fenders. The Chevrolet and Bel Air scripts were gilded for 1957, and so were the V-8 ornaments on models where this engine was fitted. Rocker sills, roof and windows outlines and the entire edge of the fins were all trimmed with rather glitzy metal moldings. Two-tone interiors were also introduced in this model year, and are apparent in this lovely example of the car, coffee 'n' cream upholstery complementing the cream and bronze bodywork.

■ *Left: This 1957 Sport Sedan demonstrates the Cadillac-inspired styling for the new Bel Air models.*

Engine: Six-cylinder overhead valve, cast iron block (V-8 also available for this model)

Displacement: 235.5 cid

Horsepower: 140 at 4200 rpm

Compression: 8.0:1

Wheelbase Length: 115 inches

Price: $2238

Number Produced: 62,751

1957 Chrysler 300-C Two-Door Convertible

The 300C was the third (following on from the C-300 and 300-B), and first convertible generation of the Chrysler 300 series. The model continued to fly the flag as the fastest production car in America. A completely new direction in styling, 'The Forward Look' had been applied to the 1957 300s by Exner and the Chrysler design team. The main features of the new body style were the elegant tailfins and masculine grille. The cars were restrained compared to the flamboyance of several contemporary models (the Chevy Bel Air Convertible, and Plymouth Fury are just two examples), but won the company several design awards. The cars were also built with a new torsion bar front suspension, replacing coil springs, that was to be used by Chrysler well into the 1980s. Motor Trend Magazine awarded the model 'Car of the Year', mainly for its excellent handling and engineering. However, in the annual league of car producers, Chrysler was back at eleventh place.

The Firepower hemi was again fitted to the car, but this would be its penultimate year in the model, the Golden Lion V-8 would be used from 1958.

Although considered part of the New Yorker series by Chrysler, the 300s were really a world away from even their production stable mates for power and handling. They were also much more simply

■ *Below: This proud ragtop C-300 demonstrates the fluid lines and elegant simplicity of the 1957 model.*

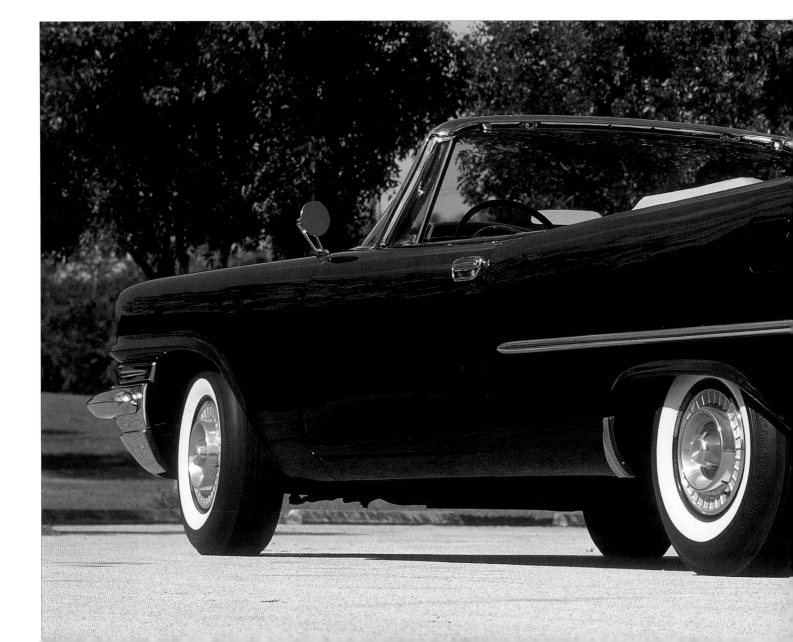

trimmed, with a just a single sidespear running along the rear the rear quarter panels on both sides of the car. The wheels, at 14 inches, were smaller than the previous model, and typical of the wheel size of contemporary US cars. The smallness of the wheels necessitated more effective brake cooling, which was achieved by adding rectangular openings under the headlamps, from where the in-coming air was ducted onto the break drums. The 300s were now produced exclusively in monotone colours, with elegant leather interiors. Two model shapes were now available, a revised two-door hardtop, and the new two-door convertible. The hardtop sold 1918 cars to the convertible's 484, but was $430 less expensive.

As well as the fantastic road car, Chrysler also manufactured a C300 with a specially enlarged V-8 set up with a standard stick shift, mainly intended for stock car racing and acceleration trials (a line of 300-Cs led the 1957 Speed Weeks parade at Daytona Beach). This optional engine developed 390 horsepower at 5400 rpm, and had a 10.0:1 compression ratio.

Engine:	V-8, overhead valve with hemispherical combustion chambers
Displacement:	392 cid
Horsepower:	375 at 5200 rpm
Transmission:	TorqueFlite
Compression ratio:	9.25:1
Number of Seats:	6
Weight:	4390 lbs
Wheelbase Length:	126 inches (overall length 219.2 inches)
Base Price:	$5359
Number Produced:	484 Convertibles

Corvette

The Corvette styling for '56, '57 and '58 remained pretty well unchanged except for modest tweaking of the chrome between model years. But the new 283 V-8s under the hood offered one horsepower per cubic inch with Chevy's new 'Ramjet' fuel injection. As the adverts of the time proclaimed, 'For the first time in automotive history – one horsepower for every cubic inch.' Of course, this wasn't actually true, the Chrysler 300 series was the first American car in this field.

The spirit of the car also remained unchanged, it was designed as a fun and economical sports car for young people, and remains so to this day. The original car was built in fiberglass to lower the initial production cost.

Amongst the standard features fitted to the car in this model year were dual exhaust pipes, all-vinyl bucket seats, three-spoke competition style steering wheel and carpeting. Seven optional colours were available, Onyx black, Polo white, Aztec copper, Artic blue, Cascade green, silver or, the colour of our photographed car – Venetian red. In two-tone cars, the 'cove' in the side panels could be picked out in white, silver or beige.

For a model that Chevy only retained to compete with Ford's Thunderbird, Corvette sales were virtually doubled from 1956, and continued to climb for the rest of the '50s.

Interesting option included a detachable hardtop ($215), Whitewall tires ($32), Hydraulic power top ($99), automatic transmission ($175), three versions of the fuel-injected engine were available (the most expensive of which could from 0-60 mph in 5.7 seconds, and achieve a top speed of 132 mph) and heavy-duty racing suspension ($725). In fact, only 1040 of the 1957 'Vettes were manufactured with fuel injection.

■ *Left: This fabulous Venetian red 'Vette has the cheeky grille of the early models.*

Engine: v-8 overhead valve, cast iron block. Fuel injection available as an option.

Displacement: 283 cid

Horsepower: 220 at 4800 rpm

Transmission: Three-speed manual floor shift, or four-speed manual floor shift or Powerglide as optional extras

Compression Ratio: 9.50:1

Induction: Carter four-barrel Model 3744925

Weight: 2730 lbs

Wheelbase: 102 inches (overall length 168 inches)

Base Price: $3,465

Number Produced: 6,339

Dodge D-500 Convertible

1957

The year 1957 saw the introduction of Virgil Exner's second generation 'Forward Look' applied to all the Chrysler products, including Dodge. The Dodge brand of the styling was denoted as 'Swept-Wing Styling' – and it was. The Dodge tailfins made the cars look as though they could take off, and with the D-500 super package, they virtually could. This supercharged version of their Hemi V-8 developed up to 340 horsepower, which put the car into some very good Chrysler company.

Body-wise, the cars were longer, lower and wider than any previous Dodge, and the wheelbase was longer than anything the company had built since 1933. The change over to fourteen-inch wheels helped to lower the silhouette of the car, and the torsion bar suspension (introduced over at Chrysler) was also new. The grille featured a gull-wing shaped bar that surrounded a huge Dodge crest. All the 1957 models had a single chrome bar along the body, and chrome trim under the rear fins. But the new styling could not disguise some quality control problems that were to dog the company and hinder sales for a couple of years.

In fact, the D-500 was actually designed as a high-performance engine that could be used in all the 1957 series, but the specifications given are for the engine fitted to two versions of the Custom Royal series (the two-door sedan and the two-door convertible) – but the model shown in the photograph is a Coronet (two-door Lancer convertible) fitted with the D-500. The Coronet was now the base Dodge model, and sales of this series made up over 160,000 of the sales figures for the year.

As a company, Dodge was performing much better, climbing to seventh in the league of sales, and produced nearly 290,000 cars in the year. Over 96% of the 1957 cars were automatics, and 93.4% were fitted with a V-8.

■ *Left: The styling of this 1957 Coronet demonstrates the second generation 'Forward Look' styling of the Chrysler Group.*

Engine: D-500 V-8 overhead valve, cast iron block, hemispherical heads

Displacement: 354 cid

Horsepower: 340 at 5200 rpm

Compression Ratio: 10.0:1

Induction: Carter four-barrel Type WCFB

Body Style: Two-door Convertible

Number of Seats: 6

Weight: 3975 lbs

Wheelbase: 122 inches

Base Price: $3635

Number Produced: 6,960 Two-door Convertibles across all ranges

253

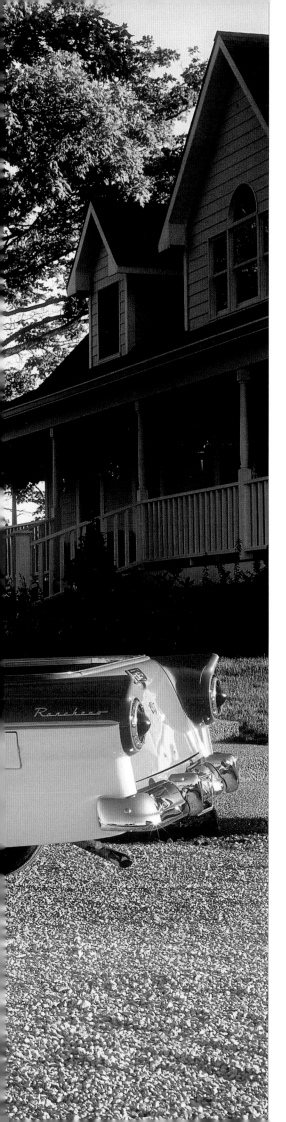

Ford Ranchero

1957

Ford made automotive manufacturing history in 1957 by offering the largest ever total of 21 production models, including the completely new Skyliner, with retractable hardtop, and the Ranchero car-derived pickup – the first production car-truck built in America. The entire Ford range was radically redesigned for 1957, the new styling based on the Mystere show car. The bodies were longer, wider and lower, with completely new trim, including jet tube taillights and the bulls eye hood ornament. The chassis were also completely revised, riding four inches lower than the facelifted '56. Mechanically, '57 engines were higher in horsepower, with increased compression from reshaped combustion chambers. The Ranchero was available with all the current engine options, ranging from the improved six-cylinder to the supercharged Thunderbird V-8. This latter option wasn't really meant for cruising, but was great for red-light challenges!

This was a critical year for FoMoCo, and Henry Ford II was so determined to beat Chevrolet in the league of automotive manufacturers, that he made it the goal of every Ford employee. The Company successfully beat Chevrolet into second place for the year by a margin of nearly 170,000 cars.

The instant success of Ranchero was a contributory factor to this, as Chevy didn't manage to get their reply to this phenomenon (the El Camino) onto the market until 1959.

Like El Camino, 'Rachero' is also a Spanish-derived word, being a man who owned a big tract of land in nineteenth-century California. But in automotive terms, it heralded a completely new kind of vehicle, a light pickup with a truck bed based on Ford's Ranch station wagon, thus employing car rather than truck components. The 1957 brochure described the model as 'More than a car! More than a truck', and it announced an automotive original that was to remain in continuous production until 1979. 508,355 Rancheros were built, uniquely based on a succession of five Ford car body styles with numerous restyle changes from year to year. For 1957, the Ranchero was available in both plain 'Ranchero' and 'Custom Ranchero' versions. The latter came with more options and more luxurious interior trim.

■ *Left: This V-8 equipped Ranchero in Dresden blue and Colonial white looks good in this country setting.*

Engine: Overhead valve V-8, cast iron block	
Displacement: 312 cid	
Horsepower: 245 at 4500 rpm	
Compression Ratio: 9.7:1	
Body Style: Pickup with flat bed	
Weight: 3,220 lbs (estimated)	
Wheelbase: 116 inches	
Base Price: $2,098	
Number Produced: 21,705	

Ford Thunderbird

Ford had first introduced the Thunderbird two-seater 'personal' car in 1955 to counter Chevrolet's 1953-introduced Corvette. At almost exactly the same base price as its more established rival, the T-bird hugely outsold the 'Vette in its first year. Buyers loved the sleek good looks of the car, and the practical lift-off hardtop. 16,155 examples were sold in the car's first model year, as opposed to a slightly pathetic 700 Corvette roadsters.

By 1957, the Thunderbird was still well ahead in the sales race, (21,380 to 9,168) although the Corvette was considerably more expensive by this model year, and followed the general trend as Fords outsold Chevys for the first time in a good while. The Thunderbird was also available as the more powerful option by the time the new 1957 model was introduced in October 1956. Whilst Chevy offered 283 horsepower via its optional Ramjet fuel injector (one horsepower per cubic inch) Ford was offering a far more massive power option. The supercharged Thunderbird Special Supercharge V-8 belted out 340 horsepower at 5300 rpm in the NASCAR version of the car. Both Thunderbirds and Corvettes were available with a single body option in 1957, the standard two-door convertible.

Thunderbirds had been heavily re-styled for the 1957 model year, as were all the cars in this decisive year in Ford's history. The redesign included a revised body shape, including huge tailfins (or 'high-canted fender blades') and the abolition of the externally mounted spare wheel. Interior changes included a new instrument panel and 'Lifeguard Design' safety features (including a padded dashboard and dished steering wheel). Six engine options were available for the T-bird, a six-cylinder version (serial number code 'A') and five increasingly powerful V-8s (serial number codes 'B', 'C', 'D', 'E' and 'F'). All kinds of optional refinements were available at extra cost – everything from power windows to white sidewall tires.

Despite its success, 1957 turned out to be the final year for the two-seater version of the Thunderbird. 1958 witnessed the introduction of the luxury four-passenger 'Square Birds'. A ragtop version was also launched. Effectively, this took Thunderbirds out of the American sports car market, and Corvette inherited the two-seater roadster market. This was doubly ironic – Ford had clearly interpreted this market far more accurately than Chevrolet, but by establishing demand for cars of this stamp, they ensured the survival of their rival's car.

■ *Left: The 1957 Thunderbird was the last two-seater version of this marque.*

Engine: Standard V-8. Overhead valve	
Displacement: 272 cid	
Horsepower: 190 at 4500 rpm	
Compression Ratio: 8.6:1	
Wheelbase: 102 inches (181.4 inches overall)	
Base Price: $3408	
Number Produced: 21,380	

1957 Pontiac Bonneville Convertible

Big things were happening at Pontiac in 1957. Semon E. 'Bunkie' Knudsen became Pontiac's new general manager in '56, the son of former GM President William S. Knudsen, he became the youngest general manager at GM at the ripe old age of 43. The change marked the quiet insurgence of Pontiac into the youth car market. Knudsen hired Pete Estes (who became Chief Engineer at Pontiac in '57) and John DeLorean to head up the design and engineering teams, together with a series of huge performance advances, their work was to positively shape Pontiac cars for years to come. The Strato-Streak V-8 was launched in 1955, it was lighter than the GM Straight 8, and cheaper to manufacture than the Oldsmobile Rocket V-8.

There was a huge emphasis at Pontiac on research and development, and a constant striving for engineering advances. The company funded an influential 'Product Engineering' department. During this period, they experimented with four-speed floor-shift, rear-mounted transaxles and supercharging.

■ *Below: This stunning Kenya Ivory and Fontaine Blue painted Bonneville Convertible is one of only a hundred surviving examples of the model.*

A unique, limited edition Custom Bonneville Convertible was released in January 1957. It was Pontiac's first Bonneville. The car was in the Custom Star Chief sub-series (series 28) in which there were four body styles. The cars were released on a one-to-a-dealer basis, and availability was very limited – only 630 production examples were built, plus two prototypes. The car was only available with a convertible top and the Bonneville V-8, an enlarged Strato-Streak, which developed an estimated 315 horsepower at 4800 rpm. The cars were also fitted with a Rochester mechanical fuel injection system. A NASCAR certified triple-carb option was also available.

The Bonnies were hugely accessorized, and were fitted with air suspension, power seats, power brakes, power windows, power steering, leather upholstery and Hydra-Matic drive. The only options were air conditioning, and 'continental' externally mounted tires.

Engine: Overhead valve V-8, cast iron block

Displacement: 347 cid

Horsepower: (estimated) 315 at 4800 rpm

Transmission: Strato-Flight Hydra-Matic

Compression Ratio: 10.25:1

Induction: Rochester mechanical fuel injection

Number of Seats: 6

Weight: 4285 lbs

Wheelbase: 124 inches

Base Price: $5782

Buick Limited

1958

The year 1958 wasn't a good year for Ford with the introduction of the horrid and unlucky Edsel, but things were even worse over at Buick. Sales in the year plummeted to fewer than 250,000 and the company fell to number five in the sales league. The designers at Buick seemed to have completely missed the plot. As the economy went into a deep (but thankfully mini) recession, and unemployment hit over 5.5 million, car buyers either stayed away in droves or bought smaller economy models, Buick chose this year to launch the big, expensive, luxury top-of-the-line 'Limited' series.

Buick resurrected this grand old nameplate for a trio of cars that were designed to vie with Oldsmobile for glitter, and even challenge Cadillac at the luxury end of the market. A four-door hardtop, two-door hardtop and two-door convertible comprised the full model range in the Limited series.

The most distinctive feature of the styling was twelve diagonal chrome louvers set in the rocket-like trim motive of the rear fenders, together with massive louvered taillights set in squared off tail fins. There was also a heavy sweeping chrome sidespear on either side of the car that swept backwards from the headlamp assembly all the way back to the rear wheel arch. The rear fender was a truly massive chromed construction complete with positively sculptural over riders.

The front fender, also heavily chromed, featured the classic Buick chequerboard effect, whilst the two double headlight assemblies appear to be heavily lidded.

The series was completely disastrous, and far more 'Limited' than Buick had hoped. Across the three models (both hardtop and convertible) only 7136 units were produced. Production of the range was cancelled at the end of the year, as Buick's designers completely revised the entire line. In fact, none of the 1958 model names survived this apocalyptic year.

■ *Left: One of the extremely 'Limited' convertibles of 1958, only 839 were produced.*

Engine:	V-8 overhead valve, cast iron block
Displacement:	364 cid
Horsepower:	300 at 4600 rpm
Transmission:	Dynaflow
Compression:	10.0:1
Body Style:	Two-door Convertible
Number of Seats:	6
Weight:	4603 lbs
Wheelbase Length:	127.5 inches
Price:	$5125
Number Produced:	839

Chevrolet Impala Convertible 1958

The worst recession year of the post-war era was 1958, and car sales fell by about 30% on the three previous boom years. Americans were seriously concerned that the Russians appeared to be pulling ahead, technologically speaking, in the Cold War – claiming that their nuclear missiles could now reach anywhere in the world. However, with an excellent selection of reasonably priced models, Chevrolet regained poll position in the sales stakes, about 1.14 million compared to just under one million Fords. Imported cars were also becoming more of a factor, cornering an unprecedented market share of almost 10%. These were mostly from Japan, and the first Toyotas (Toyopets) and Datsuns arrived for sale for the first time in America in 1958.

1958 saw the introduction of two luxurious 'Impala' models to the already up-market Bel Air series. For Chevrolet, the cars were launched with relatively stiff retail prices, and were an attempt to reach upmarket. Despite the generally poor trading conditions, the innate class and style of the Impalas meant that they sold very well. The Impala name itself was almost immediately destined for positively iconic status amongst the cognoscenti. A hardtop sport coupe, and a hardtop convertible were simultaneously introduced – both two-door vehicles. The most powerful engine option for the Impalas developed 300 horsepower from a V-8 engine block. The trim features for the new cars included Impala script insignia, broad ribbed sill panels, large dummy chromed air scoops just ahead of the rear wheelwells and triple taillamp arrangements. Inside the car, there were competition style two-spoke deep hub steering wheels, and several Impala script emblems.

Technologically, the cars were built with full coil spring suspension, anti-dive braking and foot-operated parking brakes.

■ *Left: This gleaming black Impala Convertible shows the distinct lines and grown-up styling of this iconic model.*

Engine: Six-cylinder with overhead valve, or V-8 with overhead valves were both available for Impalas

Displacement: 235.5 and 283 respectively

Horsepower: 145 at 4200 rpm, 185 at 4600 rpm

Weight: 3522 lbs (2841 lbs with a V-8)

Price: $2724 ($2841 with a V-8)

Number Produced: Note: After 1957, Chevrolet production totals are only available by series, no breakdown is available for each series, model or engine type. 142,592 Sports Coupes were sold by the company in 1958, plus 55,989 Convertible models

Dodge Coronet Sedan 1958

The 1958 Dodges, including the Coronet, used the 1957 swept-wing body shell with minor restyling, except that the grille and headlights were completed revised. The grille now consisted of side-to-side horizontal bars with a single low fender and two shorter bars at the sides that housed the parking lights. The headlights followed the general market trend by adopting the quad-light format. The revised model offered the public plenty of style at a relatively reasonable price, and sold 77,000 units in the year.

The main preoccupation at Dodge in this model year was power. The engine was now the 'wedge' shaped single rocker head design. This became standard across the Chrysler Group, and was cheaper to produce than the Hemi V-8s. In fact, six engine options were available to all Dodge models, ranging from the Inline six-cylinder right through to the super-powerful electronic fuel injection V-8, fitted with the Bendix EFI assembly. However, although this model could develop 333 horsepower at 4800 rpm, only six such cars were built in the year, and were later recalled for the unreliable injector to be replaced with an ordinary carburettor.

Surprisingly, the demand for six-cylinder engines actually increased in the year. Maybe it was the general recession that made buyers more economical. However, 94.4% of the 1958 cars were fitted with automatic transmission, and 62.5% had power steering. General production fell disastrously in the auto industry as a whole, but Dodge production was particularly badly affected, falling by more than 50%, and retaining only a 3.1% of the market. The 65,000 employees of the company only accounted for approximately two cars each during this dreadful year. Labor problems with the workforce in 1958 had a knock-on effect to 1959 production, and even the introduction of exaggerated styling couldn't gloss over ridiculously long delivery times.

The 1958 Coronets were assembled in three Dodge plant locations – six-cylinder powered models in Detroit and Newark, V-8s in Detroit, Newark and Los Angeles.

■ *Left: This two-door hardtop 1958 Coronet demonstrates the subtle styling up-date from the Dodge's of the year.*

Engine:	Red Ram V-8 overhead valve
Displacement:	325 cid
Horsepower:	245 at 4400 rpm
Compression Ratio:	8.0:1
Body Style:	Two-door hardtop
Weight:	3540
Wheelbase:	122 inches
Base Price:	$2644
Number Produced:	Dodge produced 77,388 Coronets in the year, but no figures for the different models were available

Ford Edsel Citation

1958

FoMoCo had realised in the late '40s that they needed a truly up-market car to offer their buyers, who would otherwise move up and away to other brands. A Special Products Division was set up in 1955, under the leadership of R.E.Krafve, to develop such as car. The plan was to use components from other parts of the group, but to develop a distinct car in its own right. FoMoCo stylist Roy Brown wanted to create a car with a unique, immediately recognisable appearance. The project was nick-named the 'E-car' (for experiment).

After several delays, the new product was scheduled for a fall 1957 launch, and a name was finally agreed upon – Edsel - after Henry Ford's son, who had died in 1942. The Ford family were initially unsure about using the name, but were talked into it by company chairman Ernest Breech. Ranger, Pacer, Corsair and Citation were chosen as the model names for the series. The Ranger was the base model, and the Citation was the most expensive, 'senior', car in the range.

Eighteen models were launched initially, including five station wagons. The model names for these were Roundup, Villager and Bermuda. Production started in 1957 in four different assembly plants. The Edsel was billed as 'The Newest Thing on Wheels', and there was a massive three-year long publicity build-up to the launch date. Four thousand cars were sold on the September 4 launch date, but within a month, this had slowed dramatically and the cracks were already beginning to show in Ford's big experiment. Having said all that, the Edsels did set an all-time record for deliveries of a newly introduced, mid-price car.

From a manufacturing point of view, the 1958 Citation and Corsair shared a single body shell, but the Citations were trimmed to a higher level. Three models were introduced with this model name, a two-door hardtop coupe, a four-door hardtop sedan and a two-door convertible. But apart from the unfortunately delayed launch date, which exactly coincided with America's sharpest downturn of the decade, the most problematic aspect of the Edsel was undoubtedly its controversial, not to say ugly, styling. The odd, pursed lips of the grille, and the clunky square body panels positively repelled the customers. On the other hand, the performance of the cars, especially that of the top-of the-range Citation was fine. The V-8 engine and three-speed Teletouch automatic transmission (with pushbutton controls) made the car easy and enjoyable to drive.

■ *Left: The Citation Convertible came with dual exhausts and vinyl-coated ragtops in black, turquoise and white. Our photographed car has turquoise vinyl upholstery and a matching cove, with inset silver beauty panel.*

Engine: V-8 overhead valve, cast iron block	
Displacement: 361 cid	
Horsepower: 303 at 4600 rpm	
Compression Ratio: 10.5:1	
Wheelbase: 124 inches	
Base Price: $3766	
Number Produced: 930	

1958 Lincoln Continental Convertible

Lincoln Introduced the Continental in 1940, and the series quickly became one of the most celebrated lines ever. Indeed, the 1940 convertible model is considered by many to be the most beautiful American production car every built. It was longer and lower than the other model year Lincolns, and introduced the 'continental spare tire' look. The original Continental cars were powered by a V-12 engine.

Lincoln's top-of-the-range series was completely re-styled in 1958, from the Mark IIs of '56 and '57. These had been a very exclusive and expensive range, and sold in modest numbers   The Mark III was the largest unibody car ever built, and became the longest American production convertible ever built at a stunning 229 inches in overall length. The chassis was dispensed with, and the suspension, driveline and engine units were fastened to the body structure. It was also fitted with the biggest contemporary American engine – the huge 430-cid V-8. Lincoln offered air suspension, but only 2% of the units sold were ordered with this option. But the cars had lost some of the elite reputation of the series. The Mark II convertible retailed for $10,000, which was nearly $3,000 more than the Cadillac Eldorado Biarritz, but the Mark IIIs were considerably re-positioned in the market, being nearly $1,000 cheaper.

The low-flying lines of this super-long car emphasised its great length, as did the lower body moldings, chrome trim and criss-cross pattern aluminium grille. The elegant streamlining was maintained by the 'disappearing top'. The fabric hood and glass rear window were fully retracted into the truck, which was hinged at the rear to allow this power-operated system to work smoothly. The luxurious feel of the model was emphasised by full leather upholstery fitted as standard.

The other 1958 Lincoln series were the base level Capris and the mid-range Premiere. The Capri was also completely restyled for this model year, whilst the Premiere used the same body with slightly more trim. All three 1958 models were fitted with the same standard equipment. Lincoln production fell to 17,134 units in this recession year, which translated to position fifteen in the league of model year production.

Engine: Overhead valve V-8, cast iron block

Displacement: 430 cid

Horsepower: 375 at 4800 rpm

Compression Ratio: 10.5:1

Weight: 4927 lbs

Wheelbase: 131 inches

Base Price: $6223

Number Produced: 3,048

■ *Right: Many people don't rate the Mark III and later Lincoln Continentals as highly as the original models, but this long and elegant car was nevertheless unique as the longest convertible ever manufactured in the US.*

1958 Plymouth Fury

Plymouth had made it back to third position in the producers' league in 1957, and retained this place in '58 with just over a 30% share of the market.

The 1958 Fury was a Belvedere sub-series containing only the high performance sports coupe. First introduced as a midyear model back in '56, the Fury was designed to heat up Plymouth's new performance-orientated image, equipped with a 240 horsepower V-8, and special gold-anodized side trim (this trim persisted into the '58 range). Like the rest of the Plymouth line, the Fury hardtop emerged from the 1957 styling bigger, bolder and better-handling than the first model, complete with a 290-horse V-8. The '58 Fury was a limited edition two-door hardtop with Fury rear fender, nameplates, bumper wing guards, padded interior, and front and rear foam seats. It was effectively a revised and super-charged Belvedere. Just as is '57, the Belvederes remained the top Plymouth range, Plazas were the base models, whilst the Savoys comprised the medium-priced series.

The '58 Furys were now powered by an overhead valve Fury V-8, and an optional Bendix fuel

■ *Below: The '58 Fury was available in a single two-door Hardtop coupe, in buckskin beige with gold trim.*

injection (EFI) system was also available for the big-block Golden Commando V-8, but these were later recalled and reconverted. These Golden Commando 'big block' wedge head V-8s were capable of 0-60 miles per hour in 7.7 seconds and could run the quarter-mile in 16.1 seconds.

The '58 model Fury is the car immortalized by Stephen King in his book Christine, but there are several inconsistencies with reality. In the King's book (as in John Carpenter's 1983 film version), Christine is red and white, but the real model was only available in buckskin beige with gold trim. In the book, King refers to the car as having four doors, but the '58 models were only available in the singe two-door version. He also mentions that car as having hydramatic transmission with a transmission lever, but the car actually had TorqueFlite, push-button transmission. Plus, the real life Furys did not kill people that insulted their owners!

Engine: Fury v-8 overhead valve

Displacement: 317.6 cid

Horsepower: 225 at 4400 rpm

Transmission: Three-speed manual with Torqueflite automatic optional

Compression Ratio: 9.25:1

Body Style: Two-door Hardtop Coupe

Weight: 3510 lbs

Wheelbase: 118 inches (206 inches overall)

Base Price: $3032

Number Produced: 5,303

Cadillac Eldorado

1959

The prevailing style of automotive styling in this year could unkindly be called 'Wurlitzer Jukebox' – and Cadillac was the supreme proponent. If the Chevrolet Impala of the same year was extreme, the Eldorado still managed to out-glitz and out-chrome its rival completely. Of course, it also weighed in at nearly $2,000 more, pushing the price of the Biarritz Convertible to over $7,400. In fact, the 1959 model attracted only 1320 well-heeled customers, but has passed into automotive history as a truly iconic car that has worshippers and detractors in almost equal number.

The car was designed by the outgoing Head of Styling at Cadillac - Harley Earl as his swan song before leaving the company later that year. The car was lower than its predecessor, but it was the body styling that really identified it. The tailfins were the largest ever to appear on a Cadillac, together with the bullet taillights and other details that so clearly reflected the national fascination with the space race. In fact, contemporaries thought the car looked positively 'Martian'. The Eldos were criticised for poor handling, but at nearly nineteen feet in length, they had been designed for good looks and luxurious cruising rather than hard driving. Despite this, the car could achieve 0-60 mph in eleven seconds, with a top speed of nearly 120mph, courtesy of an enlarged V-8 engine block.

Cadillac itself retained tenth position in the league of cars sales in the US, selling just over 140,000 units. The increased competition from imported cars may have somewhat affected sales, but Cadillac is still the biggest volume manufacturer of exclusively luxury cars in America.

Ironically, just as Cadillac's jukebox look reached its Zenith in the '59 Eldos, the death of Buddy Holly, Ritchie Valens and J.P. 'The Big Bopper' Richardson together in a single air crash signalled the end of the 'Happy Days' rock 'n' roll era, and the flamboyant styling it had inspired.

■ *Left: Though massive, this 1959 Eldorado Biarritz looks strangely delicate and poised for flight.*

Engine: V-8 overhead valve, cast iron block

Displacement: 390 cid

Horsepower: 345 at 4800 rpm

Compression: 10.5:1

Body Style: Two-door Eldorado Biarritz Convertible (Two-door Eldorado Seville hardtop also available)

Weight: 5060

Wheelbase Length: 130 inches (225 inches overall length)

Price: $7401

Number Produced: 1320

Chevrolet El Camino

1959

El Camino is Spanish for 'the road', and when Chevy launched their new two-door wagon in 1959, it was the beginning of a long journey for the car-derived model that went through twenty-seven re-styles until it was finally discontinued in 1988 (although El Caminos were temporarily off the market between 1960 and 1964). The El Camino's most successful year was 1973, when 64,987 were produced.

In essence, the El Camino was Chevy's answer to Ford's similarly conceptualised Ranchero, but it was almost always the winner in the annual sales race between the two models, and out survived the Ranchero by nine active production years.

The El Camino was conceived as a mating between car and truck. In fact, all of Chevrolet's first commercial vehicles were cars morphed into trucks. Their first attempt at the El Camino was basically a two-door station wagon with its rear roof section removed, and a pickup box fitted (with rather fetching chrome trim around the lip). Yet their 1959 sales for the model surpassed 22,000 vehicles, compared to the 14,100 Rancheros that were sold in the same period. The reflected the general trend, with 1959 Chevys outselling Fords – though by the rather slim margin of 11,000 vehicles.

But the real beauty of this eccentric model was that it was fun. It was never really designed as a workhorse, but more as an adjunct to an active lifestyle, where you just might need to tow your powerboat, or pick up a really heavy shop from the store. The El Camino was also available with various hot engine options that meant performance did not have to be sacrificed for convenience, and it could just as easily be driven as a passenger car.

Just like its companion Chevy's of this model year, the El Camino had the same rakish lines - flyaway roofline, bat wings, chrome body accents and wraparound back window - of its more conventional stable mates. But unlike the ritzy interiors enjoyed by them, the El Camino cab interior was relatively plain and serviceable. Technically, El Caminos were built with an updated suspension that included rear springs and shocks, and were available with the usual full range of Chevy engine options.

Today, the most direct descendant of the El Camino is probably the stunning Chevrolet SSR (starting at a not-so-modest $41,995). Just like itspredecessor, the new car is part roaster, part pickup – and runs off a V-8 power source.

■ *Left: The 1959 El Camino wagon was the first in a distinguished line of vehicles that continues to influence Chevy production to this day.*

Engine: Six-cylinder, V-8 (6 options)	
Displacement: 235.5 cid or 283 cid	
Horsepower: 135 at 4000 rpm, 185 at 4600 rpm	
Compression: 8.25:1, 8.5:1	
Wheelbase Length: 119 inches	
Number Produced: 22,000	

1959 Chevrolet Impala Convertible

If the nineteen fifties was the decade of the tailfin, then 1959 saw the absolute apogee of this style in several models, including the Cadillac Eldorados (q.v.) and Chevrolet Impala Sport models of that year. The appendages on the Impalas were more 'batfin' than tailfin, and looking liked something off the Batmobile itself. Both cars were simply outrageous, dripping with chrome, with acres of glistening glass and unbelievably lustrous paint jobs in the most in-your-face colours possible. They were the ultimate in rock 'n' roll glamor and excess, cars for fun, dating and cruising. The model name remains in use by Chevrolet to this day, but the cars on which it appears are completely lacking in verve and personality compared to the originals. This dreariness is reflected in the fact that a first class example of the '59 model can command a price tag of three to four times that of the current model.

The confidence and joie de vivre of the Impalas reflected the fact that the automotive industry itself was bouncing back with a bumper production year, up nearly half a million units on the previous twelve months. The 'upper crust' that the cars were designed for had given up on the economy models, and was seduced into purchasing 65,800 Convertible Impalas over the life of this model style.

The Impala range was considerably extended in 1959, to include a four-door passenger sedan, a four-door Hardtop Sport Sedan and a re-styled Nomad Station Wagon. It had now moved into a higher market position than the Bel Air range, and the cars were, typically, a couple of hundred dollars more expensive. Like the Bel Airs, Impalas were all available with both six-cylinder and V-8 engines.

A tremendous range of extras was available for the Impalas, everything from six types of V-8 engine (including Turbo-Fire and Special Super Turbo-Thrust) to Magic-Mirror deep lustre acrylic paint and Safety Master brakes.

■ *Right: This magnificent Impala Convertible must be one of the reddest cars in the world.*

Engine: Six-cylinder of V-8 – both with overhead valve and cast iron blocks

Displacement: 235.5 cid or 283 cid

Horsepower: 135 at 4000 rpm or 185 at 4600 rpm

Compression: 8.25:1 or 8.5:1

Number of Seats: (Impala Convertible) 5

Weight: 3660 lbs (or 3650 lbs with V-8)

Wheelbase Length: 119 inches, overall length 210.9 inches

Price: $2849, $2967 with V-8

DeSoto Adventurer, Sportsman   1959

First introduced to the DeSoto model line in February 1956, the Adventurer two-door hardtop coupe was a limited production speciality car. Technically a Fireflite sub-series, the car was heralded as the 'Golden Adventurer' because of its ritzy gold trim accents. The car had a special high-performance engine (with enlarged valve ports, high-lift camshaft, large diameter valves and stiffer valve springs) developing 320 horsepower at 5200 rpm. This original Adventurer also had a dual exhaust, and custom finish.

A convertible Adventurer was introduced in the following year, and the Adventurer engines were now fitted with dual four-barrel carburettors. This engine provided one horsepower per cubic inch of displacement. In effect, they were vying for power with the Chrysler 300s. In the 1958 model Adventurer, a fuel injector (manufactured by Bendix) was offered as an option. The cars could now perform at 345 horsepower at 5000 rpm.

By 1959, there were still two models in the Adventurer, the two-door Sportsman hardtop, and the two-door convertible coupe. All Adventurers carried the model script on both front wings, and were even more richly trimmed in gold, with fold color sweep inserts affixed, grilles finished in gold, and gold trimmed hubcaps. The hardtop of the Sportsman was finished with simulated Scotch-grain leather. Standard equipment was the same as for the Fireflite series from which this line had evolved, but the car could now develop 350 horsepower at 5000 rpm, as opposed to the Fireflite's 325 at 4600 rpm. Sadly, the company's fortunes were going the other way, with an output of only 45,734 units in the year.

In fact, the Adventurer went down in history as the final model produced by DeSoto in 1961, the company's last production year, providing all of the meagre 3,104 sales for that year. Even so, the car had undergone a modest face lift (following the new styling introduced at Chrysler). The power train had also been improved, and was now able to provide 265 horsepower at 4400 rpm. But this was not enough to save the model, or the company, which ceased trading after 32 illustrious years.

■ *Left: In this year of the most outrageous Eldorados and Impalas, the styling on the Adventurer looks relatively staid, belying its performance statistics.*

Engine: V-8 overhead valve, cast iron block

Displacement: 383 cid

Horsepower: 350 at 5000 rpm

Compression Ratio: 10.1:1

Weight (Sportsman): 3980 lbs

Wheelbase: 126 inches

Base Price (Sportsman): $4427

Number Produced: (Sportsman) 590
(Convertible) 97

Ford Edsel Corsair Convertible | 1959

The 1959 Corsair was the senior model in the Edsel range. But in reality, the car was a Ranger with slightly more trim and a larger engine. It really exemplified the demise of the Edsel, no longer did it have the longer wheelbase and unique design of the 1958 Corsairs, or completely different engine options.

Whereas the availability of four Citations had meant that only two Corsairs were available in '58, four versions of the car were offered in '59, reflecting the discontinuation of the more expensive line: a four-door sedan, a four-door hardtop sedan, a two-door hardtop coupe and a two-door convertible. The new Corsairs were actually quite a bit cheaper – over $500 cheaper in fact.

The marque was now a member of the Mercury-Edsel-Lincoln Division, headed up by Ben D. Mills. These '59 models were also manufactured in the single Edsel plant at Louisville, but the production problems that had dogged the earlier versions seem to have been somewhat ironed out.

But any improvement came much too late to help the Edsel. Every problem a car could have seemed to be stacked against it. The name of the line was unappealing. The styling was bizarre and universally derided. The economic downturn had reduced car sales overall, and Edsel in particular. The build quality had been suspect. The final coupe de grace was the fact that dealers no longer wanted to carry the Edsel models.

The Edsel was discontinued in November 1959, just after the introduction of the 1960 models (now just two series, Ranger and Villager). Its ill-conceived launch was reputed to have cost Ford over $350 million. Although he had assured the public that the Edsel was to be a permanent member of the Ford family, by November Henry Ford II seemed philosophical about the disaster, 'We couldn't sell them, we were losing money, so we made a decision, 'Let's quit'... I'd rather admit the mistake, chop it off, and don't throw good money after bad.' Ironically, the 1960 models looked 100% better, the horse collar grille was gone for ever. Perhaps the Edsel could have had a future after all.

■ *Left: This final Corsair Convertible in Snow white and turquoise is still heavily chromed.*

Engine:	V-8 overhead valve, cast iron block
Displacement:	332 cid
Horsepower:	225 at 4400 rpm
Compression Ratio:	8.9:1
Induction:	Two-barrel Model PB9E9510-8
Weight:	3790 lbs
Wheelbase:	120 inches
Base Price:	$3072
Number Produced:	1,343

1959 Ford Skyliner Two-Door Hardtop Convertible

When the Skyliner was introduced as a midyear model in the seminal Ford year of 1957, it was the first truly convertible hardtop in American automotive history, and a first for Detroit. Introduced as part of the completely redesigned Fairlane 500 series, the Skyliner was completely unique with its fully retractable metal roof. All the cars were built with V-8 engines. The Skyliner sold 20,766 units in its first year.

Many car connoisseurs consider the 1959 'Ford Family of Fine Cars' to be the most attractive range ever styled and built by FoMoCo. Indeed, the lineup for the year was awarded the Gold Medal for Exceptional Styling at the Brussels World Fair. With elegance, and understated styling the cars were classy and tasteful, and looked like they could take off into interstellar orbit. The re-style was more of a toning down on that of the previous year, and much chrome trim was dispensed with. The Galaxie was introduced as the most up-market car in the Ford range for 1959, and the Skyliner was absorbed into this category.

■ *Below: Although the 1959 Skyliners were re-classified as Galaxies midyear in 1959, this car still carries the Fairlane 500 script. Sales for these models were included in the Galaxie figures, however.*

The main difference between the new Galaxies and the Fairlane 500s was the styling of the top. In the Galaxies, the standard top was used with a thunderbird style 'C' pillar. The combination resulted in one of the best-looking models ever released by Dearborn.

Generally, automotive manufacturers produced over 30% more cars in 1959, after the mini recession of '58. Even so, Ford trailed Chevy's model year production, although only by a very modest 11,000 plus cars on an output of nearly 1.5 million.

Sadly, the beautifully revised Skyliner attracted only 12,915 purchasers. It was the most expensive 1959 Ford by several hundred dollars (excluding the T-bird models). Still, this was nearly three thousand more sales than the Thunderbird convertible. But the days of the 'retrac' were numbered by this poor performance, and this was its final model year.

Engine: V-8 overhead valve, cast iron block

Displacement: 292 cid

Horsepower: 145 at 4000 rpm

Transmission: three-speed manual, automatic overdrive, Ford-O-Matic and Cruise-O-Matic

Compression Ratio: 292 cid

Induction: Holley two-barrel carburetor

Weight: 4064 lbs

Wheelbase: 118 inches

Base Price: $3346

Number Produced: 12,915

1959 Oldsmobile Dynamic Eighty-Eight Holiday Hardtop

If American car manufacturers had moved into an automotive space age in 1958, then the '59 models were the epitome of this outrageous style. The completely revised '59 Oldsmobile designs, designated the 'Linear Look', heralded a range of all-new bigger and more streamlined models. It was a substantial move away from the 'chromesmobile' excesses of '58. All '59 Oldsmobile models were now powered by the Rocket V-8 engine. The GM divisions now shared a basic bodyshell, but the styling was substantially different for each different marque.

The Dynamic Eighty-Eights has stunning 'go-faster' lines that emphasised their great length (218.4 inches overall) and, in the final flourish of the age of tailfins, theirs were fairly substantial (though nothing to rival those of their Eldorado GM stable mate). The particularly thin-pillar roofline of the Oldsmobile hardtops prompted the 'SceniCoupe' tag for these models. There was a total of six models in the range, including two- and four-door Holiday Hardtops in the new 'flat top' styling. The four-door model was the company's second most popular offering in this year, whilst the two-door hardtop accounted for 18 per cent of the total Oldsmobile production. Standard equipment for the series included an oil filter, turn signals, air scoop brakes and a safety spectrum speedometer. An innovative new option was the pull out 'Trans-Portable' transistor radio.

Super Eighty-eights were the middle series for '59, and could be distinguished by their dual exhausts and air cleaners (although both of these were also optional on the Dynamics). Olds retained the ninety-eights as its successful top series format, built on a slightly longer wheelbase.

Oldsmobile had been at number four in the league of automobile producers in '58 - their 50th anniversary year – but fell back to fifth position in '59. Even so, they maintained a 6.9 per cent market share, continuing to make 'good cars for good people', whilst introducing technical innovations. Lee Petty continued to race Oldsmobiles at Daytona (though minus factory support). He took a two-door hardtop to a photo finish in the first Daytona 500-Mile stock car race.

Engine: Overhead valve V-8, cast iron block

Displacement: 371 cid

Horsepower: 270 at 4600 rpm

Compression Ratio: 9.75:1

Weight: 4235 lbs

Wheelbase: 123 inches

Base Price: $2958

Number Produced: 38,488

■ *Right: All Hardtops were 'Holidays' in '59. This one is the Dynamic '88' two-door version, with 'SceniCoupe' styling.*

1959 Plymouth Sport Fury

Plymouth sales leapt a full 11.6 per cent in their 30th anniversary model year of 1959, holding third position in the industry sales charts. Although its actual share of the market was reduced – overall production was raised by over 30 per cent. The unsuccessful fuel injection option was deleted from the list of available options. General Manager Harry E. Cheesbrough marked the production of the company's eleven-millionth car.

All Plymouths were heavily re-styled for 1959, gaining huge tailfins and a tire bulge on the trunk lid. Technologically, not much had changed for the 1957-58 models, though.

Furys became a separate series in the 1959 production year, rather strangely grouped together with the Sport Suburban station wagons. They were marketed as higher-level Plymouth offerings and came only with V-8 attachments. The cars were equipped with all the Belvedere options, plus several unique to the new series, such as a deluxe steering wheel with horn ring, lockable glove box, cigar lighter and disc wheel covers.

A Fury four-door hardtop was converted into the latest in a series of Chrysler turbine-engined cars, making a 576-mile cross-country reliability run.

Sport Fury was the highest Plymouth range of all, and was designated as their only 'premium' series. It was a hybrid luxury/performance model. Two body styles were manufactured, a sports coupe and a convertible, available only with 'Sport Fury' or 'Golden Commando' V-8 power. The Sport Fury V-8 developed 260 horsepower at 4400 rpm, as opposed to the 230 generated by the regular V-8. Golden Commando 395 V-8 produced 305 horsepower at 4600 rpm. The huge torque generated by Golden Commando necessitated a beefed-up transmission.

Standard equipment for the model included everything the Fury had, plus swivel front seats, sport deck lid tire cover and custom padded steering wheel.

Engine: Sport Fury V-8, overhead valve

Displacement: 317.6 cid

Horsepower: 260 at 4400 rpm

Transmission: three-speed manual transmission, with PowerFlite automatic as an option (standard with Golden Commando V-8)

Compression Ratio: 9.0:1

Weight: 3670 lbs

Wheelbase: 118 inches

Base Price: $3125

Number Produced: 5,990

■ *Right: The Sport Fury Convertible was new for '59, with huge tailfins to emphasise its improved performance.*

Pontiac Catalina Convertible   1959

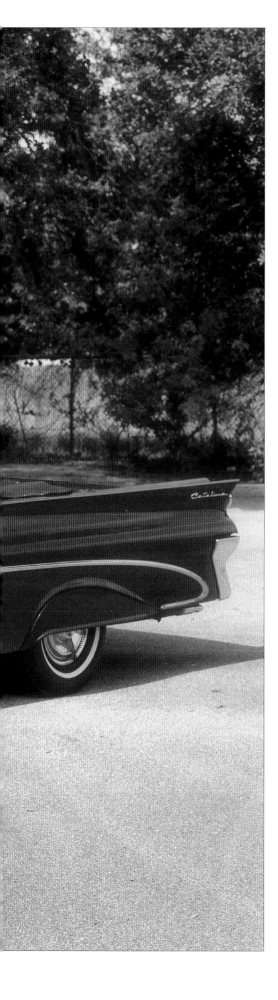

Major styling changes followed Harley Earl's retirement from GM, nowhere more so than at Pontiac. Their handsome 'Wide-Track' models and reputation for performance cars really appealed to the '59 buyers and motor journalists alike, and the company leapt to fourth position in the car producers' league (with an output of 383,320 cars, representing a 6.9 per cent market share). Motor Trend Magazine voted Pontiac as the 1959 'Car of the Year'. The new styling included longer, lower bodies with more interior room, crisp twin-fin rear fenders, 'V' contour hoods, increased glass area and a new twin grille theme. This latter element was destined to become a hallmark of the marque. In fact, all of the GM models shared a basic bodyshell in this model year, but styling was so different from division to division, that the finished products remained completely distinctive.

The old Chieftain model line was renamed 'Catalina' which was now used as a series, rather than a body style designation. Pontiac's new name for the pillarless hardtop coupes was 'Vista'. The cars were cleanly trimmed, with simple 'sweep spear' moldings and undecorated projectile flares. Standard equipment for the series included turn signals, electric wipers, dual sun visors, dome lamps, a cigarette lighter, dual headlamps, front and rear ashtrays, coat hooks, dual horns, tubeless tires and an interesting-sounding instrument panel Snak Bar.

The '59 instrument panel was even glitzier than that of the previous model year, and being virtually all bright metal could literally dazzle drivers on a sunny day. 'Buckety' front seats in a patchwork of many colours were also available, and the overall effect was dramatic.

Seven body shapes were available in the range from the two-door convertible in our photograph to a nine-seat four-door station wagon. The latter had a fold-away third row of rear-facing seats. A couple of El Camino-like pick-ups, 'El Catalinas' as they were nicknamed were also built using the series chassis. Nearly all the '59 Catalinas were fitted with Hydra-Matic (221,622 versus 9,939).

The 1959 Pontiacs were successful in the year's stock car races, and victorious at the Daytona 500 and Darlington 500. The 280 horsepower Catalina Sport Coupe (two-door hardtop) was road tested doing 0-60 miles per hour at 8.8 seconds, or 16.9 seconds over the quarter mile.

■ *Left: This top-spec Catalina Two-door Convertible looks fantastic in co-ordinated red.*

Engine:	V-8 overhead valve, cast iron block
Displacement:	389 cid
Horsepower:	280 at 4400 rpm
Compression Ratio:	10.0:1
Weight:	3970 lbs
Wheelbase:	122 inches
Base Price:	$3080
Number Produced:	14,515

1960 Buick LeSabre Convertible

Buick arrived in the '60s, having experienced a difficult end to the '50s, and their fifth decade of production. They had found themselves completely out-of-step with the market, offering massive cars with unpopular styling just when the recession-struck customers were looking for smaller and more economic cars. The wild styling of the '59 line had lacked any frame of reference to the earlier Buick models. It had been coolly received in the showrooms, and the company had slipped down the auto producers' league. From a production of nearly three-quarters of a million cars in 1955, production plunged to fewer than quarter of a million units by the end of the decade, or 4.2 per cent of the auto market. They began the '60s in ninth position, which was the company's lowest since 1905.

Buick decided to take radical measures, and dumped the names of their entire product range. Goodbye Roadmaster, Special (until 1961), Limited and Century. Hello LeSabre, Invicta and Electra. A new President, Edward D. Rollert was also committed to resolving the quality problems that the company had experienced.

Buick was committed to retaining the unpopular basic body of '59 for the '60 models, but a heavy restyle blunted the paper-fold edges, and smoothed the lines of the new models into a much softer look, whilst clipping the wild fins. For 1960, Buick introduced 'Three magnificent series: Buick LeSabre – Buick Invicta – Buick Electra'.

The LeSabre Convertible headed up Buick's entry-level model range, and gained slightly improved sales. The two-door LeSabre sedan was their price-leader from the seven models in the range. Classic Buick ventiports appeared in trios on the front fenders, and a bright lower body molding accented the car's other bright metal. The cars were equipped with a luxurious Custom interior that included deep-pile carpeting, a padded instrument panel and optional deluxe door handles, window cranks and armrests. All of the cars had Mirromagic adjustable speedometer and instrument dials, electric windscreen wipers, cigar lighter, dual sunshades, Step-On parking brake, dual horns and a single-key locking system. Mechanically, the car was fitted with finned aluminum brake drums for 'complete reliability' and responsive turbine drive transmission. Power steering and brakes were optional. The car exemplified the best of Buick for 1960, with 'The serene feel of security at Buick's All-time Best'

Engine: V-8 overhead valve, cast iron block

Displacement: 364 cid

Horsepower: 250 at 4400 rpm

Compression Ratio: 10.25:1

Wheelbase: 123 inches

Base Price: $3145

Number Produced: 13,588

■ *Right: Ventiports were back at Buick in 1960, here gracing the LeSabre convertible.*

1960 Chevrolet Corvette

The 1960 Corvette was the best yet, not because of substantial change, but carefully considered modifications. A complete restyle had been scheduled for this model year, but never made it from the drawing board due to financial constraints. Chevrolet produced 10,261 Corvettes in 1960, cracking the break-even point for the first time in its eight-year life. After Ford enlarged its Thunderbird to a four-seat, square body, Ed Cole had hoped that disaffected two-seater enthusiasts would come over to Corvette, but not so many of these materialised.

Ed Cole was still the car's engineer, and William L. Mitchell was in charge of design. He had become senior Vice President of GM in 1958 at the age of 46, having started as a stylist in the company 22 years earlier. His father had sold Buick cars for the group, and filled his office with his son's fantastic drawings of classic cars. When he got the senior appointment, Mitchell's first action was to change the name of the department from styling (which implied a superficial add-on) to design (essential to the car's identity). His motto was 'Be Brave'.

The existing '58-'59 body was retained for 1960, with its sweet and cheesy grin and classic cove in silver or white. Half were sold with a detachable hardtop, slightly more than half with the optional four-speed manual gearbox. In his quest for reduced weight, engineer Duntov attempted to replace as many steel parts as possible with aluminium and set to work trying to produce aluminium cylinder heads. But these proved too unreliable to be used on the production model. However, his work on the handling was much more successful. The heavy-duty springs were deleted, the diameter of the front antisway bars was increased, and one was added at the back of the car.

A RPO (production racing option) was offered on the car, with quickened steering and sintered-metallic brake linings inside drums cast with large cooling fins. The top engine option was fitted in this option package, with 290 horsepower. In the production models, tachometers, sun visors, dual exhaust, carpeting, outside rearview mirror and electric clock were fitted as standard.

Racer Briggs-Cunningham entered three 1960 hardtops into the 24 Hour Le Mans race, known as the 'Sting Rays', that had been specially prepared by Alfred Momo (assisted by Chevrolet's Frank Burrell and Zora Duntov). The team reached eighth position. One car reached 151 miles per hour on the four-mile long Mulsanne straight. This racing season established the Sting Ray as the racing Corvette, a beautifully balanced car to the eye and on the road.

Engine: V-8 overhead valve, cast iron block

Displacement: 283 cid

Horsepower: 230 at 4800 rpm

Compression Ratio: 9.25:1

Base Price: $3872

Number Produced: 10,261

■ *Right: The 1960 Corvette was available in eight exterior finishes, black, white, turquoise, blue, silver, green, red and maroon.*

Chrysler 300 F

1960

Chrysler improved their production by 25 per cent in 1960, but remained at twelfth position in the auto producers' league. On the corporate level, Lester L. Colbert replaced William C. Newberg as President of Chrysler around midyear in 1960, but was forced to resign in a matter of months.

A new Chrysler era began in 1960, as production was switched to welded monocoque unit bodies. The 'Uni-Body' cars were styled with a new trapezoidal grille, sloping tailfins, boomerang-like taillights, a false spare wheel cover on the trunk lid and white sidewall nylon tires. But the major changes were on the engineering side. A major feat being the introduction of ram-induction manifolding, which acted like a turbocharger on the performance of the car.

The 'sixth in a famous line' edition of the letter series 300 was introduced in this model year, continuing its tradition as a high-performance musclecar. The huge engineering advances applied to the car seemed to return the model to the fierce heritage of the first Letter cars, built for performance, not parading. Besides its all-new styling and unibody construction, big engineering improvements were also evident, with the unveiling of a Ram-Tuned induction manifold option. Two different horsepower versions were available in 1960, 375 for road cars, or an optional RPO 400. A limited number of nine ten cars (including a very rare convertible) were built with the 400 horsepower engine and a French 'Pont-a-Mousson' four-speed gearbox. Inside the car, the extraordinary AstraDome dashboard made its appearance – a bizarre glass bubble illuminated by avant-garde electrical luminescence. All New Yorker features were included on the car, plus power swivel bucket seats.

The 300F Special Gran Tourismos continued the racing career of the Letter cars by winning the first six places in the Flying Mile competition at Daytona, with driver G. Ziegler achieving a top speed of nearly 145 miles per hour. B. Shaw and H. Faubel were also team drivers. Between them, the Chrysler drivers obliterated the times set by a 300B at Daytona in 1956. These were the 'Pont-a-Mousson', short Ram equipped models, the only Letter cars fitted with factory air conditioning. Perhaps they can be fairly described as the ultimate Chrysler 300 Letter car of all time.

■ *Left: This rare 300F is now the most sought-after Letter car ever, and the most expensive to buy. It weighs in at about two '59 Eldorados.*

Engine: Overhead valve V-8, cast iron block

Displacement: 413 cid

Horsepower: 375 at 5000 rpm

Compression Ratio: 10.1:1

Wheelbase: 122 inches

Base Price: $5811

Number Produced: 248 (plus 964 Hardtops)

Dodge Dart D500

Dodge introduced a new crest in 1960, but more importantly, the structure of their entire model range was revised with new model names and target markets. In addition to the full-size Doge models, Chrysler also introduced the new 'downsized' Dart series, with a shorter, 118-inch wheelbase.

The newly introduced low-priced Dart was Dodge's big seller for 1960, and doubled their sales for the year (367,804 as opposed for 156,385). Dodge ran the model head-to-head with Plymouth, and almost achieved their rival's output for the year, hindered as their opponents were by their rather old-fashioned 'jukebox on wheels' styling. The Darts were built on the same wheelbase length as the Plymouth models.

Dodge's basic rationale in entering the Darts onto the market had been to compete directly with the 'big three' manufacturers (Ford, GM and Chrysler). The Dart was also the forerunner to their compact models of 1961. The Seneca was the entry-level model, and boasted Chrysler's new overhead valve 'Slant Six' engine, which was destined to be a corporate mainstay for three decades. The other Dart engine option was the 'A' block, small series V-8.

The Darts had a unitised body/chassis that was designed to give the car greater rigidity. Body styling remained recognizably Dodge, but the Darts were slightly more subdued in their trim than the other Dodge models. The side styling was simple with a single horizontal chrome strip, beginning at the front wheel well and ending at the rear bumper. The headlight 'eyebrows' disappeared, to be replaced by chrome bezels. The taillights were also surrounded by chromed bezels. Dodge also offered an unprecedented, long line of luxury extras, including air conditioning.

The Darts were tiered in three levels of trim. The Seneca was the base model, the Pioneer intermediate, and the Pheonix the top-of-the-range. All three tiers were available with the D-500 performance option, a 361 or 383-cid V-8 engine with cross-ram induction and dual four-barrel carburettors giving a supercharged effect. 1960 was the epitome of it's power, the engine was detuned in '61. A D-500 modified Dart Pheonix, driven by Norm Thatcher set three world records at Bonneville in the 'B' class races for supercharged gas coupes. The supercharged 383-cid V-8 equipped Dart achieved a top speed of 191.8 mph.

■ *Left: D-500 was a performance option available for all three levels of Dart trim.*

Engine: V-8	
Displacement: 381 cid	
Horsepower: 310 at 4800 rpm	
Compression Ratio: 10.0:1	
Wheelbase: 118 inches	
Base Price: $2607 (plus $418 for D-500)	
Number Produced (all Darts): 306,603	

1960 Ford Edsel

The Edsel line-up had been drastically cut back for '59, down to ten models, but the advertising slogan of the year 'Makes History by Making Sense' had fallen completely flat and only 44,861 cars were built in the year. A substantial number, as it turned out, compared to the meagre 2,846 cars sold in 1960.

The 1960 Edsels were put on sale on October 15 1959, now limited to seven car options, plus two Villager series station wagons. The ad slogan for the year was 'New – Nifty – Thrifty'. In fact, the Edsels of this year were little more than face lifted Ford Fairlane. The bodies were completely new to Edsel, with a lower silhouette that was also longer and wider. They came straight from Bud Kaufman's Ford design studio. Many engineering advances were also introduced, including horizontal coolant flow in the radiator. New styling was fairly conclusive to the distinctive appearance of the marque, as using an elaborate die-cast grille meant dropping the unfortunate horse-collar grille that is now so synonymous with the car. The Edsel side trim for '60 was also borrowed, strongly resembling that of the 1959 Pontiacs. The unusual headlight treatment made them look as though they were floating in front of the chrome grid. A one-piece front bumper was used for the first time, and the rear bumper was also a single piece. In fact, it was so difficult to tell the cars apart from their Ford parents that counterfeit Edsels are now produced. Ironically the lack of success for the '60 Edsel range means that the cars are now rare and valuable.

Standard power for all 1960 models was the 292-cid V-8 with the six-cylinder engine available as a delete-option in all models except the convertible. The larger 300-cid V-8 was also an option at extra cost. The cars were quite successful in their position just above the low-priced three, and gave good value for money. Automotive News awarded the car their plaudit of 'Best Buy' for 1960 domestic cars.

Despite Henry Ford II's assurances to the remaining Edsel dealers that the brand would be a permanent member of the Ford family of cars, Ford announced that Edsel production would cease on November 19 1959. The reasons given were poor sales and steel shortages. They had said that they were going to support the model for the long term, but obviously decided that this would mean sending good money after bad. All the 1960 models were actually constructed in 1959, at the Louisville Kentucky, factory.

So the Edsel line came to a disappointing end, after surviving for only three model years, and an output of 110,847 units.

Engine: V-8 overhead valve, cast iron block

Displacement: 292 cid

Horsepower: 185

Compression Ratio: 8.8:1

Number Produced: 777

■ *Right: This two-door Ranger sedan was the entry-level model for the final year in which Edsels were offered for sale. Thirty-eight two-tone combinations were available to order.*

1960 Ford Starliner

All three main Ford lines were completely redesigned from the ground up in 1960, and introduced to the public in October 1959. The square-bird Thunderbird retained it existing body. At this time, the new thinking in the US auto industry wasn't tending towards high performance, but to the compact market. Interest in performance kicked in later in the decade. But apart from the little Falcon, that promptly ran away with the compact market, all of the Fords other new models were sold on their size and roominess.

Only the engines and drivelines were retained from the previous Ford model year, the rather controversial styling was completely new, and was one of the smoothest model year designs ever to come from the Dearborn drawing boards. The new models were longer, lower and wider than earlier cars, and trim was restrained compared to many market offerings for this year. All the cars featured a single chrome strip that swept from the top of the front bumper all the way back to the small horizontal fin at the rear of the car. Large semi-circular taillights were housed in an aluminium escutcheon panel directly above a large chrome bumper. At the front of the car, a new meshed grille housed dual headlights.

The Galaxie model was essentially FoMoCo's sporty people mover. It was available with powerful engines and sporty styling. The cars were also drag-strip performers, and regularly outpaced their Thunderbird stable mates. They were considered one of the first muscle cars of the decade. The Galaxies were introduced in 1959 as the crème de la crème of the Ford range, although it was hard to tell apart from the Fairlane's in this model year (even by price). But the cars were given completely new bodies in 1960, and were easier to tell apart from other Fords by their unique rear quarter-panel ripples.

The re-designed Galaxie and Galaxie Special series were the top trim level cars for 1960, and included the Starliner (two-door hardtop) and convertible Sunliner. The five Galaxie and Galaxie Special models were available with both standard six-cylinder and 292-cid 'Y' block V-8 engine options, and were categorised as two series according to engine type. A four-door Town sedan, two-door Club sedan and four-door Town Victoria were also available in the series.

Engine: Ford Six-cylinder

Displacement: 223-cid

Horsepower: 145 at 4000 rpm

Compression Ratio: 8.4:1

Wheelbase: 119 inches

Base Price: $2610

Number Produced (six-cylinder and V-8 models): 68,641

■ *Right: The simple styling of this Starliner hardtop shows the unusual lateral styling of the tailfins.*

Plymouth Sonoramic Commando 1960

By the mid-fifties, Plymouth had an excellent reputation as a very reliable family car was long and well established. But this was becoming fairly ordinary, so the car-buying public began to look for new selling points from the auto industry, technical advances and styling changes.

Plymouth entered a difficult decade for the company in 1960. Their sales plummeted during the sixties, with only brief recoveries. The rather ugly tailfins of the 1960 Savoy, Belvedere, Fury and Suburban Plymouth models ensured that they were rather coolly received by the market. But things didn't improve with the introduction of the compact models in '62, which the buying public shunned in favor of larger Ford and Chevy models.

However, 1960 was a significant year for Plymouth in several regards. It was the final model year for the famous, unattractive 'fins' (or stabilizers as they were called in the sales literature. The cars were also the first manufactured with the 'unibody' construction. This offered weight and material savings over the then conventional body-on-frame construction. It also stiffened the body. This is a practically universal construction method used to this day.

Technically, 1960 also saw the introduction of two legendary engines. The slant six, and the Sonoramic Commando V-8, complete with the cross-ram induction intake manifold, the Plymouth version was available on the 383 and 361-cid 'B' engines. These were first introduced as race tune engines for use in the NASCAR series, then as 'Street Hemi' production options. The package also included heavy-duty suspension and oversized brackets. Richard Petty raced these to three Plymouth victories at the NHRA Nationals in Detroit. His winning time for the quarter mile was 14.51 seconds at 87.82 mph.

Our photographed car is the two-door Belvedere hardtop sedan, which was also available with the slant six-cylinder engine and the standard Plymouth V-8. The Sonoramic Commando option added a further $389 to the base price of the model, plus a further $211 for the necessary Torqueflite transmission. The passenger car Belvederes had the model script on the rather bizarre front fender 'coves' and three shield medallions on the tailfins.

■ *Left: The Belvedere is ornamented with the 'Sonoramic Commando Power' badge on the front fender – or, as they were called in the '60s, 'scare emblems'. The badge continued to be used in '61.*

Engine:	Sonoramic Commando V-8
Displacement:	383-cid
Horsepower:	330 at 5000 rpm
Transmission:	Torqueflite
Induction:	Dual four-barrel carburetor
Weight:	3505 lbs
Wheelbase:	118 inches
Base Price:	$2545
Number Produced:	14,085

Pontiac Ventura

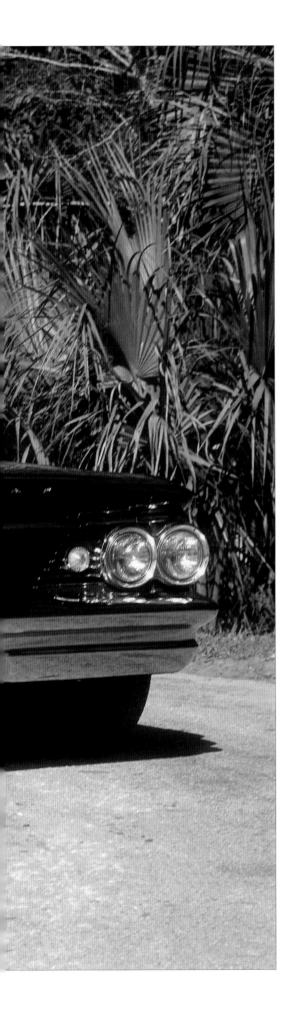

Starting with the 1959 models, the image of a sporty, youthful car with appeal across the spectrum of car buyers emerged at Pontiac, in sharp contract to its previous 'dull but reliable' image. This resulted in a six-year period in which the company's output was dominated by low-slung, 'Wide-Track' full-size performance cars that performed well in the sales league, and on the track.

Pontiac's major styling changes for the 1960 line included undivided horizontal bar grilles, straight full-length side trim moldings, and a new deck lid that seemed to almost rest on the fenders. The base Catalina models, of which there were seven, had plain beltline moldings. Standard features included turn signals, an oil filter and five tubeless tires. Ironically, the divided grille that had been evident in 1959 was to return and become a trademark of the division. The Catalina range was Pontiac's sales leader for 1960. The new cars were introduced to the public on October 1 1959.

The Ventura model range cars were effectively custom-level Catalinas. They were offered in two options – a four-door Vista Hardtop and a two-door hardtop, both models sold fairly equal numbers, which totalled 56,277. Venturas shared the short wheelbase of the Catalina models. They also had plain belt moldings. Venturas had all the Catalina features, plus custom steering wheel, electric clock, deluxe wheel discs, full carpeting, triple-tone Morrokide seats, right-hand ashtrays and special décor molding.

Nearly all of the cars were fitted with Hydramatic automatic, only 2,381 were built with synchromesh gears.

Pontiac produced 396,716 cars in 1960, to reach fifth position in the automakers' sales league. This gave them a 6.6 per cent share of the market. 1960 was also the year when Pontiac began to assert itself in the NASCAR racing series, of which they won four. Jim Wangers also drove a 1960 Pontiac to the NHRA 'Top Eliminator' title. Mickey Thompson, on the other hand, fitted four Pontiac engines in his Challenger I World Land Speed Record car and drove it at 363.67 mph... How things had changed.

■ *Left: This two-door hardtop Ventura features the single-year undivided grille theme.*

Engine:	V-8, overhead valve, cast iron block
Displacement:	389 cid
Horsepower:	283 at 4400 rpm
Transmission:	Hydra-Matic
Compression Ratio:	10.25:1
Body Style:	Two-door Hardtop
Weight:	3865 lbs
Wheelbase:	122 inches
Base Price:	$2971
Number Produced:	27,577

1960 Chevrolet Corvair Wagon

Semon E. 'Bunkie' Knudsen was Chevrolet General Manager in this year, and he steered the company back to number one position in the auto producers' league. The introduction of the compact Corvair was the big news at Chevrolet for 1960, and it may well have heralded the origins of the most significant American model range of the post-war era. Initially, the car was only available as a four-door sedan, but the Corvair turned out to be a revolution in American car design, with its rear-mounted, air-cooled, aluminium six-cylinder engine (echoing the German Volkswagon), front luggage trunk, fully-independent coiled spring/swing axle suspension and clean styling. The length of all the cars in the range was contained at 180 inches overall. By comparison the compact rivals from Ford and Plymouth (the Falcon and the Valiant) were merely scaled-down versions of larger models.

Initial sales were disappointing, but the introduction of two-door models, and the luxurious Monza Club Coupe in the middle of the year sent sales shooting up. The luxury interiors and bucket seats of the Monza, combined with its agile handling, effectively established the market niche for the entire Corvair line, as economical sporty cars, rather than small family compacts. The range quickly developed a loyal following amongst auto enthusiasts, and the Corvair was nominated as 'Car of the Year' by Motor Trend Magazine. The Corvair models continued to multiply, and by '61, there were a total of eight options in three ranges (500, 700 and Monza 900), including two four-door station wagons, a van-type sports wagon and three half-ton trucks. Promoted as the lowest price Chevys, but badged as Corvairs, the series sold nearly 300,000 units in the 1961 model year.

The Lakewood 700 station wagons were part of the mid-priced six-cylinder Corvair range, and wore '700' nameplates on the cowl side of the fenders. The Lakewood was fitted with all the base equipment for the range, with plusher interior fittings, and exterior chrome decal. The model appeared in both the 500 and 700 Corvair ranges. With the back seat folded, the station wagon had 58 cubic feet of load space. The 500 version of the Lakewood appeared just once for '61.

Despite the sales success of the Corvair range, its handling was considered so unpredictable, that it very unflatteringly inspired Ralph Nadar's expose of the dangers posed by contemporary American cars in his book 'Unsafe at Any Speed'. The book itself influenced a raft of US auto safety legislation that continues to be introduced to this day.

Engine: Horizontally opposed six-cylinder, overhead valve, aluminum block

Displacement: 144.8 cid

Horsepower: 80 at 4400 rpm

Compression Ratio: 8.0:1

■ *Right: This Lakewood station wagon sports the two-tone paint option, available for $11.*

1961 Chevrolet SS 409

The production Chevrolets for '61 followed the General Motors pattern in adopting a brand new downsized body, but they also retained the engineering, contrary to the other GM divisions. The front grilles were generally rather flat and square, whilst the Impalas were instantly recognisable at the back by their triple taillight treatment and crossed racing flags insignia in the center of the rear deck.

The company manufactured 1,604,805 units in the year, to keep them at number one in the auto producers' league. This included a modest 142 Impalas equipped with Super Sport equipment, but though they were few in number, these cars really carried the torch for Chevy's continuing love affair with the musclecar. They showcased the car's top specification for unrivalled looks and performance, and charmingly described themselves as having been designed 'for young men on the move... (who) won't settle for less than REAL driving excitement'.

Chevrolet had been the first US car manufacturer to offer real power to the masses with 'the hot one' back in 1955. The 409 was the inheritor of this mantle of power, identified by its massive horsepower and identified by the capacity of its engine the mighty 396 cid V-8 developed 409 horsepower. The car was an immediate hit, and the car quickly made its way into popular culture, celebrated in Brian Wilson's Beach Boy lyrics in 1962 ('She's real fine, my four-oh-nine' – complete with engine noise on the backing track). The original engine had been conceived in '58, carved

■ *Below: The 1961 Sport Coupe body was the perfect base for the Super Sport.*

from the classic Chevy 'W-head'. But the block was actually recast to increase the bore, and new forged aluminium pistons were fitted in pairs. A forged steel crank was fitted, together with reinforced connecting rods, and aluminum bearings. A massive Carter AFB four-barrel pumped air into the engine, and a Delco-Remy ignition sparked the heady air and gas mixture. This all boosted output to 360 horsepower. A stiffer sway bar at the front, sintered-metallic brake linings, heavy-duty springs and shocks, power steering and brakes all contributed to the feel of a really hot car, and were included in the LPO (Limited Production Option). Zero to 60 miles per hour took only seven seconds.

The exteriors of the cars were equally impressive, their image super cool, with Special Super Sport Trim, tri-blade spinner wheelcovers and narrow band whitewalls. Inside, the cars were equipped with a padded dashboard, and a grab bar across the glovebox. A 7000-rpm tachometer on the steering column was fitted as standard.

The 1961 Impala SS established Chevrolet's SS dynasty, and was the performance buyers' dream until 1969.

Engine:	W-head V-8
Displacement:	409 cid
Horsepower:	360 at 5800 rpm
Transmission:	Muncie four-speed manual
Compression Ratio:	11.25:1
Induction:	Single Carter four-barrel carburetor
Body Style:	Two-door Hardtop Sports Coupe
Number of Seats:	5
Weight:	3,737 lbs
Wheelbase:	119 inches
Base Price:	$3,500 (approximate)
Number Produced:	142

1961 Dodge Polara D-500

The 'new for '61' Dodges didn't sell at all well. Their styling was controversial, and some dealers even rejected the division's offerings for the new model year. Sales went down to just over a quarter of a million cars, falling away by over 100,000 units from the previous year and Dodge dropped three places in the league of auto producers to ninth position.

The downsized Darts remained as Dodge's bestseller for '61, when a heavy facelift made the car look more like the company's senior models. Their rather bizarre 'reverse slant' tailfins were a dubious Dodge idea that appeared for this year only. Dodge also introduced the compact Lancer in a three-level model range in '61.

The Polara (RD1) was now the only full-sized Dodge series on offer, with the classic 122-inch wheelbase. Six models were offered in this complete range. This senior line assumed a Dart look-alike appearance with an identical grille, though its taillights were deeply recessed. These were contained in the wraparound sweep of the tailfins, and looked like nothing less than jet plane exhausts. The model trim featured chrome moldings around the front windshield and rear window and a split chrome side strip with a contrasting aluminum insert. An odd 'Flight Sweep' trunk lid wheel cover was also optional.

The standard engine fitted to the line was the 265 horsepower 361-cid V-8, with an optional 383-cid version. The D-500 V-8 and Ram-Induction D-500 V-8s were also available as optional extras for the Polara. Both featured an unusual intake system with two Carter AFB four-barrel carburettors mounted on a 30-inch long intake manifold. The carburettor mounted on the right (over the valve cover) actually fed the left bank of the engine and vice-versa. The extremely long manifolds produced incredible low-end torque. This was known as the 'Sonoramic' long ram engine.

Polaras have a great following today, they look like the essence of '60s space travel on wheels, with their bizarre styling and sputnik-like ornaments. The equipment nomenclature of the line thoroughly reinforced this impression, with its 'MirrOMatic' rear-view mirror, 'Satellite' revolving clock, 'Tower Bank' front seats and 'Astrophonic' radio.

Engine: V-8 overhead valve, cast iron block

Displacement: 383 cid

Horsepower: 325 at 4800 rpm

Compression Ratio: 10.0:1

Weight: 3765 lbs

Wheelbase: 122 inches

Base Price: $3252

Number Produced: 14,032 built in 1961

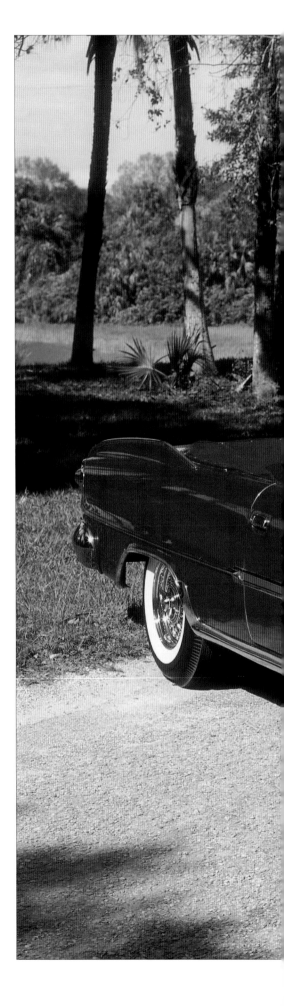

■ *Right: The Kelsey Hayes wire wheels and whitewall tires set off the sporting good looks of this D-500 equipped convertible.*

1961 Ford Galaxie Sunliner

The year 1961 saw the third major restyle of the full-sized Fords in as many years. From the beltline down the cars were completely new, but the upper body structure was retained from the previous year. The new front-end styling was highlighted with a full-width concave grille with a horizontal dividing bar. At the back, the Galaxies were fitted with tiny tailfins. A similar chrome strip was used to that in the previous year, and was complemented by a ribbed aluminium stone guard on the Galaxies.

The horsepower race was back up and running by '61, and Ford and Chevrolet were becoming increasingly competitive. Chevy was in front, and Ford strove to catch up by introducing all kinds of technical innovations, such as fuel injection in '57. But the Automobile Manufacturers Association ban on factory racing involvement (designed to promote greater car safety) badly affected Ford in the late fifties. This was because the company followed the AMA edicts to the letter, whereas other producers, such as Chevrolet and Pontiac, continued to support their performance programs as though nothing had happened.

But by 1960, the 'Blue-Oval' boys were back in the race for real, and began designing bigger and better engines for the high-performance cars they wanted to re-introduce to the market. Going through several stages of V-8, Ford finally arrive at their first 400 horsepower engine via a dealer-installed 6V induction system. This consisted of three Holley two-barrel carburetors, which could be dropped straight into the space vacated by the 375/390 horsepower engine with single-carburetor intake. This option was available for an extra $260.

Among the first drivers to take advantage of this big beast was drag racer Les Ritchey, who went racing at the 1961 NHRA Winternationals, with a top speed of 105.5 miles per hour at the wheel of his 401 horsepower Ford, despite its great weight of two tons.

This big new engine option was offered on all 1961 Fords, except for the extensive range of stations wagons, including our Sunliner convertible from the Galaxie range. The engine elevated the car from being a big cruiser available with all the usual kit (fender skirts, continental kit and special hubcaps) into a performance beast with 'No Lag. No Drag. Just flashing power'. The Sunliner was truly one of Ford's 'Lively Ones' complete with modern Borg-Warner transmission, beefed-up suspension and strengthened brakes.

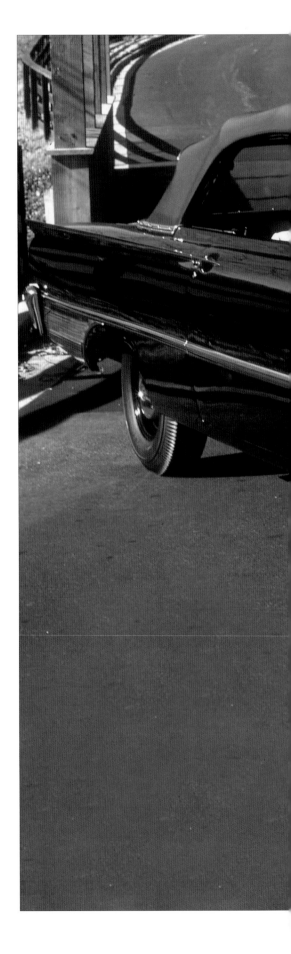

■ *Right: The '61 Sunliner was complete with Ford's top-shelf Galaxie-line trim, and was a flagship for the series.*

Engine: FE series V-8

Displacement: 390 cid

Horsepower: 401 at 6,00 rpm

Compression Ratio: 10.6:1

Wheelbase: 119 inches

Base Price: $2,847

Number Produced: 44,614

Lincoln Continental

The Continental was one of those ultimately rare cars that became a classic almost as soon as it was introduced. As part of FoMoCo, the company adopted the corporate styling for much of the '50s, but the prestigious Continental model reappeared in its Mark II incarnation in 1956. This model captured the spirit of the original car, but was thoroughly modern in design.

Lincoln's reputation was diminished by the enormous cars the company produced between 1958-60. In some states, the cars were obliged to carry red reflectors at the back of the car, and amber clearance lights at the front. The cars were widely criticised for their sheer bulk, and the beautiful and stylish models of the early '60s were a reaction against this. The 1961 Continental was a classic example of how beautiful an American production car could be. The car was so successful that the basic styling for the model was retained until the Mark III Continental was introduced in the 1969 model year.

The benefit of this consistent styling was the so-called 'Continental look', that not only made the cars themselves instantly recognizable, but was also used to make other Ford models 'classier' and more desirable.

The Lincoln-Continental was the only series offered by Lincoln in '61. What a series it turned out to be, proving that the company had not lost its ability to make beautiful cars. The model became one of the most influential of the decade, and was awarded a bronze medal by the Industrial Design Institute. The Continentals were now offered in just two versions, a four-door sedan and a four-door convertible. The four headlights were embedded in a criss-cross pattern grille, and the front and rear bumpers blended well in to the overall design. Side trim was discreet, limited to a full-length upper body molding and a chrome rocker panel. The rear doors opened to the center. All 1961 Continentals were automatics, and were fitted with a radio with rear speaker, heater, power brakes, power steering, power windows, walnut appliqué or padded instrument panel, carpeting and power door locks as standard. Sixty-five per cent of the '61 cars were also fitted with optional air conditioning.

Quality control for the cars was extreme - every new Continental was subjected to a twelve-mile road test before it left the factory.

■ *Left: The 1961 Continental was one of the most stylistically influential cars of the sixties, and was awarded a bronze medal by the Industrial Design Institute.*

Engine: V-8, overhead valve, cast iron block	
Displacement: 430 cid	
Horsepower: 300 at 4100 rpm	
Compression Ratio: 10.0:1	
Weight: 4927 lbs/5215 lbs	
Wheelbase: 123 inches	
Base Price: $6067/$6713	
Number Produced: 25,160	

1961 Pontiac Catalina Super Duty 389

Bunkie Knudsen moved to Chevrolet in 1961, and Estes took over at Pontiac. Under his able management, the division continued to grow both in sales volume, and performance reputation. The Tempest, a radical new compact model introduced in 1961, projected the company to number three in the autoproducers' league with its great success. Traditionally, this was a hot spot for competing manufacturers, but Pontiac managed to dominate this rung on the ladder for most of the decade.

The Super Duty performance cars ended Pontiac's formerly staid image forever, preparing the ground for the GTO models that came later in the sixties. Jim Wangers, winner of the 1960 'Top Eliminator' title, was a Pontiac promotions guy who drag- raced the company cars in his spare time. He and group of keen young Pontiac engineers were instrumental in bringing the Super Duty race-car options together. By their very nature the Super Duty Pontiacs were limited-production special options. The Catalinas were most often fitted out with the racing package, being the smallest and lightest cars full-size cars in the Pontiac stable.

The 1961 version used the 389 cid (6.1 liter) Super Duty engine, and took Pontiac to success in 21 of 52 NASCAR Grand National stock car races. But the omnipresent threat of the big Chevy 409 engine meant that engine power was increased to 421 cid (6.3 liters) in 1962, becoming the ultimate Super Duty engine option. It was strengthened with forged pistons and four-bolt main-bearing caps. The strength was no more than the engine required, as it developed a reputed output greater than 500 horsepower. In 1963, the engineers added a McKellar solid-lifter camshaft with dual-valve springs and transistorised ignition. This brought the rating right up to 550 horsepower. To maximise the effect of this huge power output, the cars were radically lightened, with reduced-weight front ends, aluminium bumper brackets, trunk lids and radiator supports. Even the glass windows could be changed to plexiglass as a dealer-fitted option. Most radical of all were the so-called 'Swiss Cheese Catalinas' with holes drilled into their chassis. This option reduced the weight of the car to an extraordinarily low 3325 lbs (considering the weight of the extra go-goodies). A Swiss Cheese Super Duty car with full providence would now be worth in excess of $100,000. So the Super Dutys reached the epitome of their developmental success, just in time for GM to impose a factory-sponsored racing ban.

Engine: Super Duty V-8

Displacement: 389 cid

Horsepower: 348 at 4800 rpm

Compression Ratio: 10.75:1

Wheelbase: 119 inches

Base Price: $2766

Number Produced: 14,524

■ *Right: This simple Catalina belies the power under the hood.*

Buick Skylark

Production climbed in 1961 to a 5.28 per cent market share, and eighth in the industry production rankings. But things went much better in '62, Buick sold more cars than in any year since 1956 – 415,892 units for a 6 per cent share of the market, and rose to sixth in the league of producers. Buick introduced the first production V-6 (developing 135 horsepower) on their entry level Special series, which gave them a price advantage in the burgeoning small domestic car market. It would be the first in a long line of Buick V-6s. The car won 'Car of the Year' for 1962.

The Skylark name had first appeared at Buick in 1953, on a limited edition model. From being part of the Special series in '61, Buick launched the name as a complete two model series for '62, a hardtop and a convertible, both with improved power. The Skylark range would ultimately serve as the basis for the mighty Buick GS line. It was their top compact range for the year, in a year that compact models were taking a bigger slice of the American market. Buick launched six series in all Special, Special Deluxe, Skylark, LeSabre, Invicta and Electra. The car's styling reflected that of the senior Buick models, and followed market trends with the installation of bucket seats. In fact, this trend was reflected in 14.3 per cent of the cars bought in this year as sporty 'personal cars' became more popular. Their styling was slightly refined for the year, and a power top convertible model was added to the range midyear.

The two-door hardtop Skylark was a true hardtop with no side window, and hugely outsold the convertible, more than four to one. Buick had abandoned torque tube drive in 1961, and now offered a four-speed manual option on the V-8 Skylarks (although three-speed was fitted as standard). At the same time, Buick changed the position of the starter. The new custom exterior styling included front and rear bumper guards, turbine wheelcovers, classic Buick ventiports (though these were now lozenge-shaped, rather than round), wrapped taillamp housings and a lower body bright rocker. A Skylark badge was positioned on the front fender. Skylark interiors were all-vinyl, and equipped with a heater and defroster as standard. Other luxuries included padded cushions, a deluxe Skylark steering wheel, front and rear carpeting, dualhorns/sunvisors/ armrests and a cigarette lighter. 1962 was also the year in which Buick launched its bid to get back into the power race with the Wildcat 401 cid engine.

■ *Left: The elegant two-tone Skylark hardtop looks almost like the series convertible, with its slim roof pillars and absence of side window.*

Engine:	V-8 overhead valve, cast iron block
Displacement:	215 cid
Horsepower:	190 at 4800 rpm
Compression Ratio:	11.0:1
Base Price:	$2787
Number Produced:	34,060

Oldsmobile Starfire

Oldsmobile were at number five in the automakers' league for 1962, on a production of 428,853 units. Oldsmobile was somewhat upstaged in the performance arena of the late '50s by the introduction of the Chrysler Hemi and high-winging Chevrolet V-8, but continued to manufacture solid, popular and comfortable cars. The company also re-asserted itself in the high performance stakes with its introduction of the tri-carb-based J-2 option that was offered on most models.

Like so many other US automakers, the early sixties Oldsmobile models looked as though they had just landed from outer space. Mid-1961 saw the introduction of the Starfire convertible that started the swing to big sporty cars. The car was fitted with standard 'buckety' front seats, and hard-to-see tachometer. The car was equipped with abundant bright trim, this had been limited in the other GM ranges for '61, but was more in evidence at Oldsmobile. Starfire became a separate range for '62, after the positive reception to the initial model in the previous year. The Holiday hardtop coupe was added to the big bucket-seat ragtop, and immediately outsold it, virtually five to one. The two cars were Oldsmobile's attempt to corner a greater share of the personal/luxury car market. To compete with the other cars in this market, they were deliberately well-equipped with all the hardware of the less expensive Olds models, plus sports console, Hydra-Matic automatic with console shifter, power brakes, power steering, brushed aluminum side trim, a dual exhaust with fiberglass packed mufflers and leather upholstery.

The big technological news at Olds for '62 was the introduction of America's first production turbocharged V-8 engine. It was launched in mid-season as the 'Turbo Rocket', and fitted to the new Jetfire coupe. Featuring 'fluid injection', the 215-cid engine-block pumped out 215 horsepower, and had lively acceleration. But initially, the engine had some reliability problems that somewhat curtailed sales.

■ *Left: This Convertible Starfire sold roughly the same number as the original '61 model.*

Engine:	V-8
Displacement:	394-cid
Horsepower:	345 at 4600 rpm
Transmission:	Hydra-Matic automatic
Compression Ratio:	10.50:1
Induction:	Rochester 4GC four-barrel
Body Style:	Two-door Convertible
Weight:	4488lbs
Wheelbase:	123 inches
Base Price:	$4744
Number Produced:	7149

1963 Chevrolet Impala SS

Chevrolet launched their widest ever range in 1963, and sold three out of every ten cars in America, over 2,300,3000 units (including Corvette and Corvair). This output was 700,000 cars more than that of closest rival, Ford. Bunkie Knudsen was still at the helm of the division. This was a vintage year for factory drag racing options, and the Chevelle launch year. At the other end of the model range, the full-size Impala was the 'upper crust' Chevy model. It was the only '63 model to receive new sheetmetal, and looked elegant and uncluttered. Impala had started life in the late fifties as a model in the Bel Air series, and soon became instantly recognisable by their triple taillight treatment. A large range of options were available for the car, including the RPO Z11 race ready package.

Impala was Chevy's largest seller, and their plushest car had most of the equipment standard on lower lines. They also had bright aluminium front seat end panels, patterned cloth and leather grained vinyl upholstery in color-coordinated materials over thick foam seat cushions. A sport-style steering wheel was fitted, and other extras included an electric clock, parking brake warning lamp, and dashboard face panels in textured bright metal. The Super Sport (RPO Z03) trim was up-rated for '63, with the addition of special chrome spinner hubs, extra emblems, matching cove inserts, bucket seats and a locking storage compartment (when the transmission was upgraded to four-speed or Powerglide automatic). Super Sports also had the option to fit the Turbo-Fire 409-cid V-8, and most of these fitted in '63 were installed on this model. This was just one of six V-8 options that were available, producing between 250 and 430 horsepower, all the way from mild to wild. The biggest engine was available only with the Z11 package, and was the prototype for the spectacularly successful 396-cid V-8 of 1965.

Motor Trend Magazine road tested two Impala SS sport coupes with V-8 engines at both ends of the mild and wild scale – the 250 horsepower 327 and the newly introduced 340 horsepower 409. Both cars were installed with Powerglide automatic, power steering and power brakes. The tester found the automatic gears tricky on both cars, and slow to shift, but liked their performance in the acceleration tests. Of course, the 409-cid engine was much quicker, covering a quarter mile in 15.9 seconds, reaching 88 mph.

Engine: (Base V-8) Overhead valve

Displacement: 283 cid

Horsepower: 195 at 4800 rpm

Compression Ratio: 9.25:1

Wheelbase: 119 inches

Base Price: $2774

Number Produced: 399,224

■ *Right: This Impala two-door Hardtop Sport Coupe could be fitted with any one of six Chevy V-8s.*

1963 Chevrolet Corvette Sting Ray Zo6 Fastback Coupe

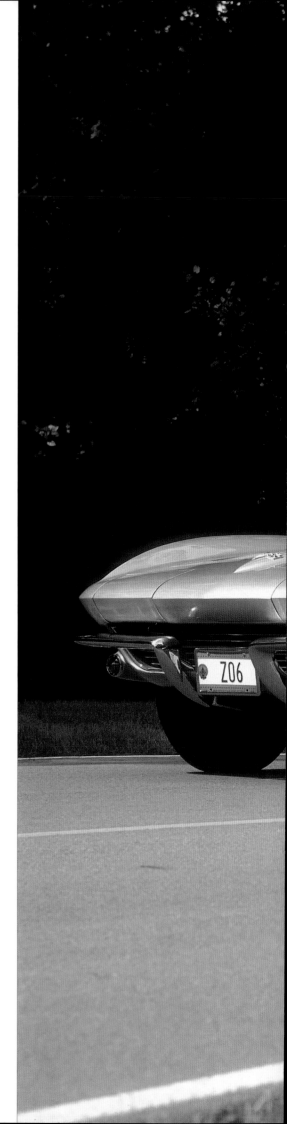

The 1963 Corvette turned out to one of the greatest ever, a brilliant synthesis of styling and performance. The cars were called 'Sting Rays' to emphasise that they were different to all the Corvettes that had gone before. The Sting Ray was the joint concept of design guru Bill Mitchell, and engineering genius Zora Duntov. Duntov had been a racing driver, and was very aware of the handling and performance of the car, while Mitchell wanted to inject the glamor of the European sports cars into Corvette. The contemporary Jaguars in particular are credited with influencing the sinuous, cat-like lines of the car. He himself drove an E-Type.

The Corvette received a major restyle in 1963, for the first time since its introduction ten years earlier. Two models were available for the first time. The traditional convertible, and the first Corvette coupe, introduced for the first time in this model year. This 'boattail' fastback would be the only Corvette ever to have the unique 'split' rear window, now highly coveted by classic car collectors. It gave the car the appearance of a kind of fish spine running the entire length of the car. Apart from this unusual feature, the rear deck view resembled that of the '62 body, but the rest of the car was unrecognisable from its predecessors. The headlights were hidden in an electronically operated panel. This was not a gimmick, but a serious attempt to improve the aerodynamics of the car. Corvette and Jaguar were two of the few marques to have grasped this concept in the early '60s. Corvette was the first manufacturer to introduce hidden headlights since the DeSoto of 1942. The recessed fake hood louvers were of the more superficial styling type, however. Mechanically, this was the year when Duntov introduced the famous ladder-frame chassis and suspension layout. The center of gravity for the car was lowered from nineteen to sixteen and a half inches (so that ground clearance was reduced to only five inches) and weight was evenly distributed between the front and rear axles. This gave the car both excellent road holding and ride quality. The interior had circular gauges with black faces. Windshield washers, carpeting, an outside rearview mirror, dual exhaust, tachometer, electric clock, heater and defroster, cigarette lighter, and safety belts were all fitted as standard.

The Sting Rays also hugely improved Corvette's performance in the market place, and the car sold over 22,000 units in the first year of this model.

Engine: V-8 overhead valve, cast iron block

Displacement: 327 cid

Horsepower: 250 at 4400 rpm

Compression Ratio: 10.5:1

Base Price: $4257

Number Produced: 10,594

■ *Right: This silver-blue Sting Ray was one of seven colours offered – the others were black, white, silver, Daytona blue, red and tan.*

1963 Chrysler New Yorker

Despite the fantastic reputation of several of its models, including the Letter cars and the New Yorker, Chrysler were struggling in '63, with falling sales in its fourth decade. They were at eleventh in the auto producers' league of output. Chrysler had finally abandoned tailfins in 1962, and there was a complete styling revamp for 1963. A tasteful slab-sided look evolved, with a minimal amount of trim. Chrysler touted this as its 'crisp, clean custom look'. But sales actually dropped and the company remained at eleventh position in the auto producers' league. A five-year or 50,000-mile warranty on the drive-train components was introduced as a marketing tool.

The 1963 New Yorkers displayed the crisp, new custom look expounded in the years advertising. They shared the 'C' body with the Newports and 300s. The new styling look gave the hood, fenders and rear deck a flat, wide look that contributed to the overall integrated styling theme. A thin beltline molding ran from front to back of the car, and the usual New Yorker trim bars were now found on the front fender, behind the wheel opening and below the New Yorker nameplate. The grille was divided into two halves, by a chromed centre bar, and egg crate inserts on either side of this, harking back to the models of the mid-fifties. The number of trim bars was reduced to six. In the interior, the car was embellished with deeply quilted luxurious Jacquard fabrics and soft vinyl trim. The New Yorker line included five model options.

Our featured car is the Salon option, a limited edition four-door vinyl-roofed hardtop with a luxurious interior, special side trim and Salon nameplates. The model was introduced as the top option in the New Yorker range, selling only a modest 593 examples. It is said that only 11 of these are still registered. The car had pillarless styling, unusual for a four-door car, with no 'B' pillar between the front and rear doors, and no framing around the window glass. In fact, there was absolutely nothing between the vent windows and the 'C' pillar at the back of the car. The Salons were fitted with leather interiors as standard, together with a load of power options including power steering, brakes, windows and door locks. Inside the car, Auto Pilot, air conditioning, seat belts, six-way power seats, an FM radio and cup holders were all fitted for a luxurious feel. Aficionados of the car say that it was the finest American car available for sale in '63.

Engine: New Yorker V-8, overhead valve	
Displacement: 413.8 cid	
Horsepower: 340 at 4600 rpm	
Compression Ratio: 10.0:1	
Wheelbase: 122 inches	
Base Price: $5344	
Number Produced: 593	

■ *Right: This Salon is stunning in Embassy Gold metallic paint, the only color advertised for the cars.*

1963 Ford Galaxie 500 427

Ford completely revised their full-size car range for the fifth year in a row. As in the previous year, the base model cars were devoid of any sculptural lines except for the beltline feature line. Each model name was carried in script on the fender immediately behind the front wheel opening. Once again, the taillights were large round units mounted at the top of the rear fenders with a stamped aluminium panel being used on the Galaxie 500 series.

There are several Galaxies model years that describe the top range as '500s'. The number does not stand for 500 horsepower or 500 cubic inch displacement. The leading rumour for the origination of the notation is the 500 miles as in the 500-mile stock car races in which the Galaxie models competed. The '63 Galaxie was a classic from the first day it rolled off the showroom floor, the car's distinctive lines and styling are timeless and are now among the most collected Fords of any era.

The Galaxie 500 series was the top trim level for the model in this year. The series contained sedans, hardtops and convertibles. The model was slightly more elaborately trimmed that the simply-styled base-model Galaxies, having an attractive full length upper and lower body side molding, and trimmed with chromed 'A' pillar and window moldings. There were also two horizontal chrome strips on the side of the car. Between the two chrome pieces, just in front of the taillights were six cast 'hash marks'. The 500 XL models were available as two- and four-door hardtops, convertible and midyear fastback model. The fastback featured a sporty new roofline with no post and Starliner type looks. The standard equipment on these cars was a deluxe offering with standard bucket seats and console, spinner wheelcovers, wall to wall carpeting, courtesy lights and contoured deluxe seat upholstery.

The 427-cid big-block V-8 was the most powerful engine option for the year. The high-performance race with other US manufacturers was in full swing by now, and this was the most powerful engine in Ford's entire history. It fully reflected FoMoCo's determination to sell more cars via racing successes. Two versions of the engine were introduced, a single four-barrel version at 410 horsepower and a dual four-barrel carburettor at an astounding 425 horsepower. Transmission types were the SynchroSmooth manual column shift, a four-on-the-floor manual, Ford-O-Matic Drive automatic and Cruise-O-Matic three speed automatic.

Engine: Thunderbird High-performance V-8

Displacement: 427 cid

Horsepower: 425 at 6000 rpm

Compression Ratio: 11.5:1

Base Price: $3268

Number Produced: 33,870

■ *Right: Options for the '63 Galaxie included power front seats, power windows/steering/brakes, padded dash/visors and Select Aire Conditioner.*

Ford Thunderbird 'M-Code' Sports Roadster

The Thunderbird was Ford's answer to the Chevrolet Corvette and debuted onto the market in 1955. It started out as a two-seat personal car, but was re-built as a four-seat model in 1958. This was the last time it would appear as a true two-seat car until 2002, but the Sports Roadster of 1962/63 was a partial return to two-seat styling. It seemed the perfect answer to the nostalgia felt for the original T-birds. The model was an attempt to revive the sporty appearance of the original 'personal' cars. It featured a fibreglass tonneau package (designed by Bud Kaufman), which covered the back seat of the car to give a two-seat appearance. The tonneau covered the twin front headrests and was 'flowed' from these to the back of the car to make the styling more aerodynamic. The convertible top could operate with the tonneau in position. The introduction of the Sports Roadster meant that the car buyer could purchase a sporty two-passenger convertible and four-passenger car in one and the same car.

For its second and final model year, the car received new doors and front fenders, and a bodyside crease. The Sports Roadster was fitted with a dash-mounted grab bar for the passenger, and four dazzling Kelsey-Hayes wire wheels. The rear fender skirts were deleted to allow clearance for the knock-off wheel centers. For performance fans, Ford offered a special 'M-code' 390-cid FE V-8 rated engine, rated at 340 brake horsepower. It was equipped with three Holley two-barrel carburettors and an aluminum manifold to keep the carbs level and at the same height. The 'M-code' option was rare, and only 145 Thunderbirds were ever built with this engine, including thirty-seven '63 Sports Roadsters.

Although the idea for the Sports Roadster was intriguing (it is usually attributed to Lee Iacocca), a combination of the model's high price and difficult tonneau-installation limited its sales. The price was so high, that the buyer could have a Cadillac Convertible for only $162 more. The Kelsey-Hayes wire wheels have also been blamed for the demise of the car, not only because they added expense (a whopping $372.30), but because they were blamed for causing wheel failure, extremely dangerous at speed. The best-known customer of the Sports Roadster, Elvis Presley, had a blow out accident at high speed that immediately hit the headlines. Ford discontinued the model in '63.

■ *Left: This 1963 'M-code' Sports Roadster is a very rare model, one of just 37 built.*

Engine: 'M-code' Thunderbird Special Six-Barrel V-8	
Displacement: 390-cid	
Horsepower: 340 at 5000 rpm	
Compression Ratio: 10.5:1	
Base Price: $5563	
Number Produced: 37	

Mercury S-55

1963

Mercury cars had first been introduced in 1939 as intermediate models, priced between Ford and Lincoln. The joint Lincoln-Mercury division was founded by Ford in 1945, and so it wasn't until the 1949 models appeared that Mercurys were able to shed their image as glorified Fords (at least for the moment). The youth-appeal of the cars was hugely improved when James Dean drove a Mercury in the cult movie Rebel Without a Cause. However, Fords and Mercurys shared body shells throughout the fifties, and early 60s so it was difficult for the marque to define itself. Later advertising also stressed the classy heritage of their stable-mate Lincolns.

Basic Monterey styling for the year was reminiscent of the 1961 models, with six taillights located in the rear deck panel, and a concave vertical bar grille housed four chrome-trimmed headlights. The Monterey Custom was the intermediate model for the year, and had additional chroming and standard features.

The 1963 Mercury Monterey S-55 was the top of the Mercury model line for this year, and was offered in four body styles – the two-door convertible, two-door Marauder Fastback Coupe, four-door Breezeway Hardtop sedan and the two-door Breezeway Hardtop. The unique and practical Breezeway roof, first offered in 1957 on the Turnpike Cruiser and reintroduced in this model year, featured a roll-down back window. The standard engine for the line was the Marauder Super 390-cid V-8, with four-barrel carburetor, but the Marauder 390 V-8 with two-barrel carburetor was available as a no-cost option. The Marauder Fastbacks were true muscle cars that were raced to victory in the 1963 NASCAR series, with 427-cid V-8s. They had been designed with aerodynamics and speed in mind. Transmission options for the production models were three or four-speed manual or Multi-Drive Merc-O-Matic automatic. S-55s were identified by marque insignia in front of the rear fender, chrome bars and special wheel covers.

The Mercury advertising slogan for '63 was 'Shift to the Real Performer! Go Mercury!' The S-55 was a real sizzler that delivered the luxury of the Monterey Custom series plus sports car features – individually adjustable bucket seats, bright-metal floor console with shift lever and storage compartment. Red and white courtesy lights were positioned inside the doors. When the doors were opened the interiors were revealed as deeply luxurious, complete with vinyl upholstery, front and rear armrests and a padded dashboard.

■ *Left: This S-55 hardtop looks cool in two-tone.*

Engine: V-8 overhead valve, cast iron block	
Displacement: 390-cid	
Horsepower: 250 at 4400 rpm	
Compression Ratio: 8.9:1	
Number Produced: 1203	

Pontiac Grand Prix

1963

The Grand Prix model was introduced to the Pontiac range in 1962, replacing the Ventura model (although Ventura-Catalinas were still available as a trim option). This first Grand Prix model was the top of the line sporty Pontiac for the year, and was available with a range of engine options. Sixteen Super Duty Grand Prix cars were built in the first model year, equipped with 421 V-8s inducted through twin Carter four-barrel carburettors. The Super Duty engine option could develop in excess of 400 horsepower, and were usually equipped with a four-speed manual transmission. The Grand Prix cars were identified by clean side styling, ornamented with a checkered flag badge in the rear concave section of the side spears. The cars also had a rocker panel molding, anodised grille insert and nose-piece and special rear end styling. The factory-fitted equipment included all the lower-model range Bonneville equipment (except the courtesy lights) and solid color Morrokide upholstery, bucket seats and a center console complete with a tachometer. A single model was offered in '62, a two-door hardtop. 30,195 were sold.

The '63 Grand Prixs were handsomely restyled from bumper to bumper. The new model brought glamor and performance to the division. The new car had a clean look with no side trim, and a grille that emphasised negative space with bright accents and enclosed parking lights. In fact, this grille was unique to the bucket-seated hardtop. The car also had grilled-over taillamps, that were mounted on the deck lid and a concave rear window treatment. Standard equipment continued to include the full list of Bonneville equipment, together with extra Grand Prix fittings. The standard engine for the model was the 389-cid V-8 engine fitted with the optional Tri Power carburetion (i.e. three two-barrel carburetors). The car boasted a smart interior, with bucket seats, console and Morrokide upholstery as well as a wood-grained dash and steering wheel. The elegant black-faced instrumentation and chrome bezels made the dash elegant and tasteful.

The Grand Prix badges were now mounted on the sides of the rear fenders and rocker panel moldings. A single two-door hardtop was still the only model on offer, but sales more than doubled at 72,959 for the year.

■ *Left: Unique eight lug aluminium wheels, as seen on this car, are now a hugely collectible option.*

Engine:	V-8 overhead valve, cast iron block
Displacement:	389-cid
Horsepower:	303 at 4600 rpm
Compression Ratio:	10.25:1
Weight:	3915 lbs
Wheelbase:	120 inches
Base Price:	$3490
Number Produced:	72,959

Ford Mustang 260

1964

The big news at Ford for 1964 was the introduction of the Mustang in April. As this was late in the model year, the cars are often known as '64-½s'. Lee Iacocca is attributed with its introduction, despite the reluctance of the Ford top brass. The Ford Studio team presented the original design in response to a brief set out by Iacocca. The cars were Ford's response to the improving economy of the early '60s, when consumers were looking for smaller cars complete with luxury and good performance. The car was designed with such clean, attractive lines that it was awarded the Tiffany Award for Excellence in American Design, the only car ever to be so honored. It was the right car at the right time, and went on to have spectacular success, selling over half a million examples in its first year of production. A million were sold in the first two years. An unbroken record to this day. This unprecedented achievement can be attributed to its clever combination of desirable features and striking design aimed at a large segment of the buying public. Not only did the Mustang spawn an entire class of family sports car, but an entire cohort of youthful Americans became known as the Mustang generation. In some regards, this is misleading, as it was the fact that the car appealed to such a large cross-section of age groups, which was the crux of its desirability.

The car was received with such a wave of universal enthusiasm that demand outstripped production for almost a year. Its combination of comfort, convenience, luxury and economy engendered a pride of ownership unmatched in this price bracket. Although the Mustang was the very first of the 'pony' muscle cars, it was first designed and marketed to be a low cost 'personal luxury' sports car. The initial production did not have serious performance engines. The base engine option was the six-cylinder 170-cid, developing a rather weak 101 horsepower. The base V-8 displaced 260 cid and developed 164 horsepower. The top V-8 option, the Challenger High-Performance (Hi-Po) engine was introduced in June '64. This powerplant developed a punchy 271 horsepower, and came with a special handling package, including fourteen-inch red line tires. Only 7273 Hi-Po Mustangs were built.

The original Mustang would diversify into an enormous range of variants, factory special editions, performance options and custom-built models. The streets of America were soon full of them.

■ *Left: This Skylight Blue Mustang is equipped with the base V-8 option.*

Engine:	V-8, overhead valve, cast iron block
Displacement:	260 cid
Horsepower:	164 at 4400 rpm
Compression Ratio:	8.8:1
Wheelbase:	108 inches
Base Price:	$2368
Number Produced:	97,705

1964 Lincoln Continental

The classic Continental model of 1961 had undergone minor re-styling in '62 (with the removal of the front bumper cars, use of a new type of individual headlight trim, and a new semi-honeycomb style grille treatment) and '63 (a different rear panel design and yet another grille treatment).

The '64 model followed the Lincoln tendency to grow a little; the wheelbase was now three inches longer than in the original. But styling changes continued to be mild and superficial. A new dashboard was incorporated into the interior, a full-length lower body molding added, together with flat side glass. This horizontal theme was continued with the trim at the rear end of the car, and the deletion of the thick center grille bar. This was replaced with five vertical bars. All Continental models continued to be automatic, and were equipped with radios, power seats, power windows, power brakes and power steering as standard. A moveable steering wheel was offered as an option, but this proved very unpopular and only seven per cent of buyers ordered this. More popular options included an air conditioner/heater, speed control, tinted glass, AM/FM push-button radio, power trunk lock, automatic headlight dimmer and directed power differential.

There were still only two Continental models on offer, the four-door sedan and four-door convertible. A single 430-cid V-8 engine option was fitted as standard. The model continued to be discreetly face-lifted, and to grew by a further 4.6 inches (in 1966), whilst being loaded with even more luxury options until the hardtop coupe Mark III Continental was introduced to the public in 1969. Essentially, this was a personal luxury car in the long hood, short deck tradition of the Mark I Continentals. The rear deck spare tire hump also recalled the earlier car. Nearly all of these cars were sold with optional air conditioning, and 83.8 per cent had vinyl hoods. The Mark III V-8 now became the standard engine for the car, with a displacement of 460 cid, and an output of 365 horsepower.

Engine: V-8, overhead valve, cast iron block	
Displacement: 430 cid	
Horsepower: 320 at 4600 rpm	
Transmission: Automatic	
Compression Ratio: 10.0:1	
Induction: Carter C3VE-9510B four-barrel	
Weight: 5393 lbs	
Wheelbase: 126 inches	
Base Price: $6938	
Number Produced: 3328	

■ *Right: This convertible Continental has wonderfully restrained styling and elegant lines.*

Mercury Comet Caliente 1964

Mercury celebrated its Silver Anniversary in 1964, and was at number nine in the auto producers' league with an output of 298,609 cars. The Comet models were produced by Mercury between 1960 and 1967. The original Comet series was based on the Ford Falcon platform of 1960. The sister cars shared many technical features, but the Comet had its own distinct bodylines, exterior ornamentation and interior trim. The first convertible Comet was introduced in the '63 line-up.

The Mercury Comets were extensively re-styled for 1964, with a Lincoln-Continental-style grille. The same theme was repeated on the rear deck panel. A wraparound trim piece was seen on the tips of the front fenders. Three thin, vertical trim slashes were on the sides of the front fenders. The signal lights remained embedded in the front bumper. Overall, the new squared-off bodyline, slightly longer than the earlier models, made the cars far more futuristic looking.

The 1964 range introduced new names to the Comet line-up, the Comet 202, Comet 404 and Caliente: three distinctive packages with the same bodylines and drivetrain components. The Caliente was the sports model Comet, with bucket seats. Six-cylinder and V-8 engines were available for the model, as were manual and automatic transmission options. The Cyclone was the ultimate Comet package with the V-8 engine as standard equipment and 6000rpm factory dashboard tachometer.

'Every bit as hot as it looks!' was how the sales literature described the Caliente series. The model trim consisted of a wide, full-length molding on its sides and a nameplate on the lower front fenders. The interior of the car was embellished with a padded instrument panel with walnut grain trim and deep-loop carpeting as luxury standard features. Caliente hardtops and convertibles were available only in solid colors. A third model, a four-door sedan was also on offer.

A team of customized Calientes, equipped with 289 cid/271 horsepower V-8s joined the Mercury muscle car club by travelling for over 100,000 miles at average speeds of over a hundred miles per hour.

■ *Left: The Caliente was the sports package Comet for 1964. This was the second year for a convertible Comet.*

Engine:	Six-cylinder, overhead valve
Displacement:	170 cid
Horsepower:	101 at 4400 rpm
Compression Ratio:	8.7:1
Body Style:	Two-door Convertible
Wheelbase:	114 inches
Base Price:	$2636
Number Produced:	9039

1964 Oldsmobile F-85 Cutlass 4-4-2

The F-85, launched in 1961, was the smallest Oldsmobile model in decades. It was a compact companion to the full-size Super 88 Holiday model, and strongly resembled this car. The four-door model, the coupe and the four-door wagons were sold in the $2300-$2900 range. F-85 output totalled 76,394 for this model year. The F-85s rode on a 112 inch wheelbase.

Sportiest of the new F-85 range was the mid-year, Deluxe-trim, bucket-seat pillared coupe called the Cutlass. This progenitor of a well-regarded Oldsmobile model name was priced at $2621 attracted 9935 sales. The car came with only one engine option – the 155 horsepower aluminum V-8.

Convertibles were added to the compact F-85 range in '62, in both base and bucket-seat Cutlass trim. The Cutlass model sold 9893. In 1963, Oldsmobile retained the trim options of the F-85s, but gave the car more of a big-car appearance, as the buyers had requested. The new Cutlass Sports Coupe hardtop was the bestselling model in the range, attracting 29,269 buyers with an attractive base price of $2592. All F-85 models were equipped with a 215-cid aluminum V-8 engine, rated with either 155 or 215 horsepower.

The F-85 went from a compact model to mid-size 'senior compacts' for '64, by adopting a handsome new 'A-body' platform, shared with several GM stablemates – the Buick Special and Skylark, the Pontiac Tempest and Le Mans and the new Chevy from Chevelle. It was completely redesigned, and gained a full eleven inches in length (just three inches on the wheelbase). The Sporty Cutlass now became a separate three-model series, which included a two-door coupe, two-door Holiday hardtop and two-door convertible. The $2784 Holiday hardtop coupe was the bestselling model in the range, with sales of 36,153. Cutlasses also now came with a new cast-iron 'Rocket' 330-cid V-8 making 290 horsepower. The aluminium block was a thing of the past.

1964 was also the introductory year for the 4-4-2 equipment package, at an extra price of $136, RPO code B09. This translated as four-barrel, four-speed and dual exhaust. Other equipment included a heavy-duty suspension, dual-snorkel air cleaner, oversized redline tires and special badges. The cars were also fitted with a heater/defroster, self-adjusting brakes, oil filter, front stabilizer and dual sun visors. Deluxe models also boasted a Deluxe steering wheel, padded dashboard and carpets. Interiors were vinyl or cloth.
The F-85 models were built in six Oldsmobile plants at Lansing, Atlanta, Kansas City, Linden, Southgate and Arlington.

Engine: V-8, overhead valve, cast-iron block

Displacement: 330-cid

Horsepower: 210 at 4400 rpm

Compression Ratio: 9.0:1

Number Produced: 36,153

■ *Right: This F-85 Cutlass Holiday hardtop was the best-selling model in the range.*

1964 Pontiac GTO

The original GTO package was initially offered for the LeMans sports coupe and convertible, but a hardtop was added to the line-up shortly after the launch. The LeMans were a sub-series of the Tempests, which were enlarged for this model year into a senior compact. The base powerplant for the line was a six-cylinder engine assembled by Pontiac Motor Division from Chevrolet-produced components. But this was a world away from the legendary 'Goat'.

The re-designed '64 Tempest body provided the ideal basis for the GTO, which effectively became America's first modern muscle car. Actually, it wasn't the hottest thing on the road, but it represented a powerfully attractive combination of power and affordability that thrust its way to the forefront of this market sector.

Pontiac General Manager Pete Estes had given the development of the GTO his enthusiastic blessing, and somehow managed to keep it away from the anti-performance top brass at GM long enough for the concept to emerge undiluted. Effectively, he bought John DeLorean and fellow engineer Bill Collins enough time to wait for the new '64 Tempest body, with its full-

■ Below: Dress-up features for this Tempest LeMans-based convertible included 'GTO' identification and a blacked-out grille.

perimeter frame and solid rear axle. Their fundamental idea was simple: take big-block engine and drop it into the lightest possible chassis, whilst keeping the price within reach of the average baby boomer. But as well as producing a car aimed at the youth market, Pontiac had also managed to produce a car for the general market by using a mid-sized body.

The multi-talented Jim Wangers, drag car racer and marketing guru, also worked with DeLorean on designing an appealing performance package. GTO was a tag borrowed from sports-giant Ferrari, which brilliantly encapsulated the aspirations of the package. The American public loved it with a passion. Pontiac sales manager Frank Bridge predicted that he would be able to sell 5000 examples of the GTO package, but 32,450 were actually ordered, and the production line failed to keep up with the demand. According to Car And Driver Magazine's David E. Davis, the GTO combines 'brute, blasting performance with balance and stability of a superior nature'.

Engine: Tri-Power V-8

Displacement: 389-cid

Horsepower: 348 at 4900 rpm

Compression Ratio: 10.75:1

Body Style: Two-door Convertible

Number of Seats: 5

Weight: 3360 lbs

Wheelbase: 115 inches

Base Price: $3400

Number Produced (With Tri-Power 389): 8,245

1964 Studebaker Gran Tourismo Hawk

Studebaker introduced the GT Hawks in 1962, and the introductory models had a squared roofline, no fins and rocker panel moldings. They were offered with six-cylinder engines, but these cars were only available outside North America. A 259-cid V-8 engine option was also offered in this market. American/Canadian GT Hawks came with a standard 289-cid V-8, which developed 210 horsepower. The Hawk name appeared on the deck lid and 'Gran Turismo' script appeared on the doors. Only one model was offered for the three years of GT production, a two-door hardtop.

The 1964 Gran Turismo Hawk had new, smooth deck lids and slightly restyled imitation side grilles. Their identifications were the same as in '62-'63, a vertical Hawk emblem in the center of the grille. A stand-up 'S' hood ornament was also fitted, but a decklid appliqués had been removed. The rear deck was now smoothed off, and a new red, white and blue round medallion added. A tremendous list of options were offered for the Gran Turismo, including a half-vinyl roof, rear deck lid radio antenna, aero strut wheel covers, door handle guards, visor vanity mirror, power steering, hill holder, air conditioning, white sidewall tires, tinted glass, transistor AM/FM push-button radio, Strato-Vue rearview mirror, license plate frames and rubber floor mats, locking gas cap, seat belts, windshield washer and adjustable shock absorbers.

As well as the standard engine option, GT Hawks were also offered with a 289 'Power Pack' V-8 that could develop 225 horsepower. Super Hawks had four larger engine options. Two 289-cid options were available, one developing 240 horsepower and the other 290 horsepower. Two 304.5-cid engines, developing 280 and 335 horsepower were also offered as options on this model. This was the final year in which Studebaker manufactured its own power plants.

A total of 1548 Gran Turismo Hawks were sold in this model year. The model was discontinued in '64, and did not appear again.

Right: This is the final year GT Hawk model

Engine: V-8 overhead valve, cast iron block

Displacement: 289-cid

Horsepower: 210 at 4500 rpm

Compression Ratio: 8.5:1

Induction: Stromberg Model WW two-barrel

Body Style: Two-door Hardtop

Weight: 3280 lbs

Wheelbase: 120.5 inches

Base Price: $2958

Number Produced: 1548

Studebaker (Lark) Daytona

As of January 1 1964, all Studebaker production took place at the Canadian plant, and the company was in negotiation with General Motors to buy in engines for their 1965-66 cars. Model year production fell to only 19,748 units, and the company fell to twelfth position in the auto producers' league. Avanti production had been discontinued in December '63, though leftover cars were on sale in '64.

The Lark name was de-emphasised in 1964, and was actually only being used in connection with the early Challenger and Commander models. Several new model names and a revised squared-up design were the major changes for this model year, including the Daytona range, which wore a neat new look. All the outer panels were new, their design was courtesy of Brooks Stevens. The overall length of the car grew by six inches. The grille became more horizontal, with an egg-crate center and integral headlamps, and a pointy new rear end carried high-set tail and backup lamps. Despite this, sales tumbled.

A new Daytona model was introduced, the four-door sedan. This joined the other three cars in the line-up, a two-door hardtop, four-door station wagon and two-door convertible. The new Daytona models were fitted with wide metal side moldings across the back of the deck lid, and had a standard circled 'S' hood ornament. Four power plants were available for the car, the 64S and SC-10 six-cylinder engines, and the 64V and VC-50 V-8s.

Studebaker's automotive division was in serious trouble by 1966. Calendar year auto production was down to a meagre 2.045 units. The corporation's other diversified holdings now represented the majority of the company's activities, and kept the corporation going. In mid-1967, the Studebaker Corporation purchased the Wagner Electric Corporation, and combined in the November of that year to form the Studebaker-Worthington Corporation. The car company had now effectively ceased to exist, with production terminating in March '66 ending 114 years of Studebaker tradition, and 64 years of car production. The only automotive survivor of the corporation was the Avanti. Two South Bend businessmen, Nathan Altman and Leo Newman revived the marque after the company left their plant in the town. They created the Avanti Motor Corporation, which was to subsequently pass through several changes of ownership.

■ *Left: This was the final year for the convertible Lark Daytona.*

Engine:	V-8 overhead valve, cast iron block
Displacement:	259.2-cid
Horsepower:	180 at 4500 rpm
Compression Ratio:	8.5:1
Induction:	Stromberg Model WW two-barrel
Wheelbase:	109 inches
Base Price:	$2797

Buick Skylark Gran Sport 1965

American car sales accelerated dramatically in the mid-sixties, partly encouraged by the launch of a host of tasty models by the big automakers and by the growth of the economy. Multi-car households were greatly on the rise, and the industry sold more than nine million cars for the first time in 1965. On the flip side of the market, some old names were on the way out, including Studebaker and Packard.

Buick slipped past both Dodge and Oldsmobile in 1965 to climb to fourth position in the automakers' league of production, with an output of 653,838 units. The 'Father of the Skylark', Edward T. Rollert moved to GM head office, and a new Buick General Manager, Robert L. Kessler, was appointed.

The son of the Skylark, on the other hand, took poll position as the epitome of the '65 Buick range. The Gran Sport was the top optional package for both three Skylark models (the two-door coupe, sport coupe and convertible) and the senior Riviera model ranges. The Riviera version was advertised as an 'Iron Fist in a Velvet Glove', the Skylark GS (a midyear introduction) as a 'Howitzer with windshield wipers'. Both cars were fitted with the Wildcat 401-cid V-8 engine 'Buick engineering wraps their potent 401 powerplant and super quick Turbine trans with a reinforced Skylark shell' proclaimed a contemporary article in Hot Rod Magazine. 'The Buick Gran Sport evolves as one of the hottest of factory-produced street/strip hybrids.' Indeed, many people view this model as Buick's first serious attempt to enter the muscle car market, although it also had a reputation for luxury and refinement. The 1965 Skylarks were plush with cloth and vinyl (or leather-grained vinyl) with bucket seats optional. Outside, the cars were adorned with unique coved styling on the exterior. This intermediate Buick range was very much aimed at the new market, which demanded both 'young' styling and high performance.

From a performance point of view, the engines produced 325 horsepower, with the addition of heavy-duty cross-flow radiators and dual exhaust manifolds with oversized pipes.

■ *Left: A red-filled Gran Sport badge on the grille of this 1965 Skylark Sport Coupe identifies the car with this elite Buick series.*

Engine:	Wildcat V-8
Displacement:	401 cid
Horsepower:	325 at 4400 rpm
Transmission:	Turbine drive automatic
Compression Ratio:	10.25:1
Induction:	Carter AFB four-barrel
Body Style:	Two-door Sport Coupe
Wheelbase:	115 inches
Base Price:	$2622
Number Produced (for Skylark model):	4501

Chevrolet Chevelle Malibu SS Z16 | 1965

Chevrolet had launched the Chevelle/Malibu range in 1964, anticipating a general improvement in the market for cars priced and sized below full-sized models – senior compacts. The car was placed between the compact Chevy II and the regular full-sized models, and was designed to take the same market share that the classic mid-size Chevys of the mid fifties had done. Projected demand was so high that Chevy even opened a new factory in Fremont, California. The model was quite square in it styling, but had curved side window glass and a 'wide' look that gave the range a distinctive new look. Eleven models were available in two basic lines called Chevelle 300 and Chevelle Malibu, with a convertible as an exclusive upper level offering. A Super Sport option was also released. The car had SS insignia, and bucket front seats were popular options.

For their second year, the Chevelles were mildly restyled. The nose was 'veed' slightly outwards and a new grille came in. At the rear, Chevy gave the line new taillights. The Chevelle Malibu SS 396 (RPO Z16) was the top-of-the-range car. It was aimed at a young, musclecar-obsessed market. Z16s were blacktop-bruising powerhouses, accurately described as 'one of the wildest pieces of equipment on wheels'. They were introduced as a special midyear package, and featured the 396- cid V-8 with dual exhaust and chrome accents. Mechanically, the cars were constructed on the stronger convertible frame, and fitted with special shocks and a brawny sports suspension with front and rear sway bars. Heavy duty cooling was also installed. The cars were also fitted with hydraulic power-assisted steering for more responsive handling, and power brakes. Fifteen-inch wide simulated mag style wheel covers were included in the package, and enhanced with Firestone gold line tires. Despite this, considering the power and cost of the upgrade to the Z16s ($1500), they were quite discreetly styled, and it was tricky to instantly differentiate them from the other Chevelles. The interiors also had an SS-396 emblem on the dashboard, and were equipped with a 160 mph speedometer and an AM/FM stereo multiplex radio.

Only 201 cars equipped in this way were built in '65: 200 hardtops and one super-rare convertible. Surviving Z16s are revered today as one of the most rare and powerful musclecars ever produced.

■ *Left: This Z16 looks good in Regal Red. The car was also available in Tuxedo black and Crocus Yellow.*

Engine: V-8	
Displacement: 396 cid	
Horsepower: 375 at 5600 rpm	
Wheelbase: 115 inches	
Base Price: $4091	
Number Produced: 200 hardtops, one convertible	

1965 | Chevrolet Corvette Roadster

The Year 1964 has seen the birth of the 'sporty compact' Ford Mustang, but as the advertising slogan of 1965 proclaimed, 'Corvette is America's one true sports car'. Even so, these first 'pony cars' had more 'youth appeal' than any other car on the road at this time with the exception of the Corvette. The Sting Rays were now offered in two body styles, five engines and three transmissions, so the car came in a good many configurations. These ranged from the plush for the 'boulevardier' to the seriously sporty for the 'aficionado' and several in-between options. The car itself was getting increasingly sophisticated in both appearance and driving enjoyment.

Every Corvette now came with four-wheel disc brakes (although drums were available as a minus cost option), fully independent suspension, retractable highlights and a bucket-seated interior. The big mechanical change for '65 was the introduction of a big block V-8. This was the height of the musclecar era in America and performance (together with 'think young' styling) was the driving force behind the phenomenal success of Detroit in this period. Introduced midyear, the engine that was to become known as the Turbo Jet came with up to 427 horsepower. In fact, it was so big that an impressive power bulge appeared on the hood lid. This 'W' engine had been used for five years already in Chevy saloons, and on the NASCAR circuits in '63. For some strange reason, Chevy had decreed that medium-sized cars like the Corvette should not have engines with a higher displacement than 400 cid, so the engine was sleeved down to 396. To handle the power of the Turbo Jet, the Borg-Warner gearbox was replaced by a home grown GM model. Manufactured at Muncie, Indiana, it became known as the 'Muncie Box'. A beefed up clutch and cooling system were also added. Duntov had to rebalance the car due to the increased engine weight, but managed to do so with characteristic precision.

The car itself had cleaned up looks, with very limited ornament. The look was more uncompromising and rather less sinuous than the early models, more piscine than panther, perhaps. The front fender vents certainly had a look of shark gills, and would become a mainstay of Corvette design. This all led to Corvette seats reaching another new high of 23,562 cars.

Engine: (standard) V-8, overhead valve

Displacement: 327 cid

Horsepower: 250 at 4400 rpm

Compression Ratio: 10.5:1

Wheelbase: 98 inches (175.2 overall)

Base Price: $3212

Number Produced: 15,377 convertibles

■ *Right: This yellow convertible with goldwall tires has a detachable hardtop (optional at $236.75). Other colours available were black, white, red, blue, green, silver and maroon.*

1965 Mercury Comet Cyclone

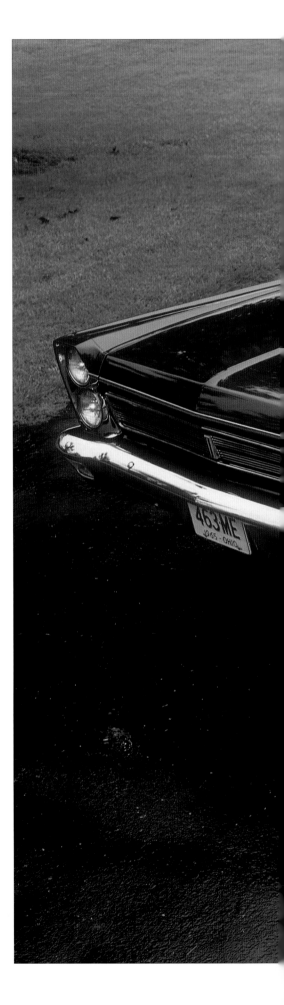

Mercury announced the first Cyclone Comet as a new mid-year model in 1964. It was available in only one body style, the two-door hardtop. The cars were equipped with a special exterior trim, which was very restrained. The car only had decoration on the wheel well moldings, a rocker panel molding and the letters C-O-M-E-T on the rear fin. A special insignia with the word 'Cyclone' and a checkered flag adorned the lower section of the front fenders. The wheel covers were made of stainless steel, which gave the appearance of chrome. The Cyclone was considered the first 'macho' Comet model. Sales literature referred to the V-8 engine 'under the hood, a whiplash of surging power' and of the 'masculine feel of black vinyl in the instrument panel'. Macho or not, the blurb also pointed out that, as a safety feature, the 'bucket seats are contoured to hold you more securely in turns'. Inside the cars, a three-spoke steering wheel, tachometer and console were fitted as standard. Even the engine was decorated with special chromed parts, including air cleaner, dipstick, oil filter, radiator cap and rocker arm covers.

7,454 Cyclones were sold in their first year of 1964. Mercury continued the Cyclone model in 1965, but made several changes to the car. Cyclones were still only available as a two-door hardtop, but styling was overhauled. The checkered flag emblems were moved to the rear fenders. The stainless steel wheel covers remained, but the interior upholstery options were updated. The cars were offered with vinyl roofs, curb moldings, a distinctive grille design and revised tachometer.

The standard Cyclone engine for 1965 was a 200 horsepower version of the small block (289-cid) 'Cyclone V-8', with two-barrel carburetion. An up-rated 289 V-8 engine, the 'Super Cyclone', with 225 horsepower, was also offered as an option. Both engines were offered with the 'dress-up' chrome of the '64 cars. Cyclones were also offered with a 'macho', but simulated, twin air scoop hood in fiberglass.

The cars had a great reputation for reliability, with the exception of the clutch, which sometimes began to slip at around 10,000 miles. Many owners changed these to the heavy-duty Cobra clutch that offered a permanent solution to the problem.

Engine: Cyclone V-8, overhead valve

Displacement: 289 cid

Horsepower: 200 at 4400 rpm

Compression Ratio: 9.3:1

Wheelbase: 114 inches

Base Price: $2625

Number Produced: 12,347

■ *Right: This '65 model is painted in a special Cyclone colour, Cypress Green Iridescent.*

1965 Mercury Park Lane

Mercury was at ninth position in the auto producers' league for 1965, on a production of 346,751 units manufactured. The Park Lane had returned to the Mercury line-up in 1964 as the top-of-the-line series. A wide band of tire-level chrome trim, running across the bodysides, set it apart from the other Mercury models. Its interior featured nylon face, biscuit-design upholstery and large walnut-tone panel inserts. The Park Lane convertible, like the Monterey version, came with a retractable glass rear window in a Breezeway roof.

The 1965 advertising for the Mercury models were described as being 'In the Lincoln Continental tradition', meaning that they were to be raised to new levels of luxury. The write-up also extolled the car's 'beautiful proportions, confident stance, elegant appointments. And its thoughtful touches'. Ford group vice-president Lee A. Iacocca was put in charge of a program to improve Lincoln-Mercury sales. He was keen to identify the line with the prestigious Lincoln reputation, but this didn't really become apparent until the 1969 model line-up.

■ *Below: This convertible Park Lane is in Porsche Red with red vinyl interior – one of five color choices.*

The 'king-size' 1965 Park Lane models had three new styling features - rectangular rear fender nameplates, chrome gravel shields and a band of molding above the rocker panels. They were equipped with more luxurious interiors than other Mercurys, including a padded dashboard, padded visors, courtesy lights, visor-mounted vanity mirrors plus a trip odometer.

A total of 32,407 Park Lanes were sold in 1965, and four body styles were offered in the range. The Breezeway was a sedan with slanting and retractable rear window. Then there were two Marauder models, a four-door hardtop fastback and a two-door hardtop fastback. A two-door convertible concluded the line-up. As well as the tilt steering wheel, locking differential and crinkle all-vinyl bucket seats, and the abundance of wood grain trim, the most important aspect of the convertible model was the Breezeway glass rear window. The advertising claimed that the window was made from 'special pliant (real) glass'. What is that?

Engine: Park Lane V-8

Displacement: 390-cid

Horsepower: 300 at 4600 rpm

Compression Ratio: 10.1:1

Induction: Ford C5AF-9510E four-barrel

Body Style: Two-door Convertible

Number of seats: 6

Weight: 4013 lbs

Wheelbase: 123 inches

Base Price: $3526

Number Produced: 3008

Plymouth Belvedere Satellite   1965

Plymouth was back in the big league by '65, having recovered from the disastrous compact model introduction of '62. They were at number four in the table of auto production, on an output of 728,228 cars. It was at the end of this model year that the fourteen-millionth Plymouth rolled off the production line. The generic Plymouth advertising slogan for the year was 'Plymouth presents the roaring '65s'.

For this model year, the standard 1962-64 Plymouth was restyled into the mid-size Belvederes. In fact, the Belvedere nameplate was no longer used to designate the level of trim and equipment, but was now used to classify the intermediate size Plymouth ranges. They utilised the same platform that Plymouths had used the previous year. The Belvederes were now offered in three model tiers. Three Belvedere I models were the base-level offerings for the range in this model year and had fairly limited standard equipment and trim. The higher level Belvedere II models (there were five of these, ranging from a convertible to a nine-seat station wagon) were far more luxuriously appointed, with carpeting, special trim and upholstery, foam cushions and back-up lights. The exterior trim was also more generous.

The sporty Satellites were now the premium level cars in the Belvedere range. They were introduced rather tenuously, as the 'New Way to Swing Without Going Out on a Limb'. The cars were endowed with rich and sporty characters, fitted with all the equipment of the Belvedere I and II models, plus front bucket seats, center console, full wheel covers and all-vinyl trim on two-door hardtop model. The side trim moldings apparent on other models were deleted, but louvers were added to the rear fenders and rocker panel moldings were used, as were trimmed wheel openings and a rear panel beauty strip. Two Satellites were available - hardtops or ragtops.

Belvederes were now fitted with column-mounted gear shifters, instead of the derided push-button models. As well as the slant six, a whole range of V-8 engine options were available for the '65 Belvederes – the 318-cid, 361-cid, 383-cid and 426-S (wedge head). Plymouth also built a relative handful (actually 27) Belvederes powered by the 426-cid/425 horsepower Hemi V-8. At an extra $1105, these cars were aimed solidly at the professional auto racer. Styling for these cars was a revamp of the '64 body, with single headlamps and a crossbar grille superimposed over a rectangular mesh background.

■ *Left: This Satellite Convertible has almost exactly the same roofline as the Hardtop model.*

Engine:	Plymouth V-8, overhead valve
Displacement:	318-cid
Horsepower:	230 at 4400 rpm
Transmission:	TorqueFlite automatic
Compression Ratio:	9.0:1
Number Produced:	1860

1965 Pontiac Catalina Convertible

tacked headlights continued on Pontiac's all new big '65 models, as did the performance oriented '2+2' package option. 2+2 was only available for the big Catalina convertible and the semi-fastback Sport Coupe hardtop. The package had first been introduced to the Catalina range in 1964, and was the first such performance option to be offered by Pontiac on the full-size models. The 2+2-adapted cars were marketed as a sort of giant five-seat luxury sports car with a long list of technical and luxury choices '...as fine as you want – or as fierce'. The top '64 engine option was a 370 horsepower version of the 410-cid V-8, which came fitted with Tri Power (three two-barrel carburetors). However, the weight of the car topped 4,000lbs, which tended to slow things down, somewhat.

Power for the 2+2 option was up-rated in the following model year, but when comparing even the revised performance of the package with the GTO option, it has to be said that even this sporty package wasn't quite as spectacular in these bigger cars as it had been on the smaller GTO models. Even so, the '65 2+2 option cars came fully loaded with a 338 horsepower, a four-barrel 421-cid V-8 fitted as standard that developed 338 horsepower at 4600rmp. Hardtops fitted with this engine could achieve 0-60 mph in 7.4 seconds, and the quarter mile in 15.8. This engine option was available for an extra price of $108 - $174 on other Pontiac models. The 2+2 421 was offered in three different strengths, including a top-rated 421, capable of 370 horsepower equipped with Tri Power as in '64. With this version fitted, the cars could achieve 0-60 mph in just over seven seconds (7.2) and the quarter mile in 15.5. Hydra-Matic automatic transmission came fitted as standard with the package.

The basic problem remained the weight/power ratio. The entire Pontiac range became bigger and wider for 1965, wheelbases lengthened to 121 and 124 inches, and the Wide Track chassis was wider than ever. The 2+2 Catalinas were muscle cars, but only just. Other styling changes for the '65 Catalina models included twin air-slot grilles, V-shaped hoods with a prominent center bulge, curved side-glass and symmetrical 'Venturi' contours with fin-shaped creases along the lower body. Coupes and convertibles with the 2+2 package were trimmed with '421' engine badges on the front fenders, 2+2 numbering on the rear fenders and deck lid, and simulated louvers behind the front wheel cut-outs.

Engine: V-8

Displacement: 421-cid

Horsepower: 338 at 4600rpm

Compression Ratio: 10.5:1

Weight: 3795lbs

Wheelbase: 121 inches

Base Price Catalina Convertible: $3103

■ *Right: The 2+2 Catalinas were musclecars, but only just. Hindered by their weight/power ratio, they were no contest for the GTOs*

Cadillac Eldorado

S afety was becoming an issue in UC car making by 1966. The Department of Transportation was set up, and The National Traffic and Motor Vehicle Safety Act and The Highway Safety Act were both passed by Congress.

Despite the fact that industry volume eased to 8.6 million cars in '66, Cadillac, the most distinguished name in US car production, enjoyed its first year of manufacturing more than 200,000 units. This enabled the company to reach eleventh position in the league of auto producers. It was the company's fifth record sales year in a row, and it turned out that 1966 was to be the best sales and production year yet. Indeed, productivity was also at a record level. An unprecedented number of cars, (5,570) were produced in one week in December '66, and in one record day in October, no less than 1,017 cars came off the Cadillac production lines.

A minor facelift was given to all the '66 year models at Cadillac, including a new bumper, grille and more integrated taillight housing. White sidewall tires were also fitted to the cars. Variable-ratio power steering was a new option, as were carbon-cloth seat heating pads. The Eldorados were the top-of-the-line model for the year, and Fleetwood type trim was seen again on this year's model. Finless rear fenders had appeared in 1959, on a long, low and luxurious body, and this look was retained for '66. Soft Ray tinted glass was available as an option. The interiors of the cars blended fabrics, leathers and walnut in a tasteful welter of luxury. The Eldorado was available with bucket seats at no extra cost, and leather upholstery was available in a delicious range of colours – green, black, white, midnight blue, gold, vermilion and antique saddle. A six-way power front bench was fitted as standard. Mechanically, the cars were full of power-operated options, including power-operated cent panes, automatic level control, cruise control and power-operated door locks.

Little change had been in evidence with the model year Fleetwood Eldorado and it turned out that the car was to be the final rear-wheel car in this line. Cadillac had decided that it was time for something completely new, and a brand new front-wheel drive Eldo arrived in the following year with completely new 'sports' styling. This car built on the unrivalled heritage and reputation of the marque, and it strengthened Cadillac's dominance of the upper end of the US car market.

■ *Left: The last of the rear-wheel drive Eldos, the '66 model nevertheless maintained the line's reputation for luxury and performance.*

Engine:	V-8 overhead valve, cast iron block
Displacement:	429 cid
Horsepower:	340 at 4600 rpm
Compression Ratio:	10.5:1
Wheelbase:	224.2
Base Price:	$6631
Number Produced:	2,250

1966 Chevrolet Corvair Corsa

Chevy trailed Ford production for the second time in the decade in 1966 – though only by a modest 6000-odd units. Both companies topped an output of 2.2 million cars, despite industry volume contracting to 8.6 million. Over at Corvair, the GM bosses mandated that there should be no further changes from the complete restyle of 1965, so the cars remained little changed. But the Corvairs remained desirable semi-sports cars and still looked terrific. In fact, its smooth-lined restyle package was to influence all the GM styling for years to come. The range had also been given a mechanical overhaul in '65 with the addition of a revised rear suspension (to correct the tendency of the cars to over-steer), and a turbocharged option.

The Corsa had been introduced as the top-of-the-line model in 1965, more richly equipped than the Corvair 500 and Monza lines, but hugely outsold by both of these. The Monzas had effectively saved the Corvair range from extinction on its introduction in 1960. It was outselling every other Corvair range by the following year. Like the Monza, Corsas were only available with 164-cid six-cylinder engines. But the Corsa engines were fitted with four Rochester carburetors that enabled them to develop nearly fifty per cent more power.

1966 marked the final appearance of the Corsa option. In its last season, the sporty high-performance Corsa clung to the few visual distinctions that set it apart from the less expensive Monzas. The car's standard interior equipment included bucket seats, carpeting, glovebox light, fold-down rear seat, ashtrays and rear seat foam cushions. The Corsa was equipped with full instrumentation, including tachometer, oil pressure gauge and temperature gauge.

The Corvair range as a whole sold 103,743 units in 1966, but production was slowed down to 73,360. In fact, the writing had been on the wall for the entire range since Ford had introduced its Mustang in 1964, whose raunchy performance was preferred by the public. Chevrolet also contributed to the drying up of demand for the Corvairs by introducing the Camaro in 1967. 'Unsafe At Any Speed' – Ralph Nadar's expose of the Corvair's poor handling, hadn't helped sales, and these plummeted to unacceptable levels for a volume manufacturer. The Corvairs limped along until 1969, when the final gold Monza coupe rolled off the Willow Run, Michigan production line.

Engine: Horizontally opposed six-cylinder, overhead valve, aluminum block

Displacement: 164 cid

Horsepower: 140 at 5200 rpm

Compression Ratio: 9.25:1

Base Price: $2519

Number Produced: 7,330

■ *Right: This Marina Blue Corsa made its final appearance in '66. The car was also available in Lemonwood Yellow and Chateau Slate.*

1966 Ford Bronco

The original Bronco's were introduced in August 1965 as a response to the needs of active Americans, who were looking for adventure as well as practical transport. It was effectively Ford's answer to the Jeep and International Scout. It was a full-time four-wheel drive vehicle, and was available as a two-door roadster (with two or four seats), sports utility (re-named the 'pickup' in '67) and four-passenger wagon. They were all made from one body as the pickup/wagon roof was just bolted on.

It's simply upright boxy shape is instantly recognizable, with its rather shapeless hood, high front fenders and round headlamps. The interior was functional and rather basic, with a simple instrument panel. Interestingly, the windshield could be folded down. These design hallmarks have made the car an icon of the four-wheel drive enthusiast. The Bronco was an immediate success, leading the emerging recreational four-wheel drive market with sales of over 18,200 in its first year of production.

The model had a ninety-two inch wheelbase. Like the other no-frills off-roaders of the day, the Bronco was extremely rugged and adaptable. The car could easily be customized with all kinds of Ford-offered factory options. These included winches, snowplow blades, locking front hubs, tow hooks, air-lift springs, an auxiliary gas tank and many other possibilities.

The original Bronco was powered by a 105 horsepower inline six-cylinder engine from the Falcon and was fitted with the 'three on a tree' a fully synchronized three-speed manual transmission with column-mounted shifter. The '66 model year also saw the introduction of the 289-cid V-8, which was upgraded to 302-cid in '69. Later versions of the Bronco became increasingly powerful and sophisticated.

The four-wheel drive was uniquely mounted for a maximum ground clearance with a solid front axle that made it ideal for off-roading.

After a break from the market, the legendary Bronco is being re-introduced as a concept SUV at the 2004 North American International Auto Show. The new version demonstrates the authentic spirit of the original, with advanced powertrain technology (including nitrous-oxide fuel injection), and sophisticated comfort wedded to the four-wheel drive heritage.

Engine: Inline Six-cylinder, overhead valve

Displacement: 170 cid

Horsepower: 105 at 4400 rpm

Compression Ratio: 9.2:1

Induction: Holley one-barrel carburetor

Wheelbase: 92 inches

Number Produced: 18,200

■ *Right: The shapeless hood of the Bronco can be folded for open top motoring, and the windscreen folded down for even greater airiness.*

1966 Ford Fairlane 427

The Ford Fairlane model range was manufactured by FoMoCo from 1955 through to 1969. The original body design was the full sized Ford body. This body started out as a family vehicle, and evolved into many different models and body styles. The exterior paint and trim options were virtually endless, with a rainbow of paint colors and massive variety of cloth trim for inside.

From 1960-62 the Fairlanes began to decrease in size and the car went from a large to mid-sized model. The first sports coupe model was introduced in 1962, which continued until 1965. These models were bigger than the Falcons, but smaller than the Galaxies and offered the best of both worlds with solid performance and great economy.

In 1966, Ford restyled all the full-sized cars for this model year, including the Fairlane. The model was getting larger again, but still not a full-size Ford. The mid-sized Fairlanes were all new for this model year, wearing swoopier GM-type styling on slightly larger dimensions, though the body weight remained pretty much the same. The new dual stacked headlamp design was popular from the start. The model now boasted many available options and performance goodies to include 427 dual-carburetor engine setups, four-speed manual transmission, bucket seats and a console. A '66 Fairlane built specifically for the dragstrip was produced with a fiberglass hood. Fifty-seven of these were built with stripped down race specifications, and equipped with 427-cid race engines. However, the great majority of 1966 Fairlaines were actually fitted with a standard 200-cid six-cylinder engine, and a 200-horsepower 289-cid as the base option V-8.

This model year also introduced the Fairlane convertible, which was available in GT, GTA, 500XL and 500 models. The GT and GTA models were offered with more of the performance accessories and were most commonly built with 390-cid big block engines and luxury interiors complete with bucket seats and consoles. The GTA was a 'GT' with an 'A' automatic transmission, GTs were fitted with four-on-the-floor manual transmission. Disc brakes weren't introduced until the following year.

Engine: Single Overhead Camshaft 8V V-8

Displacement: 427 cid

Horsepower: 657 at 7500 rpm

Transmission: Four-speed manual

Compression Ratio: 12.1:1

Induction: Two Holley four-barrel

Body Style: Two-door Hardtop Coupe

Wheelbase: 116 inches

Base Price: $2649

■ *Right: The 427-cid V-8 was the performance option. This car has the optional 'Ram Air' hood scoop.*

1966 Ford Galaxie 500 7-Litre Series Convertible

Ford finally made it to number one in the production league table for 1966, under the leadership of Donald N. Frey. FoMoCo continued its policy of major annual re-styling for several model lines. While 1965 and 1966 full-sized Fords bear a resemblance to each other, they are quite different cars. The hood is the only interchangeable exterior body component. The '66 models featured more rounded lines than the previous year, though the feature lines were in exactly the same positions.

Galaxie was the intermediate Ford trim for 1966, and offered a full range of seven different series containing nineteen different models. The series were the LTD, the Galaxie 500XL, the Galaxie 500 –Litre, the Galaxie 500 and Custom 500, and the lower trim levels also existed as a parallel V-8 format. Hardtops, sedan and convertible Galaxies were on offer. The model became known for both its clean lines and performance options.

The LTD had a rather different look with a distinctive trim, ornamentation and interior trim. The 500 XL was the ultimate Galaxie in '66 with deep foam contoured bucket seats, full-length console, wall-to-wall carpeting, padded dashboard and visors and special 500 XL exterior ornamentation. Ford also offered an impressive eight different engine choices, all the way from a standard economy six-cylinder to the 'side oiler' 427-cid engine with dual carburetion and 425 horsepower. FoMoCo also introduced a new 428 cubic inch Thunderbird V-8 that was standard equipment on the Galaxie 7-Litre model.

The 7-Litre was the high performance version of the Galaxie 500 XL, equipped with Cruise-O-Matic transmission. The four-speed manual was also available as a no-cost option for those who chose the even sportier driving characteristics it imparted. The cars also had low restriction dual exhausts, a non-silenced air cleaner system and power disc brakes. The model also had a Sport steering wheel, of simulated English walnut. The Galaxie exterior was available in fifteen Super Diamond Lustre enamels, in twenty-three two-tone combinations. Vinyl-covered roofs were also on offer. Inside the cars, forty-two different upholstery choices were available. The '66s had several power options, for steering, windows and seats together with optional disc brakes and air conditioning.

Engine: Thunderbird Special V-8

Displacement: 428 cid

Horsepower: 345 at 4600 rpm

Transmission: Cruise-O-Matic automatic

Compression Ratio: 10.5:1

Number Produced: 2368

■ *Right: The Galaxie 500 7-Litre model was available as either a Fastback Coupe, or this Convertible.*

Ford GT40

Ford was at number one in the 1966 league of autoproducers. This was in part to their successful introduction of production performance cars like the Torino, Mustang and Thunderbird. These were both inspired, and initiated by technological advances learned at the classic American races and at Le Mans. As far back as 1962, Henry Ford II had decided that Ford should participate in the International Competition field.

The prototype Mark II GT40s made their first appearance at the 1965 LeMans, featuring a NASCAR approved 427 cid V-8. Unfortunately, the cars were obliged to retire with transmission problems. Ford and racing partner Shelby American spent the rest of '65 developing the Mark II for the 1966 endurance-racing season. They refined the big block 427, reducing the engine weight by fifty pounds by using aluminium heads with smaller valves and other modifications. Shelby American did most of the work on the chassis and suspension, reinforcing and revising these where necessary. The GT40 body consisted of a semi-monocoque construction of 0.61mm steel, hinged front and rear panel sections and doors of reinforced fibreglass.

Their work was fully justified. The cars not only took 1-2-3-5 at the first 24-hour Daytona Continental race, but 1-2-3 at the '66 LeMans. In fact, the GT40 was the first American car to win this prestigious race. The winning car was driven by Bruce McLaren and Chris Amon, and set a new average race speed of 125.4 mph. It had a top speed of 205 mph. This is where the GT40 earned its reputation as a 'Ferrari eater', proving more than a match for the P3.

Despite failing to win at Monza and the Nurnburgring 1000km race in Germany, Ford took the constructors' championship for prototype and series production cars. This resulted in the GT40 Mark II becoming the vehicle that showed the world that heavier, larger displacement cars could deliver spectacular performance. It was a victory for American talent, and gained a reputation for the GT40 as the being the best supercar of the era. As well as the fifty-plus cars that FIA rules insisted upon, Ford also had to produce at least 1,000 units of the car for public sale to qualify for competition in the production car series. These were known as the GT40 Mark III cars. Several changes had to be made to ensure that the car complied with safety regulations. The engine was changed to the 289-cid used on Shelby 350 Mustangs, but the clutch and transmission were identical to the race set-up.

■ *Left: The 1966 GT40 appeared as the race-ready Mark II and the production Mark III model.*

Engine: V-8	
Displacement: 427 cid	
Horsepower: 485 at 6200 rpm	
Weight: 2450 lbs	
Wheelbase: 95 inches	

1966 Oldsmobile 4-4-2 W-30

Oldsmobile entered the supercar sweepstakes in April '64 with a self-explanatory name four-four-two – four-barrel carburettor, four-on-the-floor transmission and dual exhausts. The name remained the same for fifteen years, even though the transmission was also made available as both three-speed synchomesh and automatic over this period.

In 1966, Oldsmobile introduced the W-30 option, which later became known as 'Outside Air Induction'. This fantastic package became Olds hottest musclecar equipment. The package consisted of a RPO list of extras, designed to boost the 4-4-2s to be suitable for super-stock drag racing. The package consisted of a 400-cid L69 big-block V-8. This 360 horsepower engine had been introduced in the November of the previous year. It was equipped with three Rochester two-barrel carburetors, designed to keep the air/fuel mixture cooler and denser, to increase the available power. The engine option was not limited to the W-30 models, however, they were also fitted to 2,129 production models, including the F-85 Cutlasses.

The W-30 equipment also included ram-air ductwork that rammed cool air into the Rochester via two authentic large plastic scoops, which were situated in two openings of the front bumper, reserved for the turn signals in ordinary production cars. The hoses took up so much room under the hood that the battery was re-located to the trunk at the back of the car, which had the additional benefit of loading some weight onto the rear wheels. Other '66 W-30 equipment included a four-bladed fan with no clutch, heavy-duty three-core radiator, close-ratio manual transmission and a hydraulic, high-lift, long-duartion camshaft. Despite all this heavy gear, no output rating change was listed for the W-30-equipped Oldsmobile.

Only 54 of these W-30 cars were built in 1966. The cars were not actively promoted at all. As soon as they were, production jumped to a far healthier 502 cars in '67. Some equipment changes were made, including replacing the carburetor system with a single four-barrel unit. This was due to a GM edict banning multiple-carb setups. An optional automatic transmission was offered.

The W-30 was most popular in 1970 when 3,100 W-30 equipped cars hit the streets. Oldsmobile continued to offer the package until 1980, but it was substantially diluted by this time.

Engine: L69 V-8

Displacement: 400-cid

Horsepower: 360 at 5000 rpm

Body Style: Two-door Coupe

Wheelbase: 115 inches

Number Produced: 54

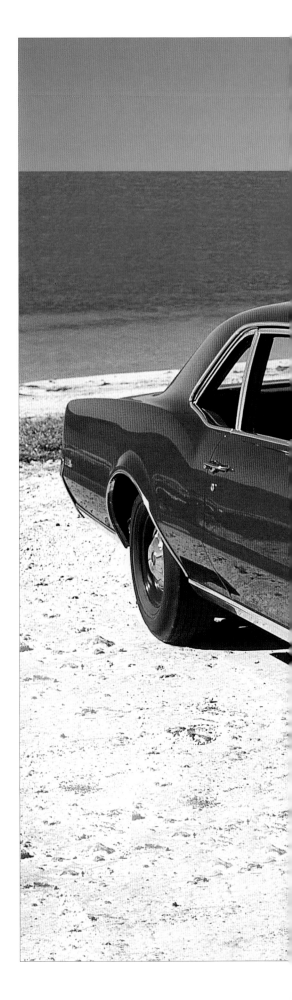

■ *Right: This W-30 equipped 4-4-2 clearly shows the simulated hood louvers.*

Pontiac GTO 1966

Back in 1964, Pontiac had succeeded in launching its first GTO option model by skirting GM head office policy do drop its most popular engine, the 389-cid V-8 into medium-sized Tempest bodies in true hot rod fashion. GTO actually stood for Gran Turismo Omologato, which was mean to imply that, like the Ferrari GTO, the car had been homologated for racing. The tag was actually quite controversial in some quarters, but as they say, there's no such thing as bad publicity. 1965 had seen a major restyle on the Le Mans/GTO and in 1966 the GTO became a series in its own right, with distinctive trim on the new Tempest sheet metal, unique grille and GTO nameplates and lettering. The GTOs were available in three body styles: a two-door (semi-fastback) hardtop, a two-door coupe and a two-door convertible.

Fully equipped, the '66 GTOs could achieve 0-60 miles an hour in 6.8 seconds. The base GTO engine was rated at 335 horsepower, whilst the most powerful option available in this model year was the 389-cid V-8 with Tri Power carburetion, rated at 360 horsepower. A convertible with this option was timed at 15.5 seconds over the quarter mile (at 93 mph). But this was to be the final year for the Tri Power set-up, as GM instigated a ban on multiple-carburetion for all models, with the single exception of the Corvette. The GTOs were also equipped with dual exhaust, plus heavy-duty shocks, springs and stabilizer bar.

Whatever the model mix, the GTOs were the undisputed kings of the musclecar market in 1966, selling more units than any of its competitors (ignoring the pony cars). This was quite an achievement considering that the market was now crowded with copycat quick-car contenders. Ford had fitted a 390-cid V-8 to the Fairlane GT and GTA models, while Mercury had metamorphosed the Comet into a veritable Cyclone. Both of these cars could also be ordered with a 427-cid (seven liter) option, and Chrysler's 426-cid Hemi was just about the hit the scene. The GM cars were at a great disadvantage from the high-handed head office decrees that stated that the intermediate cars could not be fitted with engines larger than 400-cid. This time, this edict actually stuck. But this did nothing to dent GTO sales (a huge 96,946 units for the '66 model year) which were positively affected by the new Coke-bottle styling. The powertrain options were also improved, with the addition of a Ram Air option for the Tri-power engine. Ram Air cars also had longer duration camshafts and heavy-duty valve springs.

■ *Left: This '66 Hardtop looks cool with the wire mesh grille and GTO badge.*

Engine:	GTO V-8
Displacement:	389 cid
Horsepower:	335 at 5000 rpm
Compression Ratio:	10.75:1
Base Price:	$2847
Number Produced:	73,785

1967 Chevrolet Camaro Z/28

Chevy was still at number one in the production stakes in 1967, and intended to stay there. Inspired by the huge success of the Mustang, Chevrolet entered the pony car race in 1967 with its sporty Camaro. Chevrolet was determined that the new model should appeal to as wide a range of drivers as possible. A massive 'building block' system of option packages allowed for the creation of many distinctive vehicles, tailored to many different types of drivers. Two basic body shapes were available, a two-door hardtop coupe and a two-door convertible. A huge range of engines from an inline six-cylinder to a 295 horsepower Turbo-fire V-8 was available for the retail models. The basic price was fairly reasonable at around $2,500, but the extensive list of options could easily push the price for an individual car past $5,000. The Camaro quickly established itself as Chevy's real contender in the sporty compact field, ousting their fast-fading Corvair, which lost its turbocharged option this year. They were soon taking market share off Ford, as sales of the new model achieved sales of over 220,000 in its first year. Unsurprisingly, the car shared the same basic profile with the Mustang, having a long hood on a visually short deck.

The Z/28 competition package Camaro was created for the recently formed Trans-Am racing series, and had a fantastic option package that included numerous performance goodies, including a powerful small-block V-8 and disc brakes. The distinctive Z/28 badging didn't actually appear until '68. In fact, the car effectively saved the Trans-Am, as the complete dominance of the Mustang in the

■ *Below: The Z/28 was capable of a quarter mile in 14.9 seconds.*

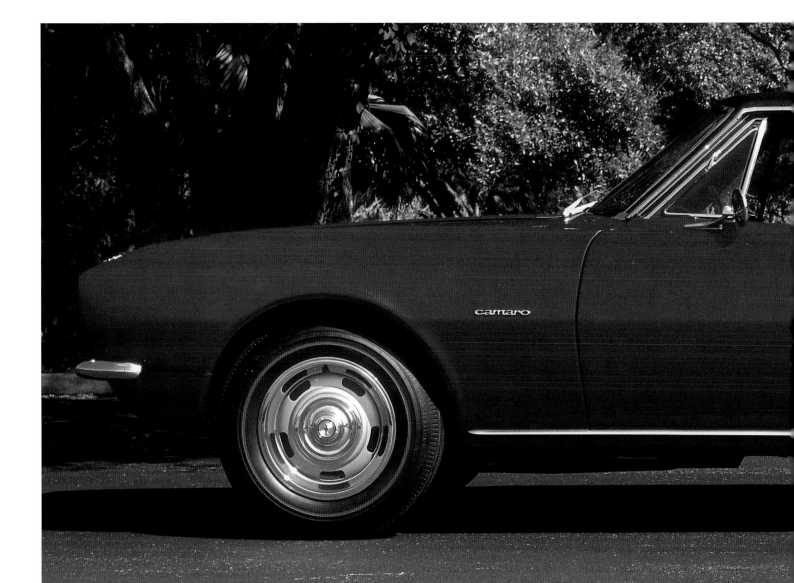

'66 season was a complete turn-off to the race goers. Chevrolet's Vince Piggins promised the organisers that he would turn up with a racecar for the next season, and then persuaded the board to back his plan to take the Camaro to the races. To be race legal, the car had to be available for general retail sale, and attract at least 1000 customers, and displace no more than 305 cid. This resulted in a huge engineering project, redesigning a hot small-block V-8 especially for the car, with a forged steel crank, L79 big-port cylinder heads, and a Holley four-barrel carburetor. Unofficially, the car was rated at over 400 horsepower. The car was also fitted with F41 stiffened suspension and a Muncie four-speed transmission. The only external signs of the powerhouse within were Corvette rally wheels with bright rims, and wide twin racing stripes on the hood and rear decklid.

Although sales were a modest 602 in their first year of introduction, this was one Camaro model that really caught on, selling 7,199 in '68, production soared to 19,000. The reviews for the car were fantastic, it was described as a 'happy and extremely potent screamer'. Apart from a two-year hiccup in the seventies, the brilliant Z/28 stayed in production until the new millennium.

Engine:	Small-block V-8, overhead valve, cast iron block
Displacement:	302 cid
Horsepower:	290 at 5800 rpm
Transmission:	Muncie four-speed manual
Compression Ratio:	11:1
Induction:	Single 800-cfm Holley four-barrel with high-rise intake
Body Style:	Two-door hardtop coupe
Number of Seats:	5
Weight:	3070 lbs
Wheelbase:	108 inches
Base Price:	$3,380
Number Produced:	602

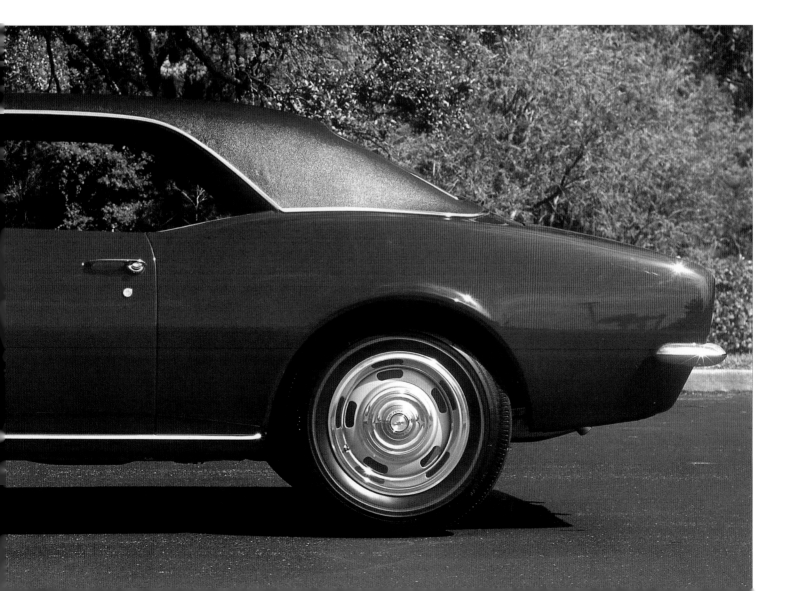

1967 Chevrolet Corvette L-88

An all-new Corvette had been planned for 1967, but development problems intervened, and delayed the new model for a year. The Sting Ray put in one more glamorous appearance, looking cleaner and meaner than ever with less decal, and retained its now familiar hood hump. The body was fundamentally that of the original '63 Sting Ray.

The special L-88 model Corvette was primarily designed as a race-ready car for the track, and anyone who tried to use it as a streetcar was destined for a shock. The car was stripped of any of the normal refinements that street Corvettes were loaded with, radio, heater, automatic choke or underhood cooling, even reliable brakes. In fact, Corvette was quite coy about identifying the cars at all in case the unsuspecting ordinary buyer might insist on purchasing one. They had originally planned to identify the cars with special L/88 badges, but dropped this idea. Chevrolet even grossly underrated the car as having 430 horsepower, hoping to steer their racer customers to the L-71 engine (rated at 435 horsepower). They only wanted to sell the cars to genuine racers. In fact, the car could not even be filled with regular gas, it required special high octane fuel of at least 103 octane to prevent engine damage.

What the car did have was a selection of specially designed performance enhancing equipment, including the (now reliable) aluminum cylinder heads, a huge four-barrel Holley carburetor and the first Corvette ram air hood forcing cool air down into it (the first Corvette to have a fully functional hood scoop). This was the result of extensive testing to identify the flow characteristics of the air coming off the windshield. The L-88s were also fitted with stiff suspension, G81 Positraction differential, J56 power-assisted metallic brakes and an M22 'Rock Crusher' four-speed manual transmission. Racing-style sidepipes manufactured by Stahl were also fitted to the car, as was a transistorised transmission. All of these modifications were supervised by Corvette chief engineer Zora Duntov.

At the Le Mans 24 Hour race of June '67, an L-88 was clocked at 170 mph before a connecting rod disconnected.

The L-88 was manufactured for a total of three years ('67, '68 and '69) and a total of 216 were produced. Rather appropriately, at least one L-88 was amongst a batch of complimentary Sting Rays given to NASA astronauts.

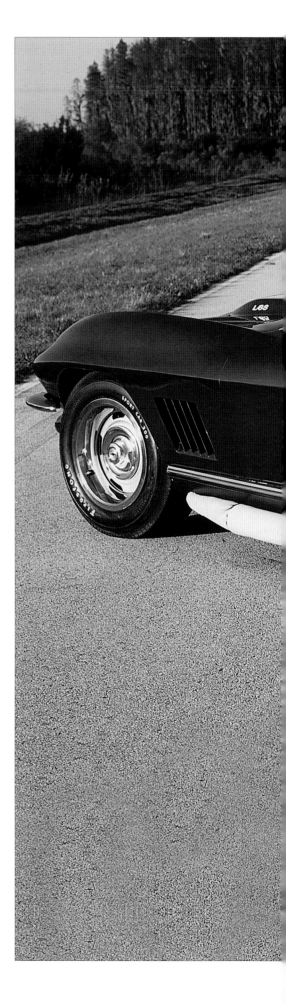

Engine: L-88 V-8, aluminum cylinder heads

Displacement: 427 cid

Horsepower: 430 at 5200 rpm

Compression Ratio: 12.5:1

Wheelbase: 98 inches

Base Price: $5675

■ *Right: This Goodwood Green coupe is one of the earliest L-88s built, and is owned by collector Bill Tower, a former GM engineer. He thinks it was the first car in the series to be built.*

382

1967 | Chevrolet Impala SS 427

GM celebrated the manufacture of its 100 millionth American-built car in April 1967. The company was now divided between the car and truck divisions. Ralph Nadar's influence continued to pervade the company thinking, with safety becoming an increasingly important issue. An energy-absorbing steering column and seat belts were both now standard. Chevy was now back on top of Ford in '67 (out-producing their rival by over 220,000 units), thanks in some part to the launch of the Camaro.

Chevrolet's Impala SS was still a separate series in '67, but would revert to option package status in 1968. Chevy introduced the big new 427 cid V-8 in this year. Although there was a growing market for compacts in the US, the full-sized Chevys, including the Impalas, held onto sales of over half a million units. The Biscayne, Bel Air, Impala and Caprice models were all built on the full-sized chassis. The basic Impala range for this year included six options, ranging from a two-door convertible to a nine-seat station wagon. By contrast, the Impala Super Sport series had two options, a two-door hardtop and two-door convertible. The cars also came with a choice of engines, an inline six-cylinder or the overhead valve V-8 in various power levels. Turbo Hydra-Matic transmission was introduced in '67, and was available as an option.

The sporting Impala once again featured an all-vinyl interior, with front Strato bucket seats and a division console that housed the shift lever were standard, although Strato bench seating was available at no extra charge). Exterior identification for the series consisted of a black accented grille, with bright metal horizontal bars, front and rear wheelhouse moldings, a black highlighted body sill and deck lid latch panel. 'SS' grille badges and specific 'SS' full wheel covers were also part of the equipment for the model. The bright metal hood louvers were simulated.

The car impressed contemporary customers with both its 'mobile creature comforts' and performance, 'which was, until recently, reserved for dragstrip specialists'. He continued that the car 'may well be the Ultimate average car – the status symbol of Everyman'. Of course, at around $5000 for the full SS 427 package, not every man could afford the luxurious, fully loaded, feel of the SS. In fact, this price tag rather blew Chevy's image as being one of the 'low-priced three'. Car Life magazine really liked the car, rating the ride good, the acceleration exciting, the handling fair to good, but the braking dreadful (with rear wheel lockup and significant fade).

Engine: V-8 overhead valve, cast iron block

Displacement: 427 cid

Horsepower: 385 at 5200rpm

Compression Ratio: 10.25:1

Wheelbase: 118 inches

■ *Right: Almost everything was good about the Impala SS, except the braking and fuel economy (10 mpg).*

Chevrolet Nova SS L79

1967

The Nova had been dropped, briefly, in anticipation of the larger Chevelle SS, but public demand had resulted in a midyear return for the model, with two new engine options. These were the first V-8 for the Nova, and the 230 inline. The convertible and 3-seat station wagon were dropped, but the 2-seat wagon continued. The Chevy II 300 series trim was deleted. '65 had heralded minor trim changes, which were reinforced in '66. The installation of more serious engines to the car in the '64-'65 period began to establish a serious reputation for Nova SS as a musclecar.

Both the Chevelles and Chevy II Novas were completely restyled in 1966. The hot ticket version of the car was the L79 version of the 327 V-8, which developed 350 horsepower. Officially, this engine option was dropped in 1967, to prevent sales being drawn away from the newly introduced Camaro range. But although the L79 option was officially deleted, production records show that six such cars were built in '67.

Only minor styling changes were introduced in 1967, to consolidate the car as one of the most clean-looking and collectible Chevys of all time. A new grille and side trim were the most visible changes to the car. Mechanically, the dual-pot barking system was fitted as standard, but disc brakes were available as an option. Revised for '67, the standard engine option for the Nova and Nova SS was a 187.6 six-cylinder inline. Optional engine variations were the RPO L22 250-cid 155 horsepower six-cylinder block, and the RPO L30 327-cid 275 horsepower V-8. The small, taut Nova Super Sport two-door hardtop coupe (series 117) continued to make an excellent high-performance car when equipped with these special options.

The exterior of the Nova SS was distinguished with a special black-accented chrome grille, complete with SS insignia low on the driver's side. Above a black painted sill area, there was an elegant chrome accent stripe, lower body moldings, and bright wheelhouse accents extending along the lower fender edges. The model had specific Super Sport full wheelcovers, fender scripts and full-width color accent deck lid trim panels. The car interiors were all vinyl, with front Strato bucket seats, optional Astro-bucket headrests, with bright seat end panels as standard. In cars where the transmission was upgraded to four-speed or automatic transmission, a floor shift trim plate was added. The cars also had a specific Nova Super Sport three-spoke steering wheel.

■ *Left: One of only six '67 Nova Super Sports built with the L79 engine option, this red hardtop coupe is a rare car indeed.*

Engine: V-8 overhead valve, cast iron block,	
Displacement: 326.7 cid	
Horsepower: 275 at 4800 rpm	
Compression Ratio: 10.0:1	
Number Produced: 10,100	

1967 Dodge Charger 426 Hemi

Dodge had slipped back to seventh in the auto producers' league in 1967, though production remained pretty steady at just under half a million. Byron Nichols was now the General Manager of the division. With its unique looks and massive powerhouse, the Charge Hemi 426 was a scary beast, especially if you came upon one on the road. Rather more sedately, Nichols described the car as 'a fresh concept in styling and engineering excellence from bumper to bumper'.

The basic body fastback Charger body was pretty much the same one that had been introduced in 1966, with the cars built on Coronet chassis. The road-going version was fitted with front fender mounted turn signal indicators and some extra chrome trim, together with front and rear bucket seats and a cigar lighter. All were fitted with V-8 engines. But these were pretty tame compared to the Hemi 426. These had been designed for one thing and one thing only – racing at the new super speedway in Daytona Beach, Florida. Owned by Bill France, this was the real testing ground for the biggest muscles in Detroit. Chrysler, of course, had a huge advantage in having the milestone hemi-head engine in its parts cupboard. The original engine was launched in 1951, but was abandoned in the late fifties in favor of the equally powerful, but smaller wedge-heads. However, the concept was revived six years later, bigger and meaner than ever.

■ *Below: The Charger's unique back row of bucket seats folded down to increase the load area.*

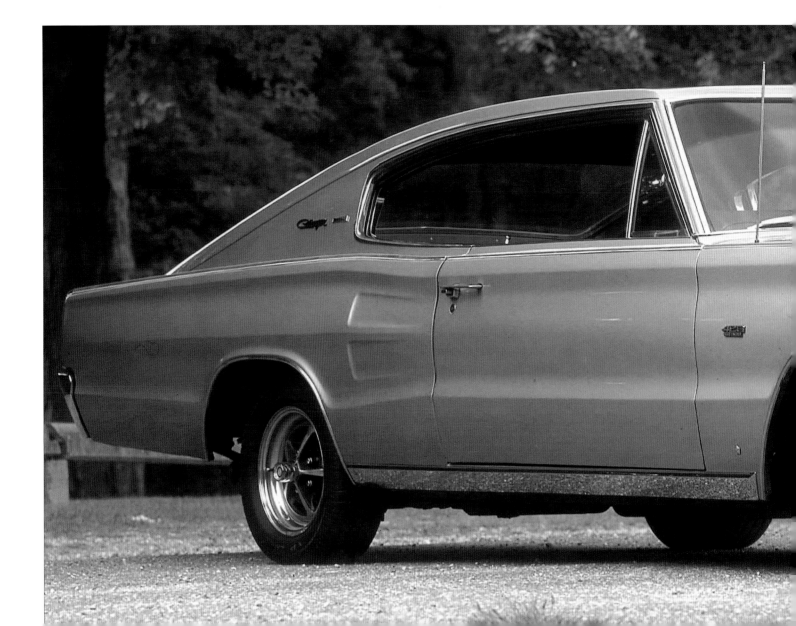

Back in 1962, Chrysler engineer Tom Hoover was asked to recreate the Hemi for the modern NASCAR circuit. They completed the job in February 1964. In fact, the engine proved to be so dominant that Bill France actually tried to ban the Hemi from the race circuit on the basis that it didn't fulfil the race rules, not being fitted to a regular production car. Chrysler got round this by offering de-tuned version of the engine to the public – the 'Street Hemi'. This engine was offered on a wide array of Dodge and Plymouth models from '66 – '71, but in the Charger version, the hot performance of the hemi was matched by the stunning looks of the car. It was first offered on this model in February '66. It was advertised as the most powerful sedan ever offered to the public.

Despite the hype, actual sales for the Charger model fell by almost half in 1967, from 37,300 to 15,788. The Hemi Chargers accounted for only 468 in '66, and despite an even larger engine option of 440-cid, only 118 in '67. Half the problem was the price, with the full Hemi engine option, the cars were almost $5000. Higher insurance costs were also problematic. The Hemi returned in a new Charger body for '68 but was finally retired in '71.

Engine: Hemi V-8

Displacement: 426 cid

Horsepower: 425 at 5000 rpm

Transmission: Four-speed manual with Hurst shifter, TorqueFlite automatic optional

Compression Ratio: 10.25:1

Induction: Two 650-cfm Carter four-barrel carburetors

Body Style: Two-door Fastback Coupe

Number of Seats: 4

Weight: 4160lbs

Wheelbase: 117 inches

Base Price: $4500

Number Produced: 118

Dodge Dart GTS (383 V-8)

1967

Engines and cars got bigger in the mid-sixties, heavier and more complex. Detroit had learnt the way to power through stock-car racing and gradually introduced what it had learnt to production models. The company's fortunes had also grown in these years, as it gradually climbed higher in the production league table. In 1967, they were at seventh place (on production of nearly half a million cars), but had made a brief stop at fifth in '66. R.B. Curry became the General Manager of Dodge in this year.

The Darts got a completely restyled unibody, 43 per cent of these were fitted with the V-8 engine option. The car was now America's largest compact and was styled with curved side glass and delta-shaped taillamps. Polara and Monaco were also extensively redesigned and built larger, riding a 122-inch wheelbase.

The restyle for the Dart was total, from the ground up. The cars retained the chassis of the previous year, but were restyled to look larger than the earlier model (although they were actually half an inch shorter). The full-width grille housed single headlights and featured a vertical bar arrangement with a large-scale dividing bar in the center of the concave grille. The side profile was rather more rounded than in the previous incarnation of the car, but carried similar lines. At the back, the taillights were almost square and fitted into a flat section on the trunk lid. The cars were trimmed with chromed windshield and rear window moldings.

The Dart was the base model of the range, the Dart 270 was the intermediate trim level, and the Dart GT was the top-level model. The GT was fitted with all the options of the entry-level models, plus a padded instrument panel, special wheel covers and bucket seats. There were two GT models, a two-door hardtop coupe and two-door convertible. The cars were fitted with two basic engine options, the slant six-cylinder and the V-8 – available with various-sized engine blocks. The convenience options for GT models included an interior console, buffed paint, a tachometer and simulated 'mag' wheel covers.

■ *Left: This convertible Dart GTS proclaims its 383-cid V-8 status with pride.*

Engine: Overhead valve V-8, cast iron block	
Displacement: 383 cid	
Horsepower: 270 at 4400 rpm	
Compression Ratio: 9.2:1	
Induction: Carter two-barrel BDD-4125S	
Weight: 3030 lbs	
Wheelbase: 111 inches	
Base Price: $2860	
Number Produced (All Dart GTs): 38,200 \including 21,600 V-8s)	

1967 Ford Thunderbird Landau

The Thunderbirds received a complete re-style for 1967. The front end of the car now featured a full-width grille with hidden headlights. As in 1966, the rear end featured a large, single taillight lens with a horizontal trim strip in the center. In addition, there were backup lights, in the center of the strip, which gave the impression of a large round taillight.

Introduced in 1955 as a luxury two-seater Thunderbird, the model range gradually evolved over the years with the open version selling only 7.5% of the total range by 1966. This was the final year that offered a convertible Thunderbird, and some say that the later series had all the luxury, but none of the sportiness of the earlier car.

For the fifth Thunderbird series, and for the first time in Thunderbird history, a four-door sedan, the 'Landau Sedan', was introduced to the model range. It was built on a longer wheelbase than the two-door hardtop and featured unusual rear doors that opened to the front, of 'suicide doors' as they were known. This model seemed to some to mark the descent of the T-birds into middle age. The production engines at least were now tuned for refinement and not performance, and the bodies looked bulky compared to the sprightly earlier two-seat models.

The base interior now included full five-dial instrumentation plus a glovebox-mounted emergency flasher. Other niceties, such as an AM/FM radio, Stereophonic tape system, six-way power driver's seat, cruise control and seat belt warning lamps were available as options.

1967 turned out to be the fourth best sales year to date for the Thunderbirds. The model sold 77,956 cars out of a total Ford production of 1,742,311 units. This was despite industrial action by the United Auto Workers that knocked out fifty-seven Ford production days. The two-door Tudor models and the new 'Fordor' Landau appeared in most of the advertising for the year, but the most popular model in the range was the Tudor Landau – despite the fact that virtually all of the year's advertising ignored it. While appearances may well suggest otherwise, almost no parts from the '67 Thunderbirds are interchangeable with the '68-'69 models. However, Thunderbird sales then declined until the introduction of the 1972 models, which reversed the decline until the disastrous effect of the oil crisis of 1974.

Engine: Thunderbird Four-Barrel V-8

Displacement: 390 cid

Horsepower: 315 at 4600 rpm

Transmission: Cruise-O-Matic automatic

Compression Ratio: 10.5:1

Base Price: $4825

Number Produced: 24,967

■ *Right: Four-door Thunderbird Landau Sedan, complete with rear opening suicide doors.*

Mercury Cougar XR-7

1967

Mercury entered the pony car race at full speed in 1967 with the introduction of the Cougar. The model was launched with some powerful performance packages.

The Cougar was one of the most handsome automobiles of 1967, and Cougar was a niche marketing success for Mercury in that it bridged the gap between the performance of the Ford Mustangs (and was slightly larger) and the luxury of the Thunderbird models. Overall, its probably leant more to comfort than performance. Its styling was more mature, featuring disappearing headlights, wraparound front and rear fenders and triple taillights (with sequential turn signals). The front and rear end styling were similar. Cougars came, equipped with all-vinyl bucket seats, three-spoke 'sport-style' steering wheel, deep-loop carpeting and deluxe seat belts. The standard transmission for the model was floor-mounted three-speed manual transmission.

There was a single base Cougar model, the two-door hardtop coupe. A Cougar XR-7 two-door hardtop coupe was introduced in the mid-model-year. No convertible or fastback models were offered until 1969. Except for a medallion on the quarter panel of the roof, it looked just like the standard Cougar model. It was also embellished with a black-faced instruments set into a simulated walnut dashboard, and a more luxurious, simulated leather, interior.

The Cougar was immediately successful, selling a total of 150,893 cars in its first model outing, accounting for nearly half of Mercury sales for the entire year. Only 7,412 of these were fitted with the optional front bench seat, and only 5.3% with the four-speed manual transmission. The most popular options were automatic transmission (96.2%), power steering (97%), tinted glass (69.7%) and power brakes (65.6%). A GT performance package was also available for a further $323. This included a firmer suspension with bigger shocks, fatter anti-roll bars, power front disc brakes and a 390-cid V-8 (rated at 335 horsepower) that required premium fuel.

■ *Left: The Cougar received Motor Trend Magazine's 'Car of the Year' award for 1965.*

Engine:	V-8, overhead valve, cast iron block
Displacement:	289 cid
Horsepower:	200 at 4400rpm
Compression Ratio:	9.3:1
Induction:	Autolite C7DF-9510-Z two-barrel
Body Style:	Two-door Hardtop Coupe
Number of Seats:	5
Weight:	3015 lbs
Wheelbase:	111 inches
Base Price:	$3081
Number Produced:	27,221

1967 Mercury Cyclone 427

Mercury offered thirteen different styles for the '66 and '67 Comet ranges, with an almost custom flavor. These cars are amongst the most desirable Mercury models ever built, gone was the economy car image of the 1960-63 Comets, and the new V-8 engine selections massively up-rated the available power. The cars continue to see great appreciation in their value in the classic car markets.

The 427 Cyclone, introduced by Mercury as their answer to Pontiac's '64 GTO phenomenon. This car was responsible for spawning several other muscle car competitors, including the Buick Gran Sport, Chevrolet's SS-396 Chevelle and Oldsmobile's 4-4-2.

Chrysler and Ford had been slow to join the club, but hoped that the Mercury Comet Cyclone would be able to take on their competitors. But the small block V-8 of the 1965 production model was no match for the GM big block big boys. The 225 horsepower Super Cyclone 289 could only manage the quarter mile in a rather sedate 17.1 seconds at 82 mph. The simulated air scoops didn't help much, either. The Cyclone model had originally been introduced to the Comet range in 1964 in an attempt to attract a more masculine, 'macho'

■ *Below: The Cyclone 427s were some of the hottest cars on the street for 1967.*

buyer, with its up-rated power train and black vinyl dash, but it soon became evident that this model wasn't muscle enough to see off the serious competition.

1967 Comet customers were offered two new big block engines, the 410 horsepower 427-cid (complete with four-barrel carburetion). Mercury also offered the even bigger and badder Ford 427 FE, complete with 425 horsepower. This engine was the king of the FE-series big-blocks, and dated from 1958. It had been growing progressively over the years, from 352 cid to 390 in '61, 406 in '62 and finally 427 in '63. It had been used to power the '66 GT-40s to a 1-2-3 finish at Le Mans. Company records show that around eight Mercurys were built in '67, complete with this single four-barrel carburetor engine option. The car was designed exclusively with drag racers in mind, and came equipped with a heavy-duty clutch, 'top loader' four-speed manual transmission and heavy-duty suspension, battery and extra-capacity radiator. Luxuries such as radio and heaters were not included

Engine:	FE-series V-8
Displacement:	427-cid
Horsepower:	410 at 5600rpm
Transmission:	Four-speed 'top loader' manual
Compression Ratio:	11.1:1
Induction:	Single-Holley Four-barrel carburetor
Body Style:	Two-door Hardtop Coupe
Number of Seats:	5
Weight:	3600 lbs
Wheelbase:	116 inches
Base Price:	$4100
Number Produced:	8

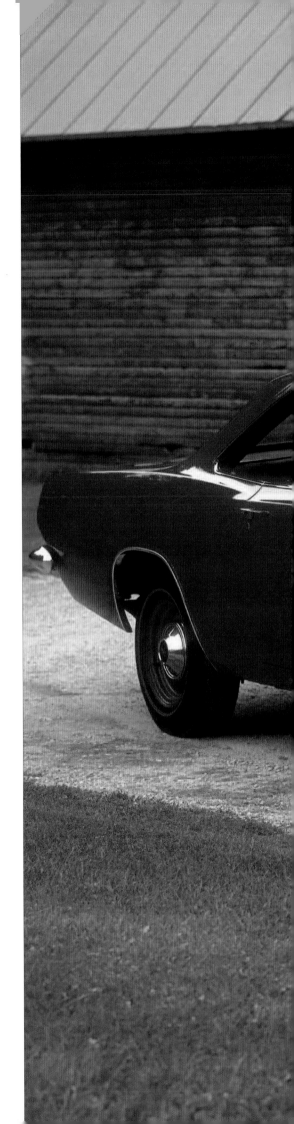

1967 Plymouth Barracuda Formula S 383-cid

The Barracuda had been launched by Plymouth in 1964, specifically designed to go head-to-head with Ford in the Mustang pony car race. It was a sporty new 'glassback' coupe with a large and distinctive wrap-over rear window treatment that gave the car a fastback shape. It also had a uniquely styled roof and deck, in which the deck lid bulged up to meet the glass. The car also boasted distinct trim features, that included a split, negative space grille with center insert and horizontal outer division bars, wide rocker sill panels and a chrome band across the base of the rear window.

A single two-door sports hardtop Barracuda model was offered in the model's first, second and third years. The news for '65 was the introduction of the Barracuda Formula S package. This included a Commando 273-cid V-8 engine, rally suspension, heavy-duty shocks, Goodyear Blue Streak tires, a tachometer and 'open wheel' covers.

For 1966, the Barracuda was offered as part of the Valiant series. The car was redesigned towards the font, but remained largely unchanged at the rear end and above the belt. It was now fitted with the split Valiant grille opening. The 'S' option package continued to be offered, and the standard engines were either the 225-cid slant six, or 273-cid two-barrel V-8.

The Barracuda models shed their links with the Valiant family in '67, and three distinct body shapes were now on offer, a two-door notchback coupe, a two-door fastback coupe (the 'Sports Barracuda') and a two-door convertible. The 'glassback' look was consigned to the past, and the cars were offered to the public with completely new styling. Barracudas now had curvy, flowing features with extremely restrained, modern trim. Contemporary motoring magazines compared the styling of the car to that of the Buick Riviera, but they were really worlds apart. The new Barracuda had single headlights, concave roof pillars (on the notchback coupe), curved side glass, a concave rear deck panel, wide wheel openings and a sleek fastback.

Standard equipment for the '67 Barracuda included three-speed transmission, and the 225-cid slant six or 273-cid V-8. The interiors were equipped with carpeting, front bucket seats (in the convertible), a fold-down rear seat (in the fastback), a padded dash and all standard safety equipment. The 'S' equipment package was still available in an up-rated form. Whatever the rationale, the '67 Barracuda doubled its sales from the previous model year.

Engine: Barracuda V-8

Displacement: 383-cid

Horsepower: 280

Transmission: three-speed manual

Number Produced: 28,196

Right: This Barracuda 'Formula S' two-door notchback coupe was fitted with the up-rated 383-cid V-8.

Pontiac Grand Prix

1967

Pontiac was at its habitual third place in the auto producers' league for 1967, on a production of 857,171 units. '67 was a big year at the company with the introduction of the Camaro-clone Firebird model, the continued presence of the GTOs, and the expansion of the Grand Prix range to include a convertible. Interesting '67 Pontiac conversions included the 'Monkeemobile' based on the GTO phaeton, made for The Monkees TV show. Racecar driver/builder John Fitch also marketed his hot performance Firebird – the Fitchbird.

The Grand Prix models underwent a transformation for 1967. Following the trend for hideaway headlights, these were now completely concealed behind the grille, and could not be seen at all, except when they were lit. The turn signals were equally discreet, positioned in recesses in the front wings. The cars were also equipped with elegant fender skirts and lower body accent moldings, on their face-lifted 'Poncho' bodies. For identification, the cars had GP letters on the left hand side of the grille and on the rear fender. Grand Prix models were built on a massive 121-inch wheelbase and the overall length of the car was almost 215 inches (nearly eighteen feet...). The Grand Prix now weighed over 4,000 pounds, and typified the mid-sixties trend towards the bigger, heavier, accessory-laden cars being built in America.

Naturally, cars of this great bulk needed equally hearty power to compensate for the extra weight. The standard engine fitted to the model was the 350 horsepower 400-cid V-8 (coming just under the wire for engine size, according to GM directives). Despite this, the sheer mass of the car meant that it was never going to be truly quick. The interior of the car was sporty, however, equipped with front Strato Bucket seats and a console (plus all the government required safely features). From the long range of options, Grand Prix could be as well equipped as a Cadillac.

The '67 Grand Prix range consisted of two models, a convertible (as shown in our photograph) being added to the two-door hardtop coupe (which lost its vent windows this year) in an effort to boost sales for this line-up. Unfortunately, the convertible attracted only 5,856 buyers, and so ended up being a one-year option only.

■ *Left: This single-year model Grand Prix convertible demonstrates the '67 Poncho styling.*

Engine:	Grand Prix V-8
Displacement:	400-cid
Horsepower:	350 at 5000 rpm
Compression Ratio:	10.5:1
Weight:	4040 lbs
Wheelbase:	121 inches
Base Price:	$3813
Number Produced:	5856

1968 Ford Mustang 428 Cobra Jet

This was another of the specialist high-performance cars initially brought to the market by enthusiastic dealers. Robert F. Tasca ran a Ford dealership in East Providence, Rhode Island, and is credited with having invented the tag, 'Win on Sunday, sell on Monday'. Tasca put his money where his mouth was, and sponsored several individual cars, plus a fully-fledged drag race team. The latter won championships at the NHRA Winternationals in 1964 and '65. Tasca Ford became a byword for everything 'hot' produced by the blue oval, under the watchful eye of performance manager, Dean Gregson.

This reputation led Tasca to feel somewhat disappointed in Ford's revised Mustang GT, introduced in 1967. This was a larger version of the original car, fitted with the big-block 390 cid FE-series V-8. Tasca made his own revises to the car. He used a 428-cid Police Interceptor short-block engine with reworked cylinder heads and carburetion. This 428 version Mustang could cover the quarter mile in thirteen seconds, and earned the soubriquet 'KR' – 'King of the Road'. Hot Rod magazine writer Rod Dahlquist polled his readers with the question – should Ford make a production version of the KR? Several thousand affirmative responses came in, and Henry Ford II duly set the ball rolling. The Dearborn technical people followed Tasca's recipe for success, but also included a 390 GT cam, PI rods and low restriction dual exhausts. Production started on the strip-ready models on December 13 1967, slightly later for the street-going models. These were launched on April 1 1968. The car was offered as a $420 Mustang option.

Ford decided not to use the 'KR' name for the car, but chose 'Cobra Jet' instead. It was offered as a fastback, coupe and convertible, and had a long list of extras available including power front disc brakes, strengthened suspensions and a black-striped ram-air hood, four-speed or C6 automatic transmission, F70 tires, chromed quad exhaust tips. GT-styled bright steel wheels and competition-style flip-open gas caps were fitted as standard. The 335 horsepower car was Ford's new shot at musclecar prominence, and they raced it to top honors at the NHRA Winternationals in Pomona, California. At the time, it was probably the fastest regular-production sedan ever built. The strip-ready model covered the quarter mile in a scorching 13.56 seconds. A total of 2827 were built, 2253 fastbacks, 564 hardtops and 10 convertibles.

Engine: Cobra Jet V-8

Displacement: 428 cid

Horsepower: 335 at 5600 rpm

Compression Ratio: 10.6:1

Base Price: $3600

Number Produced: 2827

■ *Right: This Wimbledon White Cobra Jet is fitted with a fully-functional black-striped ram-air hood.*

Plymouth Road Runner   1968

Plymouth launched the Road Runner in 1968 as a mass-market muscle car. It remained in production until 1974. There were plenty of rivals to the car, but they tended to be expensive and exclusive, and out of reach of the very young pockets they were aimed at. Most of the cars that could do the quarter mile in 100mph were at least $3,300 – nothing below this price mark could cut the mustard.

Plymouth were looking to give more bang for the buck, and aimed to build a car that could reach the quarter mile at 100 mph, for less than $3,000. Luxuries and non-essentials were pared down to an absolute minimum. Resources were concentrated on the performance package instead, the 'go-goodies'. The suspension was stiffened and a A833 four-speed manual column change gearbox was fitted. Despite the sporty image of the car, bucket seats were not included. But outside, the car was pretty glamorous with a blacked out Sports Satellite grille and GTX hood. All '68 Road Runners were either hardtops or coupes, a convertible option was offered for a single year in '69.

But Plymouth also made the car fun. It was named after a cartoon character! The Road Runner had decals of its namesake, and a droll horn that played the recognizable 'beep beep beep bccccp beep'. Even so, it was the muscle car image and power of the car that made it a success – it was only $2,900 and full of go. Plymouth engineers had concocted a 335 horsepower V-8 from off-the-shelf equipment that enabled them to offer lots of car for the power. In fact, it was heralded as the first car since the GTO to be offered specifically at American youth. Demanded for the car skyrocketed, 44,599 were sold in '68, and the car became the second most successful production musclecar in America, behind the Chevy SS 396 Chevelle.

Despite the modest price of the car, options could be added to build it up to be either more luxurious or more powerful. The 426 Hemi engine was offered, but at the hefty price of $715. Fitting the Hemi also necessitated fitting Torqueflite automatic transmission, at a further $139, and a whole lot of beefed up equipment, including a K-member subframe and further-stiffened suspension. This raised the price of the car to around $4,400. Even so, the car was rated as probably the fastest production sedan on offer. About 840 coupes and 169 hardtops were built with this option.

■ *Left: This cheery red Hemi-equipped Road Runner has the Warner Brothers' character decals on each door and the trunk lid. The ads described the car as 'acceleratii rapidus maximus'.*

Engine:	Hemi V-8
Displacement:	426 cid
Horsepower:	425 at 5000 rpm
Compression Ratio:	10.25:1
Wheelbase:	116 inches
Base Price:	$4,400
Number Produced (Hemi):	840

1968 Pontiac Firebird 400

Pontiac introduced the Firebird in 1967, as the Chevy Camaro-clone of the division. Both cars were designed to go head-to-head with Ford's Mustang. The first car was made at Lordstown, Ohio in early January 1967, and was officially released in the February of that year. Two basic models were launched (the two-door hardtop coupe and two-door convertible), but the cars were marketed in five 'model-options' created by adding regular production options (RPOs) in specific combinations. All Tempest and GTO powertrains were available for the car, a total of four major engine types (two six-cylinders, and two V-8s). All others were described as optional equipment. Sales were excellent, with 82,560 model units being sold.

Styling for the second year Firebird models was almost identical to the original cars, and continued to be offered as two-door hardtop coupes and two-door convertibles. Body styling was sculptural with twin grilles of a bumper-integral design, front vent windows, and three vertical air slots on the leading edge of rear body panels. Federal safety side-marker lights made use of the Pontiac logo. The only major change was that the vent windows were now replaced with one-piece side door glass. The cars were also fitted with outside mirrors, side marker lights, E70-14 black sidewall wide-oval tires with a Space Saver spare. Cordova vinyl tops were available, as were wire wheel covers. Inside the car, apart from the standard GM safety features, front bucket seats continued to be fitted as standard, as was vinyl upholstery. The dash was simulated burl woodgrain. Astro-ventilation was now offered on the cars.

The Firebirds were now offered with seven different engine options, ranging from a base 175 horsepower six-cylinder, to a fire-breathing Ram Air II 400-cid V-8, rated at 340 brake horse power. This top option (available for an extra $616) could blow even the Mustang GT off the strip, and was fitted with twin functional hood scoops and a de-clutching fan. The V-8 options were revised to be more emissions-friendly. Technical changes to the '68 model included bias-mounted rear shock absorbers and multi-leaf rear springs.

'68 Firebird sales were even better than in the launch year, with the model attracting a total of 107,112 buyers. This was despite the number of cars now competing for 'pony car' sales. Every major US car manufacturer was now in on this act. The Firebird sales were a significant contribution to Pontiac's total model year total of 910,977.

Engine: Firebird 400 V-8

Displacement: 400 cid

Horsepower: 335 at 5000 rpm

Compression Ratio: 10.75:1

Base Price: $3397

Number Produced: 90,152

■ *Right: This Firebird 400 is identified as having the Ram Air package by the twin hood scoops – functional of course.*

1969-70 Ford Boss 302 Mustang

Like its 'big brother' the Boss 429, the Boss 302 was developed for racing – in this case for the SCCA Trans Am series. In developing the car, Ford probably ended up with the best handling, ultimate muscle car. The Ford engineers made sure that the car could corner, Bunkie Knudsen had demanded a car that was 'absolutely the best-handling street car available on the American market', and had plenty of power to call upon. The car was designed to be light, and fitted with an effective powerplant, it gave an excellent power-to-weight ratio. The car not only handled well, it could plough a straight furrow – and fast. Boss 302s could cover the quarter mile in 14.62 seconds at 97.7 mph and reach 60 mph in 6.5 seconds. Top speed was 118 mph. The power was delivered by a 302-cid V-8, rated at 290 horsepower, and the car could deliver 290 pounds per feet of torque at 4300 rpm.

The Boss 302 listed at a base price of $3,'720, almost $1000 more that the base price Mustang. Some would argue that this was cheap at the price, as the car on offer was virtually ready to race out the showroom, and included all kinds of race-fit options such as quick ratio steering, competitions suspension (designed by engineer Matt Donner), E70x15 fiberglass belted tires, front disc-brakes and four-speed manual transmission.

The car owed its inception to the broad-minded Bunkie Knudsen, who had been GM's youngest ever General Manager at Pontiac. He oft-quoted maxim was 'You can sell a young man's car to an old man, but you'll never sell an old man's car to a young man'. He believed that young men hankered after hot cars, the hotter the better. He view was that the market was full of ponycars, but that what distinguished the successful cars was power and performance. The Mustang was in his sights. Knudsen had poached plenty of talent from his old bosses at GM, and one of them was designer Larry Shinoda, who had created the sporty image of the Z/28 Camaro, and had worked on the Corvette Sting Ray. Knudsen wanted him to out-Camaro the car over at Ford, and the car was ultimately named after him – the 'Boss'. Shinoda styled and named the car, but Kar Kraft in Brighton, Michigan developed the prototypes, and delivered the first in August 1968.

On the track, honors were fairly even between the Boss and Z/28, who shared similar-sized engines. Camaro took the SCCA championship in 1969, and Parnelli Jones, driving the Ford, won in 1970.

Engine: Boss V-8

Displacement: 302-cid

Horsepower: 290 at 5800 rpm

Compression Ratio: 10.5:1

Body Style: Two-door Fastback Coupe

Number Produced: 7,013

■ *Right: The 'Boss' was named for its instigator, Bunkie Knudsen.*

Ford/Shelby Mustang GT 350 1969

FoMoCo hitched up with ex-racer Carroll Shelby in late 1964 to build an all-new sports car, based on the Mustang fastback. The goal was to create a car with the grunt to compete directly with the Chevy Corvette. The first Shelby GT350 was launched on January 27 1965. At first glance, the car looked just like an ordinary fastback Mustang, but that was the only similarity. The car's drive train and technical equipment was all seriously beefed-up, and the engine power raised considerably. Effectively, the GT350 was a full-bred race car that could be purchased direct from a Ford dealer. The car underwent some minor changes in '66, which Ford directed in an attempt the make line financially viable. This meant making the specifications of the car closer to those of the production Mustangs. Hertz ordered 1,000 GT350s in '66, which were known as Hertz Shelby GT350s, and had gold-stripe decals.

In 1967, the Shelby body styling was quite a radical departure from that of '66, with the extensive use of fiberglass to modify its appearance. The car was given a big rear spoiler and dual hood-mounted air scoops. The driving lights were moved to the outside of the grille. '67 also saw the introduction of the Shelby GT500s, equipped with a big-block 427-cid Medium Riser engine. The range was virtually unchanged for '68 but the cars were now known as the Shelby Cobra GT350 and GT500. A production convertible was now added to the model range, and the Cobra Jet 428-cid engine was introduced.

1969 saw the introduction of the final Shelby Mustangs (though some of the cars were held over until 1970). But, effectively, this was the last year of this fine heritage line-up. This was due to a change of thinking at Ford, who now believed that sales were less relative to high-performance marketing. Engine availability was changed from '68. The 302-cid V-8 was still fitted as standard, but the GT350s were also offered with a 351-cid four valve Ram Air cooled engine. The GT500s were offered with a single engine option, the Ram Air cooled 428. This was also the year of 'scoops' – the NASA styled hood was equipped with five, there was one on both front fenders, and one on both rear quarter panels. The Lucas driving lights were now mounted below the front bumper and the dual exhausts now exited through a massive aluminum outlet mounted in the center of the rear valance panel. The cars were fitted with five-spoke Shelby mag wheels. Technically, the car was equipped with power disc brakes and steering. Safety was accommodated with an integral rollbar and shoulder harness seat belts.

■ *Left: This 1969 Shelby GT350 fastback is equipped with a total of nine air scoops.*

Engine:	V-8
Displacement:	351 cid
Horsepower:	290 at 4800rpm
Compression Ratio:	10.7:1
Wheelbase:	108 inches

Mercury Comet Cyclone Spoiler II   1969

The Comet had been restyled for 1968. It is described as looking like a full-size Mercury that had gone on a diet. The new car had a horizontal grille, rocker panel moldings, side market lights and chrome-encase vertical taillights. Among the standard safety features for the car were an energy absorbing steering wheel and column, padded dashboard and sun visors, plus front and rear seat belts. Two speed windshield wipers and washers were also fitted. '68 Cyclones had a mid-tire level body tape stripe. Those with the GT option had an upper body racing stripe, bucket seats, wide tread whitewalls, special wheel covers, all-vinyl interior and a special handling package.

The '69 Comet Cyclone was lightly face-lifted, and only the Fastback body style returned for this model year. The GT option was reduced to just an appearance group option. The hot new Cyclone was the CJ. The Cyclone had a special blacked-out grille, Cyclone emblem, wheelwell opening moldings and a dual exhaust. The car came with the 428 Cobra Jet rated engine, which developed 335 horsepower. It was also fitted with the Competition Handling Package, and a plain bench seat interior.

But the hottest of the hot was the Cyclone Spoiler II, which was modified to improve its aerodynamics for NASCAR drag racing. A total of 519 Spoiler IIs were built.

Spoilers came in two trim versions, both named after Mercury NASCAR drivers. The Dan Gurney Spoiler had a dark blue roof and striping, with a signature decal on the white lower portion of the car. The Cale Yarborough edition featured red trim and a signature decal. These Spoiler signature editions had Windsor 351-cid engines, rated with 290 horsepower, and FMX Cruise-O-Matic.

The Cyclone was based on the Mercury Montego for 1970, and thus became bigger and heavier. It is said that this changed the car from a true contender to a full size pretender... The model was discontinued in 1971.

■ *Left: The Cale Yarborough Cyclone Spoiler II models enjoyed special striping, badging and a rear spoiler.*

Engine:	Windsor V-8
Displacement:	351-cid
Horsepower:	290 at 5200 rpm
Transmission:	FMX Cruise-O-Matic
Induction:	Autolite four-barrel
Body Style:	Two-door Hardtop
Number of Seats:	6
Weight:	3273 lbs
Wheelbase:	116 inches
Number Produced:	519

1969 Oldsmobile Hurst

By the end of the sixties, Oldsmobile's market share was wavering slightly, they were now at sixth position in the auto manufacturers' league, and would begin the seventies at seventh position.

Continuing their muscle-car collaboration, Hurst/Oldsmobile again offered a Cutlass-based hardtop coupe. The car was a fine example of a pure-bred muscle car. Hurst was (and still is today) one of the premier U.S. gearbox manufacturers. When they teamed their expertise with that of Oldsmobile, a truly memorable product was born. The car was based on the Cutlass 4-4-2 two-door 'Holiday' hardtop, and was equipped with a massive 455-cid V-8 engine, and had a special Firefrost Gold and White paint scheme. The engine power output was a tasty 380 horsepower. Nine hundred and six cars were produced for this model year.

The Cutlass models were offered in three ranges for '69, the base Cutlass, the Cutlass Supreme and the 4-4-2s. The Cutlass was the next step up the Oldsmobile ladder from the base level F-85 models. The two-door Cutlass SS had a shorter wheelbase than the four-door models. A potent W-31 performance package was available for both the Cutlass and Cutlass Supreme models, as performance became important throughout the range. It was based on a 'Force-Air' inducted 350-cid V-8 with special equipment included hood louvers, an insulated fibreglass hood blanket, nylon blend carpeting, special molding package and Deluxe steering wheel. Upholstery was vinyl or cloth.

Cutlass Supremes were the ultimate luxury in the range. This three-model series was one of Oldsmobile's best sellers and was equipped with standard supreme equipment plus a few luxury extras.

The 4-4-2 series was now in its second year. Not only could the buyer for this series order the classic 4-4-2 option, but they could also order the super-stock drag racing package, the W-30. Properly tuned, these cars were among the fastest show room stock cars available on the domestic market. The Hurst/Oldsmobile two-door hardtop was included in this four-model range, and was the most expensive option by far.

Engine: V-8 overhead valve, cast iron block

Displacement: 455 cid

Horsepower: 380 at 4800 rpm

Transmission: Hurst Dual-Gate Shifter

Induction: Rochester 4GC four-barrel

Weight: 3900 lbs

Wheelbase: 112 inches

Base Price: $4500 - $4900

Number Produced: 906

■ *Right: This 4-4-2 based Hurst/Oldsmobile two-door hardtop sports its special White and Firefrost Gold paintjob.*

Plymouth 'Cuda 440-cid

1969

By the late 1960s, the Plymouth Barracuda was a quintessential muscle car, and the bigger engined versions were difficult in insure. But the original car was quite a different, milder creature all together. The model was launched in '64 as a fastback version of the Valiant Sedan, and aimed at young, sporty American drivers, who wanted some fun transport. These sound just like Mustang drivers... Handily, the car was fitted with a fold-down rear seat that offered 7 feet of fully carpeted 'anything' space.

The original model was by no means hot, available with a single 273-cid V-8, developing a modest 180 horsepower. Eve so, a four-speed manual gearbox with a Hurst shifter was available. Handicapped by this low performance rating, the car got off to a rather slow start, selling only 23,000 in their first eight months of production.

Luckily, Plymouth soon realised where they were going wrong, and revamped the model considerably. The V-8 remained at 273cid, but with a four-barrel carburetor and higher compression ratio, the car could now push out 235 horsepower, and was tested at 0-60mph in 8.2 seconds. The car was also offered with a Formula S performance package, with stiffer suspension, wide wheels/tires and rally stripes. The car now appealed to the market far more, and sold 64,000 in this incarnation.

For '67, the Barracuda became a line in its own right, and had a bigger and hotter engine – the 383-cid, 280 horsepower engine, coupled with a Carter four-barrel carburetor and front disc brakes.

By '69, the 'Cuda was available in three models (two-door hardtop, two-door fastback and two-door convertible). The cars were hardly changed from the '68s, except for slightly face-lifted hoods and grilles. The cars also had new side marker lamps that were rectangular. The standard engine V-8 engine option was the 318-cid, but the tried-and-tested 225-cid Slant Six was also on offer. However, higher performance options were also available, including the 440-cid Hemi V-8. The cars were fitted with standard government-required safety equipment (deep dish steering wheels and padding), all-vinyl interiors, bucket seats, Pit-stop gas cap, rally lights and red or white stripe tires.

■ *Left: Our '69 'Cuda 440 is the fastback, complete with red stripe tires. Cars fitted with this powerful engine had a reputation for poor handling and braking.*

Engine:	GTX V-8
Displacement:	440-cid
Horsepower:	375 at 4600rpm
Compression Ratio:	10.1:1
Weight:	2987lbs
Wheelbase:	108 inches
Base Price:	$2813
Number Produced:	17,788

Pontiac GTO Judge

1969

Pontiac's still at number three, and 'Here come da Judge' – a new $332 option package for Pontiac's '69 GTO, complete with 366 horsepower, Ram Air III induction, 400-cid V-8. For $390, the buyer could step up to 370 horsepower with Am Air IV. With this option, the car could go from 0-60 mph at 6.2 seconds, and cover the quarter mile in 14.5. The car was decorated with loud 'The Judge' decals, and was a 'hairy' looking car indeed. The first 2,000 Judges were finished in a true pop-art color, Carousel Red, and came complete with extrovert spoiler, and stripes. This in-your-face decorative style was becoming a muscle car tradition, and buyers were almost as interested in the 'look' as they were in the power under the hood.

The Judge model was introduced to try and halt the decline in GTO sales. The LeMans-based car was falling between two stools – it wasn't a budget musclecar, but neither was it a premium model. Other Pontiac models, such as the HO-powered Tempest developed almost as much power, and were cheaper to insure. An important consideration for the young drivers these cars were aimed at. The Judge was designed to be a top-of-the-range GTO, to mop up customers who were looking for something with more style and power than the regular models. For an extra $332 over the price of a standard GTO, the car came fully loaded with Ram Air III induction (later upgraded to Ram Air IV for $558), the '68 400-cid HO power unit, three-speed gearbox with floor shifter, (automatic was optional), Rally II wheels, heavy duty suspension and 14-inch tires. The cars were offered in hardtop and convertible forms, but the convertible sold only a meagre 108 units, whereas the hardtop scored nearly 7000 sales. Considering that the convertibles were over a thousand dollars more, this isn't too surprising. As well as the standard equipment, Pontiac also offered the cars with an enormous range of options, ranging from the handy to the downright bizarre (including a litter basket in several color choices, and a reading lamp). Inside the car, carpeting was fitted as standard, and there was a choice of bucket or notchback seats.

Although the Judge was now the best-equipped musclecar available for the money, it was only temporarily successful in halting the slide in GTO sales. The car was reasonably successful in it's own right, but its image did not seem to reflect on the rest of the range, and GTO sales slid by nearly 20 per cent to just over 72,000 for the '69 model year. Worse was to come. Sales really slumped as the '70s arrived, falling to fewer than 40,000 in 1970, and to just over 10,000 in '71. This was largely due to the spiralling insurance costs generated by the car's own scary performance image.

■ *Left: 'Here come da Judge'*

Engine: Ram Air V-8	
Displacement: 400-cid	
Horsepower: 370	
Number Produced: 6725	

1969 Pontiac Trans Am

Apart from the Corvette, The Pontiac Trans Am Firebird has the longest heritage of any American muscle car, its production running uninterruptedly from the mid-sixties right up to the new millennium, and was cancelled only recently. Even GM cousin, the Camaro, can't equal this record, as their production was stopped between 1974-77.

The original Trans Am debuted in 1969, originally as a low-production speciality vehicle with stock car racing the driving factor in their conception. They were designed to compete in the Sports Car Club of America's 'Trans Am' American Sedan Championship races. Get it?

But, as always, manufacturers had to retail a certain number of cars to make them race legal, and had maximum displacement criteria of 305-cid. The Mustang had been an early leader in this race series, and was ideally equipped to compete, with its 289-cid small-block V-8. The cars dominated the races, until the Mustang's performance was out-stripped by that of the Chevy Z/28 Camaro. The series effectively developed into a showcase for America's latest pony cars, and all the major manufacturers started developing and selling 'homologated' hot rod cars, basing their investment on the adage 'Win on Sunday, Sell on Monday'.

Pontiac Motor Division had introduced the musclecar to the American scene, with the Trans Am Firebird in 1968. The car was launched to the public in '69. Although the manufacture started conventionally, as a route to race legal status, the cars soon became sought after in their own right, and became a long-running success. Demand initially outstripped supply, but as soon as it caught up, the cars raced out of the doors. Ironically, the engines in the first Trans-Ams were too big (at 400-cid) to be SCCA legal in any case, but the street-racers loved the car, and it sold in big numbers right from the start. The classic 'Trans Am Performance and Appearance' cars were offered in blue-accented Cameo white paint jobs, ram air hoods, flat racing spoilers and fender-mounted air extractors. Technically, the cars were equipped with a strengthened chassis, stiffer shocks, Safe-T-Track differential and front disc brakes. The power unit was the 335 horsepower Ram Air II 400-cid V-8, and a bigger 345 horsepower Ram Air IV option was available for extra cost. Transmission options included a Muncie four-speed manual, Turbo-Hydramatic or the standard heavy-duty three-speed manual. Only 55 of the '69 cars were fitted with the more powerful option.

The car got rave reviews, and was particularly praised for its handling and suspension, that were habitually criticised in other performance Pontiacs. Hot Rod Magazine rated it only second to the Corvette.

Engine: Ram Air III V-8

Displacement: 400-cid

Horsepower: 335 at 5000 rpm

Compression Ratio: 10.75:1

■ *Right: Sports wheels were standard on the Trans Am. As well as the hardtops, the model sold eight convertible models.*

1970 AMC AMX

The AMX (American Motors Experimental) was a two-seater car, based on a shortened (97 inch) version of the Javelin wheelbase. It was launched in 1968. The AMX was one of the best-handling cars of the era, and being relatively light, was also nimble, capable of quarter mile times of 10.73 seconds at 128 mph in its super stock times. American two-seater sport cars were incredibly rare during this time, the only well-known model of this kind being the Corvette. Sadly, the hot little AMX was destined for a much shorter, three-year lifespan. Its wheelbase was also slightly shorter than that of its long-lived rival.

AMC loaded the Kenosha, Wisconsin-built AMX with top performance goodies, such as heavy-duty suspension, sway bar and shocks. The highest option engine for 1970 was the 390-cid V-8, now rated with 325 horsepower. Interiors were fitted with woodgrain dashboard and woodgrain racing steering wheel, complete with AMC roundel. Having no room for a back seat, the rear area was simply carpeted.

The original AMX concept dated back to 1966 also featured a two-seater cabin, and was body-built in fiberglass. It was this prototype that inspired the steel-bodied production spin-off. When the real AMXs were revealed at the February 1968 Daytona Speed Week, they attracted rave reviews. Styling guru Richard Teague was responsible for the car's startling and yet timeless good looks, and lovingly referred to his creation as a 'hairy little brother to the Javelin'. Group Vice-President Vic Raviolo was responsible for the concept development, and referred to the car as a 'Walter Mitty Ferrari'. Like the other pony cars (the Camaro, Cougar and Firebird), the AMX followed in the venerable hoofprints of the Mustang. But the crisply defined body styling of the AMX, with its long-hood/really-short-deck profile almost succeeded in redefining the image of the ponycars. The cars also offered good performance and AMC were very hopeful that this style/power combination ensured good prospects for their 'runt'.

■ Below: The 1970 AMX was awarded Milestone Car status by the Milestone Car Society.

The company projected sales of 10,000 for 1968 and 20,000 for each ensuing year. But sadly, AMX sales never took off, and even a revamp for the 1970 model year (including a sexy power bulge on the hood, and simulated 'sidepipe' rocker trim) could not reverse the sagging sales figures for the model. Only 19,134 AMXs were ever sold. AMX sales fell to an all-time low of 4,116 units in 1970, and AMC decided to discontinue the model.

Engine: V-8

Displacement: 390-cid

Horsepower: 325 at 5000 rpm

Compression Ratio: 10:1

Number Produced: 4116

1970 Buick GSX Stage1

By the end of the '60s, Buick had loyal followers in many sectors of the American car market. Never a huge part of the Buick sales picture, but still catered to with great care, were Buick's performance customers. The hi-po market at this time was dominated by GM, whose Pontiac GTOs and Oldsmobile 4-4-2s had started the whole supercar race. Buick followed in their footsteps with the launch of the first of their long-running Gran Sports models, based on the mid-sized Skylark. The Gran Sports cars were built in Flint, Michigan, where Buick constructed their classier models. But the gentlemanly image of these 'better' cars didn't mean that Buick weren't serious about tapping into the muscle market. This was particularly evident in their Stage 1 GSX engine package.

Stage 1 GSXs were blessed with a great combination of good musclecar looks and zinging performance. Only coming as hardtops, the package started out as a 1970-71 option for the Gran Sport 455 coupe and was developed to offer what is now considered to be one of the musclecar era's highest profile image treatment packages. This featured two special paint colors (Apollo White and Saturn Yellow), color-coordinated headlight bezels, wild hood and bodyside stripes in black and red, front and rear spoilers, hood-mounted tachometer, dual racing mirrors and G60-15 Wide-Oval tires. Interiors were only available in all black, with bucket seats, consolette, Rallye steering wheel, gauges and a Rallye clock.

The standard power plant for the GSX was a 315 horsepower 400-cid V-8. But the Stage 1 version of the car was equipped with a modified Rochester Quadra-Jet four-barrel carburettor (topped with a ram-air hood) and a hotter camshaft so that the car developed 360 horsepower. This equipment enabled the car to cover the quarter mile in 13.38 seconds, and caused Motor Trend Magazine's Bill Sanders to remark that the car was like an 'old man's car inbred with a going street

■ Below: This Saturn Yellow GSX looks like a real muscle car, despite its gentlemanly Buick background.

bomb... performance verges on a precipitous mechanical hysteria'.

In fact, the car was loaded with performance features. Go-goodies included the Buick Rally Ride Control Package, Positraction rear axle, four-speed manual transmission with Hurst shifter/Turbo Hydramatic, heavy-duty suspension and power front disc brakes.

The GSX carried a hefty price tag, and was effectively a $1,199 option package on the GS455. It was a special limited edition model, and sold only 678 cars in 1970, including 400 with the Stage 1 package (only 124 in '71). Many commentators feel that the car was held back by Buick's staid image, and reflected on how much better it would have sold as a GTO. Today, however, the GTX is a rare classic, and one of the most sought-after seventies Buicks.

Engine: Stage 1 V-8

Displacement: 455-cid

Horsepower: 360 at 4600 rpm

Transmission: Turbo Hydramatic automatic

Compression Ratio: 10.5:1

Weight: 3920lbs

Wheelbase: 112 inches

Base Price: $3920

Number Produced: 400

Chevrolet Corvette LT-1 1970

Corvette production dropped by half in 1970, due to a prolonged workforce dispute at the St. Louis factory. This had had the knock-on effect of extending dealer delivery times to over two months, which reduced orders to only 17,316 cars. This was the lowest Corvette production volume for over a decade, and means that cars from this 'limited-production' model year are now both rare and sought after. Other market factors were also mitigating against the success of high-performance cars at this time. High gas and insurance prices, together with a general feeling of economic uncertainty made selling this kind of luxury/power auto package tricky. In real terms, the cars were becoming obsolete. But despite their problems, Chevrolet continued to subtly revise the car to keep it in the forefront of design and performance.

Corvette's big block V-8 engine grew even bigger in this year – to a high point of 454-cid (producing 465 horsepower). This LS-7 option was designed for competition, and could cover the quarter mile in around 13 seconds at 110 mph. The LS-7 package wasn't fitted to regular road cars. The LT-1 engine option was also introduced to the range in '70. This was a solid-lifter 370 horsepower version of the small block engine. The LT-1 package included sharper valve timing, a bigger bore exhaust, and the same carburetion as the big-block with cold air induction. The LT-1 was actually advertised as a 350-cid set-up to accommodate Federal emissions regulations. These anti-performance government restrictions were to negatively affect all the pony car runners in the 1970s, obliging them to put an increased emphasis on comfort and luxury features to sell the cars.

The basic aerodynamic styling introduced to the Corvette in 1968 effectively persisted until 1983, but it was refined and revised for 1970. Corvettes were available as sport coupes and convertibles in this model year. The car's four fender gills were replaced by an ice cube tray grille, which was echoed in the (non-functional) radiator intakes at the front of the car. Corvette designers were aware that the lower portion of the car was susceptible to stone-chip damage from material flicked up by the wheels, so they flared the wheel arches to offset this problem. The twin tail-pipes were squared-ff to become rectangular rather than round. Inside the car, the seats were improved, in an attempt to give better support and more headroom, and improved access to the luggage area. This was crucial, as the cars still weren't fitted with trunk lids. Inertia-reel seatbelts were now fitted as standard.

■ *Left: This 1970 Corvette inadvertently became a limited-production model, and is now extremely desirable.*

Engine:	LT-1 V-8
Displacement:	350-cid
Horsepower:	370
Weight:	3153lbs
Wheelbase:	98 inches
Base Price:	$5469
Number Produced:	10,668

Dodge Challenger R/T

Short for 'Road and Track', R/T was to the Dodge musclecars what 'SS' was to Chevrolet, although the cars were far thinner on the ground, and their profile was much lower. Sadly, they were never quite as cool. From its humble beginnings in 1967, the R/T package consisted, most importantly, of the high-powered big-block Magnum V-8. A beefed-up chassis was necessary to handle the greater output of the engine.

The package was initially fitted to the Coronet in 1967 and a Charger in the following year. Both cars were fitted with either a 375 horsepower 440-cid V-8 or the optional 426-cid Hemi. A third version of the R/T based on the new Dodge Challenger 'pony car' debuted in 1970. This car was something of an answer to Plymouth's Barracuda.

To fit in as many go-goodies as possible, the Dodge designers utilized the slightly longer wheelbase to create a slightly different slant on the same long-hood/short-deck theme. The 'S' body Challenger was offered in three different forms, a hardtop, convertible and 'sports hardtop' that featured Dodge's Special Edition package, which included a vinyl-covered roof and reduced size rear window.

This new Challenger R/T package came with a whole range of engine options, starting with the 383-cid Magnum four-barrel V-8 (335 horsepower), then came the 440-cid V-8 (375 horsepower), the 440-cid Triple-carb V-8 (390 horsepower) and the 426-cid Hemi. The last three engines were only available on the R/T models. A range of gearboxes was also available in various engine combinations. A three-speed manual, four-speed manual and Torqueflite automatic came with the various packages. Other R/T extras included the Rallye suspension package, heavy-duty drum brakes and Wide-Tread F70x14 tires (Hemi models had 15 inch tires). Inside the cars, the Rallye instrument cluster was included, as were a simulated woodgrain panel, 150 mph speedometer, a tachometer, trip odometer, clock and fuel oil and temperature gauges. The outside of the cars was decorated with either a body-long stripe, or a stripe around the tail. Rallye wheels, the functional Shaker hood scoop and spoiler were all optional. The competition-style fuel filler was standard.

Dodge built 76,935 Challengers in 1970, 14,889 of which were Challengers. 3,979 R/R hardtops and 963 R/T convertibles were produced with the Special Edition package.

■ *Left: This R/T Challenger is painted in mouth-watering 'Plum Crazy'.*

Engine: Big-block V-8	
Displacement: 440-cid	
Horsepower: 375 at 4600 rpm	
Compression Ratio: 9.7:1	
Wheelbase: 110 inches	
Base Price: $3266	
Number Produced in this format: 916	

1970 Mercury Cougar Eliminator

Throughout the sixties, Cougars, Z28s and Javelins fought it out in the Tran Am racing series, taking turns to take the honors. The Cougar also fought it out in the pony car sales stakes, but was beaten by its archrival the Dodge Challenger in 1970. At this time, the car was effectively an upmarket version of the Mustang, having the same performance options but more luxurious interior. Like so many worthy Mercury models, the car seemed to roll out straight into the shadows.

The Eliminator was Mercury's hottest ever pony car, and had fabulous styling to boot. It was also roomier than its Mustang cousins and had loads more class. Convenience was also on offer with a long list of optional extras available. Like the Ford Boss 302, the Cougar was designed by engineer Larry Shinoda (who had also been responsible for the lovely GM Sting Ray of '63). He had been poached over to Ford by his boss Bunkie Knudsen, and when the Boss Mustang became successful, the Lincoln-Mercury bosses hoped that he could work the same magic for their baby ponycar.

The Eliminator (named for the famous dragstrip) was originally launched as a prototype in October 1968. The front and rear spoilers were very attractive, and reputedly functional. Virtually all the

■ *Below: The image for this Boss Eliminator was designed by Larry Shinoda, who blessed the car with his signature spoiler, striping and blacked out grille.*

styling elements of the prototype, including the hood scoop, bodyside striping and blacked-out grille were given to the production model. Unfortunately, the bosses refused to give in to Larry Shinoda's longed-for sporty mag wheels. These were available as a cost plus option. Other standard equipment included F70-14 Goodyear Polyglas tires and the Competition Handling Suspension. The prototype had been painted in Flaming Orange and the six production colors were similarly eye-catching.

Power came from a range of power sources, ranging from the base 351-cid four-barrel small-block Cleveland V-8, through a 320 horsepower 390-cid big-block V-8 to the 335 horsepower 428 Cobra Jet. The latter came with a further up-rated suspension, and a functional Ram Air hood scoop. The Cobra Jet suspension package was also partnered with the Boss 302 small-block to give the car a brilliant combination of power and excellent handling. Even so, the car was never a serious rival to Mustang for popularity.

Engine:	Boss V-8
Displacement:	302-cid
Horsepower:	290 at 5800 rpm
Transmission:	Four-speed manual
Compression Ratio:	10.5:1
Induction:	Single 780 cfm Holley four-barrel
Body Style:	Two-door Coupe
Weight:	3610 lbs
Wheelbase:	111 inches
Base Price:	$3200
Number Produced:	450

Oldsmobile F-85 Rallye 350   **1970**

Olds had launched the F-85 in 1961, as an entry-level car to it's range. This was the first time that the company had broken with its three series format. Smaller than any other post-war Oldsmobile, the first F-85 models were powered by a unique aluminum 215-cid V-8. It was launched to compete with the small car offerings of Buick and Pontiac. The Cutlasses were launched as part of the F-85 series in 1962. The cars were restyled and re-sized over the years, and went from compact to midsize in 1964. The cars gained a handsome new 'A' body platform, which was shared with the Buick Special and Skylark, the Pontiac Tempest and Le Mans and Chevy's new Chevelle. F-85s were also used as the platform for several of Oldsmobile's high-performance options, including being the first body for the 4-4-2 in 1965. This was the Oldsmobile answer to the Pontiac GTO option. The full name for the option was 'Option B-09 Police Apprehender Pursuit'. 25,003 4-4-2s were ordered in that year.

By 1970 the F-85 line was reduced to a single model sports coupe, and Cutlass was by now the next level Oldsmobile intermediate series. The F-85 was available with both a six-cylinder and V-8 engine option. At the performance end of the scale, the W-45, Rallye 350 package was installed on 3,547 Cutlass 'S'/F-85 coupes. This enabled Olds to offer a range of what might be called 'junior musclecars'. Although cars like this were sometimes eclipsed by the 'big-block' tire burners, the Rallye 350 was actually 'big-block quick'.

Oldsmobile launched the Rallye 350 in 1970, as a kind of bargain bruiser musclecar in the tradition of Pontiac's GTO Judge. Like 'da Judge', the car also had eye-catching livery, including an eye-scorching Sebring Yellow paint job with black and orange stripes and cool black decals. You also got hood louvers and a spruced-up interior trim. Power for the car was a 310 horsepower 350-cid V-8. This engine could also be up-graded with the scary W-31 forced induction system that boosted the horsepower rating by 15 – up to 325. A typical 310 Rallye with a three-speed manual shifter could cover the quarter mile in around 15.5 seconds at speeds of just below 90 mph. It could get from 0-60 mph in just under eight seconds.

The low sales of the F-85 Rallye 350, a mere 1020, meant that the model did not return in 1971. The hallucinogenic graphic treatment had scared off too many buyers.

■ *Left: These wild-looking musclecars draw a premium from collectors today.*

Engine:	V-8
Displacement:	350-cid
Horsepower:	310 at 4600 rpm
Compression Ratio:	10.25:1
Wheelbase:	112 inches
Base Price:	$2676
Number Produced:	1020

1970 Plymouth Road Runner 426 Hemi

Plymouth had gone to Hollywood in 1969, adopting the popular Warner Brothers Road Runner cartoon character as both the name and symbol for a new range of low-priced, medium-sized, high-performance musclecars. The Road Runners were instantly popular. The base price for a GTX was below $3000 and this was for a car that featured a 383-cid, 335 horsepower V-8 Hemi. Performance was shattering and the cars had loads of personality, complete with their jolly 'Beep! Beep!' horn.

The Road Runner, and 'Superbird' models were developed in a wind tunnel to develop a body that would cut through the air, straight to NASCAR stock car race victory. Qualifying speeds of over 190 mph were recorded at the super speedways like Daytona and Talladega, and highly tuned cars were capable of around 200 mph. The model dominated the 1970 NASCAR season. Pete Hamilton won the 1970 Daytona 500 in a Superbird at an average speed of 150 mph, and Superbirds rode to victory in 21 Grand National races. Plymouth was obliged to manufacture in excess of 1500 cars to homologate the model for the NASCAR series. They actually produced around 1,935 of these 426-cid Hemi V-8 fitted race-going cars, but they was obliged to discount the price of the model to stimulate demand.

The cars were replete with Plymouth heavy-duty 'fuselage' styling, which included loads of vents and scoops, both dummy and functional. The car was derived from the 1969 Dodge Charger Daytona, and employed an identical, massive aerodynamic, front-end extension that covered the headlights, and a towering rear spoiler mounted on struts above the trunk.

Production models of the car were equipped with the 383-cid V-8 that developed 335 horsepower. They also had a four-barrel carburetor and TorqueFlite automatic transmission. Options included a four-speed manual transmission and a 390 horsepower, 440-cid Street Hemi with the 440 'Six pack'. A Super Trak Package designed with racers in mind was also available, this constituted of a heavy-duty manual four-speed transmission (instead of the standard three-speed) and a 9¾-inch Dana Sure Grip rear axle.

But sadly, 1970 was the third and final year for the Road Runner body style. NASCAR changed their rules to bring the Superbird's brief reign to an abrupt end. But the iconic status of the car was assured.

Engine:	Superbird V-8
Displacement:	440-cid
Horsepower:	375 at 4400 rpm
Compression Ratio:	9.7:1
Wheelbase:	116 inches
Base Price:	$2896
Number Produced:	15,716

■ *Right: Only 74 Road Runner Coupes were fitted with the Hemi engine option in 1970. Forty-four of these had the four-speed manual transmission upgrade.*

1971 Dodge Charger R/T Hemi

By 1971 the muscle car era was drawing to a close, but Dodge decided to integrate both Super Bee and R/T musclecars into their newly restyled Charger series. The changes to the Charger series were largely instigated to further segregate the models from the lower-level Coronets. The cars now rode on a new 115-inch chassis, and the model range was expanded to six coupes and hardtops in three series, the Chargers, Charger 500 series and Charger R/T (one car) series. All Chargers were now semi-fastback coupes featuring rear quarter window styling that swept up from the fender to meet the sloping upper window frame. The full-width bumper-grille shell was split by a large vertical divider on all Chargers and the rear end of the car featured a small trunk lid spoiler. Six square taillights were located in the oval rear bumper.

The top-of-the-range R/T model was the most luxurious and high-performance Charger model. It included all the standard equipment fitted to the 500s, together with a 70 amp/hour battery, heavy-duty brakes and shock absorbers; pedal dress-up kit; extra heavy duty Rallye suspension; Torqueflite automatic or four-speed manual transmission. Interiors were kitted out in keeping with the contemporary trend, and were awash with white-pleated vinyl and plastic wood. The exterior of the car was dressed with a black R/T decal.

Engine options were the 440 Magnum (fitted as standard) and the Hemi was available as a $707 option. Some cars (178) were also equipped with the 440-cid 'Six Pak' V-8. The Hemi Chargers were equipped with twin Carter four-barrel carburetors and had a compression ratio of 10.25:1 producing 425 horsepower. According to Mopar authority Galen V. Govier, 63 R/Ts were fitted with the Hemi engine option (30 four-speed manuals, and 33 TorqueFlite automatics). These cars were feared at dragstrips up and down the country.

NASCAR performance limitations severely reduced Dodge's interest in this race series, and they cut back heavily on their factory backing of stock car racing. Following 22 Grand National wins in 1969, and 17 in 1970, there were only eight Dodge victories in 1971. 1971 also marked the final year when the Hemi engine was offered for sale to the public, in either the street or racing form. Insurance premiums were astronomical on these high-performance cars and beginning in 1972, all cars had to be run on regular gas. Dodge decided to retire the Hemi while it was still in front. It returned in 1992, for sale to racers and restorers via the Chrysler Performance high-performance parts division.

Engine: Street Hemi V-8, overhead valve with hemispherical combustion chambers

Displacement: 428-cid

Horsepower: 425 at 5600 rpm

Compression Ratio: 10.25:1

Number Produced: 3,118

■ *Right: The R/T was one of the last cars equipped with a Hemi for over twenty years.*

1971 Ford Mustang Mach 1

Ford had broken the mold to offer the first Mustang to the American public in April 1964. The car was a completely unique fusion of Detroit's power and comfort, with the styling of the classic European sportscars. The Mustang was an immediate run-away success, and for the moment, the first of the ponycars was ahead in a one horse race.

One of the main reasons for the success of the Mustang range was always the breadth of its appeal. Ford was careful to offer a selection of cars to appeal to different kinds of buyers, from the boy-racer to the more sedate middle-aged customer interested more in image than performance. The first Mach 1 was introduced in 1969 as a middle-of-the-road Mustang, with musclecar heritage in a relatively civilised road-going package. The car was styled with the new Ford Sportsroof (the latest version of the fastback). Mach 1s were immediately successful, and sold 70,00 units in their introductory year.

By 1971, Mustang production peaked at 149,678 unis, and the division was known as the Ford Marketing Corporation. The Boss Mustang 351 was now the most serious package on offer. But for buyers who wanted something slightly less hairy, but still with a sporty flavor, the Mustang Mach 1 remained the street-friendly alternative for this model year. The car came complete with a full sports appearance package and was available with a range of power plant options. These varied from the relatively mild 210 horsepower 302-cid V-8 all the way through to the Cobra Jet 429, or even the completely wild 370 horsepower 429-cid Super Cobra Jet fitted with Ram Air induction. In fact, only five othese cars were reputedly built, and 1971 was the final year that this big-block 429 engine was on offer. The 351-cid Cleveland four-barrel V-8 was another engine on offer with the Mach 1, and developed an impressive 285 horsepower. Other sports goodies could also be included in the package, including E70 tires and Special Handling suspension.

Mach 1s were also blessed with the classic good looks you would expect from such a fine musclecar heritage. Buyers got a blacked-out hood with twin NASA-style air scoops, a mean black spoiler and side striping, with Mach 1 decals. The package was completed with a honeycomb grille with driving lights, color-keyed mirrors and bumpers, black or 'argent' colored lower bodysides. Inside, the buyer could upgrade the interior with high-backed bucket seats and a center console. The Mach 1 perfectly reflected a market that was now tending towards appearance, rather than performance concerns. But with the range of power-plants on offer, Mach 1 buyers could still specify a seriously hot car from the Mustang stable.

Engine: Cleveland V-8

Displacement: 351-cid

Horsepower: 285 at 5400 rpm

Number Produced: 36,499

■ *Right: The black spoiler can just be seen at the rear of this Mach 1.*

Plymouth Duster 340 1972

Dusters were members of Plymouth's entry level Valiant Group series, as were Scamp two-door hardtops and Valiant sedans. Interestingly, the mighty 'Cudas had also started out as Valiants back in '64, but by this time, the 'Cudas were configured on the larger 'E' Mopar body. The Dusters soon eclipsed the sales of the bigger car.

Dusters were engineered in 1969 for a 1970 launch. The name would ultimately outlast 'Valiant'. The 340 Duster achieved a great power-to-weight ratio that allowed the car to out-perform many larger cars fitted with more powerful engines. Car Life rated the 1970 model with a 0-60 mph time of just 6.2 seconds, and a quarter mile time of 14.7 seconds at an average 94 mph.

The 1971 Valiant models had set great sales levels, with a volume of 256,930 units in that year. Consequently, there was very little impetus to change this successful model. Only details of the model taillights and grille were changed. The front side marker was also now slimmer and longer. The base Duster model for '72 shared this pattern of light revision, but the side market lamps were moved an inch or two higher above the lower feature line. Base Duster equipment included ventless side windows, a concealed spare tire and two-speed wipers. Outside, the car had a lower deck tape stripe, bodyside tape stripe, a unique grille, roof drip rail moldings and wide tires. Mechanically, the car was fitted with the 340-cid V-8 with dual exhaust, a three-speed manual floor shift, optional axle ratio, heavy-duty suspension and dual snorkel air cleaner. Duster interiors had been upgraded in 1971, and the car was equipped with an optional fold-down rear seat, optional electrically heated window defogger and had front and rear fender guards as standard. Lowback-style seats were a Duster option, and the car also had a locking glovebox.

Just as they had done with the Demon, Plymouth offered a mighty little compact in the shape of their 1972 Plymouth Duster 340. Like the earlier Demon, the car also made use of fun 'character' graphics to appeal to a young audience, and this 340 version had a wide tape strip running the full length of the car along the beltline with bold '340' lettering on the rear fender edge. Effectively, the Duster was Plymouth's entry-level musclecar and came fully loaded with both plenty of performance goodies and a wallet-friendly price. The car continued to be a great success in '72, with almost identical sales to the 1971 model. Its fun image and targeted marketing was right on the money.

■ *Left: lthough the Duster 340 was the most expensive member of Plymouth's Valiant Group, it was still a great little musclecar for the money.*

Engine:	V-8 overhead valve, cast iron block
Displacement:	340-cid
Transmission:	Three-speed manual
Compression Ratio:	8.5:1
Base Price:	$2728
Number Produced:	15,681

1972 Pontiac Trans Am

During the 1971 calendar year, Pontiac captured third place in the US auto producers' league for the tenth time in eleven years, but the image of the division was simultaneously losing interest from the buying public, and things were very difficult by 1972.

Pontiac had launched the Trans Am as a $725 Firebird option package in 1969. A 335 horsepower engine was offered as standard, with the option of a 345 horsepower Ram Air IV. Buyers got a limited slip differential and three-speed manual transmission. Despite its name and heritage, the Trans Am never actually raced in the eponymous series. Nevertheless, with 0-60 mph times of 6.5 seconds and quarter mile times of 14.3 seconds (averaging 101 mph), they were undoubtedly fully loaded in the performance department.

The Trans Am was heavily restyled in 1970, and the model was fitted with a new 'bull nose' front grille and streamlined fastback profile that made the car look longer, lower and wider. The 1972 Trans Am series reflected the same look, but was now fitted with the 300 horsepower 455-cid V-8 as standard. The Trans Am interiors had the same standard features as the Firebirds, plus a Formula steering wheel, engine-turned dash trim, rally gauge cluster with clock and a tachometer. Outside, the cars were equipped with a front air dam, wheel flares front and back, full-width rear deck spoiler, shaker hood, 15-inch Rally II rims with trim rings and black-textured grille inserts.

Sadly, a combination of circumstances almost resulted in Pontiac axing the car in 1972. Part of the problem was that buyers were deserting musclecar models in the fuel conscious seventies. But this wasn't the only problem Pontiac had to overcome in this year. The most damaging was a five-month long strike on the Firebird/Trans Am manufacturing line at the Norwood, Ohio plant. This resulted in the loss of thousands of cars, and millions of dollars. It very nearly caused the company to drop the model altogether. Further complications arose from the increased volume of Federal safety regulations. These generally resulted in a lessening of performance, and this was certainly true for the Trans Am. Compression ratios were scaled back to cope with lower octane fuel and stricter emissions limits.

Despite all its problems, the Trans Am turned out to be a real survivor, and it was a best-selling model by 1974.

Engine: V-8

Displacement: 455-cid

Horsepower: 300 at 400 rpm

Compression Ratio: 8.4:1

Wheelbase: 108 inches

Base Price: $4256

Number Produced: 1286

Right: Almost dropped from the GM range in '72, The Trans Am turned out to be a tough survivor.

1973 AMC Javelin

The Javelin had first been added to the AMC range in 1968, fitting into the slot vacated by the unsuccessful Marlin. It was AMC's attempt to follow in the 1964 hoofprints of the Ford Mustang, and like the classic ponycar, boasted four seats. The car was built on a 109-inch wheelbase platform, and had an overall length of 189 inches. Power for the car was varied, supplied by either a 232-cid six-cylinder, or a 343-cid V-8. The top Javelin option, the SST was fitted with the 390-cid V-8 that worked so well in the Rebel Machine. This option was introduced late in the '68 model year – so late that it didn't make it into that model year's brochures. At first, Javelin power was hampered by the wide-ratio three-speed manual gearbox, but the car came into its own in '69 with 'loud and proud' options aimed squarely at muscle car aficionados. This option was called the 'Go-Package'. It included heavy-duty suspension and wide wheels together with a selection of garish paint colors, including Big Bad Orange and Bid Bad Green. If even a standard Javelin 390 wasn't quick enough to fit the bill, there were tuning parts that could be dealer-fitted. AMC was undoubtedly keen to leave its sensible image in the past.

Original styling characteristics for the model included a split grille with blackout treatment and form-filling bumper, single square headlamp housings were integrated into the fenders, and round parking lamps were integrated into the bumper. The Javelin had a clean-lined body with smooth-flowing lines and a semi-fastback roofline with wide, flat sail panels.

The Javelin was given new styling in 1973, which it substantially shared with the AMX sports hardtops. Both cars featured a new, smooth roofline. A new taillight treatment was adopted, with twin-pod lamps at each side of the car. The base level Javelin now had a recessed plastic grille that incorporated rectangular Rallye lights. Bucket seats were standard in the car along with interior styling of the aircraft cockpit-type.

Race driver Mark Donohue drove a Javelin in the 1970 Trans Am race series, and lost the championship by just one point to Parnelli Jones in the Boss Mustang. The car proved itself to be both powerful and reliable, and was a great combination with this experienced and talented driver. The car went on to win seven out of ten races in 1971, to take the championship. George Follmer repeated this feat in 1972, but pulled out of the races in '73.

Engine: Base V-8, overhead

Displacement: 304-cid

Horsepower: 150 at 4400 rpm

Compression Ratio: 8.4:1

Base Price: $2983

Number Produced: 25195

■ *Right: The Javelin was AMC's attempt to follow in the hoofprints of the Mustang*

Ford Gran Torino Sport   **1973**

The full-size Fords were for '73 the only models to receive significant restyling. The new full-size LTD was honoured by Motor Trend Magazine as the 1973 'Full-size Sedan of the Year'. Road Test Magazine went further, calling it the 'Car of the Year'.

The rest of the Fords received only minor trim updating. More federally mandated safety requirements were initiated. They were reflected in the form of massive 'park bench' safety bumpers, designed to tolerate a full-on impact at five miles per hour without any damage. Pollution standards were tightened, and engines were detuned. Sadly, this had the negative effect of making some of the least fuel efficient and poorest performing engines ever built. The embargo on fuel imports from the Middle East brought fuel economy into the spotlight.

Ford also attempted to make the 1973 models thief and vandal proof. For example a new fixed-length type of radio antenna was adopted, and the hoods could not be opened from outside.

The Torino and Gran Torino series were built on a slightly shorter wheelbase than the full-size models. They were slightly modified for '73, with revised grilles having slightly more rectangular openings than those of '72. There was a larger front bumper, and the technical equipment was also up-graded. The rear brakes were enlarged, an interior hood release was fitted, and there was an optional spare tire lock. The Torino models were the base trim for the series, and were offered in three body styles. The Gran Torinos were the top trim series models for the year, and included all the Torino trim, plus manual front disc brakes, cloth and vinyl upholstery trim, carpeting, and chrome trim on the foot pedals. A deluxe two-spoke steering wheel was fitted.

The Gran Torino Sport was the sporty version of the Gran Torino line and included all the Gran Torino features, plus the 302-cid v-8 engine that developed 138 horsepower. Upholstery for this model featured pleated, all-vinyl trim, hood scoops, color-keyed dual racing mirrors and a unique grille.

Well-known names on the FoMoCo board during this year were Chairman Henry Ford II, Corporate President Lee Iacocca and Ford Marketing Corporation Vice-President and Divisional General Manager B.E. Bidwell.

■ *Left: Note the subtle shading on the go-faster stripes on this Gran Torino Sport.*

Engine:	Overhead valve V-8
Displacement:	302-cid
Horsepower:	135 at 4200 rpm
Compression Ratio:	8.0:1
Weight:	3670 lbs
Wheelbase:	114 inches
Base Price:	$3154
Number Produced:	51,853

1979 Ford Indy Pace Car Mustang

The year 1979 started with Jimmy Carter telling the nation about his six-point plan to combat America's oil crisis. Inevitably, this led to a search for better gas economy.

Mustang had already decided to end their run of Mustang IIs, and introduced their third generation – Mustang III - models in 1979. In fact, the basic idea for these dated back to 1974, even before the second generation Mustangs were launched. These were based on the new 'Fox' Ford global platform, and it was hoped that it would be possible to manufacture the car in Ford factories worldwide. Unfortunately, this 'world car' concept proved impractical. Ford commissioned four different design teams to style the car, including Ghia in Italy. The chosen design came from Jack Telnack's group at Ford's own North American Light Car and Truck Design department. The new cars had a longer wheelbase and roomier cabin, yet they weighed 200 pounds less than the previous models, and were far more aerodynamic. Mustang IIIs were offered as a two-door booted model, or a three-door hatchback. A convertible wasn't added to the range until 1983. The car still had the live rear axle, but the front suspension was a new MacPherson strut layout. Three levels of ordinary suspension were offered, and a Special Suspension package was optional, complete with cast aluminium wheels. The same engine range was initially retained, but even so, the improved weigh-to-power ratio and wind tunnel tested lines imparted far better performance to the car.

The new shape Mustang proved to be an immediate success, boosting model sales by over 80%, and was credible enough to act as a pace car for the 1979 Indianapolis 500 Race. The true 'pace' cars used a highly modified 302-cid engine.

Ford built around 6,000 Indy Pace Car replicas to celebrate this honor. These were fitted with either a turbo four-cylinder, or 5-litre V-8. A Front air dam with integral fog lamps, non-functional rear-facing hood scoop, rear spoiler and sunroof were standard features on Pace Car models, together with a special silver, black orange and red paint scheme. But the factory left the lettering decals to be fitted, or not, by the dealer or customer.

Almost 2.5 million Mustangs built on the IIIrd generation platform between 1979 and 1992, with only minor changes to the front and rear of the body.

Engine: V-8 Cast iron block

Displacement: 302-cid

Horsepower: 140 at 3600 rpm

Compression Ratio: 8.4:1

Base Price: $5,000 plus

Number Produced: Approximately 6,000

■ *Right: Around 6,000 Indy Pace Car replicas were built in this special silver, black orange and red livery.*

De Lorean Sport Coupe

1981

John Z. De Lorean began his career in the automotive industry with Chrysler in 1948, later moving to Packard and General Motors. But after a remarkable record during sixteen years of service at GM, De Lorean left the company in 1974 to follow his dream. He started to raise money to build a revolutionary American sports car to rival the Corvette. Production of the first De Loreans began in early 1981 at a revolutionary new mass-production factory in Dunmurry, Northern Ireland. A first shipment of 500 cars arrived in the US in that April. The car had unique styling by Giugiaro. It was a two-seater, rear-engined sports coupe with gullwing doors, Y-shaped chassis and a unpainted stainless steel body. Power came from a Renault OHC V-6 with electronic fuel injection, and a five-speed manual gearbox.

Although the engine location compromised the power of the car, it could still offer some fairly impressive statistics – with a top speed of 124 mph, and 0-60 mph in 9.6 seconds. The main downside was the handling characteristics – the car tended to understeer when cornering. The basic problem with the De Lorean was that it was fundamentally a prototype, launched too early. Being a self-financing independent company meant that testing time was very limited, and the cars had to pay their way. Without the reputation for mechanical problems, the cars may have sold better. It's looks were certainly stunning, movie-star quality in fact. The De Lorean was the star of the movie 'Back to the Future'.

Two 24-karat gold-plated De Loreans were produced, ordered as part of an American Express promotional campaign for 'Gold' cardholders. They appeared in the December 1979 American Express catalog. The cars cost a princely $85,000, and insurance ran out at over $1,000 a month. It was calculated that a door ding would cost over $24,000 to correct.

Unfortunately, although the cars sold well in the first place, unsold cars soon began to pile up at the factory. De Lorean simply ran out of time and money. By February 1982, the factory had gone into receivership, after De Lorean failed to raise further funding. The Enron-inculpated accountancy firm, Arthur Andersen, were implicated in the failure, and the British Prime Minister, Margaret Thatcher, blamed them for the company's demise. Ironically, the cars are very collectible today.

■ *Left: The DMC12 was built between 1979 and 1982. Some motor journalists credit it with being one of the 100 best cars of the twentieth century.*

Engine:	V-6 Cylinder
Displacement:	174-cid
Horsepower:	145 at 5500 rpm
Transmission:	Five-speed manual
Induction:	Fuel injection
Base Price:	$25,000
Number Produced:	6,500

1983 Chevrolet Cavalier

Chevrolet introduced the Cavalier in May 1982. It was Chevy's next-to-base model, just senior to the subcompact Chevette. This new front-wheel drive, four-passenger Chevy was described as subcompact on the outside, with compact roominess inside. Chevy described the car as a 'high-content vehicle' which meant that it was fully-loaded with a good array of standard equipment, including a radio, power brakes, reclining bucket seats, stabilizer bar and remote trunk/hatch/tailgate release. Four models were offered in this opening line-up, two- and four-door sedans, a two-door hatchback and a four-door wagon. These models were arranged in three tiers of trim, the low-budget Cadet, interim base and high-end CL. Only a single engine was offered in the first place, a transverse-mounted 112-cid, four-valve engine, rated at 88 horsepower equipped with four-speed (overdrive) manual transmission. The Environmental Protection Agency fuel rating was 30 mpg for city driving. A two-liter version was announced but did not arrive for the moment.

The cars were designed with low, horizontal-style grilles, single recessed rectangular headlamps, and taillamps split into two sections by a horizontal divider. In 1983, the basic appearance of the model line was similar to that of '82, but a modified standard equipment list allowed significant price cuts to the subcompact Cavalier. This was due to General Manager Robert C. Stempel's new 'pricing strategy' that reduced the sticker price of over half the 1983 Chevrolets. These new base prices were as much as $1868 lower than in the previous year. But quite a few items that had been standard on the original cars were now classed as options. The range now included seven models, on three trim levels. The top line-up was the CS while the CL now became an option package. A new convertible model was available in the CS range. The convertibles were built by American Sunroof in Lansing, Michigan. Produced in limited numbers, it was the first Chevrolet ragtop since 1975. The car was equipped with tinted glass, power steering, power windows and twin sport mirrors (the left-had mirror was controlled remotely). The budget-priced Cadets were dropped completely, along with the base hatchback coupe.

The US Economy picked up in 1983, but the position at Chevrolet remained precarious. Model year sales improved by nearly six per cent, but other domestic manufacturers improved theirs by nearer seventeen per cent. Ironically, most of the improved sales came from mid- and full-size models, rather than the subcompact and compact models like the Cavalier.

Engine: Four-Cylinder
Displacement: 121-cid
Horsepower: 88 at 4800 rpm
Compression Ratio: 9.3:1
Number Produced: 627

■ *Right: Production of this limited edition convertible was out-sourced to American Sunroof in Lansing, Michigan.*

Avanti GT

Raymond Loewy was approached by Sherwood Egbert, the President of Studebaker, in March 1961, with a brief to design a completely new car for the company. Loewy was probably the most important industrial designer of the twentieth-century. When the car was introduced to the world the following April , the Avanti inspired immediate acclaim, even though it was launched in what was possibly the most imaginative auto design era in history. 'Avanti' was derived from the Italian for 'go forward' and the car was aptly named. It represented a great leap forward both in design and technological advances, and was a brilliant hybridisation of American know-how and European styling. As the Avanti was built from fiberglass, it was possible to use completely unique sinuous styling. The material also offered safety and practicality.

Unfortunately, Studebaker was already in a dire economic position, and was unable to give the Avanti and its other two new models (the Lark and the GT Hawk) long enough to float the company out of trouble. The last true Studebaker was produced on March 17 1966. But the Avanti model remains in production, still highly recognisable, to the present day.

In 1965, Nathan Altman and Leo Newman set up The Avanti Motor Corporation in Studebaker's old factory in South Bend, Indiana, to manufacture the Avanti II. This car was in not a replica of the original, but a continuation of the original Studebaker production. They used the original tooling. As Studebaker no longer manufactured engines at this time, Avanti decided to use Corvette powerplants, but the frame, suspension and body panels remained unchanged. The company was sold to Stephen Blake in 1982. Blake made some changes to the car, including dropping the 'II' from its name, and introducing a convertible version in 1985. But quality control problems and an erratic management style resulted in bankruptcy. Avanti's remaining assets were purchased by Mike Kelly in 1986. Kelly then formed the New Avanti Motor Corporation, with financial backing from John J. Cafaro. He believed that he was 'handcrafting the finest motorcar in all the world', but he and Cafaro were unable to agree as to whether the company should pursue the performance or luxury markets. Kelly sold out to Cafaro in 1988, and Cafaro became the penultimate owner of the trade name. Under his leadership, a design team formed by Jim Bunting and Tom Kellogg, who was a member of the original Avanti design team of the sixties, created a car resulting from the fusion of an Avanti with a Pontiac Firebird.

The current company, Avanti Motor Corporation is based in Villa Rica, Georgia. Avanti is the largest independent carmaker in the US, and is now in its 40th year. The company manufactures several cars, including an Avanti-derived model based on the Bunting/Kellogg version, and a prototype 'Studebaker Xtreme' SUV.

■ *Born ahead of its time, the Avanti continued to outpace the industry for many years.*

Engine:	V-8 OHV
Displacement:	305.4-cid
Horsepower:	180 at 4000 rpm

1985 Chevrolet Monte Carlo SS

Chevrolet made a big claim in 1985, that they were offering 'America's highest-mileage car, America's fastest car... America's most popular full-size car and America's most popular car, regardless of size'. That just about covers it. But internally, 1985 was a year of refinement and evolution rather than revolution. Several interesting models and engine options were announced, including the IROC-Z Camaro, and high performance Z24 Cavalier.

The first Monte Carlo was introduced by Chevrolet back in 1970, at the height of GM muscle car power. The car was designed to compete with the Pontiac Grand Prix and Buick Riviera. But just as soon as it was introduced to the market, performance fell out of favor, and the model's brief life as a musclecar was over almost before it began. However, this first generation of Monte Carlo's was a great hit with the buying public, who snapped up 145,975 of the cars in their launch year. The top model in the range was the SS 454, bought by 3823 performance-inspired souls. The car was equipped with the mighty Chevy 454 big block, and was came fully-loaded with go-goodies, including heavy-duty suspension, a heavy-duty battery, automatic level control suspension, air shocks and 15x7 inch rally wheels. Ten Monte Carlos sneaked off the line equipped with the LS-6 454 engine – rated at a massive 450 horsepower.

The car evolved over the years, as did the SS model. By 1985, the standard Monte Carlos were equipped with a 130 horsepower powerplant, which was aimed at V-8 fans looking for improved gas mileage. Chevrolet claimed that it was almost as 'frisky'. The SS model 'cousin to the Grand National stock cars' racing on the NASCAR circuit was very strongly marketed. Formerly offered only in a white or blue body, this year's car came in silver, maroon, white or black with gray or maroon interior trims, and either bench or bucket seats. This street version of the NASCAR model had special instruments, sport suspension, rear spoiler, sport mirrors and steering wheel and special rally wheels. The car had very plain styling, and only discreet badging. The blackout grille was simple crosshatch pattern, flanked by recessed quad rectangular headlamps with deeply inset park/signal lamps below the forward crease line. The car was fitted with the RPO L69 up-rated version of the familiar 305-cid V-8, now with four-speed overdrive automatic transmission. The car now had beefier equipment, SS mufflers grew in capacity and axles got larger ring gears. Removable black roof panels were to become available on the SS later in the model year.

■ *Right: The 1985 Monte Carlo SS. Chevrolet continues to offer a modern version of car to this day.*

Engine: V-8

Displacement: 305-cid

Horsepower: 180 at 4800 rpm

Compression Ratio: 9.5:1

Number Produced: 35,484

457

1986 Ford Mustang SVO

Ford launched the second edition of the Mustang, Mustang II back in 1974, in part as a reaction to the prevailing oil crisis. They described it as 'the right car at the right time'. But the car was far removed from the inspiration at the inception of the ponycar concept, and many aficionados were disappointed by the relatively lack lustre performance. But sales held up, and buyers were eager for Mustang III, which arrived with all new sheet metal in 1979.

Performance was also back. The Boss 302 V-8 came back on the scene in 1982, even stronger than before. The revised model line-up now contained a GT instead of the old Cobra option, but sales declined for the third year in a row.

Things looked up in 1983, when a convertible re-joined the line-up. Mustangs also received a restyled front and rear end, and the power of the V-8 was boosted to 175 horsepower. The turbo model also rejoined the Mustang family, now with multi-port fuel injection. Borg-Warner's close-ratio five-speed gearbox could help the GTs hit 60 mph in around seven seconds.

The SVO (Special Vehicle Operations) department had been established in 1981, to oversee the company's renewed involvement in motorsports and limited edition production. Its first fruit -the SVO- appeared in 1984, with an air-to-air intercooler on its turbocharged four-cylinder engine. The car also had Hurst linkage, four disc brakes and big 16-inch tires. The car was immediately heralded as 'the best driving street Mustang the factory has ever produced' by Motor Trend. Road & Track magazine claimed that the SVO 'outruns the Datsun 280ZX, out-handles the Ferrari 308 and Porsche 944... and it's affordable'. Praise indeed. By 1986, SVO turbos were capable of 200 horsepower, ready for the Hurst-shifted five-speed. The cars retained their single-slot grille and luxury interior. In fact, high performance was a serious theme at Mustang between '84 and '85 for both hatchbacks and convertibles, and the cars were taken to heart by the V-8 brigade.

The Mustang line-up for 1986 was made up of five models, with the hatchback SVO Turbo Four the ultimate Mustang of the year. The car now carried a computer-controlled 200-horsepower 2.3 liter four cylinder engine with inter-cooled turbocharger and multi-port fuel injection. Set up in this way, the engine delivered a hefty amount of power, delivering acceleration that rivalled the big old V-8s. A five-speed transmission, with Hurst shifter that offered short, quick throws, was standard. Disc brakes were fitted all round. Mustang was the only Ford model to show a sales increase for 1986. The Mercury Capri was off the market in this year, so the Mustang mopped up some of its buyers.

Engine: Four-cylinder

Displacement: 140-cid

Horsepower: 200 at 5000 rpm

Compression Ratio: 8.0:1

Base Price: $15,272

■ *Right: Mustang celebrated its twentieth anniversary in 1984, the year of the first SVO.*

1990　Corvette ZR-1

Launched In 1953, the Corvette had had to adapt to survive. Although the hefty rise in the price of gas, Federal emissions regulations and the 55 mph speed limit had conspired to make the car redundant, the Corvette retained and developed a loyal customer base that survives to this day. The half-millionth Corvette came off the St. Louis production line in 1977. The Silver Anniversary car of 1978 was effectively more of a luxury tourer than a sports model. Manufacture of the cars was subsequently switched to Bowling Green, Kentucky to a specialist Corvette plant.

Jerry Palmer, the Head of Chevrolet Three Studio and Dave McLellan, the Corvette design engineer, were now developing a new model, that would combine aerodynamic styling, nostalgia and modernity to create a new, sixth generation Corvette that would launch in 1984. The car was so successful in everything it set out to do, that it remained the basis of the car until its fortieth birthday in 1993, even its fiftieth in 2003.

The '84 car cleverly combined the great heritage of the model, while looking new and exciting. Styling was restrained, but all the signature Corvette features were still there to be seen – fold-away headlights, four round recessed taillights, wraparound rear window and fender vents harking back to the indented coves of the '56 model. Top speed was measured at 140 mph, and the car could get from 0-60 mph in 6.7 seconds. The car was, in fact 'one of the half-dozen fastest production automobiles in the world.' However, it soon became evident that the brilliant new 'backbone' chassis and tough suspension could handle even more power. This resulted in the decision to rework the thirty-year-old 427-cid V-8 engine. The result would be known as the ZR-1. It was Corvette's intention to rival the performance of the hot Europeans – Ferrari, Aston Martin and Porsche at a fraction of the price. Tuned port fuel injection, gas-pressurized shocks, an oil cooler, ABS from Bosch, and six-speed manual gearbox were all added to the Corvette during the eighties.

When it arrived in 1990, the super-performance ZR-1 was effectively a seventh series Corvette, which had cost around 24 million dollars to develop. It was worth it, the car is one of the all-time greats. It was fitted wit the fantastic Texas-built LT5 engine, complete with huge acceleration, high top speed, masses of torque, and fuel efficiency. It all added up to making the car one of the most potent machines ever to hit the streets, that held the driving experience as its paramount raison d'etre.

Engine: V-8

Displacement: 350-cid

Horsepower: 370 at 5800 rpm

Compression Ratio: 11.0:1

Base Price: $58,995

■ *Right: The 'King of the Hill' ZR1 was launched with the highest price tag ever for a GM product.*

Pontiac Firehawk Firebird

1992

The third generation Firebird made use of many unseen build improvements in its final model year of 1992. These included the use of improved structural adhesives, improved body panel fit and finish, reinforced structure for rigidity and silicone impregnated weather striping. Even so, GM were still concerned about the forces generated by their big 5.7 liter Firebird engines, and wouldn't allow this option to be ordered with either T-tops or a manual transmission.

1992 was the dawn of a new era of serious performance with the introduction of the Formula Firehawk. This was the fastest, most extreme, hard edged, Firebird ever. 250 cars were slated for production (in street and competition versions), but only 25 actually made it into production, including a single convertible.

This Firehawk, Option code B4U, was the fastest street Pontiac ever produced. It arrived as a new model to the Firebird line-up as a special kind of Formula model. The cars were actually normal Pontiac-produced Firebirds that were then sent to development partner SLP (Street Legal Performance) for the Firehawk package to be installed – for a hefty sum. The SLP package included a number of engine and suspension upgrades (including heavy duty 4-bolt main engine blocks with forged crank), Brembo brakes, a tire and rim package – and the Firehawk graphics. The upshot of this was sparkling performance: 0-60 mph in 4.6 seconds, quarter mile times of 13.2 seconds and a top speed of 160 mph. Amazingly, the car still gave good gas mileage at 25 mpg, and was street legal in fifty states.

'Mandatory Red' was the standard color option for the 1992 cars, but single Artic White, Medium Quasar Blue Metallic, Medium Green Metallic and Dark Jade Gray Metallic examples were built. Two of the cars were fitted with the Super Duty 366-cid engine that was rated at 375 horsepower. SLP had built a prototype Firehawk to develop the package. Early Firehawks also got a special interior package, including Recaro racing seats, and a full roll bar. After the full SLP treatment, the cars retailed for around $40,000, easily the most expensive Pontiac ever to hit the streets. It was Pontiac's hot ticket for performance, designed to compete with the Mustang 5.0 LX Notchback coupe. The Firehawk helped the company to regain its position on both the street and the track with an infusion of pure performance. SLP began to install a similar package to Camaros in the late '90s.

■ *Left: Firestone were the owners of the Firehawk trademark, and only and handful of the cars were equipped with the decal, due to copyright disputes.*

Engine:	V-8, 90 Degree
Displacement:	350-cid
Horsepower:	350 at 5500 rpm
Compression Ratio:	9.9:1
Wheelbase:	101 inches
Base Price:	$39,995
Number Produced:	25

1994 Chevrolet Camaro Z28

G M launched the Camaro in 1966, and the GM copywriters went into full swing, 'Meet the masked marvel. Meet Camaro'. The car was very well received, despite the difficulty that GM had had in naming the car. They were looking for a European-sounding name that began with a 'c', in the Chevy tradition. Evidently, what they turned up actually means 'shrimp-like creature' in Spanish.

But it wasn't until the Z28 models were first introduced that GM really had a car that could run head-to-head with the Mustang. Z-28s were built specifically for racing in the Trans Am series, and necessitated a substantially new car. You can always tell when a concept really works – its keeps coming back over and over again. The tag actually remained in use right up until the end of the twentieth century.

Like the Corvette, the Camaro was redesigned over several generations. By the early 1990s, the wedge-shaped Camaro, that had looked so radical when it was first introduced in 1982, looked old and stale. In the meantime, a whole new generation of two- and four-seater Japanese sports cars had entered the American car market, with a degree of technical sophistication that somewhat overcame their small engine sizes. The fourth generation Camaro, first launched in 1993, was a real product of the 1990s, with soft, smoothed over lines. The car was a totally new product from nose to tail. But the Z28 performance option remained a true American under the bodywork, complete with traditional V-8 power and rear-wheel drive. The new Camaro was introduced as a single model hatchback coupe, but a convertible was added to the range for the following year after a year's absence. It was offered in both the base V-6 and Z28 series, as were the coupes. The new convertible had a sleek new body of composite panels fixed to a steel structure. The front suspension and rack-and-pinion steering were also new.

When the Z28 package was fitted to the convertible, it meant a V-8, rather than V-6 powered the car, and raised the Camaro to the musclecar league. The associated go-goodies, including aluminum cylinder heads, Borg-Warner six-speed manual gearbox, ABS brakes and eight-inch wheels with Goodyear 235/55R16 tires meant that the car actually had to be speed limited – to 108 mph. With Z-rated tires, the real top speed was over 150 mph. This meant that this Z28 was the fastest road-going factory-built Camaro to date.

Engine: Z28 V-8

Displacement: 350-cid

Horsepower: 275 at 5000 rpm

Compression Ratio: 10.5:1

Base Price: $18,745

Number Produced (Base and Z28): 7260

■ *Right: Car and Driver Magazine rated the 1984 Z28 Camaro as the best car in its class.*

Chevrolet Impala SS

1994

Back in the sixties, the Impala was a car with classic musclecar potential, a prime candidate to be beefed up for the performance brigade. The car had been downsized in the early '60s, and the lowered weight meant greater performance potential. This had been a reaction to the compacts that hit the market at this time, including the Ford Falcon and Chevy's own Nova. Coupled with the size issue was the range of powerful Chevy V-8s available. For example, there was the meaty 348-cid Turbo Thrust available with either 340 or 360 horsepower, or the 409 Turbo-Fire that inspired the Beach Boys song. This could offer up to 409 horsepower, equipped with twin four-barrel carburetion. An SS (Super Sports) handling package could also be fitted, complete with power steering and brakes, heavy-duty springs and shocks, sintered metal brake linings and a tachometer. But although the Impala could offer a truly hot package, and was a serious contender in the NASCARs of the early 1960s, only a moderate number of buyers were convinced.

Over the years, SS status was sometimes compromised, badges were affixed to cars with no performance equipment at all, but the legend persisted.

Chevrolet has often been inspired to resurrect old and evocative names from its rich and varied history. The Impala SS of 1994 came out of this impetus. The original SS had been capable of generating 400 horsepower, quarter mile times of around twelve seconds, and fierce admiration on the streets. Thirty years later, kids who had been too young to drive when the first cars were available had their dreams brought to life by Chevrolet. The new Impala SS was based on an ordinary Caprice Classic Sedan, but the engine was up-rated to the Law Enforcement 260 horsepower V-8 and suspension, complete with sequential fuel injection and all-wheel disc brakes. This propelled the car to fantastic performance. The Caprice was already a popular model, and its big smooth shape look really good when lowered. The all-black body of the SS, contrasted with polished aluminum wheels looked great straight from the factory. The interior was slightly dull, in grey cloth, but performance was the inspiration behind the car. The model was offered for only four years, but sold in excess of 40,000 units. It was living proof that the original muscle car concept of four-seater cars still had a loyal following.

■ *Left: The Impala SS, a muscle car on the original four-seat template.*

Engine:	LT1 Corvette V-8
Displacement:	350-cid
Horsepower:	260 at 5000 rpm
Compression Ratio:	10.5:1
Weight:	4218 lbs
Wheelbase:	115.9 inches
Base Price:	$22,920

Chrysler LHS

1994

There were big changes to Chrysler's line-up for 1994. In fact, it was vastly different to that of the previous year, with the 'new' New York LH sedan and LHS sedan joining the remaining LeBaron models and the Concorde Sedan. The LeBaron ranks were thinned considerably. Gone were all the coupe models and the base and LX convertibles. The LE and Landau sedans and the GTC convertible were offered again, but it was the final year for sedan availability.

The New Yorker LH series was introduced in May 1993, and featured the cab-forward design sported by most other Chrysler models in this year. Running changes, from one model year to the next were planned as an intrinsic aspect of the model range. Standard features of the car included dual air-bags, anti-lock four-wheel disc brakes, air conditioning (with non-CFC R-134A refrigerant), stainless steel dual exhaust, solar control window glass, windshield wipers with vertical speed sensitive operation, and courtesy lamps with fade off time. The 'Fall' model of the car also had variable-assist speed-proportional power steering and aluminised exhaust system coating, 'Simplex' wheel covers and touring wheels and tires.

The LHS series was the new top-of-the-line Chrysler, and senior member of the New Yorker series. The cars were identical to the New Yorker LH cars, and it too was subject to a program of rolling model changes. The power train was the same for both cars, and they shared most of the standard equipment. The difference was that variants that were optional on the LH were standard on the LHS. These included low-speed traction control, automatic temperature control, vehicle theft security alarm system, eight-way power driver and passenger seats, automatic headlights with delay feature, automatic day/night rearview mirror and power moonroof.

Both cars also shared the same wheelbase and chassis, and were offered in the same range of colors, Black Cherry, Radiant Red, Char-Coal, Emerald Green, Black, Bright White and Bright Metallic Silver. Interiors were available in Agate, Medium Driftwood, Medium Quartz and Slate Blue.

Chrysler's model year production was 209,386 units.

■ *Left: This Chrysler LHS is cool in Bright Metallic Silver.*

Engine:	V-6 overhead valve
Displacement:	214-cid
Horsepower:	214 at 5800 rpm
Compression Ratio:	10.5:1
Induction:	Sequential fuel injection
Body Style:	Four-door Sedan
Wheelbase:	113 inches
Base Price:	$30,283
Number Produced:	44,739

1994 Ford Mustang GT

Ford first introduced the Mustang in 1964 and it is the progenitor of the entire ponycar herd. The car was designed and marketed to be a low cost sports car, and did not have any serious intent to be a performance model. But as the series developed, all kinds of high performance options were offered in the line, beginning with a 'Hi-Po' 289-cid 271 horsepower engine only a few months after the car was first launched. The first generation of Mustang was offered between 1964-1973, first as a two-door sports car and later as a four-door. The Mustang II's rolled out in 1974. Initially they weren't very well received, but were soon selling well, and several special models were added to the line with extra power options. The cars were restyled again in 1982 onto the Ford Fox platform. This model persisted until 1993, and was the base for all kinds of performance models including GTs, Cobras and several SVO (Special Vehicle Operations department) cars.

In 1994, in its thirtieth anniversary year, the long-overdue next-generation Mustang was unveiled in two body styles – notchback coupe and convertible – and three separate series: the base level Mustang, GT and limited edition Cobra. The sheetmetal was completely new, but the exterior and interior dimensions were virtually unchanged. The three-door hatchback, four-cylinder engine and LX series were now all things of the past. Engine options were now the 3.8 liter V-6 fitted to the base model, or the 5.0 liter V-8 fitted to the GTs and Cobras. The Cobra's sequentially fuel-injected engine was modified through the use of GT-40 cylinder heads, roller rockers, stronger valve springs and a tuned-length cast-aluminum upper intake manifold. Other changes included an oil-cooler and a lightened flywheel. The cars were still rear wheel drive, but all-wheel disc brakes were now fitted as standard. The gears in the Cobra's T5OD five-speed manual transmission were coated to better handle the engine's 240 horsepower output. Standard equipment in all Mustangs included dual airbags.

The 1994 Mustang convertible was now assembled in house. These now included power tops and glass rear windows with optional rear defogger.

The new 1994 Mustang was named as Motor Trend Magazine's 'Car of the Year', and a Mustang Cobra paced the 1994 Indianapolis 500. Mustang production totals for the year were almost double that of 1993.

Engine: V-8

Displacement: 302-cid

Horsepower: 215 at 4200 rpm

Compression Ratio: 9.0:1

Wheelbase: 101.3 inches

Base Price: $21,960

Number Produced (all coupes): 78,480

■ *Right: Mustang celebrated their fortieth anniversary with the launch of generation IV.*

1994 Pontiac Trans Am 25th Anniversary Model

Pontiac launched their fourth generation Firebird/Trans Am in 1993. The cars were completely reengineered and redesigned into a well-balanced package that was both in tune with stringent government regulations and the high expectations of the performance-buying public.

The twenty-fifth anniversary model of 1994 was the epitome of this early fourth generation car. It followed a Pontiac tradition of issuing anniversary models that had begin in 1979 with a ten-year anniversary model, and was continued in 1989 with a twenty-year commemorative car. The most outstanding feature of the 1994 special edition is its unique styling. The car was white with a blue 'screaming chicken' decal on the nose, and blue stripes running up the hood of the car, down the deck lid and over the rear spoiler. These were borrowed from the 1970-72 Trans Am model years. The door bottoms also had blue twenty-fifth anniversary Trans Am script. The car also had special lightweight rim, five spoke wheels that were painted white to match the car. There were also ornamented with the blue bird, and twenty-fifth anniversary Trans Am logos.

The cars interior was white and black, with white leather Prado seats decorated with blue embroidered twenty-fifth anniversary Trans Am script, and white door panels.

All the 1994 anniversary models were powered by the LT1 350 'Corporate' V-8 and equipped with a four-speed automatic transmission. They could be ordered as hardtops, T-tops or convertibles. In fact, for the whole 1994 Trans Am line-up, convertibles were added to each series, in addition to the coupes offered in '93.

Sadly, Firebird production was discontinued in 2003, in the thirty-fifth anniversary years of the car. Pontiac issued a 'Collectors' Edition' car with special 'Collector Yellow' color scheme, detailed interior appointments and special edition emblems. A Gold Rush Trans Am show car was also manufactured to be displayed at car shows around the country.

Engine: LT1 V-8

Displacement: 350-cid

Horsepower: 275 at 5000 rpm

Transmission: Four-speed automatic

Compression Ratio: 10.5:1

Weight: 4200 lbs

Wheelbase: 101.1 inches

Base Price: $21,395

Number Produced (total Firebirds): 51,523

■ *Right: The Twenty-fifth anniversary Trans Am of 1994 was one in a long line of Pontiac commemorative cars.*

1995 Lincoln Continental

Until 1994, the long established Continental was a six cylinder (170 horse power) giant economy car, but although the moniker didn't change, the hefty revises of 1994 transformed the car into a small luxury model with a trimmer body design and far more exciting styling. The new inheritor of the long-established Continental heritage now featured a new transverse V-8 engine with dual overhead camshafts. The new car had more contemporary styling with a curved character line that ran the length of the car in an eye-pleasing update of the slab-sided appearance of the previous Continental. Lincoln openly acknowledged that they hoped to make the new car a hybrid sports sedan whilst retaining its traditionally luxurious feel. With its new four-speed automatic transmission, the new V-8 could now generate a sparky 260 horsepower. The body shell of the car was also a great deal stronger than that of the old model. Standard equipment on the car included dual airbags, antilock braking, automatic climate control and an air-filtration system to trap dust and pollen. A redesigned instrument panel displayed virtual-image graphics. These were strikingly bright at night, but difficult to read on a sunny day. The driver could also adjust the ride quality and the steering assist with dashboard buttons.

The Continental was now much quicker, and a bit more agile, although it retained its original front-wheel drive and was thus given to serious under-steer. It was loaded with desirable electronic gadgetry. In acceleration, the newly energetic car could match a Cadillac Seville SLS, going from 0-60 mph in about eight seconds. However, the gas mileage was unimproved at 16.3 mpg, and premium fuel was recommended. Interior space in the car was very good, with plenty of leg space for the occupants in the front and rear. Storage was also capacious with a wide, deep and long trunk.

The new Continental was positioned in an extremely competitive market sector, positioned against more powerful Cadillac Seville, the superb Lexus LS 400, plus BMW and Audi models. Although none of these other cars came close to the Lincoln for electronic wizardry, the new Continental had only modest success, and after some changes and add-ons in the intervening years, the distinguished model was discontinued in 2002.

Engine: V-8 DOHC

Displacement: 281-cid

Horsepower: 260 horsepower

Compression Ratio: 9.0:1

Wheelbase: 109 inches

Base Price: $40,750

Number Produced: 32,851

■ *Right: Although rather bland looking, the new Continental was an extremely capable car.*

1996 Dodge Viper GTS

The Corvette is widely known as 'America's sports car', and the fiberglass two-seater has reigned supreme for over fifty years. Of course there have been contenders for the title, such as the Thunderbirds, the Avanti, Cobras and the AMX. But the Corvette outlasted them all, and sold in increasingly large numbers.

But if ever there was a serious threat, it came from the Viper. Dodge developed a prototype for the car by 1988, and showed it to the public for the first time on January 4 1989. A pre-production version of the car went on to pace the 1991 Indianapolis 500, and a production version was finally introduced to the marketplace in 1992. But the open-air cockpit and very basic nature of the comforts on offer didn't really go down well at all. Even the fantastic V-10 engine caused offence, it was truly loud. AutoWeek Magazine's writer Matt DeLorenzo said that the Viper RT/10 roadster sounded like a 'UPS truck at idle'. Hardly surprising, as the beast under the hood was actually borrowed from Dodge's truck line. Dodge saw the obvious solution on offer. In 1995, they offered a closed version of the roadster, which they hoped would make the car a little more civilised and less of a handful. The slicked back hardtop also offered huge improvement to the aerodynamics of the car. The car was launched as a 1996 model. It looked rather similar to the Shelby American Dayton coupe, which was no surprise as Carroll Shelby was one of the inspirations behind the car. The

■ *Below: The Viper's sinister headlights made the car look like the ruthless animal it was.*

Viper Blue and white striped livery was a combination directly copied from Shelby's victorious car of 1964.

Dodge managed to keep the weight of the GTS coupe down to that of the RT/10 roadster, and this was achieved by cutting down the weight of other components – like the engine. The block was now eighty pounds lighter. Elsewhere, the car had a little more sophistication, with a softer suspension, electric windows, adjustable foot pedals, dual airbags and more convenient instrumentation. However, the roof made the car totally unsuitable for the claustrophobic.

But the power under the hood was fantastic. The V-10 was revised to make a huge leap in power. As well as being lighter, it had a stronger camshaft, better-breathing heads and revised exhausts. Everything conspired to jump from 415 horsepower all the way to 450. This was the most powerful engine offered by Detroit in this year, and for sheer muscle, nothing American could beat the Viper in 1996.

For the second time, the Viper was chosen as the pace car for the Indianapolis 500. This time it was the GTS coupe. The car was hailed as instantly collectible, one of the world's greatest touring cars.

Engine: V-10 overhead valve

Displacement: 488-cid

Horsepower: 450 at 5200 rpm

Transmission: Six-speed manual

Compression Ratio: 9.6:1

Induction: Electronic Sequential Multi-port Fuel Injection

Body Style: Two-door coupe

Number of Seats: 2

Weight: 3445 lbs

Wheelbase: 96.2 lbs

Base Price: $66,045

1996 Ford Cobra Mystic

The base, GT and Cobra Mustangs all returned for the 1996 model year. Ford's SVO team (Special Performance Operations) had developed a convertible to add to the range, but this did not go into production until the spring of 1996, whilst the coupe was available at the beginning of the year. The Cobras were just slightly longer than the other Mustangs, at 182.5 inches. Under the hood was where the major changes for this season occurred. The 5.0-liter V-8 previously fitted to the GT and Cobra Mustangs was discontinued, replaced by a modular 4.6 liter V-8. Teksid cast the aluminum cylinder heads. They are an Italian company that also works for Ferrari Road and Formula One cars. In fact, the engine had such great performance that it was voted one of the ten best by Ward's Auto World for 1996. The Cobra also now used a new T45 five-speed manual transmission, which replaced its predecessor, the T5.

The already stiff chassis was furthered stiffened and rigidized by the addition of a redesigned front crossmember. This also provided clearance for the deep oil sump fitted to the engine. Also new for the Cobra was a 3.27:1 rear axle ratio. Standard equipment on all V-8 Mustangs now included the Passive Anti-theft System.

In this model year, Mustang production totalled 124,698. 2,000 'Mystic' Cobra coupes were finished in ultra-technological light-reflecting Mystic Clearcoat paint (produced by BASF), as an $815 option. These cars were the first to wear a paint developed with this color-shifting technology. The paint contains special 'light-interference' pigments, which allow the paint to show drastic color transformations as the observer's angle to the car changes, or the angle that light hits the car alters. The microscopic paint layers act like tiny prisms, and the color produced is controlled by precise variances, measured in atoms, in these prismatic layers. As Todd Hayes wrote for the North American Auto Writers Syndicate, 'The car literally changes from emerald green to violet blue, magenta, burgundy, amber, and a dark brown. It is truly fascinating and the object of many open-mouthed stares on the freeway'.

A second line of 1000 'Mystichrome' painted Cobras was launched in 2004. This special optical paint was manufactured by DuPont.

Engine: V-8 90-degree, dual overhead cam

Displacement: 282-cid

Horsepower: 305 at 5800 rpm

Compression Ratio: 9.85:1

Induction: Sequential Fuel Injection

Wheelbase: 101.3 inches

Base Price: $24,810

Number Produced: 5496

■ *Right: There is a huge fascination around these slightly bizarre-looking cars, and a web site for Mystic Cobra owner to register their cars.*

Ford Thunderbird

1997

Ford introduced the Thunderbird in 1955 as their answer to Chevrolet's Corvette. But whereas the Corvette remains true to its two-seater sports car origins to this day, the Thunderbird was more of a do-everything car, and has been through many changes, restyles and rethinks over its existence of more than four decades.

The Thunderbird has always been about style, refined power and creature comforts and the combination of these elements made it a good seller right from the start. The original car came only as a two-seater convertible, but it was soon available as a hardtop coupe and with a back seat and even two more doors. It wasn't really until the 1957 car that Thunderbird got serious about performance and new versions of the 312-cid 'Y' block V-8 were offered.

Several Thunderbird restyles were initiated by Ford over the years, the final makeover took place in 1989. The car became trimmer in its overall dimensions, but the wheelbase was actually nine inches longer than that of the previous model. Fully independent suspension was introduced with this model, which came in two versions, the base and LX. Power came from a choice of V-6s, the base being a 3.8 liter with four-speed overdrive automatic, all the way through to a 210 horsepower V-6 fitted to the Super Coupe. V-8 power was re-introduced to the line for 1991, with a five liter engine rated at 200 horsepower. Thunderbird launched four models for 1992, the base Thunderbird, Sport, LX and SC. There was also a light facelift for this year. The line-up was trimmed back to two models in the next season. Just the LX and Super Coupe were offered in 1993. Performance was back under the spotlight in 1994, with the introduction of an overhead cam 4.6 liter V-8. By 1996, the line was tapered further to just a single car, the Thunderbird LX, and this remained the situation in 1997. Several revisions were made to various aspects of the car for 1997, including a new instrument cluster, decklid spoiler with integrated stoplight, and three new exterior colors and a single new interior color, Light Prairie Tan. New optional equipment included 16-inch wheels and an upgraded suspension. At the end of the year, Ford announced that it was going to discontinue Thunderbird production after forty-two continuous years. But watch this space...

■ *Left: The stylish but portly Thunderbirds of the 1990s were roomy and comfortable, but no performance giants.*

Engine: V-8	
Displacement: 281-cid	
Horsepower: 205 at 4250 rpm	
Compression Ratio: 9.0:1	
Body Style: Two-door coupe	
Wheelbase: 113 inches	
Base Price: $19,015	
Number Produced: 73,814	

1998 Corvette C5

The eagerly awaited C5 fifth series Corvette was launched in January 1997 at both the Detroit and the Los Angeles Auto Shows. A new line was to have been introduced in 1993, but due to the dreadful financial problems at GM, the development of the new car had been delayed. The body shape was now reworked, and completely engine and chassis were introduced simultaneously. In fact, there was almost no carry-over from the previous series. The new chassis was based on a pair of immensely strong hydro-formed rails, stiff enough to support the fiberglass body. Ride quality was improved by the lengthening of the wheelbase to 104.5 inches, and this also gave the cars a more spacious interior. Five-spoke alloy wheels were fitted as standard, recalling the ZR-1.

In its 45th anniversary year, the Corvette returned to offering convertible and coupe models with the debut of a topless version. The convertible's glass window was heated and the top had an Express-Down feature that released the tonneau cover and automatically lowered windows part way at the touch of a button. But essentially, it remained manually operated. One of the most-welcome innovations of the new convertible was the provision of a trunk lid! This convenience hadn't been seen on a ragtop 'Vette since the early sixties and was greeted with great enthusiasm. It even featured remote opening via a control button the key fob.

New for this model year was the magnesium wheel option featuring lightweight wheels with a unique bronze tone. Two new exterior colors were offered and a new light oak leather interior color was available. Standard features included stainless steel exhaust system, Extended Mobility Tires capable of running for 200 miles with no air pressure, dual heated electric remote breakaway outside rearview mirrors, Daytime Running Lamps and five-mph front and rear bumpers. The LS1 V-8 and four-speed automatic transmission were again offered as standard, with the T56 six-speed manual transmission available as an option.

Corvette was also able to celebrate its fourth selection as the pace car for the Indianapolis 500, with Indy 500 veteran Parnelli Jones driving the wild purple and yellow car (with black and yellow leather interior). Corvette had first been given the honor in 1978, then in '86 and '95. Corvette also made a long-awaited return to Trans-Am racing in '98, achieving a first place in the season's opening event – a street race around Long Beach, California. The winning car was the Number 8 Autolink Corvette driven by Paul Gentilozzi.

■ *Right: This seventh generation Corvette convertible looks stunning.*

Engine: V-8

Displacement: 346-cid

Horsepower: 345 at 5600 rpm

Compression Ratio: 10.1:1

Base Price: $44,425

Number Produced: 12,090

Ford Contour SVT

1998

Ford launched the Contour in the spring of 1994. It was their new 'World Car', the replacement for the Tempo. It was designed to run against the Honda Accord and the other imported compact and mid-size sedans. Mercury offered a similar four-door sedan, the Mystique. Both cars were based on the European Ford Mondeo model. Contours were offered in a three-tier range – the GL, LX and sporty SE. Ford took a huge step forward in performance, refinement and overall execution with this compact sedan, and many felt that the car was a formidable rival to both the Japanese imports and domestic cars such as the Chrysler Cirrus and Dodge Stratus. There were only two criticisms levelled at the car, that the exterior styling was bland, and the legroom in the back of the car was limited. Dual airbags were standard on the cars, as were impact resistant bumpers that could absorb an impact of five mph. Antilock brakes and traction control were optional on all models. The base engine option for the range was the four-cylinder with a 170 horsepower six optional. Both engines were available with a five-speed manual gearbox or an optional electronic four-speed automatic transmission.

Ford added a high-performance car to the range in 1998, in the shape of the SVT (for Ford Special Vehicle Team). The car was equipped with the same Duratec 2.5 liter (155-cid) V-6 available on the other Contours, but this one was tuned to deliver 195 horsepower. This was a full 13 per cent more power. Developing 76.6 horse-power per liter of displacement in a non-supercharged engine, and a top speed of 143 mph gives the SVT some of the best performance figures in the business. The car also came with a five-speed transmission as standard. Antilock brakes, sport suspension, larger tires and other go-goodies were optional. Road-testers felt that the SVT felt responsive, but that the driver really had to work the transmission to develop all the available power. They also felt that the car felt more German than American to drive, with its precise steering, sporty handling and firm ride.

The SVT designers showed a great deal of restraint in the exterior restyling of the car, the only differential between them and the rest of the Contours were sports rocker panel extensions, a modestly restyled front fascia with round fog lamps and 16-inch alloys. They managed to avoid the customary spoiler. The SVT interior was distinguished with black-on-white gauges, SVT logos and dark blue leather upholstery. The SVT was retained for the 1999 model year, but was only available through selected Ford dealers by 2000.

■ *Left: The SVT Contour is something special, with mainstream ride comfort and exceptional all-round performance.*

Engine:	DOHC six-cylinder
Displacement:	155-cid
Horsepower:	195
Wheelbase:	106.5 inches
Base Price:	$22,405
Number Produced:	5,000

Ford Escort ZX-2

1998

The 1981 introduction of the front-wheel-drive subcompact Escort heralded a whole new era for Ford. Ford described it as 'The World Car' due to its international presence. The car was equipped with a CHV (hemi) engine, and immediately became Ford's best-selling model. Within a year, the car was also the best-selling car in America. The GT model was offered with turbocharging in 1984, and a Mazda-built diesel could also be ordered. The Escort line-up was revised for the 1986 model year, with the GT model fitted with a high-output engine. The car continued to sell well, although Ford's overall sales fell, leaving them with less than 12 per cent of the market. But Escort's continued sales successes helped Ford to bounce back to the top in 1987. The company broke all records, netting $4.6 billion in income (out-performing GM) and $71.6 billion in worldwide sales. Escort continued as America's favorite for 1988, and by 1989 the car was approaching its three millionth sale. Ford continued to maintain a high level of product development for the line, and launched an all-new Escort design in both 1990 and 1997. Fewer body styles were now on offer and both the two- and four-door hatchback models were discontinued. A new SE series was introduced to the line. The wheelbase remained unchanged, but the overall length of the new model went up by four inches. The new body design featured completely new body panels and frameless door glass. It weighed 120 pounds more than the previous version so even increased horsepower meant performance was by no means sparkling.

The ZX2 two-door coupe was launched in January 1997 for the 1998 season, and was available in 'cool' and 'hot' trim versions. The 'cool' package had limited options and a manual five-speed gearbox. The 'hot' option had more options available, including a choice of wheels, plus rear defogger and air conditioning fitted as standard. ZX2 exterior and interior styling was unique, and the car had a sportier suspension setting. It was aimed at younger buyers with an average age of 32, who got peppy performance from the Zetex 2-liter, four-cylinder, that developed 130 horsepower. Optional equipment included anti-lock brakes, a premium sound system, power windows, power moonroof, remote entry system and an automatic transaxle. Three packages were offered with the car, 'Comfort Group', 'Power Group' and 'Sport Group'. The latter featured 15-inch alloys, a rear spoiler, foglamps, upgraded bucket seats and special badging. The performance coupe sold well, but some auto reviewers considered the ZX2 to be unacceptably noisy. Sadly, Ford discontinued the stalwart Escorts in 2001, and the ZX2's final model was launched in 2003.

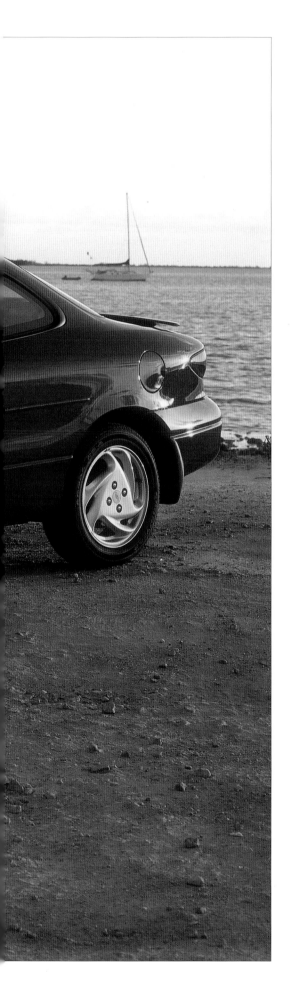

■ : Left: Ford's 'hot' package ZX2 for 1998.

Engine: In-line Four-cylinder
Displacement: 2-liter
Horsepower: 130 at 5750 rpm
Compression Ratio: 9.6:1

1998 Lincoln Navigator

In the full-size SUV category, the Lincoln Navigator is the only vehicle with 'Made In America' stamped on its rocker panel. This is even more surprising in the light of the fact that this Yankee challenger comes from a marque with no history of truck development. Lincoln launched the Navigator in 1998, a full-size Lincoln sport-utility vehicle, based on the Ford Expedition model. The difference was in the styling. The Lincoln had unique (and much more lavish) front and rear styling, extra sound deadening, softer suspension tuning, plus standard leather upholstery and walnut trim. Of course, Lincoln is no stranger to luxury on a grand scale, its current Town Car sedan, a perennial favorite with limousine services, is the biggest passenger car sold in the US.

The main rivals to the Navigator included the GMC Yukon/Denali, Land Rover Range Rover and Toyota Land Cruiser. Quality control on the model was good with a special post-assembly inspection and a twenty-five mile pre-shipment road test.

These first Navigators were available with either rear-wheel drive or Ford's Control Trac four-wheel-drive system, which could be left engaged on dry pavement. The 4x4 option came with automatic self-levelling air-ride shock absorbers at front and rear. On rear-wheel 2WD Navigators, these was fitted at the rear only. Antilock four-wheel disc brakes were standard either way. A three-seat third-row bench seat was installed, with a three-seat split middle row seat available at no extra charge. The Navigator could carry a total of eight people in great comfort. Towing capacity for the truck was 8000 pounds – or four tons to you and me.

Navigators were equipped with a single engine, the Ford Expedition's larger V-8, the 5.4 liter, rated at 230 horsepower. Although Lincoln's SUV is too big and heavy to drive like a car, it does have reasonable acceleration for such a large vehicle. Although the model is not truly agile, it handles reasonably well on twisly roads. The main demerits of the Navigator are its dismal fuel economy (at just over 12 mpg in either two- or four-wheel drive), and parking difficulties due to its sheer bulk in all directions. Despite this, the model has been a hot seller since its introduction, attracting buyers in their forties, much younger than the average Lincoln purchaser. The model remains in Lincoln's line-up.

Engine: SOHC V-8

Displacement: 5.4-liter

Horsepower: 230 at 4250

Transmission: Four-speed automatic

Body Style: Five-door SUV

Weight: 5150 lbs

Wheelbase: 119 inches

■ *Right: The Lincoln Navigator has been described as sumptuous, silent and strong.*

Mercury Cougar

1999

Very different from the overweight Thunderbird-related Cougars of the past, the revived 1999 Cougar was a compact, front-drive sports hatchback coupe with seating for four. It's stated goal was to liven up Mercury's staid image, whilst being true to the heritage of the 1967 Cougar by combining style with performance. Although the styling of the car was sharp edge, the basis for the car were the Ford Cougar/Mercury Mystique sedans. The Cougar was an inch longer than both of these and was designed with a more luxurious feel. The three cars shared engine options, but the Cougars were set up to feel sportier, with firmer suspension and tighter steering.

The power options were a base four-cylinder 16-valve Zetec equipped with a manual shift, rated at 125 horsepower. For around $600 more, the buyer could order a 24-valve, 2.5-liter V-6, rated at 170 horsepower. This engine came with a four-speed automatic as standard. Five-speed manual and traction control were both V-6 options. Although the four-cylinder engine had better fuel economy, road-testers rated it to be noisy and to have excessive vibration, preferring the smoother ride of the V-6. They also preferred the five-speed manual transmission for better pick-up times and a sportier feel. Some felt that both engines were outperformed by those fitted to their Japanese rivals (particularly the Mitsubishi Eclipse and Honda Prelude). The car handled reasonably well, but the long wheelbase diminished its twisty-road agility.

The strongest selling point of the car was its revised 'high tech' design, specifically designed to attract trendy young buyers. These would be different from the usual Mercury customers, better-off middle-aged people. The New Edge Ford styling, of sculpted surfaces and sharp intersections, also incorporated some strong European references. These included the roof-mounted radio antenna and many other subtle details that were attractive to the image-conscious market. As well as the detail, the design fundamentals were right in the car, such as the basic body styling and exemplary driving dynamics.

A sport packages was available for $775 on theV-6, which included fog lamps, four-wheel disc brakes, a leather-wrapped steering wheel, leather shift knob, spoiler, 16-inch aluminium wheels, a center armrest and more distinctive bucket seats. The interior featured a blend of good styling and ergonomics, and commentators were reminded of Ford's European Puma model.

■ *Left: The redesigned V-6 Cougar was aimed at driving enthusiasts in the market for a sports coupe.*

Engine:	V-6
Displacement:	2.5-liter
Horsepower:	170 at 6250 rpm
Compression Ratio:	9.7:1
Weight:	2941 lbs
Wheelbase:	106.4
Base Price:	$17,095

1999 Pontiac Trans Am – 30th Anniversary Edition

The Trans Am turned thirty in 1999, and Pontiac celebrated by launching a special, limited run of a Cameo White Trans Ams trimmed in Lucerne Blue stripes... and a set of rather bizarre blue alloys. Coupe and convertible models were offered. The livery is pretty much the same as that given to the car on its twenty-fifth birthday model, all of which helps to underline the fact that the Trans Am is the longest-running, continuous, performance nameplate in America – as there was no 1983 Corvette, and Camaro Z28 production was discontinued between 1975 and mid-77.

The special paint scheme pays tribute to the WS4 option package of the very first Trans Am of mid-year 1969. At the time, Ford Mustang and Chevy Camaro seemed unassailable in the SCCA Trans Am series, and to be taking it in turns to take the honors. Pontiac's basic problem was that even its smallest engine was too big to be race legal for the series – Trans Am stipulated that engines could be no larger than 305-cid, theirs was 350. The street Trans Am was launched in this year, and Pontiac were obliged to pay a royalty to the SCCA for every Trans Am sold. The single-choice paint scheme didn't help sales, and they built just 697 of this landmark model. The most popular model of the year was the Ram Air III with a four-speed gearbox.

The 1999 car follows a more 1990s aesthetic, with a monochromatic paint scheme, white inside and out.

■ *Below: Only 1600 Thirtieth Anniversary Trans Ams were ever built, each with a numbered console.*

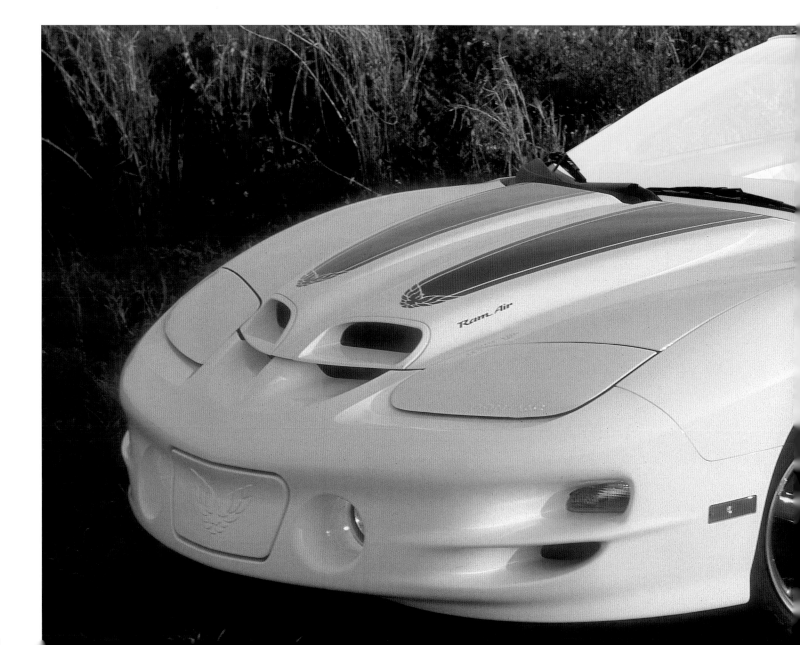

Inside, white leather bucket seats carried special '30th Anniversary' embroidery on their headrests. But the 17-inch five-spoke 'medium-blue-tinted clearcoat' metallic rims were either loved or loathed. But part of the design success of the new Trans Am is the many nods it gives to its own past. The 'screaming chicken' hood emblems (though they were quite discreet by now) and the twin hood scoop, for example.

The car also came with the customary serious muscle power under the hood. It is equipped with a slightly detuned version of the C5 Corvette's 5.7-liter LS1 V-8. The car went straight to the top of the contemporary muscle class. The fully functional WS6 Ram-Air hood punched up the power even further. For transmission, there was a choice between four-speed automatic of six-speed manual. The Pontiac performance and handling package was fitted as standard, including power-assisted four-wheel ABS disc brakes.

Sadly, GM has recently cancelled its F-body line, and the Pontiac Firebird Trans AM has been consigned to history. This will probably translate into soaring collector-car values for the anniversary models.

Engine:	V-8, aluminum block and heads
Displacement:	346-cid
Horsepower:	320 at 5200 rpm
Transmission:	Four-speed automatic
Compression Ratio:	10.5:1
Induction:	Sequential-port fuel injection
Body Style:	Two-door convertible
Number of Seats:	5
Weight:	3474 lbs
Wheelbase:	101.1 inches
Base Price:	$35,495
Number Produced:	535

Ford Focus Sony Edition

2000

Just as Ford's old stalwart, the Escort was fading, the company brought out the replacement Focus. The first Focus hit US dealerships in October 1999, and quickly became one of the ten best selling cars in America, and yet another winner from the Ford stable. In fact, it outsold every other economy model except the Honda Civic. It went on to win the title North American Car of the Year for 2000. The Focus combined a tall cabin and upright seating to create massive interior room, especially for the rear passengers. It was offered as a hatchback, sedan and wagon. This compact model was designed to appeal to the highly influential Generation X (20-25 year olds) and the Echo Boomers (aged 19 and under). To understand their market, Ford executives immersed themselves in the youth culture of major cities such as Los Angeles, New York and Miami. The execs soon realised that this age group is passionately interested in music, fashion and the internet. Ford instigated a huge 'live' advertising campaign to promote the car, the biggest since the '50s. This involved all kinds of media plugs for the car, that were aimed at the target age group, such as the 'Dawson's Creek National Sweepstakes'.

This strategy also led to the first hitch up with an electronics brand in automotive history, with the launch of the Sony Edition Focus in 2000. Responding to the popularity of Sony products with their target market, FoMoCo teamed up with Sony Electronics to create a car featuring custom-designed Xplod red and black speakers and amplifiers. Sony had launched these Xplod products in the previous year, and they were already a big hit with 16-24 year-olds across America. The incorporation of this advanced equipment into the car effectively turned the Focus into a kind of mobile sound system.

Seven thousand Sony Limited Edition Ford Focuses were manufactured. The cars displayed special decals on each front door panel, and were equipped as four-door SE Sport Focus models with a 60/40 split rear seat, air conditioning, power mirrors, all-door remote entry and powerlocks, 15-inch painted aluminum five-spoke wheels, five-passenger seating and black cloth or optional black leather seats. The car was offered in three standard Ford colors, Rainforest Green, Infra-Red and Pitch Black plus one new color made exclusively for the Sony Limited Edition models – Going Platinum.

Ford also made a special edition Kona Focus, supplied complete with its own 'Out of Bounds' Kona mountain bike and bike rack.

■ *Left: 7000 Sony Limited Edition Focuses were built, this one is in Going Platinum.*

Engine: Four-cylinder	
Displacement: 121-cid	
Horsepower: 130	
Wheelbase: 103 inches	
Base Price: $15,535	
Number Produced: 7000	

2001 Chevrolet Corvette Z06

Millenium celebrations over, American car enthusiasts found something new to celebrate in the shape of the new hardtop Corvette, the Z06, resurrecting the heritage racing model designation. The car shared the revised aluminum engine block design of the mighty LS6 V-8, which raised the power output to 385 horsepower, making it even more powerful, and half-a-second quicker than the ZR1 of 1992. The engine block was fitted with red covers. The car was exclusively fitted with the M12 six-speed manual transmission.

In effect, the car was a more sporting development of the hardtop Corvettes, and reminded Corvette aficionados of Duntov's first Z06 production racers of 1963. The car arrived as Corvette's highest priced variant at $47,500. Corvette brand manager Jim Campbell said that the car was 'aimed directly at the diehard performance enthusiast at the upper end of the high-performance market'.

The 2001 chassis was rigidized with a stiffer rear leaf monospring, a larger diameter front stabilizer bar and revised front camber settings to improve cornering. The Chevrolet second-generation active handling package was standard on all 2001 Corvettes.

■ *Below: The Z06 was described as 'simply the quickest, best handling production Corvette ever.*

The exterior of the car was accented with stainless steel highlights, and the model was available in five colors: Quicksilver Metallic, Speedway White, black, Torch Red and Millenium Yellow. It also sported fully operated brake vents and unique wheels that were even wider than those fitted to the coupe and convertible, fitted with Goodyear Eagle Supercar tires, supplied complete with a sophisticated puncture repair kit. The interior of the car was slightly less refined that those of the coupes or convertibles. It's nature was slanted towards performance at the expense of touring. The interiors were available with only two color choices, black, and black with Torch Red accents.

In 2002, standard Corvettes were rated at 350 horsepower, and the Z06 was rated at 405 horsepower. This increase in power was achieved by the removal of two of the pre-catalytic converters from the exhaust system: a well-known NASCAR engine-builder's trick. The Corvette went on to pace the Indy 500 for the fifth time in 2002, but unlike previous years, Chevrolet produced only three pace car replicas that didn't go on sale.

Engine: LS6 V-8

Displacement: 346-cid

Horsepower: 385 at 6000 rpm

Transmission: Six-speed Manual

Compression Ratio: 10.5:1

Induction: Electronic Sequential Fuel Injection

Body Style: Two-door hardtop coupe

Number of Seats: 2

Weight: 3115 lbs

Wheelbase: 104.5 inches

Base Price: $47,500

Number Produced: 5,773

Ford Thunderbird

2002

Ford restored a famous name to its line-up with its 2002 Thunderbird. The car had reverted to a two-seat convertible, and was designed with a retro panache that recalled the classic model of '55. Like the Thunderbirds of the mid-fifties, the new car has reverted to the 'Personal Luxury Car' formula. The new T'bird was built on a shortened version of the rear-wheel drive platform employed by the Lincoln LS and Jaguar S-Type sedan, and was equipped with a power-fold soft top with a heated glass rear window. A removable hardtop was also available, with the marque's trademark porthole windows.

The Thunderbird 2000 is the production version of the concept car that was launched to great acclaim in US auto shows of 1999 and 2000. Although the car's design is very evocative of the car's heritage, the new Thunderbird uses the latest engineering technologies to install confidence in the driver. It is a balanced rear-wheel drive car that utilizes a rigid, computer-engineered chassis and a fine-tuned four-wheel independent suspension system employing lightweight materials to improve the car's responsiveness. The car also has rack-and-pinion steering assembly, four-wheel anti-lock disc brakes, electronic brake force distribution, seventeen-inch cast aluminium wheels and all-season tires. The car was also equipped with an optional all-speed traction control system, which gave the car excellent start-up on slippery surfaces and improved its cornering stability. Although the car was successful in achieving the feel of a relaxed cruiser, it is too big and heavy to be sports-car agile, especially in tight manoeuvres.

The standard engine for the car was an all-aluminum 3.9-liter dual overhead cam V-8, producing an estimated 252 horsepower at 6100 rpm coupled with a specially engineered close-ratio, five-speed automatic transmission. The entire assembly gave great performance and efficiency along with minimal levels of noise, vibration and harshness. The car had good acceleration, with 0-60 mph times of seven seconds. But the acceleration between 35 and 50 mph was soft, due to a failure to downshift promptly. Fuel economy wasn't sparkling either, at around 17.4 mpg. The car's interior felt luxurious with leather seats and leather-wrapped steering wheel.

The car was launched into a hotly competitive sector of the market, running against the Acura TL, Lexus ES 300 and BMW 3-Series. Although originally successful, there has been talk of discontinuing Thunderbird production, but for the moment it remains in the Ford line-up.

■ *Left: The styling of this Whisper White 2002 Thunderbird ragtop echoes the car's heritage, but is far more technologically advanced.*

Engine: DOHC V-8	
Displacement: 3.9-liter	
Horsepower: 252 at 6100 rpm	
Weight: 3775 lbs	
Wheelbase: 107.2 inches	
Base Price: $35,390	

2004 Pontiac GTO

Pontiac built their original GTO 'Goats' between 1964 and 1974, and to many these were not only the original American muscle cars, but also the 'best of breed'. They produced over half a million during this period, and they were the best selling muscle car between 1964 and 1968. If you couldn't afford a Corvette, this was the car for you. Unfortunately, GM had discontinued their F-body in 2002, so no rear-wheel V-8 platform was available to Pontiac. Pontiac got around this by using the Australian Holden Monaro GM model as the basis for the new car. This was a two-door coupe first seen at the Sydney motor show in 1998.

When the new car hit the streets in 2004, it was met with rave reviews. In fact, the car was universally well received both by aficionados of the original muscle cars, and newcomers to the scene alike. The car was introduced to fill the gap left by the retiring Trans Am, and was put together in just 17 months from conception to delivery. Pontiac put this speed down to their 'focus on customer enthusiasm' and their consummate desire to 're-energize the car market with vehicles that command attention and excite the customer's senses'.

The main source of the model's undeniable excitement was under the hood. The LS1 V-8

■ *Below: According to Car And Driver the fabled letters stand for 'God-bless-America performance wrapped in a sleek and refined package at a price the rest of us can afford'.*

(Corvette's standard powerhouse since the 1997 debut of the C5) was fitted to the car. It was rated at 350 horsepower, and was mated to a standard 4L60-E four-speed automatic transmission. A close-ratio Tremec six-speed manual (as seen on the Z06) was optional.

The car was also equipped with power-assisted four-wheel ventilated disc brakes (complete with four-channel anti-lock system), four-wheel independent suspension, power rack-and-pinion steering, and 17x8 cast aluminum wheels with BF Goodrich 245/45ZR-17 tires. The car was adorned with a low profile spoiler, GTO identification, full instrumentation and comfortable bucket seats. Compared to the Z06, the car was still reasonably priced at $33,000, and could milk the available power to achieve a 0-60 mph time of 5.3 seconds, or a quarter mile time of 13.62.

Like the Z06, the 2004 GTO is another new-wave musclecar for the twenty-first century: a high-powered time machine. As for the future, a reborn 'Judge' GTO is rumoured to be on Pontiac's mind. Here come da judge?

Engine: LS1 pushrod V-8

Displacement: 346-cid

Horsepower: 340 at 5200 rpm

Transmission: six-speed manual

Compression Ratio: 10.1:1

Induction: Electronic Sequential-Port Fuel Injection

Body Style: Two-door coupe

Number of Seats: 5

Weight: 3,821 lbs

Wheelbase: 109.7 inches

Base Price: $33,000

Number Produced (projected): 18,000

2005 Chrysler 300-C

Nothing is ever new under the sun and in 2005 Chrysler's original "beautiful brute" re-emerged once again fifty years after the first car in 1955 (see page 214).The new car displays styling hints of the original car , like the deep square sectioned grille.As the company was owned by Mercedes-Benz at the time, the Chrysler 300 used components derived from the E-Class, which included the rear suspension design, front seat frames, wiring harnesses, steering column, and the 5-speed automatic transmission.The front suspension was a double wishbone system derived from the S-Class. The Chrysler 300-C was first shown at the 2003 New York Auto Show as a concept car. Sales in the U.S. began in the spring of 2004 as an early 2005 model year car. Designed by Ralph Gilles, the new 300-C was built in the same spirit as the original "letter car" as a high performance, full- size,sporty sedan. The car uses a 345 cu in Hemi V8 in common with its ancestor. Using the Multidisplacement System (MDS), this engine can run on four cylinders when less power is needed in order to reduce total fuel consumption.. When all 8 cylinders are needed, the 300-C can make 340 hp and 390 ft/lbs of torque. It uses a 5-speed automatic transmission and comes standard with 18 inch chrome-clad alloy wheels. The Hemi engine features a pushrod induction tube, located on the side of the engine-block. This tube makes the 300-C more fuel efficient and quicker, because of the air being "pulled and pushed" into the engine's induction area. The engine uses a double rocker configuration, with a cam-in-block, overhead valve (OHV) pushrod design. There are two spark plugs per cylinder to effect a complete fuel/air mixture burn and to decrease emissions. Chrysler also introduced the SRT-8 version of the car in 2004. This had a formidable 370-cubic-inch Hemi V8 producing 425 hp allowing a 0-60 mph time in the low 5-second range and quarter-mile in the high 13-second range. It went on sale in February 2005 at the not inconsiderable sum of US$43,695. Additional features included leather SRT-8 performance-embossed seats and 20-inch forged, polished aluminum wheels, Brembo brakes, and a rear lip spoiler. The 2007–2008 SRT-8 models had a rear spoiler molded into the body, which became standard throughout the entire 300 line-up. The 2007 models had a lower air dam at the front of the car which increased cooling to the engine by as much as 30%.

■ *Right: The latest Letter Car fulfills the promise of the original "beautiful brute."*

Engine: Hemi V-8

Displacement: 345 cid

Horsepower: 340

Transmission: 5-speed automatic

Wheelbase: 120 inches

Length: 196.8 inches

Base Price: $30,000 depending on options

2008 | Dodge Challenger SRT8

When Barry Newman (as Kowalski) heads into oblivion in his 1970 Dodge Challenger, a legend was born. A legend that would re-emerge in 2008.The original concept of the model was as a "pony car competitor" for the Ford Mustang. The Mustang had its day of fame in the movie *Bullitt* (1968), the Challenger had its three years later in *Vanishing Point*. Both films achieved cult status. Vanishing Point was re-launched in 1998 as a not-so-successful TV film. But the Challenger was to fare better with its metamorphosis in 2008. The new version of the car is a two-door coupe. It shares common design elements with the first generation Challenger, despite being significantly longer and taller. The chassis was a modified version of the LX platform (with a shortened wheelbase) that underpins the 2006 to the current Dodge Charger, the 2005-2008 Dodge Magnum, and the 2005-Current Chrysler 300. The LX platform was adapted from the Mercedes E Class, reflecting Mercedes-Benz's ownership of Chrysler at the time. All (7119) 2008 models were SRT8s, equipped with the 370 cu in Hemi and a 5-speed AutoStick automatic transmission. The entire 2008 US run of 6,400 cars was pre-sold. The 2009 SRT8, while still equipped with the 370 cu in Hemi V8, was virtually identical to its 2008 counterpart. The main difference was the choice of either a 5-speed automatic or a 6-speed manual transmission. Standard features included Brembo brakes, a sport suspension, bi-xenon headlamps, heated leather sport seats, keyless ignition, Sirius satellite radio, and 20-inch forged aluminum wheels.

The extras were in addition to the amenities already offered on the R/T and SE models, such as air conditioning and cruise control. In addition, the 2009 had a proper "limited slip" differential. A "Spring Special" SRT8 Challenger was offered in B5 Blue, but due to rolling plant shutdowns, only 250 Spring Special Challengers were built before the end of the 2009 model year. For 2010, SRT8 models added Detonator Yellow to the range of available colors (at extra cost), and only as an optional "Special Edition Group" car. Yellow Challengers would only be built for a limited time (October/December 2009) for the 2010 model year. Another retro color, Plum Crazy Purple, was also available during the Spring 2010 production, this was offered exclusively in the "Spring Special" package. Another retro color, Furious Fuchsia (similar to the Panther Pink of the 1970s) was limited to a single production day at Chrysler's Brampton, Ontario plant.

Engine: Hemi V-8

Displacement: 345 cid

Horsepower: 425

Trans: 5-speed automatic/6-speed manual

Wheelbase: 116 inches

Length: 197.7 inches

Base Price: $40,095

■ *Below: The exciting new Challenger SRT lives up to its heritage.*

2010 Chevrolet Camaro

Chevrolet are keeping retro styling cues high on their agenda with this the fifth generation Camaro. The car happily just misses the complete retro look, combining retro styling cues with modern functionality by using the very latest technology and modern components. It seems that most informed reviewers are hard-pressed to discover anything disappointing with the exterior appearance of the car, and early customer response has been really good. However, while the exterior has been universally praised the interior has received some slightly critical reviews as it is felt to be "rather more vintage than retro" with its high-mounted gauges and center stack that look cool, but prove to be "ergonomically challenging" in operation. With the car's high belt line and low roof, coupled with its dark upholstery, there have been comments about the interior being gloomy. This Coupe, based on the GM Zeta platform, comes in five different trims: the LS and LT versions are powered by a 217 cubic inch V-6 producing a very respectable 304 hp. The SS versions use two different V-8s. The SS, with 6-speed manual transmission, is powered by a GM LS3 unit of 376 cubic inches putting out 426 hp at 5900 rpm. Presumably, this version is aimed at all-out performance freaks with little concern for economy. By contrast, the auto version uses a GML99 V-8. This develops 400 horsepower, and features an Active Fuel Management system which allows the engine to run on just four cylinders during light-load driving conditions (such as highway cruising) to improve fuel economy. Other features of the model range include a fully independent four-wheel suspension system, variable-rate power steering, four-wheel disc brakes standard on all models (four-piston Brembo calipers on SS models), a StabiliTrak electronic stability/traction control system, Competitive/Sport modes for the stability system offered on SS models, launch control on SS models equipped with the six-speed manual transmission, and six standard air bags that include head curtain side-impact air bags and front seat-mounted thorax side air bags. An RS appearance package is available on LT and SS trim levels, which includes HID headlamps with integrated halo rings, a spoiler, and RS-specific tail lamps and wheels. Rally and hockey stripe packages are also available in several colors. Importantly, despite its modern sophistication the sporty element of the original car is not lost in this fifth generation Camaro. *Automobile Magazine* says that, "out among traffic, the Camaro sticks out," and not simply because of its unmistakably loud exhaust note.

Engine: (SS) GM LS3 V-8

Displacement: 376 cid

Horsepower: 426

Wheelbase: 112.3 inches

Length: 190.4 inches

Weight: 3750 lbs

■ *Right: The new Camaro's exterior styling is a happy combination of retro and ultra modern lines.*

2011 Ford Mustang GT

Mustang attracts two kinds of drivers - those under 30 and those over 30. Really, that's its strength. America's most popular nameplate transcends demographics and socio-economic trends, because Mustang is really more than a car. It's an icon that's been woven into the fabric of America for 60 years and running. The all-new, all-American 2011 Mustang is a bold, clean, and contemporary version of possibly the most celebrated muscle car in the US. It is a purely American sports car. The new design is fresh and contemporary, but harks back to the venerable Mustangs of the past. Mustang was launched by Ford back in 1964 and just twelve months later it had broken auto manufacturing records by selling 419,000 cars in its first production year. By the end of its second year, 1,000,000 Mustangs were out on the roads of America. Somehow, Ford had managed to tap into a reservoir of un-catered for demand. Young, performance orientated, fun-loving, and glamorous, the car reflected many buyers' view of themselves for the first time. It was the start of a love affair that would continue to the present. Through over 300 film appearances, including *Bullitt* and *Gone in 60 Seconds* the image of the Mustang is entwined in American pop culture and continues to have resonance to this day. It's a bad-boy car, hip, smooth and definitely trouble. The 2011 Ford Mustang GT has an all-new 5.0-liter V-8 engine which features four-valve Twin Independent Variable Camshaft Timing (Ti-VCT) which will deliver 412 horsepower and 390 ft.-lb. of torque. This development, coupled with a pair of new six-speed transmissions, one manual and one automatic, will enable the new Mustang to take advantage of the flexibility and fuel economy benefits of having six forward ratios. For example, the six-speed automatic transmission in the 2011 Mustang GT will deliver fuel economy of 25mpg highway and 18mpg city. Alternatively, Mustang GT drivers who prefer a manual gearbox, will enjoy the short throws and direct feel of the shifter, along with the relaxed cruising permitted by the extra top gear ratio. The car also boasts Standard AdvanceTrac® Electronic Stability Control, which complements the all-speed traction control. A standard Anti-lock Braking System (ABS), helps keep the car under control in all driving conditions. GT owners can run with the traction control system on, off, or in a special "Sport Mode." The ride of the car has also been improved, with the addition of a three-link rear suspension with a panhard rod. In addition, Ford have adjusted the springs, stabilizer bars, and shocks to balance the ride, steering, and handling. A Brembo brake package upgrade is available for serious enthusiasts which includes 14-inch vented front discs from the Shelby GT500®, unique 19-inch alloy wheels, and summer performance tires.

Engine: Ti-VCT V-8

Displacement: 305 cid

Horsepower: 412

Length: 188.1 inches

Weight: 3,750 lbs

■ *Right: Ford's Mustang GT features a brand new 5-liter, all-alloy V-8 with independent variable camshaft timing.*

Cadillac CTS-V Coupe

2011

Available from summer 2011, the Cadillac CTS-V Coupe combines massive muscle performance disguised as a luxury sports coupe, complete with all the toys. Aimed at driving enthusiasts, the car oozes both finesse and power. As Bryan Nesbitt, Cadillac general manager said, the "The CTS-V Coupe marries our most potent and sophisticated technology with our most dramatic production design." The car is equipped with a whole of technological goodies including Magnetic Ride Control, racing-bred Brembo brakes, and an (optional) automatic transmission with paddle-shift control.

The V-Series Coupe includes a unique grille that doubles the car's air intake volume, an important enabler for its high-performance capabilities. It is also visually identified by a raised center section of the hood that provides clearance for the supercharger, as well as specific front and rear fascias. Like the CTS Coupe, its exhaust is centered inside the rear fascia, but with unique twin outlets. The car rolls on 19-inch cast aluminum wheels and Michelin Pilot Sport 2 performance tires.

The CTS-V Coupe's rear track is nearly an inch wider than the CTS-V Sport Sedan, adding to the car's aggressive stance and enabling an extra measure of handling capability. The current CTS-V Sport Sedan has quickly established itself among the world's highest performing luxury sedans, becoming the first production four-door on street tires to break the legendary 8-minute barrier at Germany's famed Nürburgring. The new V-Series Coupe's sleeker shape and slightly lower mass ensure a similarly high level of performance.

The CTS-V Coupe's design is a clear visual statement of the technical precision and performance intent of the car. Sharing the CTS-V Sport Sedan's wheel base, the Coupe is about two inches (51 mm) lower and two inches (51 mm) shorter. Key design features of the new Coupe include classic hardtop styling, with no conventional B-pillar; touch-pad operation for the doors, which removes the need for conventional door handles, a faster windshield angle (62.3 degrees) and a nearly horizontal backglass, which give the car a seriously aerodynamic profile.

The car's supercharged powertrain consists of a LSA 6.2L supercharged V-8, rated at 556 horsepower (415 kW) and 551 lb.-ft. of torque (747 Nm): this is the most powerful engine offered in Cadillac's history. But the car does not sacrifice comfort for power. The 2+2 cabin combines performance with refinement and luxury. Recaro performance driving seats are optional, providing excellent support for spirited driving, together with a microfiber-covered steering wheel.

■ *Left: Cadillac's CTS-V Coupe features the most powerful engine in the history of the company.*

Engine:	Supercharged V-8
Displacement:	6.2 liter
Horsepower:	556
Acceleration:	0-60 mph in 3.9 seconds

Acknowledgements

Mike Mueller, Tracy Powell at Automobile Quarterly,
Chevrolet/General Motors, Ford Motor Company, Chrysler LLC.

Picture Credits

Automobile Quarterly, Mike Mueller, Mirco de Cet,
General Motors/Chevrolet, Ford Motor Company.